THINKING SOCIOLOGICALLY
SOCIAL SCRIPTS AND EVERYDAY LIFE

RICHARD MACDONALD

KENDALL/HUNT PUBLISHING COMPANY
4050 Westmark Drive Dubuque, Iowa 52002

CONTENTS

PREFACE   **V**

PART 1

CHAPTER 1   Scripts from Here and Around the World   7

CHAPTER 2   Thinking Sociologically   11

CHAPTER 3   More on Social Scripts   27

PART 2

CHAPTER 4   Role Models and Moral Entrepreneurs   49

CHAPTER 5   The Basics of Interaction   67

CHAPTER 6   Small Groups   77

PART 3

CHAPTER 7   Organizations   93

CHAPTER 8   Spheres of Activities   105

CHAPTER 9   Societies   111

CHAPTER 10   Social Structures   119

PART 4

CHAPTER 11   Political and Economic Scripts   135

CHAPTER 12   American Contradictions   145

CHAPTER 13   Conformity and Deviance   157

CHAPTER 14   Crime and the Criminal Justice System   169

PART 5

CHAPTER 15   Social Stratification   191

CHAPTER 16   American Minorities   205

CHAPTER 17   Sex Scripts   223

CHAPTER 18   Courtship, Marriage, and the Family   233

REFERENCES   **245**

GLOSSARY   **249**

PREFACE

Thinking Sociologically uses the idea of **social scripts** to convey the basic concepts sociologists use when they study social life. The focus on social scripts provides continuity when examining everything from interpersonal relationships and group processes to organizations and societies. Once the logic of social script analysis is mastered, its fundamentals can be easily applied to a wide variety of social activities.

Boldface is used throughout the book to **highlight concepts** and **ideas** that are the essence of learning how to think like a sociologist. **Definitions of concepts** are accompanied by **illustrations** to help you learn how to apply them. Paying attention to definitions and illustrations is the key to making them a part of your vocabulary. The more you learn to apply concepts and sociological ideas to your everyday experiences, the more you will benefit from this course.

The book is divided into **five parts.** Each part contains several chapters. **Study guides** for the chapters contained in a part of the book appear before them. The study guides list the key concepts discussed in a chapter. As you read the material in a chapter you can turn to the appropriate study guide and write down brief notes to help you remember a concept. Sometimes all that it takes is to write a word or two next to the concept on a study guide. One strategy is to select a word from the definition in the text or glossary that best reminds you of the concept.

You should become familiar with the **glossary** at the end of the book. You may find it useful to look up some terms that appear on a study guide from the glossary before reading the chapter. Writing study guide notes in pencil is advised because as you become more familiar with the vocabulary you may want to make some changes.

The first chapters contain numerous illustrations that have been concocted to help you understand how to apply concepts. You should pay closer attention to **fact-based illustrations,** such as those using prominent public figures or advertising campaigns. You should also pay close attention to **historical facts** and **data** that is used more extensively in later chapters.

PART 1
STUDY GUIDES

CHAPTER 1
SCRIPTS FROM HERE AND AROUND THE WORLD

Culture as a Social Script

Scripts from Around the World

Eye Contact

Handshakes

Women and Public Places

Time

Social Bonds

Blood, Marriage, Community

Scripts Here in America

Fourth of July

Memorial Day

Labor Day

Super Bowl

Mardi Gras

Senior Proms

Cultural Disputes

Sacred/Secular

Home Life

Everyday Life

CHAPTER 2
THINKING SOCIOLOGICALLY

Psychology

    Individual

    Personality

Culture and Personality

    Social Self

        Superego

            Guilt

            Pride

        Ideal Self-Concept

        Actual Self

        Self-Esteem

Psychological Concepts

    Bipolar

Thinking Sociologically

    Social Scripts

    Social Behavior

Social Encounters and Relationships

Social Scripts

Types of Social Scripts

    Personal Social Scripts

        Self-Preferences

            Self-Compliance

        Interaction Preferences

            Interaction Compliance

        Hypocrisy

        Compatible and Incompatible

        Magnitude of Conflict

Emergent Social Scripts

Shared Social Scripts

Script Typologies

Typical Relationships

Values and Beliefs

Value Intensity

Belief Conviction

Highly Scripted Relationships

Rewards

Self

Social

Magnitude

Costs

Self

Social

Magnitude

Balancing Rewards and Costs

Staying/Leaving an Encounter/Relationship

Negotiating Social Scripts

Negotiation Tactics

Gestures of Disapproval

Physical Threats

Economic Threats

Guilt Manipulations

Constraints on Negotiation Tactics

Definition of the Situation

Self-Preferences

Self-Rewards/Costs

Interaction Preferences

Social Rewards/Costs

Illustration

Classroom Perceptions

Awareness

Self

Social

Stereotypes

Self-Fulfilling Prophesies

Self-Disclosure

Personality Variable

Cultural Variable

Socialization

Awareness and Acceptance

Not Socialization

Social Awareness

Resocialization

Behavioral Rationalizations

Personal

Social

Superficial Relationships

The Dyad

Social Change

CHAPTER 3
MORE ON SOCIAL SCRIPTS

Cultural Themes

Some American Cultural Themes

Ideal and Real Culture

Ideal and Actual Selves

Resolving Contradictions

    Dissonance

    Dissonance Reduction

Popular Culture

    Mass Culture

Popular Culture and Lifestyles

The Scope of a Social Script

The Duration of a Social Script

    Rituals

    Fads

    Fashions

The Diffusion of Social Scripts

Music as a Social Script

Circumstances and Social Scripts

    Cultural Lag

Master Scripts

Official and Unofficial Scripts

Public and Private Scripts

Frontstage and Backstage

Taken-for-Granted Scripts

Single or Multiple Scripts

Ethnocentrism

Cultural Relativism

Identifying with Outsiders

Personal Judgments

Proselytizing

Searching for Alternative Experiences

Group Recruitment

Gossip   .

Pluralistic Ignorance

    Appearance of Consensus

Pluralistic Ignorance and Social Movements

The Silent Majority

The Sociology of Emotions

Emotion Contagion

The Degree of Personal Expression

Predicting Interaction

    Personality

    Social Scripts

Scripts and Everyday Life

Getting in the Door

CHAPTER 1
SCRIPTS FROM HERE AND AROUND THE WORLD

The emphasis throughout this book is on teaching you how to think like a sociologist. To do so requires looking at how **social scripts** come to shape human events and activities. Social scripts are similar to the scripts written by authors of plays and movies, although their origin is not always so obvious. Just like a play or a movie script directs the actions of performers, so too do social scripts.

Eventually you will have to acquire a relatively extensive vocabulary in order for you to be able to analyze social scripts more extensively. This vocabulary or terminology represents the tools you will need to fully understand the dynamics associated with the processes by which social scripts shape our activities. But now is the time to help you get a sense of what social scripts involve by looking at the general notion of culture and some illustrations taken from here and around the world.

CULTURE AS A SOCIAL SCRIPT

The term **culture** can be described as a **social script** or **blueprint** that structures generalized customs, rituals, and other activities in a society. Sociologists and anthropologists use the concept of culture to compare and contrast life in different societies. Sometimes there is a generally agreed upon social script that functions as a blueprint in a society that applies to most people and is passed on from generation to generation. Sociologists have also discovered cultural disputes within societies.

SCRIPTS FROM AROUND THE WORLD

Suppose that you are visiting a country for the first time. It is natural for you to take for granted many customs based upon your own experiences. But your familiar ways of responding to others may not play well on your visit. Your new experiences may teach you just how much social scripts differ across societies.

Let's look at some cultural script differences involving greetings. Americans are often taught the importance of directly looking at someone in the eye when meeting them for the first time. But in some societies it is considered rude and offensive to make direct eye contact. You can imagine the potential for misunderstandings when customs governing greetings differ.

Other greeting differences occur between cultures. American men favor a short firm handshake. In some African societies it is more customary for men to engage in a limp and lingering handshake. It is not difficult to imagine the potential discomfort many American men might experience when shaking hands with someone from that culture.

Other social script problems can arise for American women when visiting other countries. In some Muslim communities women are not allowed in public without clothing that completely covers them. Women in some of these societies are not even allowed to leave the house without a male family member present. Nor are they allowed to drive a car. These cultural differences have caused conflicts for American women serving in Iraq or stationed in countries like Saudi Arabia.

How different societies deal with time is another fascinating cultural difference. In some cultures a concern with time is almost nil compared to how it is dealt with in the United States. The cultural custom of exhibiting patience and taking it easy that is found in these societies stands in stark contrast to Americans who are impatient and always seem to be in a rush to get things done. Imagine the tensions that could arise in exchanges between people who relish spending extensive time lingering over a coffee and those who are in a rush to get on with their next tasks.

Cultural differences are also evident in the amount of time people spend thinking about the past or the future. If you visit some Asian societies you may find that the focus on living is the present. Expressions of this are found in the Asian philosophy of living in the here and now. Thinking about what has transpired or will occur in the future is discouraged.

Compare this with the more typical American obsession over the past or future. Americans often experience difficulty in letting go of something that happened in the past and learning how to live in the present. Living in the present is also forfeited when too much attention is placed on making lists and planning for the future.

The nature of social bonds in different societies is another basis for different cultural scripts. Americans often have difficulty understanding the extent to which social bonds in more traditional societies such as Afghanistan and Iraq are based upon local factors such as blood, marriage, and community. It is often hard for people in these societies to think nationally when their everyday life reinforces thinking locally. The difficulty Afghanistan and Iraq are experiencing in developing a national government is due in no small part to this dynamic.

SCRIPTS HERE IN AMERICA

There are many annual scripted events in the United States. Celebrations on the Fourth of July began with the signing of the Declaration of Independence from Great Britain on July 4, 1776. It was not until 1941 that the government formally recognized it. Today parades, fireworks, and family gatherings are just some of the scripted activities that have become associated with this famous holiday.

Both Memorial Day and Labor Day have long histories. Labor Day celebrations for social and economic advancements created by working class Americans date back to 1882 when the first large parade took place in New York. Memorial Day remembers those who have died in American wars. It dates back to when the Commander of the Grand Army of the Republic first established it on May 5, 1868. It was first observed on May 30, 1868, when flowers were placed on the graves of fallen Union and Confederate soldiers buried at Arlington National Cemetery.

Many still celebrate the original significance of these two events. But both Memorial and Labor Days have taken on additional significance. Memorial Day officially signals the beginning of summer vacation while Labor Day signals the end of summer and the beginning of the new school year.

Many celebrated events in the United States have not been given an official stamp of approval by Congress like the just mentioned federal holidays. The Super Bowl has turned into a huge event since its humble origins in 1967 as the first championship game between the champions of the National and American Football Leagues. After domination by the NFL in the first two games, interest spiked when an upstart quarterback named Joe Namath (aka Broadway Joe) predicted that his AFL New York Jets would beat the favored NFL Baltimore Colts. When his team won the clash by a score of 16–7, what has become known as the Super Bowl began to look like a real contest.

Since these early origins the Super Bowl has become one of our most-hyped national events that has generated scripts far beyond the contest itself. Now the scripts include everything from marketing new TVs to enthusiasts and record sales of beer and snacks to record high prices for advertisers and promotions of the Halftime programs as a great opportunity for viewers to witness the show of the year. Occasionally the Halftime shows become known more for the controversies they generate, such as Janet Jackson's wardrobe malfunction.

Mardi Gras, which runs in New Orleans until midnight the night before Ash Wednesday, is another favorite American tradition. Its origins can be traced back to 1827 when Americans gained control of New Orleans and parading in masks was permitted. During the 1850s the elite of New Orleans threw grand Mardi Gras parties that became major invitation-only social events. Some years later the first Krewe (secret society) was formed with a mission to plan parades and other Mardi Gras events. Since then such secret societies have proliferated and their floats provide some of the most colorful events during the Mardi Gras celebration. Even the official colors of Mardi Gras have been scripted. Purple represents justice, green represents faith, and gold represents power.

What is interesting about Mardi Gras is the extent to which scripts evolved among people who have little or no understanding of its origins. One of the most publicized events at Mardi Gras is the spectacle of women bearing their breasts on balconies overlooking Bourbon Street to crowds below. Interestingly enough, this spectacle is seen by many local Mardi Gras fans as a sideshow mainly for tourists. For them the real Mardi Gras centers on private parties and events that occur outside the French Quarter.

Senior proms represent yet another scripted event in the United States. It has become a symbolic rite of passage celebration for graduating seniors. For many it is the most important social event of their lives. Dress codes are highly scripted. Tuxes are often seen as the appropriate dress for males and many females spend hundreds of dollars on dresses. To not be invited to the prom remains a sore spot for some of those who were denied this rite of passage.

Heavy drinking on prom night has become a scripted tradition in many communities that worries parents. Parental concern about binge drinking on prom night and driving accidents have prompted the emergence of a number of related scripts. In some communities affluent parents hire limousines to drive their children and their dates from preparties to the prom to postparties and home. Scripts announcing the dangers of drinking have surfaced in many schools.

CULTURAL DISPUTES AND CHANGE WITHIN SOCIETIES

We need look no further than the United States to witness cultural wars involving conflicting scripts. One of the most pronounced conflicts, and one that played an important role in the reelection of President George W. Bush, revolves around sacred and secular viewpoints. Some insist that religious ideas, more particularly Evangelical Christian ideas, should be the foundation of government. Advocates of a more secular position insist on the separation of church and state.

Cultural change within a society can be illustrated from American history. Compare the image of families traveling West in prairie schooner wagons and settling in small crude cabins surrounded by danger with that conveyed during the 1920s in the popular song "My Blue Heaven":

> When whippoorwills call and evening is nigh . . . you see a smiling face, a fireplace, a cozy room, a little nest that's nestled where the roses bloom. Just Mollie and me and baby makes three. We're happy in my blue heaven.

The changes suggested by these images only touch the surface of the dramatic changes in the home life of Americans. Before World War II most Americans lived on farms or rented apartments or houses in cities. After World War II new circumstances arose that dramatically altered these housing patterns. The expansion of highways and low-interest mortgages for returning servicemen created opportunities that led to a massive increase of home ownership and the migration of people to the suburbs. Now rather than renting a flat in the city, people could buy their own one bath and three-bedroom home in the suburbs. Soon garages integrated into the design of homes became common. Wow! Talk about changing scripts for how people live!

EVERYDAY LIFE

All cultural scripts play out through interaction in everyday life. It is through everyday transactions that cultural scripts are adjusted, modified, or changed by the people who are involved. This is important to realize because it is people who transmit and alter cultural scripts through their daily activities.

Everyday life is also where more personal social scripts play out. Friction can arise between college roommates because one is a slob and one is compulsively tidy. Exactly how those differences are resolved depends upon the personalities of those involved. Some roommates can work out a compromise, while for others the only solution is to split and get another more compatible roommate.

CHAPTER 2
THINKING SOCIOLOGICALLY

Looking at some cultural scripts from here and around the world gives you some notion of what it means to think like a sociologist. Now it is time to move beyond the metaphor that compares social scripts to scripts that direct the activities of performers on the stage or in movies. We begin by contrasting sociology with psychology. Both fields offer great insights into human behavior, but knowing the difference between what psychologists and sociologists study is an essential step in learning what it means to think sociologically.

PSYCHOLOGY

The **primary unit of analysis in psychology is the individual.** The term **personality** captures the essence of this focus. **Personality** refers to the **attitudes, emotions,** and **behaviors** of a given **person.**

This does not mean that psychologists give equal time to studying all of these dimensions of personality. Psychologists differ over what aspects of personality they choose to study. Some psychologists study behavior. Other psychologists are more interested in studying emotional dispositions such as fears, anxieties, and phobias. Still others study attitudes and other cognitive components of personality such as learning.

The **focus** among psychologists on the **individual** is evident in **therapy.** Although therapists vary in terms of what aspects of personality they treat and how they go about trying to help people, their client is always a single person. The goal of all therapy is to improve the ability of that patient or client to cope.

CULTURE AND PERSONALITY

Many psychologists are interested in how **cultural experiences** influence the **development of personality.** Two prominent psychologists will be used to illustrate the different ways psychologists incorporate the concept of culture in their theories of personality. Both see **culture** as providing the basis for developing a **social self** as a component of personality.

Freud divides personality into several components (Hall, 1954). To see how Freud incorporates culture into his theory of personality it is only necessary to examine two of these components. The **Id** represents the sex drive that all humans possess. The sex drive is essential for human reproduction and the survival of the species. The **Superego** represents the social self based upon cultural learning. As a product of culture, the Superego channels the sex drive into acceptable expressions.

Many of Freud's patients experienced sexual repression. **Sexual repression** occurs when someone is unable to acknowledge or come to grips with their own sexuality because of cultural learning. The problem is that their superego forces them to repress thoughts and behavior that would make them feel guilty because of what their culture taught them.

Rogers offers a different slant on the relationship between culture and personality. Our **ideal self-concept** is who we think we **ought** to be. Rogers viewed culture as the primary source of our **ideal self-concept.** This can differ from our **actual self.** Our **actual self** is **who we really are.** People who cherish bravery as an ideal but in reality are cowards illustrate the difference.

Self-esteem, or feelings of **self-worth,** is a function of compatibility between ideal and actual selves. **Compatibility** between ideal and actual selves **enhances** a sense of self-esteem or self-worth. Any **disparity** between our ideal and actual selves diminishes our feelings of self-esteem or self-worth.

Many people are able to realize their ideal self, but others must deny who they are in order to rescue their self-esteem. An example would be a young athlete whose ideal self-concept of being the best exceeds reality. To preserve his/her sense of self-esteem may require exaggerations of personal accomplishments, excuses when performances do not excel, or degrading the accomplishments of others. Mental health requires a balance between the motivational benefits of an ideal self-concept without distorting reality in order to maintain a sense of self-worth.

Denial of the actual self requires an enormous expenditure of psychological energy and can be dangerous. A mother who denies she sometimes gets angry with her crying baby is more likely to explode than a mother who accepts that element of her personality. Rogers recommended that therapists create a supportive and accepting atmosphere to encourage patients to learn about who they really are.

PSYCHOLOGICAL CONCEPTS

Psychologists have an array of concepts that they employ to diagnose and/or treat an individual. The concepts themselves represent general categories, but the focus in psychology on the individual means that they exist to be applied to specific individuals. The concept of a bipolar personality is a case in point.

Bipolar is a term used to describe someone who experiences **dramatic mood swings** ranging from **mania** at one extreme and **depression** at the other. The manic stage is characterized by an acceleration of thoughts and activities. One feels confident and may even think in grandiose terms. The depressed state is characterized by a slow down in thoughts and activities, even to the extent of not being able to respond to other people and surroundings. Hope and exhilaration are replaced by feelings of despair and self-doubt. Nothing is fun anymore, nothing tastes good, and thoughts that one can do anything are taken over by the conviction that one is a worthless fraud.

The mood swings for someone who is bipolar may be severe enough to make it difficult to function normally. The concept of bipolar is a diagnostic tool that a psychologist can use to determine whether or not it is relevant to problems experienced by a client. To some degree the diagnosis can be therapeutic by helping the person and others better understand what is going on. This can be beneficial for someone with mild mood swings, but more severe cases usually require more extensive therapy.

THINKING SOCIOLOGICALLY

Sociologists are not interested in focusing on a single person. Instead, sociologists focus on **how social scripts shape social behavior between two or more people.** The discussion begins by establishing what is meant by a **social behavior.** It is followed by comments on the difference between a **social encounter** and **social relationship.** Once these terms have been explained, attention will turn to what is meant by a **social script.**

SOCIAL BEHAVIOR

The interpretation of social behavior used here was inspired by the thinking of a famous German sociologist. Max Weber (1922–1958) defined an act as social whenever someone takes another person(s) into account and acts on that basis. In other words, **if your act is influenced by either the actual or imagined presence of someone else, it qualifies as a social behavior.**

The **actual presence** of someone else is self-explanatory. It occurs whenever you are interacting with someone else who is present at that time. The other person need not be physically present for your actions to qualify as social behaviors, a conversation with someone on your cell phone or an exchange of e-mail would qualify.

The **imagined presence** of someone occurs whenever you are thinking about someone else but that person is not present at the time. If thinking about someone who is not there influences your choices of actions, then those actions qualify as social behaviors. Preparing for a date is one example. If thinking about how your parents might react influences your decision to study or party with your friends, then that choice would qualify as a social behavior even though your parents were not present at the time.

SOCIAL ENCOUNTERS AND RELATIONSHIPS

A **social encounter** is a **single episode** of interaction between two or more people. A **social relationship** is a **series of social encounters** over time. A social encounter is like a single snapshot, and a social relationship is more like a series of snapshots over time.

The difference is important if you want to learn to think like a sociologist. Witnessing a single encounter between two or more people in a relationship may or may not be typical of exchanges among them. A good rule of thumb is that as a sociologist you should never generalize based upon observing a single encounter. Good research requires getting a better sample of encounters before trying to characterize what typically transpires between those involved in a social relationship.

SOCIAL SCRIPTS

Social scripts contain the **behavioral preferences** people bring to social encounters and relationships. **Behavioral preferences** refer to the behaviors that people think are **acceptable** or **unacceptable.** The terms **appropriate** and **inappropriate** can be substituted for acceptable or unacceptable. **Behavioral preferences** also include behaviors that people **enjoy** or **hate** doing **themselves** or that they **enjoy** or **hate** when others engage in them.

Sometimes behavioral preferences involving what someone thinks is appropriate conflict with preferences based upon what that person enjoys or hates. Someone may think that it is appropriate as a student to study but actually hates to study. This creates a conflict that does not exist for someone who thinks that students should study and enjoy it.

TYPES OF SOCIAL SCRIPTS

Social scripts contain the behavioral preferences people bring to social encounters or relationships. These preferences reflect what they think is appropriate behavior as well as what they find enjoyable or unpleasant. There are three basic types of social scripts. They are (1) **personal social scripts,** (2) **emergent social scripts,** and (3) **shared social scripts.**

PERSONAL SOCIAL SCRIPTS

A **personal social script** contains the **behavioral preferences** of a **specific person.** Each person involved in a social encounter or relationship brings a personal social script to that situation. The behavioral preferences within a personal social script have two different applications.

A **self-preference** is a behavior **someone thinks is appropriate for himself/herself** and/or what **someone enjoys or despises doing.** Loving to talk with other people or hating to talk with other people illustrates what is meant by a self-preference. So too would behaviors that you engage in that make you feel proud or guilty about yourself.

An **interaction preference** is what **someone thinks is an appropriate response by someone else** and/or the **behaviors of others that someone enjoys or despises.** Your interaction preferences apply to how someone else behaves toward you or how they treat other people. If you disapprove of how someone treats you or another person, that disapproval is based upon an interaction preference. The same is true when you approve what someone else does.

TWO OR MORE PEOPLE

Because sociologists are interested in studying social behavior, the distinction between self-preferences and interaction preferences applies to all those engaged in a social encounter or social relationship. Person A and Person B will be used to illustrate how this works. Person A has both self-preference and interaction preferences for Person B. Person B has both self-preferences and interaction preferences for Person A.

Interaction compliance with **interaction preferences** occurs when Person A and Person B engage in behavior that is compatible with their interaction preferences for each other. **Self-compliance** occurs when Person A and Person B engage in behaviors that are compatible with their own self-preferences.

Hypocrisy exists when self-preferences and interaction preferences are not the same. Not practicing what one preaches is hypocrisy. Parents are hypocritical when they insist that their children refrain from what they do. Politicians are hypocritical when they engage in acts that they publicly denounce. Religious leaders are hypocritical when they commit the same sins that they preach against.

COMPATIBLE AND INCOMPATIBLE PERSONAL SOCIAL SCRIPTS

Compatible personal social scripts exist when the **personal social scripts** that people bring to a social encounter or relationship are in agreement. **Full compatibility** is when both self-preferences and interaction preferences match. **Partial compatibility** exists when there is some agreement but not full compatibility.

Incompatible personal social scripts exist when the preferences contained in the **personal social scripts** that people bring to a social encounter or relationship conflict. There are a number of different types of conflicts that can occur and cause tensions. Each type reflects different combinations of preferences that cause conflict.

Incompatible self-preferences represent the first combination that causes conflict. An example would be an athlete who likes to succeed but also thinks that it is wrong to use steroids but uses them. For this athlete, the use of steroids may increase success but it is at a cost. The cost is the guilt felt over using steroids. The dilemma is that not using steroids can have the cost associated with a loss of self-esteem because of diminished performance.

Incompatible self-preferences and the **interaction preferences of others** is the second combination that causes conflict. You might prefer to stay home and study when your friends prefer that you party with them. This creates a dilemma. Staying at home and studying may have its rewards, but not having fun with your friends is a cost. Going out with your friends may be rewarding, but flunking an important exam may inflict a serious cost.

The third combination that causes conflict occurs when two or more people impose **incompatible preferences on someone else.** If your parents want you to spend the holiday with them and your friends want you to be with them, you face a dilemma. If you decide to be with your friends, your parents may get mad. If you decide to spend the holiday with your parents, your friends may get upset. All of this occurs without factoring in your own preferences.

Factoring in your own preferences demonstrates how a variety of combinations can result from the three that have been identified. Complexity in making a choice is increased beyond how others will react if you prefer to be with your friends but feel guilty about abandoning your parents. None of these complexities would exist if all of the behavioral preferences were compatible.

THE MAGNITUDE OF CONFLICT

The **magnitude of the conflict** brought about by **incompatible behavioral preferences** depends upon the **intensity** of those preferences. The more intense the preferences that are involved, the more intense are the consequences. If you or someone else is relatively ambivalent about a preference, the rewards or costs of complying or not are likely to be low. If you or someone else feels strongly about a preference, then the rewards or costs associated with complying or not is likely to be high. More will be said about rewards and costs shortly.

EMERGENT SOCIAL SCRIPTS

An **emergent social script** is a script that unfolds over time and structures the relationship between two or more people. If agreement exists, that is to say, their personal social scripts are compatible, then the script that emerges will unfold accordingly. When disputes arise between the personal social scripts participants bring to a social encounter or relationship there can be a variety of outcomes that shape the emergent script that comes to structure their relationship.

One possibility is that one person is able to **impose** his/her preferences on others. If this occurs, the emergent social script structures interaction will be according to that individual's personal social script. Another possibility is that none of the participants are able to impose their will on the other participants so they decide to **compromise.** A compromise means that the emergent social script that comes to structure their interaction requires them to modify their own personal preferences. More will be said about these possibilities in Chapter Five.

SHARED SOCIAL SCRIPTS

A **shared** or **agreed upon social script** exists whenever the preferences of everyone in a group, community, or society match. In other words, their personal social scripts, along with their self-preferences and interaction preferences, are the same. The type of social script reflects the interpretation of a social norm as a generally agreed upon standard of conduct within a group, community, or society.

Whenever a **shared** or **agreed upon social script** exists, what is seen as appropriate and/or enjoyable is the same. A shared or agreed upon social script must also contain similarities concerning what is seen as inappropriate or despicable. As a blueprint for interaction, a shared social script creates the basis for harmonious relationships. Within a group, community, or society different personal social scripts are the basis for disputes, tensions, and conflict.

The same is true for relationships between groups, communities, or societies. Harmonious relationships are a function of the extent to which the agreed upon preferences that they apply to themselves are compatible with those contained in the agreed upon scripts of other groups, communities, or societies. Script disputes between groups, communities, or societies are the foundation for tensions and conflict between them.

SCRIPT TYPOLOGIES

Often **sociological research** uncovers certain **commonalties** in the **behavioral preferences** of people. Identifying these commonalties is the basis for constructing social **script types.** An example is patriarchy. **Patriarchy** refers to a type of social script where men are privileged and dominate. **Matriarchy** refers to a different type of social script where women are privileged and dominate. **Egalitarian** is yet another type of social script that describes situations where men and women share privilege and power.

A **script typology** is a set of script types that deal with a similar theme. The patriarchy, matriarchy, and egalitarian script types form a typology based upon how power and privilege are distributed within groups such as the family, organizations, communities, or societies. A script typology identifies possibilities that sociologists look for when studying groups, organizations, communities, and societies.

Confusion can arise with **labels** used to **identify** a **script type.** The key is looking for defining characteristics. For instance, comparing traditional and liberated women involves script types based upon the distinction between patriarchy, matriarchy, and egalitarian script types. When coming across such distinctions you should try to see if the author/speaker has provided a definition or whether or not you must infer a script type. One possibility is that a traditional woman is someone who accepts male privilege and power advantages and that a liberated woman wants to convert society into one where women have the privilege and power advantage. An alternative is that a liberated woman is someone who seeks fairness in the distribution of power and privilege between men and women. This reflects the egalitarian script type that is quite different from the matriarchy script type.

VALUES AND BELIEFS

Values and **beliefs sustain** the **behavioral preferences** found in social scripts. To think sociologically requires knowing how to distinguish between a value and a belief and the part that both play in supporting behavioral preferences contained in the social scripts people bring to social encounters and relationships. Knowing the difference between values and beliefs helps explain why people hold certain behavioral preferences.

VALUES

Values are **emotional sentiments** that express **generalized likes and dislikes** held by people. Values express what people admire, celebrate, or find disgusting. To value something is to feel that it is important. Examples include when someone values something such as freedom, equality, small government, limited taxes, education, rock and roll music, or quiet moonlight strolls along beaches.

It is easy to demonstrate the link between a value and the behavioral preferences in a social script. Suppose that you strongly feel that government should stay out of our lives. This sentiment represents a value. If it is an important generalized value for you, then it would dictate that you would find any policy that requires government intervention as unacceptable. The emotional sentiment attached to the more generalized value would extend to your personal behavioral preferences (script) concerning more specific practices.

Sometimes commitment to a generalized value can cause personal conflict for someone. If you value life above all else, then your antiabortion stance would be predictable, but if you also support the death penalty, then you would have a conflicting view. Whenever such conflicts arise, people usually scramble to come up with qualifications that dismiss the tension. Characterizing the embryo or fetus as innocent, while simultaneously characterizing those deserving to die with a lethal injection as villains might do the trick. But there is a cost. You really can't claim that you value life above all else.

Notice that values are generalized likes or dislikes. Liking sweet food, for instance, is more general than liking M&Ms or ice cream. Valuing freedom is more general than being against a single instance where freedom is denied. Valuing freedom is a generalization that applies to multiple instances.

VALUE INTENSITY

Value intensity is the **severity of emotional sentiments** attached to a **generalized like** or **dislike.** Those who value freedom intensely are enormously gratified when it occurs and become outraged when it is denied. The greater the value intensity, the greater the emotional response when a related behavioral preference is realized or violated.

The significance of value intensity can be seen among the extremes involving the issue of abortion. Adamant pro-life advocates and adamant pro-choice advocates are not likely to compromise on their behavioral preferences. People with less intense values and behavioral preferences concerning abortion are more likely to reach a compromise.

BELIEFS

A belief is a different form of a value. A **belief** represents a **truth claim** about the nature of reality. Examples include believing in the existence of God, that SUVs are responsible for our energy crisis, that the globe is warming, or that politicians are untrustworthy.

Beliefs combine with values to **sustain** a **behavioral preference.** Someone who values life and believes that pollution lowers life expectancies is likely to embrace a behavioral preference within his or her personal social script that is against an industrial plant that pollutes. Someone who values life and believes that emissions from that plant are not dangerous is more likely to embrace a behavioral preference against imposing pollution controls on that plant.

BELIEF CONVICTION

Belief conviction is the **extent** to which someone thinks that a **truth claim** is **true.** Belief conviction, while it can be based upon factual information, is not limited to factual information. Medieval monks were unwilling to give up their convictions based upon the authority of the Holy Scriptures when confronted with contrary scientific evidence.

Just like with values, it is relatively easy to illustrate how a truth claim (belief) can sustain a specific behavioral preference (script). Suppose that you are convinced that poor people are lazy and responsible for their plight. Would you support a government jobs program for them or would you think that it would be a waste of tax dollars?

Truth claims used to sustain a behavioral preference and counter claims that dispute the same preference are common. Your parents may justify restricting your freedom to stay out late at night with the truth claim that it is too dangerous. You may counter with the truth claim that they are wrong and that staying out late isn't so dangerous. If you prevail with your argument, your parents are likely to retreat. But even though you don't believe their truth claim it may not matter if your parents have the capacity to force you to comply.

VALUE INTENSITY AND BELIEF CONVICTION

The **more intense the value(s)** and **belief convictions** that support a **behavioral preference** the **more intense will be reactions** to **compliance** or **deviance** from that behavioral preference. The less intense the value(s) and belief convictions that support a behavioral preference, the less intense reactions to compliance or deviance will be from that preference. This applies to both social rewards and costs as well as to self-rewards and costs.

SCRIPTED

Exchanges between people can be described according to the **extent that they are scripted. Highly socially scripted** relationships are highly **predictable.** Often events such as weddings and funerals that are governed by a **socially shared script** qualify as highly scripted. This is because what transpires is quite predictable and familiar.

But relationships can become **highly scripted** without a **socially shared script.** Over time the personal preferences of a married couple may create an **emergent social script** that makes their relationship highly predictable but not necessarily agreeable. Both may come to accommodate their preferences with the result being a highly predictable but less than satisfactory relationship.

When social situations are **governed by socially shared scripts,** knowledge of the scripts makes prediction possible with little or no knowledge about the specific participants. In less scripted situations, knowledge of the specific personalities involved is necessary to make predictions about what will transpire. An example would be a friendship where personalities have a bigger influence on what transpires than a friendship script.

Even highly scripted relationships can change. An example would be an individual who had a difficult and highly predictable relationship with a parent as a teenager, and then finds that as an adult that relationship became more enjoyable. Daughters who had bitter exchanges with their mothers as teens now find sharing scripted activities such as shopping together quite enjoyable.

REWARDS AND COSTS

Both **rewards** and **costs** must be factored into choices of behavior that people make when thinking about or confronted with someone else. **Behavioral preferences** establish the circumstances under which a response by self or others will be rewarding or inflict a cost. **Compliance** with behavioral preferences is **generally rewarding** while **deviance** from behavioral preferences **creates costs** to the person whose preferences have been violated.

These general considerations frame a more extensive discussion on rewards and costs as they apply to social encounters or relationships. A **reward** is the **actual or anticipated reaction** of self or others that **encourages** someone to repeat the act that produced it and/or continue in the encounter or relationship. A **cost** is **the actual or anticipated reaction** of self or others that **discourages** someone from repeating the act that produced it and/or continuing the encounter or relationship.

A **social reward** is the actual or anticipated **reaction of others** based upon their interaction preferences for us that **encourages** us to repeat the behavior that produces it and/or to continue in the encounter or relationship. An example would be when one anticipates that an act that generated praise from others in the past will do so in subsequent situations. Anticipating praise is not only an incentive to repeat the act but it can also be an incentive to continue with an encounter or relationship.

A **self-reward** is an actual or anticipated **personal reaction** to a **self-preference** that **encourages** us to repeat it in subsequent situations and/or continue with the encounter or relationship. An example would be when we found that something we did in a past encounter or relationship felt good. This personal reaction can be self-initiated, like when we felt good about helping someone else independent of how they reacted. In other situations it is a reaction by someone else that triggers the self-reward. In either case, the effect of an actual or anticipated self-reward is to encourage repetition of what we did that caused it and/or to continue the encounter or relationship that produced it.

A **social cost** is an actual or anticipated **reaction by others** to a violation of an interaction preference that they have for us that **discourages** us from repeating the act that produced it and/or continuing the encounter or relationship. An example is when someone greets something we do with a frown, nagging, or anger and their response discourages us from repeating what we did in future encounters with them. Additionally, it may be sufficiently discouraging to the point that if given the choice, we would terminate the encounter or relationship.

A **self-cost** is an actual or anticipated personal response to a **self-preference** that **discourages** us from repeating the act that produced it and/or continuing the encounter or relationship. Feeling guilty about having done something in the past, or anticipating that we will feel guilty if we do something in a future situation, operates as a self-cost when it diminishes the likelihood that we will repeat the act that produced it and/or continue with an encounter or relationship. Not enjoying being with someone else can be a self-cost that discourages us from continuing with the encounter or relationship that caused it.

The **magnitude** of any **reward or cost** is proportional to the importance participants attach to the behavioral preferences that are involved. The severity of consequences for complying or defying the preferences others have for you or your own self-preferences depends upon the importance that you or that person attaches to that preference. Deeply offending somebody is likely to have more serious costs than if that person laughs off your indiscretion. Complying with what is extremely important to someone else is likely to generate higher rewards than if that person is relatively indifferent about the matter. Similarly, the magnitude of guilt or pride you experience is a function of the importance you attach to the underlying self-preference.

BALANCING REWARDS AND COSTS

The **motivation** to **continue** or **terminate** an encounter or relationship is proportional to the **net balance** of **rewards** and **costs.** That **net balance** is based upon the **returns you experience** in that encounter or relationship combined with **expectations of returns elsewhere.** Deciding to continue a conversation with someone you just met at a party suggests that on balance it is better than your other options. Conversely, deciding to terminate a conversation with someone you just met at a party suggests that you feel you could spend your time more productively alone or with someone else.

These same considerations apply to relationships. Deciding to continue with a job that you may not really like suggests that you may have no other options. If options do exist and the cost of exercising those options is not too great, then changing jobs is a likely possibility.

The same applies to personal relationships. Deciding to continue to date someone may be based upon high rewards and low costs or it could be based upon a lack of other options. The more options someone has, the more flexibility that person has in deciding to continue or terminate the relationship. Someone with fewer options may have to endure a less satisfactory ratio of rewards to costs.

People may decide to stay in a relationship if they think that the possibility of improving the net balance of rewards to costs exists. One reason is that the other person promises to improve and change. If the promise results in improvement, the relationship may become more stable. A different reason occurs when the leverage of one person increases because of what the other person did. The offense is greeted with "I may never forgive you for what you did," or "You owe me big time." What really is happening is that this offense becomes a bargaining chip that can be used to leverage preferences in the relationship.

NEGOTIATING SOCIAL SCRIPTS

Negotiating social scripts involves **tactics** that people use to **encourage compliance** with their interpersonal **behavioral preferences.** Anything from throwing a glass across the room or a frown to a hug or a smile can function as a negotiation tactic. Sometimes negotiation tactics are deliberate, while on other occasions they are not. The job for sociologists is to identify negotiation tactics and see how they work in given situations.

Children who pout and carry on when they don't get their way are engaging in a negotiation tactic with their parents. Smiles or pats on the back by parents to encourage a child to repeat a behavior that they approve of are also negotiation tactics.

Gestures of approval that greet conformity are meant to **encourage** the same behavior in subsequent meetings. **Gestures of disapproval,** such as frowns and glares, are meant to **discourage** the same behavior in subsequent encounters. Whether or not such gestures are successful as negotiation tactics is a separate issue.

GESTURES OF DISAPPROVAL

Gestures of disapproval that serve as **negotiation tactics** when **script disputes** exist come in a variety of packages. Often the **gestures of disapproval** amount to **negotiation tactics** based upon threats. **Physical** and **economic threats** are probably the most common. Another common negotiation tactic when script disputes exist does not involve a threat. **Guilt manipulation** relies instead on tapping into the conscience of the other person.

Physical threats are the negotiation tactic of bullies. Comply or else you will get hurt or even killed. Physical threats are a favorite among men who abuse their girlfriends or wives and who establish credibility for carrying out their threats by hitting and punching their victims. Even if someone has not been actually harmed, bullies can effectively use threatening gestures to get their way. Screaming or hitting walls may be enough to suggest that they are mad enough to carry through on their threats. Often physical threats are conveyed verbally, while on other occasions by acts such as punching a hole in the wall.

Economic threats can be just as effective as physical threats in controlling the behavior of others. Sometimes economic threats are an option used by people who are unable or unwilling to use physical threats. For an economic threat to have credibility, the person issuing the threat must be in a position to grant or deny someone money or its equivalent. Bosses use economic threats whenever they threaten to fire someone who doesn't comply. Parents use it when they threaten to withhold allowances if a child disobeys.

Guilt manipulations are yet another familiar negotiation tactic when script disputes arise. Guilt manipulation is based on efforts to make the other person feel guilty for behaving in a manner that is seen as offensive. The hope is that triggering feelings of guilt will cause someone to self-regulate the offensive behavior because they don't like to feel guilty. Whether or not an attempt at guilt manipulation works depends upon whether or not the targeted personality is responsive because of what they have internalized.

Often guilt manipulations **play off** the **ideal-self concept** of someone. Not living up to one's ideal self is a vulnerability that can be exploited. This is what a marine drill instructor is trying to accomplish when he ridicules a new recruit who fails to complete an obstacle course. Calling the recruit a name such as a "girly boy" is meant to trigger efforts to restore self-esteem by complying with the drill instructor's demands.

CONSTRAINTS ON NEGOTIATION TACTICS

There are basically **two constraints** to the **choice of negotiation tactics** that someone employs. The **first** is the **conscience** of that person. The second is the **ability to successfully use a negotiation tactic.**

The role of conscience is easy to illustrate. Some people are unable to consciously use violence to enforce their behavioral preferences. A parent who believes that it is wrong to strike a child is one example. For that parent other negotiation tactics such as economic threats or guilt manipulations may be more acceptable.

Being able to effectively use a negotiation tactic is separate from conscience constraints. Someone who is willing to use violent threats may simply not be credible. To threaten violence to someone who is amused by it implies that the person making the threat suffers from a credibility problem. Sometimes physical attributes are involved, whereas on other occasions, the capacity of the others to protect themselves and inflict pain and suffering on the person issuing the threat is what affects credibility.

The success of someone who is willing to employ economic threats depends on many variables. Is the person seen as capable of withholding things of economic value? If so, does the targeted person have other options? Threatening someone who has other options or is economically independent is less likely to succeed than when they are dependent upon the person issuing the threat.

With guilt manipulations **two factors** are significant. The **first** is the fact that no one can manipulate guilt if it is not there to be manipulated. If the **guilt potential** is there, then the **second** factor kicks in. Some people are terrific at making other people feel guilty. Others are so bad at manipulating guilt that they should not waste their time on the effort.

DEFINITION OF THE SITUATION

So far the emphasis has been on the **behavioral preferences** and their relevance to social encounters and relationships. Now the focus shifts to an equally important consideration. It involves the **perceptions people have of themselves and others** and how these perceptions impact their behavioral choices. **These perceptions are really beliefs or truth claims about the self and others.**

We turn to the American sociologist W. I. Thomas for insights into this process. Thomas (1937) characterized the **subjective meanings** that we attach to social situations as our **definition of the situation.** There are a variety of ways to think about what he meant. The easiest one is to think of **defining a situation** as a process of **sizing up a situation.** Sizing up a situation involves taking others into account. What is taken into account is their potential behavioral preferences and possible reactions should you comply or deviate from their preferences.

The physical characteristics of a situation can influence how a situation is defined. Walking into a bar creates a different definition of the situation than walking into a church. The main point is that our choice of behaviors will depend upon how we read or size up the situation that we are involved in at the time.

Thomas made a classic observation about perceptions of situations and behavior. He stated that **if people define a situation as real, it is real in its consequences.** By this he meant that people act upon what they believe and not necessarily the reality of a situation. Mistakes in perception or beliefs can easily lead to mistakes in behavioral choices.

Adverse reactions to mistaken perceptions and behavioral choices by others can provide a corrective input. Once the message is understood that they don't approve of your original behavior, you can factor that in during subsequent encounters. People are constantly receiving feedback that can affect their subsequent definitions of a situation.

ELEMENTS IN HOW PEOPLE DEFINE SITUATIONS

Let's take a moment and review the basic elements involved in how people define a situation. The first set of elements involves the people that we interact with in a social encounter or relationship. The second set of elements involves our own self-preferences and sanctions.

One involves perceptions concerning the **interaction preferences** that the **other people** in the encounter or relationship have for us. Knowing that a friend needs a lot of attention translates into a behavioral preference for you to give them attention. Knowing that a friend hates to talk about something translates into a behavioral preference for you to "not go there."

A related element is anticipated **social rewards and costs** based upon attributing certain interaction preferences to others. Will they respond favorably or unfavorably? Sometimes we have to balance the self-reward of doing what we prefer with potential social costs inflicted upon us when we offend someone else.

Our perceptions concerning possible **self-imposed constraints** by the other person is yet another element. You may know that doing something will make someone else unhappy but you are not worried because you doubt that they will do much to retaliate. Contrast this to the perception that they will respond violently because there are no self-constraints on their reaction.

Perceptions involving **self-preferences** and related **self-rewards and costs** are also elements that go into how someone defines a situation. Someone may decide not to join the military because they perceive that it is likely to require behaviors that violate that person's self-preferences. An example would be someone who has strong feelings against killing other people. The anticipated guilt should this be required is the perceived self-cost in that person's definition of the situation. Whether or not this perception is true is not the issue. What counts is if it influences their choice of a behavior.

One casualty of war is those who are never able to deal with the guilt suffered by their actions. This includes those who perceived at the time that they joined that they would not have any trouble killing someone else. Conversely, there are those who were drafted into the Vietnam War who resisted because their ideal self-concept told them that it is wrong to kill. Those among them that killed but felt no remorse had feedback that could affect how they define future situations. Perhaps the perception of guilt that had restrained them in the past is no longer a constraint on their behavioral choices.

AN ILLUSTRATION

During the 1960s, student activists often relied on predictable reactions from professors, deans, and university presidents when they confronted them. A common anticipation was that while their university adversaries might get angry and huff and puff, professors, deans, and university presidents were unlikely to resort to violence. This anticipation was based upon the assumption that whatever else they might be, professors, deans, and university presidents have self-preferences that regulate their responses to arguments and perhaps some emotional flare-ups.

Apparently, student agitators chose the wrong professor on one occasion. Having seated themselves in his large lecture hall during class they proceeded to heckle him. But rather than exhibiting the restraint that they anticipated, the professor stormed off the stage and began assaulting them. What is the lesson to be learned? Sometimes people do not accurately define a situation. But once acquainted with the response from that professor, new courses of action could be plotted. One would be to avoid that professor and select ones less likely to be violent. Another choice might be to bring in camera crews from the local TV station to record what transpires in a future confrontation.

We need only turn to the police and likely responses by them to student agitators to fully understand how anticipations about the self-preferences and self-cost/reward mechanisms of others influence behavioral decisions. During confrontations in the 1960s, name-calling and throwing stones and rocks at cops often produced a predictable outcome. Agitators depended upon the cops to wade into the crowd beating and forcefully subduing offenders. It made great political copy on the evening news!

Eventually, in some jurisdictions, police programs were developed that taught discipline to officers and made it clear that those who embarrassed the department by playing into the hand of agitators would be disciplined. Such sanctions were meant to override self-norms among officers who felt that using such tactics is appropriate. The programs were new scripts designed to minimize bad publicity.

HOW DO WE BECOME AWARE OF PREFERENCES?

The answer to this question is quite simple. We become aware of our own self-preferences and the interaction preferences of others through personal experience and what we learn from others. **Self-awareness** pertains to what we **believe** about ourselves. **Social awareness** pertains to what we **believe** about the values, beliefs, and interaction preferences of others.

The accuracy of our self- and social awareness varies. Sometimes what we know about ourselves is true. Sometimes it is distorted and erroneous. The same holds true for our social awareness. What we attribute to others in terms of their values, beliefs, and interaction preferences may be true. At other times it is wrong.

A key sociological assumption is that people behave according to what they believe about themselves and others. Behavioral decisions based upon what is believed at the time generate self-reactions or reactions of others that confirm or discredit how we defined the situation. These reactions provide feedback that can alter our self- and/or social awareness that cycles forward and influences how we define subsequent situations.

STEREOTYPES

Using generalizations in place of personal knowledge about others to define situations is commonplace. Many of our daily transactions are based upon such generalizations. When we make a deposit at our bank, our definition of the situation is based upon certain assumptions about what will be done with our money by people we don't personally know. If we encounter a police officer on the street we don't personally know, our general assumptions about cops informs how we define the situation.

Stereotypes are also generalizations that operate in the absence of personal knowledge about others that also influence how we define situations. The difference is that **stereotypes involve stubborn generalizations** about people in a category that resist information to the contrary. Racial stereotypes are a familiar example. It is the **rigidity of belief** in the generalized characterization of others that is the defining characteristic of stereotypes.

There are basically two responses to information that violates a stereotype. The first is we can **rationally process** the information and **adjust** our future perceptions of those characterized by the stereotype. The second is that we **resist** the new information so that we can **preserve** the original stereotypes. This response is based upon belief rigidity.

Here are some signs of the **belief rigidity** associated with stereotypes. When confronted with information that contradicts a stereotype, one sign of rigidity is an effort to discredit the information. Let's use a hypothetical situation where you offer a friend information that is contrary to a stereotype that friend holds to illustrate how this can unfold. The first response by your friend may be to ask you "where did you hear that?" If you cite a source, then your friend may attack the credibility of the source. If you say that it is based upon your personal experience, your friend may suggest that "maybe they were just faking it to mislead you." If this doesn't work and your friend cannot shake your conviction concerning the contrary data, the form of resistance may change to characterize your contrary information as selective and not typical. Characterizing contrary evidence about a stereotype as an exception means that for all practical purposes your friend will resort to the original stereotype when thinking about them in the future.

STEREOTYPES AND SELF-FULFILLING PROPHECIES

A **self-fulfilling prophecy** occurs whenever actions based upon a stereotype causes an outcome that justifies the stereotype. Denying women access to the opportunities necessary to compete at the Indianapolis 500 because of the belief that women are incapable of driving high performance cars sets a self-fulfilling prophecy in motion. The absence of women competing is used to justify the belief that only men are capable of competing in the event.

Gatekeepers in society often use negative stereotypes to discriminate against people in other groups. **Gatekeepers** are people in positions of power who control access to opportunities. Religious gatekeepers often call upon Scriptures or other holy documents to justify the exclusive right of men to rule. This self-fulfilling prophecy still prevents Catholic women from entering the priesthood and Muslim women from positions of authority in their religion. For more than a century after the Founding Fathers limited the vote to men, male politicians justified their refusal to allow women to vote with beliefs such as women are not capable of exercising rational judgment.

SELF-DISCLOSURE

Questions involving stereotypes as generalizations, and how information relevant to them is processed, apply to people that we don't personally know. But just because we know someone does not mean that we have an accurate picture of that person's values, beliefs, and personal social scripts. People who are low on self-disclosure make the process difficult.

Self-disclosure refers to the degree that people are **willing to reveal** their personal behavioral preferences, values, and beliefs to others. There are a variety of circumstances that affect self-disclosure. In all instances, **whenever circumstances encourage self-disclosure, the capacity for accurately defining the situation in terms of other participants increases.** Conversely, **whenever circumstances prevent self-disclosure, the capacity for error in defining the situation in terms of other participants increases.**

What are some of these circumstances that affect self-disclosure? One involves self-disclosure as a **personality trait.** Often **repression,** which prevents someone from knowing themselves, is the problem. Self-disclosure is not likely if people are unaware of their true feeling or beliefs.

A different circumstance is when people are **aware of themselves** but are **unwilling to disclose** it to others. Often the reason for not disclosing is based upon a concern over how others will react. Because the unwillingness to self-disclose is based upon perceptions of how others might react to what is revealed, the same people may reveal aspects of themselves that they believe others will judge as acceptable.

These more **personal circumstances** are related to **culture** because both repression and perceptions about how others might react are culturally based. But there is another way culture can play a role. Some cultures encourage self-disclosure, while others strongly discourage it. People in some cultures are amazed at how easy Americans reveal personal information about themselves. People in cultures that are lower on self-disclosure are less likely to learn about personal feelings and beliefs that can inform how they define situations.

HOW DELIBERATE IS THE PROCESS OF DEFINING A SITUATION?

Sometimes we are quite deliberate in how we go about defining a situation. Preparing for a job interview often involves carefully thinking about what the interviewer will be looking for. Of course, careful planning is not a guarantee that how someone defines a situation will be accurate. Its accuracy is a function of the accuracy of the information upon which that definition of the situation is calculated.

In everyday transactions, the process of defining situations we are involved in is often less calculated. If we are familiar with the situation, we may actually be on autopilot and not even consciously think about our anticipations. Only when something unpredictable occurs are we likely to switch to more deliberate and conscious appraisal of the situation.

When dealing with strangers, the manner by which people define situations involving them is more deliberate. Some may bluster forth oblivious to the possibility that strangers might hold different views, but generally speaking we are more alert when we encounter people who are unfamiliar. It is more like testing the water to see what scripts these people who we are unfamiliar with embrace.

With such encounters we may be consciously aware of the extent to which we are looking for clues so that we can predict their reactions. This often occurs when we travel to a new country. Even if we have read about the customs of people in that country, we are likely to be more aware of how we define situations involving them than when we are interacting with old friends.

SOCIALIZATION

Socialization refers to the process by which people are **made aware** of and come to **accept** the behavioral preferences, values, and beliefs of others. To say someone has been socialized into their group, community, or society is to say that his/her personal social scripts match those of the other members. If someone comes to accept the social scripts, values, and beliefs of people outside their group, community, or society, then socialization has also occurred.

The term **internalization** is used to describe the process by which people come to **incorporate** the values, beliefs, and behavioral preferences of others into their own personalities. What is internalized from others forms the basis for someone's **social self.** Freud used the term Superego to describe the social self, whereas Rogers associated the social self with someone's ideal self-concept.

The concept of socialization provides insights into script disputes. It helps explain why parents are often alarmed at media and video game images and messages that they believe encourage kids to embrace attitudes and social behaviors that they find unacceptable. **Trying to prevent children from exposure to scripts that parents find unacceptable is really trying to prevent them from exposure to what they might internalize and incorporate into their personalities and behaviors.**

The first appearance of a gyrating Elvis Presley on television triggered a chorus of criticism by parents and others who were worried that his sexuality would encourage unacceptable behavior among American youngsters. Pressures were placed on the networks to edit his sexual gyrations by filming only above the waist. Whether or not Elvis was responsible for moral decay in America is still debated by some.

NOT SOCIALIZATION

Socialization requires **becoming aware** of the values, beliefs, and social scripts of others and **internalizing** them. Only if both conditions of **awareness** and **acceptance** are met does socialization occur. **Socialization is not the same as social awareness.**

Social awareness is limited to an awareness of the values, beliefs, scripts, and how others socially reward compliance or impose costs for deviance. One need not agree with someone else for social awareness of that person to be an influence. You don't have to agree with cops stopping people for speeding for that awareness to impact your choices of behavior.

Social awareness shapes how we **define situations** in terms of the other people who are involved in a social encounter or relationship. **Socialization** is responsible for the personal scripts that we bring to social situations. **Social awareness** provides the basis for calculating how other people will respond to our behavior, whereas **socialization** affects what behaviors we think are acceptable.

RESOCIALIZATION

Resocialization refers to a **change in behavioral preferences** brought about by a **change** in **situations.** The classic example is when a father who prioritized his career and had little time to spend with his children retires and now prioritizes spending time with his grandchildren. Another example is when someone is sent to prison and is socialized into prison culture.

Just as with socialization, it is important to separate behavioral choices based upon social awareness from resocialization. For resocialization to occur, the person spending time in prison must incorporate prison culture into his/her social self. It must become the basis for his behavioral preferences. This is different from learning about prison culture in the form of social awareness. Knowing how to act may be critical for survival, even though it does not entail buying into the prison script.

BEHAVIORAL RATIONALIZATIONS

Behavioral rationalizations are the **excuses** people use to justify their actions to themselves or others. There are two basic types of behavioral rationalizations. **Personal rationalizations** are the excuses a person uses to abate or deny personal guilt. An example would be people who express hostility toward others by telling them an unpleasant truth about themselves, but who justify it by saying that they are only interested in helping that person.

Social rationalizations are excuses that are shared and offered by members of a group to justify their behavior. One justification for the loss of civilian lives in the invasions of Afghanistan and Iraq was that we were trying to help them. A related justification is that these efforts were necessary to make Americans secure at home. A justification that juvenile gangs often use for inflicting violence on others is that the others were enemies out to harm them. Whether or not a social rationalization is a true belief claim is not the ultimate issue when considering its purpose. What counts in situations like these is whether or not it works, and it works if it provides a sufficient justification to overcome guilt.

Awareness of both personal and social rationalizations affects our choices of behavior. Knowing that someone is going to rationalize his/her behavior in a particular manner can provide clues as to how one might counter it. Anticipating that your child is going to claim that "everyone does it" may require you to come up with a rebuttal such as "if everyone jumped off a cliff would you?"

Socially shared rationalizations are often more difficult to counter because of the extent that they are socially reinforced in the group. Having others chime in with the same rationalizations usually gives it more credibility than if it is expressed by an isolated individual. An illustration is the extent to which gangs justify violence in the name of protecting the "family."

Behavioral rationalizations can also be appropriated from outsiders, like when kids get excuses from musical lyrics. Parents who want to censor media messages may be worried about more than those images creating new dispositions in their children. What may concern them is that those messages may provide excuses that will release existing dispositions.

SUPERFICIAL RELATIONSHIPS

A **superficial relationship** is one that **persists over time** but is **relatively shallow.** Regularly saying hello to a neighbor and commenting on the weather is an example. Keeping the relationship superficial is what works. Not talking about other things prevents unwanted and potentially disruptive information from surfacing.

Superficial scripts that govern guys who like to hang out together with their buddies often exhibit such limitations. Blithering on about sports may be accompanied by a prohibition about talking about personal feelings. Sport talk is rewarded, whereas personal talk is discouraged as whining.

Superficial relationships with relatives can be much more satisfactory than really getting to know them. This is why some people prefer to be with their relatives only on special occasions. Superficial relationships with coworkers may involve little more than exchanges of pleasantries.

There is nothing inherently wrong with superficial relationships. Those involved may prefer it. But problems can arise if one person prefers superficiality while the other insists on more self-disclosure. Insisting on self-disclosure for someone who is repressive is likely to increase tensions in a relationship.

Insisting on more self-disclosure can cause another problem. Learning more about someone may be disturbing. It can reveal thoughts that create conflicts rather than improving a relationship. An example would be when a boyfriend insists that his girlfriend tell him if she still thinks about her ex-boyfriend.

THE DYAD

A **dyad** is a **relationship** between **two people** and only two people. **The dyad is the minimal unit of analysis** in sociology. This is what distinguishes sociology from psychology, where the focus is on the individual.

The sociological interest in studying social encounters and relationships reflects this emphasis on the dyad as the minimal unit of analysis. It takes at least two people to form a social encounter or relationship. Our definition of a social behavior also reflects the emphasis on a dyad. The actual or imagined presence of someone else is necessary before an act qualifies as a social behavior.

This difference in emphasis between sociology and psychology can be seen from a different angle. To **describe a social relationship** is to **describe the history** of a **relationship** between two or more people over time. In psychology, history is limited to describing what happened to an individual over time.

SOCIAL CHANGE

Social change occurs whenever there is a **change in participants** and/or the **activities** of people. Social change means a change in social scripts. An example was when the script that denied women access to corporate manager jobs changed to include women.

Care must be taken to distinguish between script changes that result in a change concerning who participates and the scripts for those in that position. Allowing women to become corporate managers does not necessarily mean a change in the organization script for managers. Women managers may be expected to function just like their male counterparts.

But change in participants can provoke changes in scripts. The presence of women may discourage men from telling sexist jokes. The presence of women may invite incorporating less masculine styles of management. What happens in specific situations is dictated by the relevant facts.

Social change is not limited to the larger society. Personal relationships often change over time. Divorce and remarriage reflect a change in participants. But even with a marriage that lasts, emergent scripts may come to replace earlier ones.

CHAPTER 3
MORE ON SOCIAL SCRIPTS

So far the strategy has been to think about how social scripts influence what people do in their everyday transactions. Beginning with everyday life makes it easy to understand how the idea of social scripts impacts on our daily lives. Thinking about how your personal script preferences may be similar or conflict with someone else, such as with the personal script of a roommate, and how this influences what script emerges between you over time, makes intuiting what it means to think sociologically quite simple. It is equally easy to appreciate how mistaking the preferences of others can cause you grief when you do something that offends them.

Now we will turn to examining some more factors that sociologists have found useful to look for when studying social transactions. We begin by looking at how general cultural themes can influence daily situations. This, along with other factors, creates a context for better understanding how social scripts influence everyday life.

CULTURAL THEMES

Culture was originally seen by sociologists as a **shared social script** that has a **pervasive influence** on those **living within a society.** A variety of questions identify important cultural themes examined by sociologists. One question concerns who has political power and how political leaders are selected. Another question concerns whether or not couples live with a husband's family, her family, or independently. Who has power within families is another question. There are also questions about how cultural scripts shape ceremonies, such as those associated with births, marriages, and deaths.

Cultural scripts also shape how **societies** interact with each other. Some societies prefer to be isolated from other societies. Other societies have cultural scripts that encourage contact and peaceful trade with other societies. Still other societies are hostile toward their neighbors or try to impose their scripts on them.

Although the term **culture** originally applied to **entire societies,** it can be used to characterize groups, communities, organizations, states, or even regions within a country. When applied to groups, it suggests different script possibilities. Would you expect the culture of a church teen group to be different from that of a street gang? The term corporate culture is used to describe different ways organizations operate. Labels such as affluent or blue-collar community suggest different values, beliefs, and behavioral preferences. In the 2004 election for president of the United States, the labels "red state" and "blue state" suggested political differences, with red signaling conservative scripts and blue signaling progressive scripts.

Other characterizations, such as rust belt states, suggest regions of the country where life has been changed dramatically. Prosperity and lifestyles based upon manufacturing have been replaced by economic downturns and struggling lifestyles. The economic downturns in the rust belt region of the Midwest are a contrast to areas of the country that are growing in prosperity as centers for information and computer technology.

SOME AMERICAN CULTURAL THEMES

The **American glorification of violence** serves as a cultural theme. This tradition began with European explorers and the conquest of Native Americans. It continued through the violent annexation of nearly half of Mexico into what is now the Southwest and California. Violence was further popularized by images of the Wild West, gunfighters, and hanging cattle rustlers. Movies, television, and video games continue to provide American audiences with daily doses of violent images.

The cultural theme that values violence helps explain current American attitudes. One such attitude is the general appeal of violence in the movies and on television. Another is the popularity of gun ownership for personal protection by many Americans. Some states have even extended this principle from protection at home to the liberalization of handgun carry permits. In 2005, legislation in Florida extended the right for citizens to use deadly force anytime they feel threatened. Even the police have tighter controls on the use of deadly force that what has been legalized in Florida. And finally, among all the top economic nations in the world, only the United States imposes the death penalty on its own citizens.

Other economically advanced societies are astonished by the American fascination with violence, especially its use of the death penalty. They refuse to extradite even terrorists to the United States unless the death penalty is taken off the table. Moreover, many of these nations simply cannot believe that the most economically advanced country on the globe has leaders that continue to glorify its gunslinger image.

American cultural scripts involving sex provide another contrast with other societies. Americans are more sexually uptight than their European counterparts. Censoring sexually explicit material is an obsession with many Americans. Sexual scandals involving politicians in the United States often become moral crusades, whereas in Europe they are often viewed with amusement.

IDEAL AND REAL CULTURE

Sociologists make a distinction between **ideal** and **real** cultures. The **ideal culture** is based upon scripts that celebrate certain values and images that members have of themselves and their society. The **real culture** involves scripts that determine what actually exists within a society.

An illustration taken from life in the United States will help establish the difference between ideal and real cultures. The United States proudly embraces its commitment to the ideal of democracy. Yet the reality is that the Founding Fathers excluded many people from participation in the government. Both slaves and women were denied the right to vote. It was not until after the Civil War that this right was formally extended to former male slaves and then scripts denying them eligibility were created in the South to make it virtually impossible for them to enact this formal right.

The hypocrisy between the ideal script that celebrates democracy and the reality of denying women the right to vote came to a head during World War I. Women asked why should their fathers, husbands, and sons fight for democracy in Europe when they and their own mothers and daughters could not vote at home? Shortly after the war ended women were given the right to vote in the United States. The year was 1920. It was hardly a landslide decision. It passed the Senate by only one vote.

IDEAL AND ACTUAL SELVES

Whenever people **internalize** elements contained in an **ideal culture,** it becomes a part of their **social self.** As we have already seen, authors use different terms to describe the social self. But the work of Rogers is the clearest on the link between ideal and real culture and its psychological dynamics.

Socialization into **ideal culture** is the basis upon which someone's **ideal self** is formed. The celebrated images offered by the ideal culture become the measure by which a person judges himself or herself. To the extent that people's actual self measures up to their ideal self is the extent to which they feel good about themselves. They experience a sense of high self-esteem or worth. To the extent that people experience a disparity between their ideal and actual selves is the extent to which they feel bad about themselves and have a loss of self-esteem or worth.

Rogers felt that therapy should be designed to help people come to accept themselves for who they are, rather than spending so much energy sustaining their ideal self through denials and rationalizations. We turn to a social psychologist to help translate Rogers's insights into social processes where denials and rationalizations are used to justify disparities between ideal and real cultures. An important ingredient is the extent to which these denials and rationalizations are socially generated and shared.

RESOLVING CONTRADICTIONS

Contradictions between **ideal** and **real cultures** create a **psychological tension** known as **dissonance** (Festinger, 1957). It is a tension that occurs whenever people fail to practice what they preach. The term **dissonance reduction** refers to the methods people use to ease their tensions over what they idealize and what they do.

There are a number of different ways people deal with dissonance. One is to change their ideals. This eliminates dissonance by making what they say compatible with what they do.

Because people often become wedded to their ideal image of themselves and their society this is not always easy. For those who can't give up on their ideal image of themselves and their society there is another option. They can simply deny the reality of what actually exists. The difficulty with this choice is that it can take a lot of energy to deny what exists.

Because it is often difficult to sustain a denial of reality, people often resort to **behavioral rationalizations.** The reality that in the land of opportunity there are millions of Americans who are poor can be rationalized by blaming them. Often the rationalization for denying women access to certain jobs is the claim that they are physically and/or emotionally unsuited for them. The fact that women are not given a reasonable chance to disprove the rationalization helps to sustain it.

POPULAR CULTURE

Popular culture (pop culture) encompasses **themes** and **activities** that ordinary people incorporate into their own lifestyles. Because popular culture is often driven by the mass media, it is sometimes called **mass culture,** but this is somewhat misleading because some popular culture is generated from the bottom up.

Even so, the most attention is given to how popular music, films, TV, magazines, books, and games drive popular culture. Watching kids incorporate rap music lyrics, jargon, and themes into their personal lives is one example of how scripts portrayed in the media are expressed by more ordinary people. Another is the huge influence that the TV show Star Trek has had on fans who share their enthusiasm by dressing up and meeting at Trekkie conventions. The Internet has contributed greatly to the spread of pop cultures, such as the one involving Trekkies. Everything from memorabilia to setting up local clubs within a worldwide network is possible.

In the world of film, few if any have had the influence on popular culture as that of the Star Wars series. While the Star Wars phenomenon is extraordinary, the enthusiasm of fans is common in popular culture. For years, Deadheads devoted their lives to following the Grateful Dead band from concert to concert. Similar addictions can be found among those devoted to video games.

POPULAR CULTURE AND LIFESTYLES

Popular culture can have an enormous impact on lifestyles of fans. Sociologists interested in studying popular culture often try to trace the influence of popular media on lifestyles. The effort is to first identify popular culture themes in lifestyles of those affected and then to see how participants modify these themes. The rise in popularity of tattoos is a case in point. As a sociologist you would want to document what media were involved in the process. Was it through print media such as popular music magazines like *Spin* or *Rolling Stone?* Did music video channels like MTV play a role? Once you get a picture of how the tattoo craze began, then you might want to see how it played out among those providing and getting tattoos. Did its popularity recruit new artists into providing more personal and creative tattoos? Another question that you might pursue concerns the role of friends or media personalities in popularizing locations and types of tattoos.

THE SCOPE OF A SOCIAL SCRIPT

Originally **cultural themes** were thought to have a **pervasive influence** within a society. This meant that **cultural themes** represented **social shared scripts** that are **agreed upon by all members of a society.** But even in the most isolated communities studied by anthropologists some **deviance** occurs, which means that not everyone agrees with the script.

Knowing that some deviance exists in societies alerts us to the necessity to ask a basic question whenever we describe a cultural pattern in a society. Rather than assume that a cultural theme is pervasive, it is more useful to determine its scope. The **scope of a socially shared script** is its pervasiveness. The emphasis on a **socially shared script** is because the question of pervasiveness only arises once at least some adherence to a cultural theme has been documented.

The **scope of a socially shared script,** therefore, is the extent to which it applies to those in a group, organization, community, region, state, or society. We begin by looking at the scope of cultural themes within societies.

To say that Americans tend to have an obsession with violence does not mean that this is a totally pervasive cultural theme. While it is true that American history often documents the extent to which the country used violence against slaves, the British, Native Americans, Mexicans, in the Civil War, and against other nations is not to say that Americans never used more peaceful methods to negotiate differences. Both diplomacy and war have been instruments of American foreign policy, with circumstances and leadership determining the preferences in specific situations.

Although the Supreme Court decided that it is constitutional for states to impose the death penalty, because it did not in their opinion represent cruel and unusual punishment, not all states have chosen that option. Moreover, even within states that have imposed the death penalty, many within those states voice their opposition to it. Thus, although the scope of the death penalty as a social/governmental script in the United States exceeds that of other economically advanced nations in the world who prohibit it, it would be mistaken to identify its scope as totally pervasive within the United States.

Mention of the difference between politically conservative red states and more politically progressive blue states are indicative of significant value/belief clusters of differences that exist in the United States. One problem is that designating a state as red or blue does not answer a significant question. What is the scope of the script suggested by the red or blue label in a given state? Does everyone subscribe to it? Was the label based upon whether or not a state voted for the Republican or Democratic candidate for President? If so, it is misleading to use such an outcome when in some cases it could have been decided by a few votes. A better picture concerning the scope of a political script in a state would be a scientific survey.

Script differences within the United States are not entirely unique. Many nations today experience internal script disputes if for no other reason than most represent cobbled together entities that were created through war, conquest, or other agreements. Nowhere has this become more evident than in Iraq, where significant religious and tribal differences resulted mostly from it being cobbled together as a country many years ago.

This is not to suggest that the scope of a cultural theme in a society is never pervasive. Even though significant differences exist between many groups in countries like Afghanistan and Iraq, the legacy of cultural patriarchy remains relatively pervasive, especially in more rural regions. Patriarchy exists in these societies to the extent that men are privileged in politics, religion, economics, and the home.

All of this should remind us that whenever we try to identify cultural themes in a group, community, organization, state, region, or society we must look carefully at the scope or extent of a particular theme. The more extensive or pervasive the theme, the greater is the scope of that theme.

You can also appreciate that looking at the scope of a script found in popular culture can be extremely useful. To say something qualifies as popular culture suggests that it affects a large number of people, but the extent is left dangling. As a sociologist you would want to explore the scope or extent of a given pop culture phenomenon in order to estimate its impact. In your research you may find that although a theme is shared, the way it is expressed may vary locally. Knowing that Trekkies exist in Germany tells us something about the scope of the Trekkie phenomenon, but it would also be interesting to see if differences exist between how American and German Trekkies interpret Star Trek themes.

THE DURATION OF A SOCIAL SCRIPT

The **duration of a social script** refers to **how long it lasts.** To talk about a social script as having a long duration usually means that it has persisted over generations in that society. **Rituals** are scripts with a long duration. We often find this in more rural societies, where ceremonies attending the birth of a baby or how the dead are grieved are transmitted from generation to generation. Anthropologists often found this among hunting and gathering societies, whose cultural themes and rituals when left undisturbed by outsiders persisted for generation after generation.

Both the scope and duration of social scripts often combined to form the religious history of a country. The Roman Catholic Church has had a persistent (duration) and pervasive (scope) influence in countries such as Italy and Spain. But in Spain an invasion from North Africa imposed a Muslim script on many regions of the country. Although Roman Catholicism was eventually restored, the Muslim invasion interrupted the scope and duration of Roman Catholicism, and its impact can still be seen in architectural marvels and cultural themes in cities like Granada.

FADS AND FASHIONS

Fads and **fashions** represent **pop culture** themes with a relatively **short duration.** The main difference between a fad and a fashion is that **fads** can be relatively private activities such as hobbies, whereas **fashions** involve public displays. With fads sociologists are interested in looking for patterns that express a wider interest in an activity that is not necessarily novel. Fads like collecting stamps or coins are not new but do fluctuate in popularity. The same is true for collecting dolls, action figures, sewing, knitting, and so forth. With fashions sociologists also try to document what was or is popular in a particular country or area of a country and the extent to which one country or area influences the popularity of fashions in another. We can see this with everything from what are popular clothes to diets and food.

THE DIFFUSION OF SOCIAL SCRIPTS

The **diffusion of social scripts** refers to the **spread of scripts** that shape the activities of people in one group or society to another. The spread of blue jean designs from the United States to Russia is an example of diffusion. Another example is when the Founding Fathers in the United States used political scripts that existed in Great Britain as models for our Constitution.

Conquest has been an important vehicle for diffusion. Under the Roman Empire, untold numbers of people were introduced to Roman values, beliefs, and social scripts. The same was true under British colonialism. Countries like India, which are now politically independent from England, still retain the legacy of language, political institutions, and rituals such as tea time.

The **diffusion of social scripts** and activities **within** a society also occur. An example would be when food that is popular in one area of the country spreads to another. Another is when music first popular in one area spreads to another. The spread of rap music from urban black communities to suburban white communities is a specific example.

Often the diffusion of social scripts is less dramatic than those involving countries or a large-scale spread within a society. Coaches often rely on strategies developed by other coaches. Such borrowing is an example of script diffusion. Cheerleaders sometimes "borrow" techniques or routines from other squads. This too is an example of script diffusion.

MUSIC AS A SOCIAL SCRIPT

Because the **composition of music** is often a private exercise, it might be surprising to think of it as scripted. Scripting is evident with different musical styles. One need not be a musician to recognize differences between styles such as reggae, rock and roll, or the blues by the sound patterns that are used. Combining composition scripts to form a new genre is to create a new emergent script.

Musical lyrics both reflect and influence social scripts that play out in everyday life. Fans can readily identify lyric themes associated with genres such as country and western, gangsta rap, heavy metal, and reggae. Identifying a song as upbeat or depressing also signals different script themes.

CIRCUMSTANCES AND SOCIAL SCRIPTS

Often **circumstances** are more important in determining the **content of social scripts** than **personal preferences.** Both **economic** and **technological changes** are prime examples. Sometimes it is just a natural disaster such as a tsunami or earthquake that dramatically change peoples' social scripts and lives.

The large number of mothers with young children who are working today is more a function of economic changes than personal choices. While some are single moms who have never married or are divorced, many are married but must work to support their families. Many married couples confronted with rising expenses can no longer afford to rely on a single income. The days of dear old dad as the single breadwinner are rapidly disappearing. Many of these married mothers would prefer to stay at home with their young children but simply cannot afford it. For single moms, economic challenges may require them to get more education or to work more than one job. This can leave them feeling guilty for not having enough time for their kids.

Technological changes can have an enormous impact on social scripts and activities. **Cultural lag** is the term Ogburn (1957) used to describe the time it takes for a society to adapt its social scripts to a technological innovation. An illustration would be the creation of word processing programs. Before the advent of word processing programs, secretaries used an electric typewriter to print memos, letters, and manuscripts. Because of the time needed to avoid making mistakes and correcting them, using electric typewriters is a slow process by comparison. New scripts to accommodate the new technology have emerged to replace old ones.

The advent of e-mail has dramatically altered daily scripts. In the days when memos were handwritten or typed and delivered through snail mail, less time was spent on responding to them. Now with the ease of e-mail, people often complain about the amount of time they must spend responding to messages that are of little interest to them.

Whenever economic or technological change arises and changes scripts in one area, it often has a spreadlike (diffusion) effect on scripts elsewhere. The transformation of the American economy from manufacturing to information and service means that there less good paying low-skilled jobs. A college education, which was once seen as only for the privileged, is now becoming a necessity for more and more people. This creates pressures throughout the educational system, where old scripts must be replaced by new ones that better prepare people for these new realities.

MASTER SCRIPTS

A **master script** is a **deliberately constructed** script that governs **diverse activities** among a **large number of people.** Master scripts differ from cultural scripts because a master script is deliberately planned. Cultural scripts unfold more naturally.

Master scripts are also more specific than cultural scripts in their sustaining values and beliefs. Cultural scripts provide a theme or context for other scripts. A master script prescribes more detailed requirements.

A **master script** can be thought of as a **master plan.** It contains behavioral requirements that regulate and coordinate conduct among a large number of people. Examples range from **corporate flowcharts** and **organizational job descriptions** to our **Constitution.**

Master scripts differ depending upon how specific they are regarding behavioral requirements. The Constitution and Bill of Rights state general principles for organizing government and protecting individual rights. The language allows for interpretation, such as what is meant by the right of people to bear arms or what constitutes free speech. Job descriptions for people working in hospitals or other complex organizations are usually more specific about required or forbidden behavior.

Interpretive latitude is the **amount of meaning** that can be read into a master script. The more general or ambiguous the language, the greater the interpretive latitude is that is available to people in positions of authority. The more specific the language, the less interpretive the latitude is that is available to people in positions of authority.

The **Supreme Court** is **the final interpretive authority** concerning our Constitution and the Bill of Rights. How these justices interpret the broad language contained in these documents has enormous significance. Their decisions on everything from abortion and the separation of church and state to due process in criminal cases affects everyone living in the United States. This is why the process of choosing new Supreme Court justices is often so contentious. Different political parties and interest groups want justices who favor them.

Corporate flowcharts and **job descriptions** that are **carefully designed** and **expressed** improve the potential for efficiency and the coordination of diverse activities within organizations. **Interpretive latitude** by those in positions of authority is diminished when worker responsibilities are clearly expressed. With more ambiguous job requirements, bosses have more flexibility to interpret job performance. Stating exactly what workers are to do gives bosses less flexibility than when a general requirement such as doing a good job is the requirement. Exactly what constitutes "doing a good job" is open to interpretation.

OFFICIAL AND UNOFFICIAL SCRIPTS

The **official script** of an organization is the formal script **endorsed** by the top executives in an organization such as a corporation or government agency. There are two different types of endorsements. The **first** endorsement is that of the **master script** (plan) that is used to identify and coordinate activities within the organization. The **second** endorsement is a **public portrayal** of how the organization operates.

Unofficial scripts are **informal scripts** that **are not officially recognized** by top executives within an organization. The difference between **official** and **unofficial scripts** within organizations **parallels** the distinction between **ideal** and **real culture.** Official scripts are like ideal culture and unofficial scripts are like real culture. The difference is between what is celebrated as an ideal and what exists.

Just as with ideal and real culture, disparities can exist between official and unofficial scripts within an organization. **One disparity** is between an **organization's ideal** concerning **worker conduct** as **officially described in a master script** and what **workers do.** Unofficial informal worker scripts may encourage behavior that counters the official organizational script. Workers may decide to slow down or go on strike to counter demands contained in the official organizational script.

Even when executives suspect that an unofficial informal script is diminishing compliance with what they prefer, it can be difficult to deal with. One reason is that workers can exert extraordinary pressures on their fellow workers to conform to their unofficial informal preferences. Management may try to encourage workers to reveal those who are defying the master script, but this too carries risks associated with retaliation by fellow workers. Installing monitoring devices can have some success, but excessive monitoring can alienate workers even more and this can cause further disruptions. Moreover, even in Supermax prisons with the latest in monitoring technology convicts find ingenious ways to defy them.

PUBLIC AND PRIVATE SCRIPTS

Public scripts shape **interaction** that occurs in the open and in front of **audiences.** Public scripts shape public behavior. **Private scripts** shape interaction that occurs **behind closed doors** and that is not observed by other members of the group, community, or society.

Private scripts can shape the behavior of one person that occurs behind closed doors or interaction among a number of people. An example of **solitary behavior** that is scripted would be a man who lives alone and shaves every morning before going to work. Spousal abuse illustrates a **form of interaction** that often occurs behind closed doors.

Public scripts can also shape the behavior of one person or interaction between two or more people. Driving to work along a deserted stretch of highway on the proper side of the road is an example of a **scripted solitary activity** that is public even though no one actually observes it. Passing another driver on the way to work represents a scripted **form of interaction** that is public.

The **difference** between scripts that take place in private and those that shape activities **observed by an audience** is of special concern to sociologists. **One concern is methodological.** What people report to a researcher concerning their private behavior may or may not be accurate.

The **other concern is similar to situations where the official script of an organization is contradicted by what goes on unofficially behind closed doors.** It occurs whenever public impressions conceal private realities. What you see may not be what really exists. The public appearance of a couple may not represent how they behave toward each other in private. A couple who never says angry words to each other in public may do so regularly when in private. The same applies to parents who adhere to the principle of never fighting or disagreeing in front of the kids.

FRONTSTAGE AND BACKSTAGE

Goffman (1963) used **theatrical terms** to describe the difference between public and private behavior. **Frontstage** refers to performances that are seen by an audience. **Backstage** refers to what goes on at rehearsals or behind the curtain.

One advantage of the theatrical metaphor is that it draws our attention to the possibility that people may rehearse their performances. A **rehearsal** involves preparing for a performance. Theatrical rehearsals take place before an imagined rather than real audience.

Rehearsals in everyday life are similar. One difference is that everyday-life rehearsals are not limited to physically practicing performances. Everyday-life rehearsals often involve **mental rehearsals.** An example would be when you think about what you are going to say when you return an item to a store.

TAKEN-FOR-GRANTED SCRIPTS

Taken-for-granted scripts are ones that have become so familiar that people never really question them. Taken-for-granted scripts are routinely enacted without much conscious reflection. Taken-for-granted scripts feature a relatively **passive image** of people who go about their activities without much thought or deliberation.

Taken-for-granted scripts result from **habit.** People get so used to the script that it becomes assumed. This is just the opposite from what happens when we encounter people from an unfamiliar culture. What is taken-for-granted by them is novel to us.

Isolation tends to reinforce taken-for-granted scripts. Not knowing about alternatives increases the likelihood that people will see their ideas and values as natural. Exposure to others may transform our taken-for-granted scripts into a more explicit awareness of them.

An example would be meeting someone who is a strict vegetarian. Before this experience, people who come from a meat-devouring culture may take their eating habits for granted. Becoming aware of vegetarian diets as an alternative may increase their awareness of their own diet habits. When we become aware of scripts other than what we are familiar with, something like our eating habits often become less taken-for-granted.

SINGLE OR MULTIPLE SCRIPTS

Cultural diversity is a term often used to describe a group, community, organization, or society where **multiple cultural scripts** exist. Terms like **multicultural** and **cultural pluralism** are also used to describe such situations. **The existence of multiple scripts increases the potential for script disputes.**

When those involved in **social exchanges share a single social script,** then the **potential for script disputes is low.** This is especially true when a group is isolated from others and interaction is limited to members who share the same script. Under these circumstances, the main source of any script dispute is the relatively rare deviant who for personal reasons does not fit in.

How **groups respond** to encounters with **groups that have scripts** that differ from their own is of special interest to sociologists. Curiosity make some groups amenable to learning more about the values, beliefs, and behavioral preferences of other groups. Other groups try to restrict exposure to their own viewpoints. And still other groups try to impose their own views on other groups. **Ethnocentrism** and **cultural relativism** are terms that help us better understand these different possibilities.

ETHNOCENTRISM AND CULTURAL RELATIVISM

Ethnocentrism occurs when **members of a group** believe that their **scripts are superior** to those of outsiders. **Ethnocentrism** involves **two conditions.** The first condition is that **ethnocentrism requires an outside group.**

The second condition is that an **awareness of an outside group elevates a group's taken-for-granted scripts into ones that are more explicitly recognized by members.** This sets the stage for making an invidious comparison between their own scripts and those of other groups. The result is that the group views the scripts of the outside group as inferior.

Cultural relativism is an alternative possibility. Cultural relativism represents an attitude of tolerance and respect for cultural diversity. Cultural relativism does not mean that people must abandon their own scripts in order to respect those of other people.

IDENTIFYING WITH OUTSIDERS

Ethnocentrism presumes that **members of a group identify** with their own values, beliefs, and behavioral preferences. But it is also possible that **once exposed** to an **outside group,** some members may come to identify with the values, beliefs, and behavioral preferences of that outside group. If this happens, the **neutrality of cultural relativism** gives way to more than idle curiosity and respect. Identifying with outsiders can inspire imitation and even efforts to leave and join them.

PERSONAL JUDGMENTS

Ethnocentrism and **cultural relativism** are **group phenomena.** Ethnocentrism describes a group that thinks that their scripts are superior to others and express disdain for those of outsiders. Cultural relativism describes a group that is tolerant and respectful of cultural differences.

A **personal judgment** is **individual.** Personal judgments are associated with whether or not someone likes or dislikes certain scripts, including those of outsiders. Dissidents who dislike the prevailing scripts of their own group or society are expressing a personal judgment just as much as someone who thinks outsiders are inferior.

PROSELYTIZING

The most **extreme form of ethnocentrism** is when one group of society actively proselytizes. To **proselytize** is to try and get people to abandon their ways and convert to your script. This is exactly what missionaries do when they go to other countries and try to spread the word.

Proselytizing is based upon a **sense of superiority or righteousness.** But not all people who celebrate the superiority of their values, beliefs, and behavioral preferences go out and try to win converts. Some simply want to be left alone.

Drawing the line between a **group proselytizing** and trying to **maintain independence** from outside influences can be tricky. Are Islamic fundamentalists trying to impose their version of the world on the United States? If so, then their activities would constitute proselytizing. Are Islamic fundamentalists fighting to maintain independence from outside influence from countries like the United States? If so, then their activities would constitute efforts to maintain independence from outside influences.

Notice that even though Islamic fundamentalists may not be trying to proselytize Westerners such as the United States, they are engaged in serious proselytizing efforts within Islamic countries. To the extent that they admit no alternatives to their schemes is the extent to which they are ethnocentric within their societies. This leads us to yet another issue.

What is the difference between the United States protecting its vital national interests and it proselytizing? To the extent that the United States is dependent upon oil and the extent to which success by Islamic fundamentalists threatens that supply is the extent to which it is a vital national interest. The basic question is whether or not spreading Western-style democracies to Islamic countries is proselytizing or simply an effort to thwart the development of Islamic fundamentalist governments and protect our national interest in preserving the supply of oil. There is no easy answer. It is entirely possible that supporting dictatorships is a better guarantee of preserving our supply of oil than placing it in the hands of an unpredictable electorate.

SEARCHING FOR ALTERNATIVE EXPERIENCES

In the past, many societies were isolated from exposure to social scripts other than their own. The only script that they knew was the one that prevailed in their society. The absence of alternatives meant an absence of options.

An **awareness of alternative scripts** increases the **potential options** people have for **alternative experiences.** But awareness of alternatives is not the same as having access to those alternatives. You might be aware of better job opportunities but do not have access to them.

The same is true of personal relationships. There may be someone that you would prefer to date but your chances are limited. The bottom line is that searching or thinking about alternative experiences begins with becoming aware of scripts that promise more gratification than present ones.

The **difference** between **being aware** and **having access** to alternative experiences is evident with people who live in small rural towns or large cities. People living in small towns today can readily access information about a huge variety of alternative experiences through media such as magazines and television. The difference is that living in large metropolitan areas gives people more access to these alternatives than those living in relatively homogenous and isolated small rural towns.

GROUP RECRUITMENT

Group recruitment involves efforts by a **group** to attract **new members.** The most common method is to base recruitment appeals on script descriptions or promises concerning the activities of the group. The impetus for joining is provided by an outside group. This differs from situations where individual initiative is the basis for gaining information about alternative scripts.

Universities celebrate their prominence, unique atmosphere (small town friendliness), distinctive programs, recreational opportunities, and so forth. Military recruiters often promise adventure, job training, and help paying for college expenses. Fraternities and sororities differ in their appeals depending upon whether or not they are professional or social organizations. Political organizations such as the Young Republicans and the Young Democrats exist on many campuses. And every campus has a variety of issue-based groups, such as those concerned about the environment or gay and lesbian rights.

Whether or not those who join a group based on its recruitment images remain depends on several factors. The degree that it lives up to its billing is one consideration. If the motivation that made that promise attractive remains significant a person is likely to remain in the group. But even if the experience is as advertised the relative strength of motives can change and this can affect the desire to stay or leave. Someone attracted to a small campus may enjoy its personal atmosphere but find that going to a larger university is necessary because it provides better educational opportunities in certain areas.

GOSSIP

Gossip is a familiar reality. **Gossip** is idle chatter about someone else that is known to those involved in a conversational exchange. The currency of gossip is rumors. It can occur between friends, members of a social group, workers, or just about anyplace that people congregate.

Malicious gossip goes beyond idle chatter about someone else. Malicious gossip disparages someone else. The intent is to ruin the reputation of that person.

Often the term **gossip is associated with someone** who is prone to it. A gossip is just such a person. Gossips often use negative talk about someone else to **elevate their own self-esteem.** ← How?

But the significance of gossip goes beyond that of the personality trait of someone who is insecure. People who are confident may use gossip to **advance their own personal social scripts** by negatively casting someone who prefers something different. Gossip can discredit a work supervisor who imposes script requirements that someone finds excessive or offensive. "Did you know that he drinks heavily or did you know that she had an affair?"

Gossip can also be used to **deflect unfavorable attention.** The ploy is to switch negative attention from oneself to someone else. "Dad, I know you don't approve of what I did, but let me tell you about what your favorite son did."

Gossip is also a good way to **establish your personal boundaries.** By criticizing someone else you announce your own personal preferences. Sometimes this is more effective than simply stating your preferences. By suggesting that you don't like what someone else did establishes a personal boundary because it suggests that you would have a similar reaction if the person you are talking to engaged in that activity.

Gossip serves a different purpose when the goal is to **gain acceptance.** In this instance, gossip provides an opportunity to win someone's favor by appealing to what you think they value or believe. A critical point is that you need not agree with your own assertion. An example would be if you are talking to a new acquaintance that you believe hates country music and you say: "Did you know that most country western stars are too dumb to even finish high school?"

Lastly, gossip can serve as a **"conversation filler."** Can't think of anything to talk about? Why not try some gossip about your other friends or coworkers?

PLURALISTIC IGNORANCE

The term **pluralistic ignorance** occurs when people in a group make **erroneous attributions** about what people prefer. **Pluralistic ignorance** involves an **erroneous definition of the situation by members of a group about themselves.** It does not apply to mistaken perceptions people have about outsiders.

Pluralistic ignorance arises whenever the **responses of people in a group** do not represent their true feelings. It often occurs when a strong leader makes members afraid to express what they really think. The result is an **appearance of consensus.**

An **appearance of consensus** occurs whenever what people in a group do does not really reflect what they prefer. This can vary from parroting what a strong leader expresses to remaining silent rather than risk aversive responses by the leader or other members of the group that you think agree with the leader. Sociologists are interested in determining when consensus within a group is **genuine** and when consensus is based upon **pluralistic ignorance** and more of an appearance of consensus.

This can be difficult because the dynamics causing pluralistic ignorance make people reluctant to express themselves. Have you ever been in a group where everyone seems to agree on a script but you learn later in a private conversation that a friend shares your disagreement with what was said? The problem is determining whether or not your friend actually agreed with you or did so just to make you feel good. Imagine your surprise if your friend doesn't support you when you boldly express your disagreement the next time you both are with the group. The same group dynamics that cause pluralistic ignorance may explain why your friend responded differently after having shared your disagreement in private.

Leaders are often quite adroit at exploiting pluralistic ignorance to their own advantage. The problem is that even through the expression of dissent, alternative ideas can remain suppressed for a considerable period of time that the underlying dissent may persist. When pluralistic ignorance does, it may prove to be the basis for social change in the future.

PLURALISTIC IGNORANCE AND SOCIAL MOVEMENTS

Social movements are unlikely unless there is a sufficient degree of **underlying disagreement** with a **prevailing script.** A key factor in social movements is the ability of leaders to overcome pluralistic ignorance. This requires making it possible for people who were previously silent to express themselves.

The women's movement is a prime example. At one time, many women who disagreed with the script that declared that they should be subordinate to men refused to express their true feelings. Suppression was based on their fear of ridicule or worse. In some societies, women were stoned for expressing disagreement. The result was the impression that everyone seemed to agree with the script.

More outspoken women were often criticized in public or through gossip and more informal means of social control. Sometimes women who knew each other well and met on a regular basis would soften their reaction to an outspoken friend with the label eccentric. Yet, even those who secretly agreed with some of what that person had to say may have continued to remain silent on the subject in terms of their own feelings.

The women's movement in the United States and elsewhere was fueled by disagreement with prevailing male-dominated scripts. Without that underlying dissatisfaction it would have been difficult to sustain momentum. This is not to say that all women were or are unhappy with male-dominated scripts. Today, one of the main cultural wars in the United States involves attitudes among both men and women concerning the role of women in society.

THE SILENT MAJORITY

The **Nixon Administration** offers a prime example of how **pluralistic ignorance can be exploited.** President Nixon was elected at a time when Americans were deeply conflicted about social issues and the war in Vietnam. He was extremely concerned that political activists might gain the upper hand.

His advisors came up with the notion of the **silent majority** to dispel the impression that there was popular support for those who opposed his policies. They defined the **silent majority as Americans who quietly go about their business** and don't express their political views. Nixon successfully sold the idea that these Americans really agreed with his social scripts involving everything from domestic policies to his handling of the war in Vietnam. This allowed him to discredit those who protested his policies as extremists.

THE SOCIOLOGY OF EMOTIONS

The **sociology of emotions** is an area of study where the interest is in determining **how social scripts** shape **emotional experiences** and **expressions.** Cross-cultural research served as the impetus for this field of study in sociology. This research demonstrated that how people experience and express their emotion in different societies varies substantially. Thinking about how emotions are experienced and expressed is scripted counters the more intuitive notion that the emotions we experience and express are pretty much natural.

Upon reflection, this conclusion is not entirely shocking. Freud introduced the world to the possibility that social scripts can cause the repression of basic emotions, such as those based on the human sex drive. The fact that this repression can occur at a deep unconscious level where people are unaware of it speaks to the enormous impact social scripts can have on emotions.

There are also profoundly different ways people express their emotions. In some societies not a tear is shed at a funeral. In other societies woman wail long and loudly over their loss.

Not all differences concerning emotions exist between different societies or cultures. In the United States it is not unusual for hear women complain about the inability of their boyfriends, husbands, or fathers to express love and affection. Male socialization plays a significant part in that process.

EMOTIONAL CONTAGION

The term **emotional contagion** refers to the **spread of intense feelings** among people in a group or crowd. Sometimes events stir the emotions of a crowd, like when bystanders become enraged by what they see. On other occasions it is not events but rather leaders who inflame a crowd. Hitler used inflammatory rhetoric and torchlight parades to incite German crowds. Islamic and Christian fundamentalist leaders use inflammatory speeches to generate powerful emotions among their followers. Situations where leaders manipulate the emotions of audiences are hardly a new phenomenon.

Sociologists are interested in the extent to which **emotional contagion** heightens the **intensity of beliefs and sentiments** associated with social scripts. Whether generated spontaneously or more intentionally by leaders, emotional contagion can transform relatively dormant scripts into intense action. Heightened emotions can make a crowd more susceptible to manipulations by a leader.

An important question is the **degree to which aroused emotions for a script can be sustained.** Often natural disasters such as hurricane can trigger a burst of helpfulness, and neighborliness that soon dissipates. Initial support for the family victims of 9/11 was enormous, but it did not take long for it to wane and people to lose interest in making sure that the families were compensated.

The question of sustainability and rallies designed to arouse emotions is equally important. Pep rallies are meant to create enthusiasm for a game, but they often have a short-lived effect. Fans are fired up for the moment, but without subsequent pep rallies enthusiasm can evaporate. Moreover, the effectiveness and sustainability of pep rallies often depends upon school traditions. Some schools have sport traditions and fan support that is exceptional. For other schools, pep rallies may be exercises in futility.

Although questions about sustainability are important, it is also important to recognize that it is not always the crucial issue. Riots can cause extensive damage even when emotions last for only hours or into the next day. Similarly, a political rally may sustain emotions long enough to collect donations, but those same feelings may soon begin to dissipate, even to the point that some donors never follow through and vote or take the actions promised during the emotional height of the rally.

THE DEGREE OF PERSONAL EXPRESSION

The **degree to which a social script permits personal expression** is another focus of sociologists. Some scripts contain only general parameters and invite personal expression by the participants. An example would be a friendship that encourages taking each other personally into account. In situations that are more highly scripted, there is less opportunity for personal expression. An example would be a job where you are expected to follow a set of requirements just like everyone else who has that job.

The degree of personal expression permitted affects people in a number of different ways. In situations that permit personal expressions, people involved in an encounter or relationship are more likely to express their personal preferences. This increases the potential that participants will have personal knowledge about each other. Situations that permit more personal expression are also more likely to see the personalities of the participants shape emergent social scripts in that relationship.

PREDICTING INTERACTION

The **degree** to which **behavior is scripted** is the degree to which personal expression is limited. In situations that are **highly scripted,** knowledge of the **social script** may be sufficient to predict what will transpire. An example would be a workplace where everything people do is scripted and there is little opportunity for personal preferences to be expressed.

In situations where **more personal expression** is **permitted** or **encouraged,** knowledge about **specific people and their preferences** is the key to predicting what will transpire. This is because the social script only creates general boundaries for behavior, rather than specific requirements. Predicting what will transpire between two friends is an example. Although boundaries exist, personalities determine what will transpire within these boundaries where most behavior occurs.

SCRIPTS AND EVERYDAY LIFE

All social scripts play out among people engaged in everyday encounters and relationships. Everyday life is the place where all social behavior unfolds. Everyday life encompasses the daily routines of people. This pertains just as much to everyday routines based upon the imagined presence of others as it does to social behavior that takes place in the presence of other people.

Because **culture predates** and **transcends** any **specific person,** too much emphasis on it can distract from this fundamental principle. It is not that looking at culture as a source for social scripts is not important. But what must be remembered is that cultural scripts are only relevant when people internalize them or respond to them. Only then can a cultural script shape the practices and routines of people engaged in everyday transactions.

GETTING IN THE DOOR

A Bacardi Limon ad in *Rolling Stone* (July 25, 2002: 41–44) illustrates how scripts work in everyday life. The tag line of the ad is "Getting Inside." The rest of the ad is advice on how to get in at some of the hottest American bars and clubs.

Here is a sample of the advice. The advice amounts to a script. "What you're wearing . . . Who you are with . . . And who you know. It can make or break your night."

The owner of The Rack in Boston strongly advises against telling the doorman that "I don't wait in lines." A co-owner at Rumi, a hot bar in Miami, suggests that "If you have to drop names, chances are you're standing outside for a reason and you're not getting in." Once inside the ad scripts how not to order a drink. Never "slam or bang on the bar, whistle, yell 'Hey' or 'Yo', wave or clap your hands, or slap the bartender on the back."

PART 2
STUDY GUIDES

CHAPTER 4
ROLE MODELS AND MORAL ENTREPRENEURS

Socialization

Agents of Socialization

    Initial

    Sustaining

    Conscious

    Unintentional

Cultural Climate

    Cultural Clone

    Cultural Innovator

Role Models

    Positive

    Negative

    Public

    Vicarious

    Acquaintance

Moral Entrepreneurs

    Public

    Acquaintance

A Two-Step Process

    Layers

Media

Media Bias

Halos and Smears

    Ad hominem

    Character Assassination

Liking and Beliefs

Counter/Opposition Research

Plausible Deniability

Reverse Outcomes

Scripts and Audience Reactions

Credibility

    Charisma

        Personal Hierarchy

        Charismatic Deficit

    Prestige

        Social Hierarchy

    Knowledge

        Expertise Hierarchy

Styles and Approaches

    Behind the Scenes Gurus

    Bootstrappers

    Endorsements

    Citing Authorities

    Maintaining Traditions

    Mavericks

    Scientific Approach

Preaching to the Choir

Hostile Audiences

Mixed Audiences

Coded Messages

Moral High Ground

    Moral Deficit

Putting People on Notice

Advertisers

    Care-Based Ads

    Virginia Slims

CHAPTER 5
THE BASICS OF INTERACTION

Principles of Social Exchange

    Cooperation

    Conflict

Free Riders

Techniques of Conflict Resolution

    Violence

    Coercion

    Compromise

    Co-Optation

    Competition

Dyad

Triad

    Coalitions

    Mediation

    Arbitration

Behavioral Preferences

    Folkways

    Mores

    Laws

Primary Relationships

Secondary Relationships

Societies

  Gemeinschaft

  Gesellschaft

Communication and Social Scripts

  Preliterate

    Observation and Imitation

    Being Told

  Literate

    Written Documents

    Observation and Imitation

    Being Told

Nonverbal Behavior

Impression Management

  Giving Off

  Role Distance

  Role Embracement

Ingratiation

  Genuine

  Instrumental

Instrumental Ingratiation

  Costs

Civil Inattention

Looking Glass Self

  Needing Approval

  Manipulating Others

CHAPTER 6
SMALL GROUPS

Definition

The Emphasis on Cooperation

    Businesses

    Productivity

Group Cohesion

Official Workplace Scripts

    Taylorization

Unofficial Workplace Scripts

    Rate-busters

    Chiselers

    Binging

Task and Expressive Leaders

Leadership Styles

    Democratic Leaders

    Authoritarian

    Laissez-Faire

Masking Authoritarian Leadership

Welcoming Authoritarian Leadership

Leadership Styles and Credit

Effectiveness

    Authoritarian Leader

    Democratic Leader

    Laissez-Faire Leader

The Iron Law of Oligarchy

Groupthink

    Authoritarian Leader

    Mindguards

    Suppress Dissent

Pluralistic Ignorance and Groupthink

Inoculation Theory

Inoculation Theory and Moral Entrepreneurs

Groups

    Primary

    Secondary

    In-Groups

    Out-Groups

    Ethnocentrism

Reference Groups

    Membership

    Outsider Groups

    Anticipatory Socialization

    Positive and Negative Reference Groups

Social Sanctions and Reference Groups

Reverse Psychology

CHAPTER 4
ROLE MODELS AND MORAL ENTREPRENEURS

Socialization involves the process by which people are **exposed to** and **incorporate social scripts** and the values and beliefs that sustain them into their social selves. Both **role models** and **moral entrepreneurs** play a significant role in the process of socialization. Both function as **agents of socialization.**

AGENTS OF SOCIALIZATION

An **agent of socialization** is anyone who shapes the **social selves of others** by getting them to **accept a social script and/or the values and beliefs that justify it.** If you model yourself after a public figure such as a rock star, that rock star qualifies as an agent of socialization. If you buy into the arguments of a radio or television talk show host, that host qualifies as an agent of socialization. If you internalize behaviors that your mom or dad advocate, then your mom and dad qualify as agents of socialization. If you accept the arguments and behaviors advocated by your local minister, priest, or rabbi, that person qualifies as an agent of socialization. If your friends persuade you that it is okay to do something that they favor, they qualify as agents of socialization. If you convince your brother or sister to do what you think is right, you are an agent of socialization.

AGENTS OF SOCIALIZATION: GENERAL TYPES

Agents of socialization operate in two different contexts. An **initial agent of socialization** is the first person who gets you to accept a script and/or its supporting values and beliefs. A **sustaining agent of socialization** is someone who reinforces what was initially internalized from someone else. For example, you may have initially internalized something from your mother that was reinforced later in school by a teacher. In this case, your mother would have been the initial agent of socialization, and your teacher was a sustaining agent of socialization.

A QUESTION OF INTENT

An **agent of socialization** may **consciously** promote a personal social script or the effort can be **unintentional.** An example of a **conscious agent of socialization** would be a high school principal that calls in a student who misbehaved and convinces that student to change his/her classroom behavior. An example of an **unintentional agent of socialization** would be someone who unknowingly serves as a role model for someone else.

For someone to qualify as either a **conscious** or **unintentional agent of socialization** that person must influence the **social self** of someone else. This occurs whenever someone accepts a social script and/or its sustaining values and beliefs preferred by someone else. Simply trying to influence someone else is not enough to qualify someone as an agent of socialization.

THE CULTURAL CLIMATE

Cultural themes establish a **cultural climate** within which agents of socialization often operate. Both Freud and Rogers believed that it was this cultural climate that provides the inputs for the development of the social self as a component of personality. This suggests that agents of socialization do not live in a vacuum, and often what they promote reflects cultural themes. It also suggests that children raised in different cultures may develop a different social self.

A **cultural clone** is an **agent of socialization** that parrots script messages found in a larger cultural setting. A priest who echoes the official positions of the Vatican and gets parishioners to do likewise is a cultural clone. A **cultural innovator** is an **agent of socialization** that modifies or alters a cultural theme and gets people to buy into that script. A radical priest who gets his parishioners to go against an official church policy is an agent of socialization that qualifies as a cultural innovator.

ROLE MODELS VERSUS MORAL ENTREPRENEURS

Role models and **moral entrepreneurs** are both agents of socialization. As agents of socialization, both influence the social selves of others. The basic difference is that **role models promote by example,** whereas **moral entrepreneurs actively try to persuade** others to buy into a set of behavioral preferences and/or the values and beliefs that support them.

Moral entrepreneurs are most likely to be **conscious agents of socialization** who are aware of their efforts to sell a script to others. **Role models** are different in that they can and often do unintentionally influence the social selves of others. This does not mean role models are exclusively unintentional because someone might consciously try to be a good role model for others such as children.

ROLE MODELS

Anyone who follows **sports** is familiar with controversies about whether or not an athlete is a **good role model.** Those who display what others think is inappropriate behavior are **condemned** as **bad role models.** In professional football, one of its most talented receivers had a long history of making remarks or gestures that embarrassed the team's owner and many fans. When he simulated mooning the visiting team's fans in the stand it was seen by many as the last straw.

Some athletes resent pressure to alter their public personas to accommodate fans or groups that insist that they must be good role models. For them the measure should be their athletic accomplishments and not their personality or lifestyle. Whatever you think about this issue, it is abundantly clear that the actions of others can and do serve as a socialization vehicle. It is the script preferences of audiences that decide whether or not a public figure represents a good or bad role model.

POSITIVE AND NEGATIVE ROLE MODELS

Positive role models are figures that exemplify the **values, beliefs,** and **behavioral** preferences that are **embraced** by an audience. **Negative role models** are figures that exemplify the **values, beliefs, and behavioral preferences** that are **condemned** by an audience. Depending upon the values, beliefs, and behavioral preferences of an audience, the same person can be seen as a positive or negative role model.

No one fully understands why the same public figure(s) or images represent a positive role model for some, while others are deeply offended and disturbed by them. Take, for instance, the notorious biker gang the Hell's Angels. Many readers found descriptions of their activities in Hunter Thompson's (1967) *The Hell's Angels*, a celebration of freedom and defiance of mainstream lifestyles and authority. Today, motorcycles still represent these qualities for many people. Harley-Davidson's huge revival in sales is due to shrewd promotion and purchases by affluent middle-aged men, which represents a significant demographic shift from the days when it was bought by blue-collar workers.

The rebellious image of the Hell's Angels was also attractive to many in the counterculture movements of the 1960s. Ken Kesey, the author of the cult favorite book and movie *One Flew Over the Cuckoo's Nest*, hosted parties where the Hell's Angels were invited. The Hell's Angels were also present in the San Francisco music scene until the disastrous night when, while working as security, they killed a fan at a Rolling Stones concert in California.

Fame for the Hell's Angels lasted much longer than the standard 15 minutes Andy Warhol once proposed as the window for most people. But by the end of the 1960s it had certainly waned. This is not to suggest that everyone viewed the Hell's Angels as a good role model. Police who witnessed the carnage created by the Hell's Angels on weekend bike outings that terrorized communities in California were hardly fans. Many cops viewed the Hell's Angels as thugs and were mystified by their popular appeal.

ROLE MODELS AS PROJECTIVE TESTS

Thinking about role models as **projective tests** offers insights into the complexities behind whether or not audiences characterize someone as a positive or negative role model. **Projective tests** in psychology are used to **probe unconscious regions** of personality. With a **projective test,** a therapist presents patients with unstructured or ambiguous images and then asks them what they see.

The general idea is that people project their unresolved conflicts into their renditions. The same may be true with a role model. Whether or not someone is characterized as a positive or negative role model may result from an underlying unresolved conflict.

People that promote the qualities of someone else as a **positive role model** may be expressing qualities that they admire and that are incorporated into their **ideal self-concept.** The process of promotion is a means to affirm their own ideal self-concept by publicly celebrating those qualities in others. If there is a disparity between that ideal self-concept and who they really are, then their promotion may be an effort to conceal that reality from themselves.

This could be just as true of people who view the Hell's Angels as negative role models, as it is of those who celebrate them. For those who condemn them, that condemnation may serve to reinforce themselves as defenders of virtue when virtue is more problematic for them than they realize. For those who celebrate the maverick image of the Hell's Angels, that celebration may reinforce their own ideal self-image of being a maverick when in reality they are much more timid.

For the most part, sociologists need not engage in such psychoanalysis to appreciate a point. Why people have intense feelings about a public figure, character, or acquaintance as a role model is not the issue. What counts is the intensity of those feelings and how they translate into admiration or repulsion for the scripts, values, and beliefs that are implied.

TYPES OF ROLE MODELS

Public role models are famous people who are known to influence large numbers of people. **Vicarious role models** are performers who give us an opportunity to imaginatively share their experiences and identify with their character. **Acquaintance role models** are people who we personally know that influence us by the example they set.

It is easy to see the difference. The personality of a well-known actor may serve as a positive or negative role model for you. In this capacity, the person is functioning as a **public role model.** This is different from whether or not you identify with a character they portray on television, the stage, or in a movie. As such, the character portrayed represents a **vicarious role model.** And, of course, moms, dads, brothers, sisters, relatives, teachers, and coaches are among those who may serve as an **acquaintance role model.**

MORAL ENTREPRENEURS

The concept of a moral entrepreneur was first mentioned by the sociologist Howard Becker. Becker (1963) likened **moral entrepreneurs** to business entrepreneurs, but with a critical difference. Business entrepreneurs sell products and services. The original thinking was that moral entrepreneurs are different because what they sell is morality. **Morality** encompasses what people see as virtuous, what people think what is right and what is wrong, and principles governing proper conduct.

It is relatively easy to see how the concept of a moral entrepreneur fits in with our discussion on social scripts and the values/beliefs that sustain them. To speak of virtue is to speak of values. To speak of right and wrong is to speak of values. Concepts such as virtue and distinctions between right and wrong all deal with principles that underscore general likes and dislikes.

Beliefs are often fellow travelers with values. Remember that beliefs deal with truth claims. In Christianity, the belief that conducting a virtuous life will lead to salvation is a truth claim that motivates compliance. Condemning those who fail to comply with eternal damnation is the other face of this motivational truth claim.

Morality is historically associated with religion, and even today is often thought about in relation to religion. But to limit moral entrepreneurs to religious leaders would be to restrict the insight Becker originally provided. Promoting social scripts takes place in all aspects of social life. The extent to which moral entrepreneurs exist in everyday life will become more evident upon reading the ensuing material.

MORAL ENTREPRENEURS AND PERSUASION

Moral entrepreneurs use **persuasion** to get people to accept the behavioral preferences in the scripts that they favor and to disparage scripts that they disagree with. To accomplish this goal, moral entrepreneurs employ a wide variety of tactics and strategies. Learning to think like a sociologist requires that you are able to identify how moral entrepreneurs operate because they are extremely important agents of socialization.

Selling social scripts involves justifying the **behavioral preferences** contained within them **by linking** them to **values** and **beliefs.** Linking a foreign policy script to the value of promoting freedom around the world or claiming that it makes Americans more secure in their daily lives illustrates how this works. Whether or not the posted value or belief claims are valid is a separate issue. Scripts are sold when value/belief appeals resonate with an audience.

Interpretations are used to **justify or explain** events associated with a preferred script. As with selling social scripts, the trick is to explain what happened in terms of the values and beliefs that resonate with an audience. When one explanation doesn't work, moral entrepreneurs often try another.

If preventing terrorists from using Iraqi-built weapons of mass destruction to harm the United States doesn't pan out as a justification for invading Iraq, simply change the reason. The real reason was to bring freedom and democracy to Iraq. Notice that in the final analysis what counts is whether or not audiences believe it and not the literal truth of the justification claim.

TRUTH AND DECEPTION

When promoting a social script or interpreting it, the key factor is whether or not an audience accepts the presentation. If a totally bogus claim is bought, its effect is the same as if it were true. Conversely, a true claim that is suspected or seen as fraudulent has the same effect as if it were false.

People are more likely to forgive a moral entrepreneur who makes an "honest mistake" when making a truth claim to justify a script than a moral entrepreneur who deliberately misleads or lies. Or, more accurately, the perception that a moral entrepreneur was deliberately misleading is more disturbing than when moral entrepreneurs are seen as having made an honest mistake.

If you believe the Bush claim that he only invaded Iraq because he was mislead by his intelligence sources, then you are more likely to forgive his erroneous (deceptive) justification for the war than if you believe he manipulated intelligence data to conceal his genuine purpose. If you believe Clinton, when he said that he "didn't have sex with that that woman," deliberately played with words to deceive Americans, you're less likely to be forgiving than if you think it was an honest misunderstanding because he thought having sex requires intercourse. Please understand that these inclinations concerning audiences are based upon their perceptions and that perceptions can be influenced by many other factors, such as admiring or hating someone.

PUBLIC AND ACQUAINTANCE MORAL ENTREPRENEURS

All **moral entrepreneurs** are **agents of socialization.** They are agents of socialization because their task is to promote social scripts and the values/beliefs that sustain them. For our purposes it will be useful to distinguish the basic types of moral entrepreneurs.

A **public moral entrepreneur** is someone who promotes and/or interprets social scripts to a large number of people in a public setting. A preacher giving a sermon is a public moral entrepreneur. A radio or TV personality who is in the business of promoting social scripts (agendas) is a public moral entrepreneur. Politicians are public moral entrepreneurs when they speak to a group, community, or nation.

Public moral entrepreneurs and **role models** are agents of socialization that influence large audiences. A **public role model** is a public figure that operates as an agent of socialization by **example.** A **public moral entrepreneur** relies on powers of **persuasion.**

Acquaintance moral entrepreneurs promote and/or interpret social scripts to people that they know personally. When parents talk to their children about what is right and wrong, they are functioning as acquaintance moral entrepreneur. When a friend tries to convince you that certain behaviors are acceptable or unacceptable, that friend is behaving like an acquaintance moral entrepreneur. A priest who counsels you in a private session has switched from being a public moral entrepreneur when he gives a sermon to an acquaintance moral entrepreneur.

It is tempting to think that acquaintance moral entrepreneurs promote social scripts in private settings. While this often is the case, acquaintance moral entrepreneurs do engage in script activities in more public situations. A mother who tells her child "not to beg for treats" while shopping for groceries is sending a message to that child in a public setting. If the child continues to misbehave, questions about her effectiveness as an agent of socialization may arise.

The difference between an **acquaintance role model** and **acquaintance moral entrepreneur** is important to recognize. An **acquaintance role model** is someone that your know who influences you by **example.** An acquaintance moral entrepreneur is someone that you know who persuades you to accept a social script.

There is intersection between public and acquaintance moral entrepreneurs that merits special attention. If you read newspapers you are likely to be familiar with **opinion columns** written by **public moral entrepreneurs** who work for a newspaper, news organization, or are syndicated as individuals. On the same pages there are also **letters to the editor** from private citizens who express their opinions. Whenever their opinions are published as letters to the editor, they qualify as **public moral entrepreneurs.** When they express the same opinions to their friends and family, they are **acquaintance moral entrepreneurs.**

A TWO-STEP PROCESS

Katz (1957) describes a **two-step process** by which the ideas of public opinion leaders are conveyed by acquaintances to more personal audiences. The basic idea is that the opinions and arguments offered by public figures offer ammunition for opinion leaders in more personal settings. This model is useful when thinking about how public moral entrepreneurs provide ammunition for acquaintance moral entrepreneurs.

An illustration would be when parents send for a brochure or attend a lecture on how to prevent children from using drugs. Another example would be when someone uses an argument heard on a conservative talk radio show. Still another example is when a student uses an argument heard in class to promote a personal social script with a friend. And there is always the use of points heard in a sermon when talking around the dinner table after church.

LAYERS OF PUBLIC MORAL ENTREPRENEURS

Public moral entrepreneurs can often be seen in terms of **layers of influence.** At the top are the public moral entrepreneurs who have the largest audience. Within the Catholic Church, the Pope is at the highest level and cardinals, bishops, and priests represent lower levels of influence. Such layers also exist in less-structured situations, such as when teachers attending a national convention hear a speaker and then convey his/her script recommendation to their colleagues at a department meeting.

Regardless of the complexity of levels, or whether someone operates as a public or private moral entrepreneur, something should be abundantly clear. **They qualify as agents of socialization only to the extent that they persuade the people they address.** To the extent that people are convinced or do not incorporate the script being promoted is the extent to which socialization took place.

THE MEDIA AND PUBLIC MORAL ENTREPRENEURS

Public moral entrepreneurs can present their messages through their own literature, speeches, and videos, but **national news media** coverage is what separates the top dogs who have national audiences from lesser-known figures. Up until recently, the national news was dominated by the print (newspapers and magazines) and network television programs. Cable news shows like CNN and Fox News have cut into network news markets.

The growing popularity of the Internet is another recent trend. While some Internet sites are based upon national media like CNN or the *New York Times*, there are more and more sites hosted by voices independent from national networks or print media. Both the Drudge Report and the Huffington Post, the latter being former conservative commentator Arianna Huffington's liberal alternative to the Drudge Report, are 2005 versions of what promises to be a growing trend. Added to all of this is rise of **bloggers** who are less-well-known watchdogs and commentators. It was bloggers who first suspected that the documents used in a CBS report on the military service of President Bush were faked.

MEDIA BIAS

Charges of media bias are common in American politics. The charge of media bias is the claim that the mass media favors certain social scripts and their related values and beliefs over others. It is most likely to occur when politicians get unfavorable coverage. Charges can apply to national print media, network news, cable news shows, and talk radio. It is a hot topic and recurring controversy among politicians.

Just scream bias if you don't like what is published or presented on TV about you or what you cherish. Rants from conservatives about the liberal bias in leading newspapers and network news are common when the news is unfavorable. Rants from liberals about the bias of conservative talk radio shows or Fox cable news programming follow a similar pattern.

Claims of bias in the media are often meant to **obscure** or **deflect questions** concerning the **truth of unfavorable news reports.** Attacking the source rather than using data to counter a news report is a common strategy among politicians. This is especially true when there is merit to the media report and it is seen as important to shift attention from the unfavorable report. Getting news outlets to cover the bias charges and forget about the original controversy is a sign of success.

This is not to say that alerting audiences to possible ideological leanings of news outlets is never legitimate. Knowing that certain news reports favor one side or the other can inspire audiences to seek multiple sources before forming their own opinion. This is probably the best guarantee for audiences who want to be informed because in the final analysis, it is not the ideological leanings of news sources that count. What counts are the facts relevant to a media report.

Here are some examples of how charges of bias in the media can unfold. In 2005, when House Majority Leader Tom DeLay had trouble shaking ethics accusations, he resorted to the old ploy of blaming his problems on a biased liberal media. When President Bush proposed a series of changes to Social Security that were challenged by the powerful American Association of Retired People (AARP), some of his supporters posted images on their Web site that implied that the AARP favored gay marriages over the lives of patriotic soldiers. Their clear intent was to dodge factual questions about the merits of the debate with an emotional appeal meant to discredit the AARP. Critics were quick to challenge the accuracy of the portrayal, but even this was beside the point. Exactly how does support of gay marriage or soldiers bear on questions about Bush's claim that allowing workers to divert some of their retirement money to personal accounts is necessary to save Social Security?

HALOS AND SMEARS

Claims about bias in the media invite discussion of how **personal characterizations** are used as emotional substitutes for factual information. In logic and debate circles such characterizations are called **ad hominem arguments** that appeal "to one's prejudice, emotions, or special interests rather that to one's intellect or reason" (Webster's College Dictionary, 1991: 17). The term refers to attacks on the character of an opponent (hominem means man) rather than the substance of an opponent's argument.

Usually ad hominem attacks are associated with **negative characterizations** of someone who offers an opposing point of view. Labeling someone as a "male chauvinist pig" is one example. Labeling someone as a "femi-nazi" is a favorite ad hominem attack by a popular conservative talk show host for women who disagree with him.

Smearing someone's reputation is the essence of **negative ad hominem** attacks. To **smear** opponents is to discredit, defame, or vilify them. **Character assassination** is a tactic that has worked time and again in political campaigns and other arenas involving script disputes.

Creating a "**halo**" for someone who is a proponent of a script is just as much a personal characterization as "smearing" an opponent. It deserves equal consideration as a characterization that begs the question concerning the merits of someone's position. The "**halo effect,**" as it is sometimes called, derives from the pure image of Heavenly Angels.

Ever wonder about all those campaign pictures of politicians holding and kissing babies or posing with their families. What could be purer than loving babies or one's family? If positive emotions are generated by such images, then a **halo effect** has been created.

Halos and **smears** are not limited to politicians. People who serve with distinction in the military are often seen as **heroes** who risked their own lives for the sake of their comrades and country. It is not hard to imagine admirers bestowing a **halo** over the head of their heroes. Once bestowed, it is often extremely difficult to tarnish a halo and the credibility it affords someone.

Dynamics involving halos and smears surfaced in the 2004 campaign for president. Supporters of John Kerry used the medals he had received for his service during the Vietnam War to create a hero/halo effect. It created an advantage over the image of Bush promoted by some Kerry supporters as a draft dodger who, through family connections, was able to meet his military obligations by serving the Texas Air National Guard.

To counter the halo and the advantages it afforded Kerry, the Bush people first tried to show pictures of Bush in uniform as a jet pilot. The strategy was to minimize the Kerry advantage on the issue by creating a "halo" for Bush. But this met with only limited success. It was hard to match the halo created by Kerry risking his life to battle the enemy in Vietnam. One rule of political campaigns is if you cannot match the halo of an opponent, knock the halo off from over your opponent's head.

To accomplish this task, Bush supporters created a group of swift boat veterans from the Vietnam War to dispute the heroics of Kerry. Finding veterans who disliked Kerry was not hard because many still could not forgive him for his public antiwar campaign that ended up in front of Congress. These swift boat veterans, who just happened to support Bush and were organized by a group promoting Bush, blasted the wartime credentials of Kerry. Charges that all of the medals awarded Kerry were bogus were issued. Images of these veterans swearing that they were telling the truth and Kerry and his supporters were lying were featured.

The swift boat ads were quite effective in diminishing the halo effect and deflecting attention from questions about Bush's service. Not only did these ads reinforce the Bush base, but they also created doubt among some Kerry supporters. It is not the truth or falsity of such claims that counts. What counts is the extent to which audiences were affected by such characterizations.

AN INSIGHT CONCERNING AD HOMINEM CHARACTERIZATIONS

Many years ago, Heider (1958), a social psychologist, presented a theory that directly bears on this question. His theory deals with the relationship **between emotions** and **beliefs.** He argued that **if we like someone** we are **likely to assume** that person is **similar** to us. Conversely, if we **detest someone** we are likely to assume that that person is **not like us.**

Heider researched the relationship between liking and disliking and the assumption that others hold similar or dissimilar beliefs. In experiments, he manipulated liking by creating positive or negative images of someone. He was able to demonstrate that by changing liking for someone, he was able to change the beliefs subjects attributed to that person. This was a remarkable finding because Heider had said nothing about that other person's beliefs. Subjects in the experiment simply filled in the blanks.

Heider also manipulated information to persuade subjects in other experiments that someone else held beliefs that were similar or different from their own. To accomplish this, he first measured the beliefs of the subjects and then manufactured information about the other person. What he found was that people who perceived belief similarities between themselves and someone else expressed emotional liking for that person. For those perceiving belief differences, he was able to manipulate the emotion of disliking for the other person.

All of this may seem pretty commonsensical. Does it really surprise us to find out that we like people who share our own claims about what is true? Does it really surprise us to find out that we are likely to dislike people who disagree with our versions of reality? What is probably more surprising is the idea that the emotions of liking and disliking trigger assumptions concerning the actual belief structures of other people.

This helps explain the significance of **halos.** Halos generate feelings of liking and fondness for someone. If Heider is correct, if you feel affection toward someone, you will likely assume that person shares your beliefs about reality. What is amazing is that Heider demonstrated this in situations where absolutely no information was provided about the other person's actual beliefs.

We can also see how this applies to **smear** campaigns. Getting people to despise an opponent may have the additional benefit of manipulating their assumptions about what scripts that person supports. You don't even have to convince them because it seems to somehow occur unconsciously.

There is an illustration of the power of emotions. In the campaign for President in 1960, the attractive appearance and personality of John F. Kennedy created an image deficit for Richard Nixon. Little old ladies seem enthralled by everything from Kennedy's smile to his stylish hair. What concerned the Nixon people was the likelihood that this audience would assume that Kennedy was for them without actually checking his record or what Nixon had to offer.

THE BEST DEFENSE IS A GOOD OFFENSE

As we have seen, **character assassination** is an attempt to destroy someone's reputation. Efforts at character assassination have personal and psychological consequences for the person targeted. A damaged reputation is especially difficult for public figures.

There are basically **two options** open to someone that has had their character attacked by an opponent. The first strategy is to **immerse themselves in positive images** in an effort to construct a halo effect to counter the negative image. The second strategy is to **dig up dirt on the opponent** and engage in counter character assassination.

Counter or opposition research is the term used to describe efforts to restore a damaged image. It includes trying to find out embarrassing information that can be used to smear and discredit someone who has mounted a negative attack. A more subtle form of opposition research is to find data that diminishes the significance of a claim that caused negative publicity. This is exactly what Tom DeLay did when confronted by charges that he had misused his power by not reporting trips paid for by special interest groups. It turns out that a relatively large number of both Republican and Democrat House members and their aides did not properly report trips paid for by outside groups.

THE SYMBOLIC SIGNIFICANCE OF CHARACTER JUDGMENTS

Americans like to **characterize public figures** as **good guys** or **villains.** This explains why so much of the press on Tom De Lay and other controversial public figures involves judgments about their character. Fans see them as heroes, whereas critics cast them as villains.

But there is more at stake than just someone's reputation. The **symbolic significance** of character judgments involves the **social script** that someone is alleged to have violated. President Clinton became the poster child for what is morally wrong with America when his infidelities were made public.

President Nixon's involvement with the illegal breaking and entering of the Democratic Headquarters in Washington D.C. tarnished his reputation. But documentation that he and top level members of his administration were complicit had a symbolic script message. Is this really the way administrations operate?

WHAT'S GOING ON THERE?

Moral entrepreneurs do more than just promote social scripts. **Moral entrepreneurs** also **interpret events** associated with the **scripts that they promote.** The necessity to provide interpretations of events is most likely to occur in the face of negative publicity.

Often the first response is to suppress negative publicity. Before pictures of abuse at Abu Ghraib surfaced (the American military prison in Iraq), the Bush Administration and the public relations people at the Pentagon presented a picture of respecting the rights of prisoners. Americans do not abuse prisoners.

Here are some of the interpretations that the Bush administration as moral entrepreneurs used to explain the pictures showing abuse. At first they denied the credibility of the pictures, but as evidence for the authenticity of the photos grew, they switched tactics. One new tactic was to accept the photos as genuine but claim that they never knew about such misconduct. Another tactic was to claim that they would never have endorsed such acts and that they represented acts of a few deeply flawed personalities. The implication was that they were good guys (halo effect) who had been let down by the disappointing acts of a few rogue guards. As evidence grew as to how widespread the abuse actually was, the claim that it was the result of a few rotten apples needed help.

To account for the relatively large number of incidents and people involved in the abuse, a different interpretation was offered. Rather than being the action of isolated, demented individuals, the explanation was that an unofficial script had emerged among some guards that encouraged the abuse. By condemning this script as unofficial, the Bush administration tried to distance itself from it. Whether or not the American public will get to know the truth about what the Bush administration knew or promoted remains to be seen.

Top executives often adopt this strategy of blaming negative events on the actions of subordinates that they were unaware of. When confronted with reports that some of his subordinates broke the law and used money from trade with Iran to buy guns for allies in a Latin American war, President Reagan pleaded ignorance. Ken Lay, the CEO of Enron, used the same tactic. He claimed that he was unaware of the unscrupulous activities that were going on during his watch at the company. There is an inherent risk is using this tactic because it suggests that top executives who are responsible for guiding a country or company didn't know what was going on.

PLAUSIBLE DENIABILITY

Plausible deniability is a tactic that elevates claims of not knowing to a deliberate ploy. It occurs whenever bosses make sure that acts of their subordinates cannot be traced back to them. The classic example is the mob boss who wants someone killed but phrases it in a way that gives him plausible deniability: "You know this guy disappoints me" may be code to having stated that he wanted him killed. An executive may encourage subordinates to be "creative," knowing full well that they are likely to explore illegal avenues.

REVERSE OUTCOMES

Reverse outcomes are results **caused by a script** that were **not intended.** Often these reverse outcomes are called **unintended consequences.** Explaining reverse outcomes can be a challenge for those who promoted the script that caused them to occur.

Politicians and the heads of corporations are often confronted with unpleasant outcomes resulting from their policies (scripts). Saying that the outcomes were unintended implies that it was not their fault. But if it was not due to faulty planning, what could possibly account for the unpleasant outcomes? The most common explanation is that reality is often more complex than we think.

Compare this explanation to ones that occur when outcomes are favorable. To get credit for favorable results, moral entrepreneurs attribute it to their brilliance. The possibility that unknown factors may have been responsible for the outcomes rather than those planned for is never mentioned. **What is interesting to sociologists is the extent to which moral entrepreneurs take total credit when outcomes are favorable and predicted and use the concept of unintended consequences to explain unfavorable or reverse outcomes.** Apparently they are masters of their domain when things go right, but victims of the uncertainty of reality when things go bad.

Of course when confronted with negative outcomes, moral entrepreneurs can always resort to denial. The war on terror offers another illustration involving responses to possible reverse outcomes. The Bush administration justified invasions in Afghanistan and Iraq on its publicly stated belief that to make Americans more secure it is necessary to take the fight to the enemy. Not surprisingly, the Bush administration claims that Americans are safer because of their aggressive policies. Critics counter that these aggressive policies are having just the opposite effect. Invading other countries and killing Muslims (even terrorists, let alone civilians) is fueling resentment toward the United States in the Muslim world, which Islamic fundamentalists are using to recruit and motivate suicide bombers. They demonstrate their point with the fact that terrorists have already killed more Americans (military and civilian workers in Iraq and Afghanistan) than any one terrorist attack since 9/11.

All of these claims are speculation extrapolated from selective data. Only time will tell us which of these claims is more accurate. It was almost ten years between the first attack on the World Trade Center in the early 1990s and 9/11 in the early 2000s. Meanwhile both proponents and opponents of the Bush policy will rely more on their underlying values and beliefs than facts to sustain their positions.

SCRIPTS AND AUDIENCE REACTIONS

How **audiences** and **moral entrepreneurs socially express** their pleasure or displeasure with acts or related scripts are **constrained by scripts. Personal social scripts** dictate the inclinations and potential responses of individuals. How someone defines the situation in terms of potential rewards and costs determines whether these inclinations will be expressed or how they are expressed.

Shared social scripts within a group provide for response uniformity. That unity creates the basis for reaffirming among group members their commitment to the specific script involved in their response to an act or social script. It can also reinforce the underlying values and beliefs that may extend to other shared scripts. Shared social scripts, should they differ between groups, provide the basis for identifying similar or different reactions of groups.

Emergent social scripts reflect what evolves as personal script preferences and/or shared social scripts unfold. The reactions of one person or group may come to prevail, or a compromise may result. With these points in mind, we can look at some more specific types of reactions that can be expressed in social situations.

Personal script preferences concerning what is an acceptable response to an act or social script vary enormously. Some people prefer polite disagreement, whereas others feel it is acceptable to scream at someone that violates a script or someone who advocates one that is seen as unacceptable. Some people are even willing to kill those who promote or enact scripts that they disagree with. This applies just as much to military action designed to create regime change in a country like Iraq as it does to Islamic terrorists.

The point that reactions to acts or scripts are themselves scripted is easy to illustrate. The claim that killing for regime change is morally equivalent to terrorist acts is likely to create firestorms among different groups. Advocates for the American invasion of Iraq for the purpose of regime change are likely to see it as morally justified, whereas the acts of terrorists are deemed morally deficient. Those using acts of terrorism to promote their vision of Islam or attack Americans are likely to see themselves as morally right, while at the same time condemning the acts of Americans as satanic.

THE CREDIBILITY FACTOR

Whenever public **moral entrepreneurs** or **acquaintance moral entrepreneurs** make **truth claims,** the **issue of credibility** arises. Independent from the credibility of factual claims, there are some considerations that sociologists take into account. All of these credibility factors influence whether or not a moral entrepreneur will be persuasive.

Charisma refers to extraordinary personality traits that make someone unusually compelling. At one time, charismatic personalities were thought to be like Gods. Today terms like charming, magnetic, and mesmerizing are used to describe a charismatic personality.

Charismatic personalities have a credibility advantage. Charisma, or the lack of it, is the basis for a **personal hierarchy of credibility** within groups, organizations, communities, or societies. A **charismatic deficit** is used to describe those who lack charisma.

The second basis for credibility is **social prestige. Social prestige** is basically the amount of social respect or esteem that is paid to someone. In the United States, wealth and power are the most important determinants of social prestige. Differences in social prestige create a **social hierarchy of credibility.**

President Teddy Roosevelt understood the significance of what we call the social hierarchy of credibility. He recommended that presidents take advantage of their position and use it as a "bully pulpit." By this he meant that presidents should take advantage of their prestige and credibility to promote programs. "Bully" for him was an adjective that meant something that is splendid or wonderful.

Sociologists are interested in determining if a social hierarchy of credibility exists within a group, organization, community, or society. If so, does it influence who is likely to be listened to or believed? Does the mayor have more credibility that other members on the city council? If so, is this due to the mayor's personality, or does the respect given the office give the mayor a credibility advantage?

The third form of credibility is based upon the circumstance of **socially acknowledged expertise.** The amount of socially acknowledged expertise that is given to individuals within groups, organizations, communities, and societies forms an **expertise hierarchy of credibility.** Those credited by others with the most expertise enjoy a credibility advantage in intellectual disputes. People lower in the hierarchy are at a credibility disadvantage.

This credibility advantage is justified to the extent that the expertise of someone places that person in a better position than someone else to evaluate a factual dispute. **But because it is socially determined, where people rank in an expertise hierarchy of credibility does not necessarily reflect their true level of knowledge.** Some people are more effective in gaining the attention necessary to get formal acknowledgments of expertise such as awards. Moreover, the social acknowledgment component favors researchers, scholars, and writers who have been around longer. Given that knowledge, especially in science, which is continuously evolving and exploring new frontiers, expertise may favor younger people who are knowledge innovators.

In the final analysis, what counts is the amount of expertise audiences attribute to a moral entrepreneur. This means that sometimes an audience is not really aware of how the peers of a moral entrepreneur would rank him or her. Even complete frauds can have a credibility advantage if they can convince an audience of their expertise. This applies just as much in science as it does with public moral entrepreneurs using truth claims to promote or challenging a social script.

COERCIVE POWER AND HIERARCHIES OF CREDIBILITY

Coercive power is based upon the capacity to force people to comply. Care must be taken not to confuse **coercion** with the various **hierarchies of credibility.** Any president has awesome coercive powers that can be used to forced people to comply with social scripts. The entire police and military are at the disposal of a president.

Personal, social, and expert hierarchies of credibility are associated with persuasion and not coercion. Using the office of president as a bully pulpit is an exercise in persuasion. If a president effectively sells a script, then coercion is not necessary to get compliance.

STYLES AND APPROACHES

Moral entrepreneurs differ in their personal styles and how they promote social scripts. **Behind-the-scenes gurus** are seldom seen but are the people who orchestrate promotion campaigns. They script messages and talking points for the public moral entrepreneurs who employ them. Often they lack the charisma or other circumstantial factors that enhance performance credibility. Karl Rove, who has been the promotion guru behind the success of George Bush, is a prime example.

Moral entrepreneurs, as well as behind-the-scenes gurus, use a variety of strategies. **Bootstrappers** never think too much about what they are doing. Instead they rely on their instincts and ability to read audiences.

Bootstrappers prefer spontaneous rather than calculated presentations. They like to wing it. This is what distinguishes them from those who use a **trial-and-error** approach. While they may begin with intuition, they don't rely on it to the extent of bootstrappers. Just like a stand-up comic who first writes down jokes and then learns through trial and error what jokes work for certain audiences, **trial-and-error moral entrepreneurs** plan and then use feedback to adjust their message.

Another popular approach is to use **endorsements** by famous people to promote social scripts. The endorsement of products is the model for moral entrepreneurs who use this strategy. We are all familiar with ads where charismatic athletes are used to sell everything from shoes and golf clubs to tickets for a benefit. Athletes with the most prestige, which often means the most money in the United States, are used for similar purposes. And, of course, athletes who demonstrate expert knowledge based on their experiences have benefit from their high rank with the expertise hierarchy.

All of this applies to athletes as moral entrepreneurs. Athletes become moral entrepreneurs whenever they promote or discredit social scripts that apply to sports or elsewhere. A question often raised by endorsements goes beyond their credibility advantages. The question is whether or not the athletes believe in the products that they promote. Using the products enhances their credibility, while not using the products diminishes their credibility.

Citing authorities is yet another approach used by moral entrepreneurs. A familiar example in the United States is when people use the Bible to justify prohibiting gay marriage. Another is when critics of the Patriot Act claim that it violates our basic Constitutional rights.

Citing the **virtue of maintaining tradition** is another strategy that is used by moral entrepreneurs. The basic argument is, why tamper with what works. This claim is based upon a hidden subtext from evolution that suggests that what exists has survived and therefore has virtue.

In the world of advertising, maintaining traditions is expressed in two ways. The first is involves loyalty. Loyalty can be to what is made in the United States or a specific brand. Brand loyalty is evident whenever someone insists that they would only buy a GM car.

A different "tradition" appeal by advertisers is to play on nostalgia. Appealing to a fondness for the past is the key. Reviving "muscle cars" or "image cars" like the Ford Mustang from past eras is one example.

The **maverick moral entrepreneur** appeals to the Americans fondness for independent thinking. Not trusting authorities is the subtext. Their motto is that they are independent thinkers, unlike those who simply parrot what authorities tell them. In recent years this style has been increasingly evident with popular radio and TV talk commentators.

A **scientific approach** begins by compiling demographic data on different audiences. This data typically categorizes and profiles the values and beliefs of people in an audience. Then focus groups based upon these categories and profiles are assembled to test the effectiveness of alternative messages. Only after messages have been tested will they be used on real audiences. Follow-ups are then used to calculate the necessity for changing messages and the process of using focus groups is repeated.

PREACHING TO THE CHOIR

Preaching to the choir is an expression used to described situations where the purpose of a public moral entrepreneur is to reinforce shared attitudes concerning social scripts rather than changing the minds of an audience. The concept derives from the image of a minister preaching what the church choir already believes. Amen, or other signs of agreement by the choir and parishioners, reinforces the script message.

Although the idea of preaching to the choir derives from a church setting, it has much broader significance. An illustration is when a political campaign manager selects an audience that totally supports the candidate for a speech covered by the media. The purpose is more than pumping up enthusiasm among those in the crowd. An equally and sometimes even more significant purpose, is to convey that enthusiasm and support to those watching through the media. The effort may be designed to demoralize the supporters of an opponent or create a sense of agreement with the candidate that appeals to audiences who want to support a winner.

Orchestrating positive images is much more useful than allowing dissenters to spoil the picture. That is why campaign managers who use the media to convey positive images of their candidate try to limit negative images conveyed by demonstrators by putting them outside camera range. The trick is to not violate their constitutional right to publicly demonstrate and express their views with the potential for negative images. Presidents often accomplish this by announcing that demonstrators pose a potential security threat and must be limited to expressing their views in a more remote location. Or the managers of a political convention may claim that a remote location is necessary because demonstrators will cause congestion that will disrupt the legitimate activities of local businesses and those attending the convention.

SKEPTICAL OR HOSTILE AUDIENCES

Preaching to the choir is easy. It is much more difficult to shape messages to convince skeptical or hostile audiences to buy into a script that they reject. The **solution** is to use **values** and **beliefs** of the skeptical or hostile audience to sell the script.

Suppose that you are a moral entrepreneur who embraces a social script that recommends eliminating welfare programs. You may be able to sell it to some audiences on the basis of reducing taxes and government. But this message may not work with other audiences who are more worried about the consequences for poor Americans. For them you may try to alleviate their concerns by citing data that suggests that the lives of people who have been forced off of welfare elsewhere have improved.

MIXED AUDIENCES

A **mixed audience** is comprised of people with differing points of view. A mixed audience can be the one that a moral entrepreneur addresses. It can also include those not present but who are privy to the message given. An example of the latter is when the text of a speech given to a religious group is made public. At that point a moral entrepreneur faces a mixed audience based upon the original that was present at the time of the speech and those who heard about it later.

To the degree which **moral entrepreneurs are isolated** from competing audiences is the degree to which they can pander to a specific audience. This holds for both those preaching to the choir and more hostile audiences. Sometimes leaks about what was said when preaching to the choir demonstrate that the moral entrepreneur in question would have been more careful had he or she known that outsiders would be informed. Similarly, whenever a moral entrepreneur spins a message for a more hostile audience there is the risk that his or her followers might become concerned or wonder if they can trust him or her if the message strays too far from what they believe is acceptable.

CODED MESSAGES

A **coded message** is often used to appeal to one audience while at the same time trying to avoid negative publicity from other audiences. A coded message uses words, expressions, and images that the target audience recognizes, but conceals the true appeal from potential for detractors. A coded messages disguises what is being said.

The politics of marriage is a good example. A candidate who supports a Constitutional Amendment that states marriage is the union of a man and woman may be implying more than a stance against gay marriage. It may be a coded message that the candidate is willing to infuse religion into government. This may appeal to Evangelical and other fundamentalist Christians who believe that the wall between church and state must be taken down.

GAINING THE MORAL HIGH GROUND

Gaining the moral high ground occurs when moral entrepreneurs get audiences to believe that the script they are promoting is morally superior to that of their opponents. **Capturing the moral high ground** requires framing scripts in terms of values that resonate among broad audiences. The values represented may be an accurate reflection of those held by the moral entrepreneur, or they may be calculated to win broader support.

The invasion of Iraq by the Bush administration can be used to illustrate the relative importance of values and how they relate to capturing the moral high ground. Casting the invasion as necessary to secure Americans from terrorist attacks captures a higher moral ground than if Bush claimed that he did it to exact revenge on the one responsible for the attempt to kill his father and other members of his family. Casting the invasion in terms of freedom certainly captures a higher moral ground that justifying it to get control of Middle East oil.

A moral deficit is just the opposite from capturing the moral high ground. A **moral deficit** occurs when audiences **believe** that the value (moral) basis for an event or proposed script is deficient. The emphasis on what is **believed** is what counts because it is what links the act or proposed script to the questionable value.

This pertains **equally to truth claims about the values** that are used to gain the moral high ground. It is what audiences believe about underlying values that determines whether or not an act or proposed scripted acts are elevated to a moral high ground or dismissed as morally deficient. Because all of this ultimately rests on what is believed, there is always the potential for a gap between what moral entrepreneurs say and the real values that drove an act or what sustain the script that they are promoting.

TRUTH OR DECEPTION

All of this brings us to a general consideration. Is the **presentation** by an **acquaintance** or **public moral entrepreneur** viewed as honest or deceptive by the audience? An **honest presentation** is one where what is stated is viewed as a true expression of what the moral entrepreneur values and believes. A **deceptive presentation** is one that is viewed by an audience as fraudulent. Notice that it is the perception of the audience that counts. A fraudulent presentation, if viewed as honest by an audience, has the same effect as if it were honest.

Moral entrepreneurs who are unaware of their deceptions are usually given more slack than those who deliberately mislead the public, their family, or their friends. Of course there is a difference between moral entrepreneurs who claim ignorance to conceal their real motivation and those for whom the claim is true. Conversely, a moral entrepreneur may have honestly been unaware, but audiences distrust him or her. In the final analysis, reactions and consequences by an audience are determined by what they believe is true and not necessarily what the moral entrepreneur in question felt or knew.

REAL SCRIPT DISPUTES

All of these factors that sociologists look for when examining moral entrepreneurs must not obscure an important possibility. The analysis of styles, methods, forms of presentation, and audience reactions is separate from this possibility. **Beneath even the most emotionally distorted or deceptive presentations there can be real script issues and disputes.**

To assume that all disputes are merely matters of expression is to invite the expectation that once the smoke and deceptions are exposed, agreement is possible. Such an expectation is justified only to the extent that the personalities or antics of those involved in a script dispute conceal underlying agreement. This is why mediators are often brought in as third parties to help everyone from husbands and wives to management and labor resolve their differences. But such resolutions require sufficient common ground for a compromise to be reached.

However, this is not always possible. It is always possible that more knowledge about each other may create the impression that it is impossible to reconcile their script differences. Or it may be that perceptions about each other are so set in stone that no amount of contact will reveal possible areas of script agreement. It is at this juncture that groups or societies are likely to resort to violence as a means for protecting their scripts and themselves from opponents or imposing their scripts on them.

PUTTING PEOPLE ON NOTICE

Moral entrepreneurs use persuasion to promote social scripts. This is quite different than putting people on notice. **Putting people on notice** involves announcing what will happen if they do not comply. Telling dissidents that they will be imprisoned or shot if they demonstrate is putting them on notice. Telling children that they will be grounded if they disobey is putting them on notice.

Putting people on notice involves coercive threats. Coercive threats are employed in the absence of a willingness to comply. Coercive threats range from threats to physically harm someone should they disobey to threatening to withhold something that they need or desire. Paying their kids to do a task, a form of bribery by parents, carries with it the threat not to pay them should they decide not to comply. Resorting to coercive threats implies that persuasion is not working.

WHY POLITICS?

Politicians are probably the best examples of moral entrepreneurs because their total existence revolves around the selling of social scripts. The same could be said of **religious** leaders who are devoted to peddling values and beliefs that sustain what they approve of as social scripts. **But there is one significant difference.** Politicians who are successful get their preferences translated into government policies. At that point, **reliance on persuasion** is joined by the **coercive power of the state** to advance their agendas.

There is another reason for featuring so many political examples in the discussions on moral entrepreneurs. Although you may not personally know much about politics, or for that matter be interested in politics, coverage in the print media, on network and cable news shows, and other programs provides some common ground for the purpose of illustration. No other area involving moral entrepreneurs gets that kind of extensive coverage.

Ultimately, it is important to remember that no matter what illustrations are used, they should never be allowed to detract from the point being made. Examples are vehicles for helping you to learn how to apply the concepts beyond those situations. The trick is to know how a concept is defined and then see how the material contained in an example illustrates that concept.

ADVERTISERS

Although politics embodies so many features that are amenable to moral entrepreneurs and script analysis, there is another rich source of illustrations. It is the world of advertising. The job of advertising parallels the work of moral entrepreneurs. Job number one is selling something. The most obvious difference is that advertisers sell products, whereas moral entrepreneurs sell social scripts.

This difference in emphasis can be deceiving. What advertisers really do is play on the values and beliefs of audiences to sell a product by inducing consumers to sustain or change their purchasing scripts. Ads designed to sustain purchasing habits (scripts) try to retain consumers, whereas ads designed to get new markets try to change purchasing scripts (habits).

All advertising requires inducing people to buy what they would not buy otherwise or don't really need. Why else would anyone pay for ads? A common tactic appeals to someone's ideal self. Mountain Dew ads associate risk taking and extreme activities such as jumping off cliffs while they're drinking their product. A different strategy is to help someone overcome guilt. Initially housewives were reluctant to have a dishwasher, apparently because they felt guilty about it shortchanging the effort hand washing and drying dishes takes. This precipitated ads that exclaimed the virtue of using dishwashers so she could have more time to spend and take care of the family!

CARE-BASED ADS

Companies whose **reputation** has become **tarnished** often resort to **care-based** ads to restore their image. **Care-based** ads are designed to create the impression that the company really cares about people. One cigarette company, who like others in the United States was tainted by testimony that their top echelon lied about not knowing the risks of smoking or that nicotine is addictive, displayed a care-based ad on television. The ad featured a woman who runs a home for runaway kids praising the company for donations that helped her cause.

Care-based images are also a favorite of politicians. The Bush administration has stressed their support for the education of women and their political involvement around the world. A favorite image is that of Americans helping open schools for girls and women in countries like Afghanistan and Iraq. The political effect of these ads is to soften criticism of these invasions. Dropping food packages in Afghanistan alongside bombs may have been intended for the same purpose.

Skeptics are inclined to distrust all care-based ads as connived or deceitful. The point is that some care-based ads are genuine, whereas others are deceitful. What counts is how audiences interpret them and whether or not a more positive image results.

A CLASSIC AD CAMPAIGN

In the history of advertising, the Virginia Slims cigarette campaign is considered to be a classic. The objective was to get more women to smoke. The original hook was the slogan that "You've come a long way baby."

The hook was meant to associate smoking Virginia Slims cigarettes with being a liberated woman. "You've come a long way" was meant to symbolically distance new smokers from past scripts where women were not allowed to make decisions. The "baby" reference plays off an older cultural script when men used the term "babe" to describe a sexy woman. Taken together, the hook promises women liberation without losing their attractiveness by smoking.

Other elements of Virginia Slims ads play on the name. Was the decision to use "Virginia" meant to imply virtue? What about "Slims"? Does this promise that women who smoke these cigarettes will fulfill the cultural emphasis on being slim? This might be particularly appealing to women who had tried to quit smoking other cigarettes because they were worried about health costs but found that they had gained weight as a result. The promise of less risk with a filtered cigarette could be seen as a solution to the weight gain problem associated with efforts to completely stop smoking.

It will probably come as no surprise to you, but the world of advertising was the first to systematically calculate how to exploit values and beliefs to sell products. The first, and classic effort, was by Vance Packard (1957) in his book *The Hidden Persuaders*. In this book, Packard draws upon insights from psychology and illustrations from advertising campaigns. Since those early days there has been an explosion of books dealing with what advertisers often call motivational research. Some feature theoretical insights, while others describe techniques for test marketing ideas. Using everything from lie detectors to devices that track eye movement to see what subjects are looking at in a picture are possibilities. The popularity of focus groups and market research by moral entrepreneurs was inspired by the world of advertising.

CHAPTER 5
THE BASICS OF INTERACTION

The **behavioral preferences, values,** and **beliefs** that people **bring to social situations** determines what **acts** will be **viewed favorably or unfavorably.** How people **define a situation** influences their **behavioral choices** at a given point in time, and **feedback** from those choices influencing **subsequent** behavioral choices. Now we will examine how **principles of social exchange** fit into all of this.

PRINCIPLES OF SOCIAL EXCHANGE

Principles of social exchange refer to **different** ways **interaction** can be structured. The **most basic distinction** is between **cooperation** and **conflict** as forms of social exchange. Other forms of exchange involve **different ways conflict can be resolved** should it exist. Included are **violent exchanges, coercion, compromise, co-optation,** and **competition.**

COOPERATION

Cooperation occurs when people **chose to work** together in pursuit of a **common goal. Shared values** determine **common goals. Shared behavioral preferences** set **boundaries** on what will be done to attain a goal. **Beliefs are truth claims** about which of the **permissible alternatives** is most likely to **create success** in goal attainment.

Cooperation can occur in social situations ranging from **casual friendships** to more **formal settings** with a **specified goal.** A **study group** represents a more formal setting where a **specific goal** such as studying for an exam or completing an assignment frames interaction. In more **casual relationships** like between friends **having fun together** is a much **less specific** goal.

Choosing to work together is a defining characteristic of cooperation. Choosing to work together suggests **volition. Volition** means **voluntary.** This means that to say people were **forced to cooperate** makes no sense. The **element of volition** is absent when people are forced to behave in a certain way in pursuit of a goal.

Cooperation creates a **win/win** situation. Both **self** and **social rewards** are **high. Self-rewards** are high because people do what they prefer to do. **Social rewards** are high because what people choose to do is greeted favorably by others. If the cooperative undertaking produces a desirable goal, then the benefits associated with that goal represent additional rewards for the participants.

This does not mean that cooperation always produces maximum rewards for all participants. Some may find the activities used in pursuit of the goal more satisfying than others. Differences concerning the significance of goal attainment can also signal different levels of return.

A study group can be used to illustrate these points. Some people enjoy the process of studying for an exam more than others. The importance of getting a good grade should it occur as a result of the study group can also vary.

FREE RIDERS

Free riders are people who **benefit from the efforts** of others but **contribute little** or nothing to the process. An example of a free rider is someone in a study group who contributes nothing but receives the same grade on a class project as those who did the work. Another is when a spouse receives benefits far in excess of what they contribute to the relationship.

Free riders are often quite effective in **manipulating others** to do the work that they are unwilling to do. Negotiation tactics such as not listening or pretending to be incompetent often frustrate others to the extent that they stop asking for the free rider to join in. The result is the free rider benefits at the expense of those who deserve it.

Morale is high when **everyone cooperates** in the pursuit of a goal. **Morale** is high when the **amount of satisfaction** or **enthusiasm** people have for a relationship that they are involved in is high. Even though **free riders** are successful in getting others to do the work, their presence lowers morale. Often the only way to restore morale is to get them to leave and not join in future situations that require cooperation.

CONFLICT

Conflict occurs whenever **script disputes exist** concerning **courses of action,** the **choice of goals,** or when **goal attainment** is a **win/lose** situation. Techniques of conflict resolution include different forms of social exchange that can take place when script disputes exist. **Violence, coercion, compromise, co-optation, and competition** are the most common techniques of conflict resolution.

VIOLENCE

Violence is the **infliction** of **bodily harm** on someone else. Violence, or the threat of violence, has two distinct purposes. The first is to force someone to comply. The second is to eliminate an opponent or someone who is unwilling to comply.

In the **first instance,** violence is more **measured.** The reason is that the **use of violence** as means to **force compliance** requires that the target is not disabled to the extent that they are unable to comply or killed, which means that they are unavailable to comply. This is why successful conquers down through the centuries have used violence only to establish control over a population and not eliminate everyone. When the Roman armies conquered new territories, control over survivors in the local populations was an important source of human labor.

Using **violence** to **force compliance** or **selectively eliminate opponents** has its **downside.** Disabling or killing friends and family of survivors can breed resentment and hatred. Attacks on the World Trade Towers were violent acts meant to intimidate Americans into changing their policies and actions in Muslim countries. Instead, the killings generated resentment and resolve to use violence to eliminate terrorist threats.

Using **violence** to **disable or kill** others means that those employing the violence see no purpose in having survivors. Those targeted are seen as expendable. Killing the head of a government that poses a serious threat is likely if it is believed that there is no purpose to be gained by letting him live.

But even the violent removal of a leader who is disliked by many in his society can have negative repercussions. American planners failed to take this into account when they thought they would be greeted as liberators after removing of Saddam Hussein in Iraq. But the amount of violence and suffering caused by the invasion created resentment that was unexpected. Violence used to quell insurgents often created civilian casualties that further alienated many in Iraq who saw the Americans more as an occupational force than liberators.

COERCION

Coercion is a form of **conflict resolution** based upon **forcing** compliance. **Coercion** results in **unilateral benefits.** It is a **win/lose** situation. The rewards go to the person(s) who are able to force others to comply. This is why coercion is seen as a situation where **benefits are unilateral** rather than shared.

In **personal relationships** as well as **relationships between groups** and **societies,** the **capacity to coerce** rests upon the **capacity** of someone to **control** what **others need. You cannot force** people to **comply against their will** unless they are **dependent** upon you for the gratification of their needs.

Threatening violence is a case in point. If the person threatened has the **capacity to successfully counter** or **avoid the violence,** that person is **not dependent** and therefore **less likely to comply.** If the **threat is real** and the target has **no recourse but to comply,** then that person **is dependent** and **more likely to comply.** Also, some people are willing and able to endure pain or accept the possibility of death. This reduces the potential for violent threats to be successful. The willingness of suicide bombers to sacrifice their lives suggests that the threat of violence is less effective in getting them to comply than others for whom death is a greater threat.

Violence, or threats of violence, are not the only means by which people can be coerced. Recognizing the link between **dependence** and the **capacity to coerce** allows us to consider other possibilities. People who are **economically dependent** upon someone else are more susceptible to coercion than when they are economically independent. Wives who are entirely dependent upon their husbands for a paycheck are more susceptible to coercion than wives who have other sources of income. Employees who have other job opportunities are less susceptible to economic threats by their bosses than employees who have no choice but to comply.

Threatening to withhold love and affection can also be a coercive tactic. To the extent that someone is dependent upon someone else for love and affection is the extent to which that person can use the threat of withholding love and affection to force compliance. Parents often use this tactic without fully realizing it. The child who conforms is given the most attention and love.

COMPROMISE

Compromise is a **form of conflict resolution** where participants decide to **reduce** their **original demands** in order to settle their differences. Often **compromise** occurs when **neither party** to a dispute has the **capacity to coerce** an outcome or pursuing a **coercive outcome** is seen as **too costly.** Sporadic attempts by Palestinians and Israel to abandon violence as a unilateral effort to force compliance and seek a compromise illustrates this point.

Compromise is a more **diluted win/win** situation than **cooperation.** This is because of what must be given up to reach a settlement. **Compromise** is more **mutually satisfying** than **coercion,** where **benefits are unilateral** and accrue mostly to those controlling the situation. The **capacity** to **coerce** others to **comply** presents the **greatest** opportunity for someone to **maximize benefits or rewards** when script disputes exist.

CO-OPTATION

Co-optation is a **form of conflict resolution** where **one side** is able to get the other to **switch sides.** It involves **getting them** to **identify** with **your script preferences.** An example is when a boss is able to change the mind of a subordinate who originally caused trouble on the job because of a difference of attitudes. The boss has co-opted that subordinate when the subordinate comes to agree with what the boss prefers.

Co-optation has an obvious advantage over **coercion.** Coercion often generates resentment. People often don't like to be bossed around. Such resentment does not exist when compliance is achieved through co-optation because now agreement exists without force.

Identification with an aggressor helps us understand a powerful advantage that people in power (coercive advantage) have over subordinates. **Freud** argued that when confronted with a powerfully threatening person, **unconsciously** becoming like that person reduces the fear of being harmed. This helps explain why some prisoners in Nazi death camps came to identify with their captors. Some prisoners went to great lengths to foster this connection. Even possessing a button from the tunic of a guard could create this impression. The extent to which an unconscious identity conversion really protects someone is a separate issue.

All of this suggests a **subtle relationship** between **coercive capacity** and **co-optation.** To the **extent that co-optation** is based upon an **underlying coercive threat** is the **extent to which the identity conversion** is problematic. Take away the coercive threat and the foundation for the identity conversion can evaporate. Co-optation in the absence of a conscious or unconscious threat is more likely to persist because someone more fully internalizes the behavioral preferences and justifications of others.

COMPETITION

With **competition,** the **conflict exists** over the fact that **winners** and **losers** will be declared. **Competition** is a **zero-sum game** where there can only be **one winner.** It is a form of conflict resolution to the extent that participants accept the results.

Acceptance of results depends upon **agreeing on rules** and **playing by those rules.** Only then will the competition be seen as a valid reason for giving disproportionate rewards and benefits to whoever wins. **Cheating** violates an agreement on the rules and playing by them. Cheating forfeits acceptance of results in a competition.

An **even playing field** is a term often used to describe a **competitive situation,** where the **rules** give some **an advantage.** If admission requirements give some an unfair advantage of getting into a college, an uneven playing field exists. Giving an advantage to those who had the opportunity to take advanced placement classes while in high school over those for whom these courses were unavailable is an example of an uneven playing field.

If people **define** a competitive situation **as fair,** then they are more likely to accept results than if they **perceive** it as **unfair.** Not knowing the built-in advantages for others is one reason people may perceive a competition as fair. Those who benefit from the rules often try to conceal their advantages.

DYADS AND TRIADS

A **dyad** is a relationship between **two** and **only two people.** A **triad** is a relationship among **three** people. The addition of a single person converts a dyad into a triad.

The existence of a **third person** is the most basic difference between a **dyad** and a **triad.** It is what expands upon possibilities. For instance, with one more person it is possible to form a **coalition.** A coalition exists when two of the participants marshal their resources against the other person. Coalitions, which tilt the balance of power in a relationship, are not possible in a dyad.

Thinking about how the potential for a coalition can change the dynamics of a social encounter can be conveyed through an illustration. Suppose that you and your roommate are arguing about an issue. Consider what can happen if someone else walks in on your argument. Now you both may direct your points to the third person rather than each other. The reason is that both of you are trying to get that person to agree with you. If you are successful in getting the third person to agree with you, then you have formed a coalition that may swing the argument in your favor.

MEDIATION AND ARBITRATION

Mediation and **arbitration** involve the use of a third person to help people resolve their conflicts. A **mediator** is someone who tries to help people resolve their differences through a compromise agreement. A mediator has no power to impose a resolution on those involved in the dispute. **Arbitration** differs from mediation in that the parties to the dispute agree to accept that third person's decision.

The use of mediation to facilitate a divorce settlement has become increasingly popular. The task of the mediator is to help the couple arrive at a settlement that both agree is fair. The effort to reconcile divorce differences through mediation stands in stark contrast to the adversarial method of using attack lawyers to settle differences in a courtroom.

Attempts to resolve both labor and management disputes often begin with mediation. If mediation is unsuccessful, then both may agree to arbitration. The decision to seek arbitration means that both parties to the dispute agree to accept the judgment of the arbitrator.

TYPES OF BEHAVIORAL PREFERENCES

Much has been said about **behavioral preferences** as the basis for **personal social scripts**. **Behavioral preferences** define what people find acceptable and enjoyable or despicable and unacceptable. But the importance and significance attached to behavioral preferences can vary. Distinctions between **folkways, mores,** and **laws** establish this variation.

FOLKWAYS AND MORES

Folkways are **behavioral preferences** that are behaviors that are less important to the actors. Folkways reflect more peripheral values and beliefs. **Mores** refer to **behavioral preferences** that are based upon more core values and beliefs.

Because the behavioral preferences contained in mores cover behavior that is taken more seriously, adherence is greeted with stronger approval than compliance with folkways. Violations of mores have much more serious consequences than deviance from folkways. One method for determining whether or not the behavioral preferences contained within a social script are folkways or mores is to watch for reactions to deviance or conformity. More intense reactions signal the existence of mores. Less dramatic reactions suggest that the relevant behavioral preferences are folkways.

It is tempting to assume that **casual personal relationships** are based on **folkways.** This confuses the casual nature of informal encounters with the issue of behavioral importance. Some behavioral preferences involving friends cover relatively unimportant areas that are ignored or mildly rebuked when violated. Harshly warning a friend not to pursue a point by exclaiming "don't go there" suggests a behavioral area of greater importance.

The temptation to assume that more **official scripts** involve **mores** must also be resisted. A formal script such as a job description contains behavioral preferences that the company views with differing degrees of importance. Behavioral importance is conveyed by consequences. Knowing that a company will tolerate being late to work suggests that it is less important than if such behavior results in termination.

LAWS

Laws are **state-sanctioned behavioral preferences.** Laws are behavioral preferences that have received a governmental stamp of approval. In the United States, governmental stamps of approval are handed out by all governmental jurisdictions. These governmental units range from local and state units to the federal government in Washington D.C.

Some confusion over what constitutes a law exists because of vocabulary. Are ordinances and regulations laws? If one considers any behavioral preference that is officially sanctioned by a governmental unit as a law, then governmental ordinances and regulations are types of laws. Here the use of the term law is meant to encompass all forms of state-sanctioned behavioral preferences.

STATE-SANCTIONED BEHAVIORAL PREFERENCES

State-sanctioned behavioral preferences are significant for two reasons. The first is that state-sanctioned behavioral preferences often have greater **legitimacy** than preferences held by others in a society. This means that a governmental stamp of approval may elevate the acceptability of a behavioral preference.

Cultural scripts can help to elevate the legitimacy of state-sanctioned behavioral preference. An example is the notion that in democratic societies, the majority of the people subscribe to whatever behavioral preferences receive a governmental seal of approval. This implies that all ordinances, regulations, and criminal or civil laws reflect a majority opinion.

If any **law is** viewed as **legitimate,** then **compliance** with it will be **voluntary.** But what happens if some citizens do not view a state-approved behavioral preference as legitimate? This brings us to the second advantage of having your normative preferences endorsed by the state. Having a virtual monopoly on power the state can **coerce** compliance.

Whether or not the state exercises its coercive power to compel compliance with its laws, regulations, or ordinances involves discretion. The government can decide to apply coercion to some but not all violators of its behavioral preferences. For instance, if the FBI directs more of its resources to terrorism, then it may neglect other areas such as corporate crime. Or a governmental unit may decide to apply more severe consequences for some violations. An example is when sentences for crack cocaine offenses are four or more times higher than the same offenses by people who snort coke.

PRIMARY AND SECONDARY RELATIONSHIPS

The difference between **primary** and **secondary relationships** is often used by sociologists when they compare types of relationships. **Primary relationships** are based on informal scripts that encourage participants to take each other personally into account. The element of familiarity is what makes this expectation possible. Because those involved are expected to take each other personally into account, the opportunity for personal expression is high in primary relationships. This is why primary relationships are often identified as **expressive relationships.**

Secondary relationships involve more formal, fragmented, and impersonal scripts. These relationships feature **instrumental relationships,** such as those between a physician and patient or an employer and employee. These relationships are more fragmented than primary ones because their focus is on a task. Bosses and workers are expected to do their jobs and not become too personally involved with each other. The underlying assumption is that personal involvement or expression diminishes task efficiency. Discouraging personal involvement and expression is what makes secondary relationships so impersonal.

In **traditional societies** like those that farm or hunt and gather, **work relationships** are more personal because everyone knows each other. **Work relationships** in more **modern industrial** and **postindustrial** societies are more likely to be **impersonal.** Although this **may suggest** that the **potential for personal expression** is **higher** in **traditional work relationships,** the matter is more complex. Sometimes the work scripts that evolve in a traditional society, such as one that hunts and gathers, are taken extremely seriously since they seem to have worked well in the past. If this occurs, then pressures to stick to the script may limit personal expression just as much as what is found on more modern and impersonal assembly lines.

PRIMARY AND SECONDARY OVERLAP

Often people **find themselves embedded** in situations where the **expectations** associated with a **primary** and **secondary relationship** overlap. A dentist working on a family member might feel conflicted over the requirements of the task script and those associated with his or her personal relationship with that person. For instance, a dentist might feel uncomfortable applying the billing practices used with other patients to a family member. Sending dear old Mom's bill to a collection agency might be seen as a bit over the top.

Similar conflicts arise regularly in family businesses. Retaining an impersonal task-oriented focus on the job can be difficult when dealing with family. The problem is that scripts concerning personal relationships collide with requirements contained in the job script. This is why physicians often prefer to have a colleague operate on a family member.

GEMEINSCHAFT AND GESELLSCHAFT

Tonnies (1887), a German sociologist, used the **distinction between primary** and **secondary relationships** to characterize different types of **societies. Gemeinschaft** societies are ones that are smaller, more rural, and where everyone knows each other. **Gesellschaft** societies are more **urban** societies, where more daily transactions are impersonal secondary relationships.

Because everyone knows everyone else in a **traditional society,** the term **gemeinschaft** is often used to describe it because of the amount of familiarity. Because **more transactions** are **between relative strangers** in **modern societies,** the term **gesellschaft** is often used to describe them. But care must be used when applying these concepts because many societies contain elements of both.

Using the term **gesellschaft** to characterize modern societies is usually based on the **increased concentration of people** in cities where more everyday life experiences involve impersonal exchanges. People living in small town America are familiar with each other so the designation **gemeinschaft** more accurately describes their daily existence.

MODERN SOCIETIES

Some welcome the relative **anonymity** that living in cities affords them. **Not being known** increases the latitude people have for choosing **alternative lifestyles,** (scripts) which abound in city life. It is the combination of diverse opportunities and the lower probability of negative repercussions brought about by anonymity that makes city life so attractive to so many. It allows people to do things that the extent of familiarity in smaller villages and towns discourages.

The potential for alternative lifestyles in cities is significant for another reason. Often it is these more leisure time pursuits that give people living in cities the opportunity to come to personally know others better and form primary relationships in the midst of the more impersonal climate of cities. For many frustrated by impersonality on the job, the familiarity that these leisure time activities allow for is therapeutic. Working out at the gym with friends that you made there is an example.

But city life is not for everyone. Some flee the city back to the small villages or towns in search of personal relationships, such as family and friends that they miss. Their quest may prove to be fruitful or a disappointment, depending upon whether or not they can capture the past. Sometimes life in gemeinschaft societies is more suffocating than their romantic images or memories suggest.

COMMUNICATION AND SOCIAL SCRIPTS

Traditional and **modern societies** differ in how scripts are **communicated.** In many more **traditional societies, literacy rates** are quite **low.** In some of these **preliterate** societies, no one knows how to read and write. In other preliterate societies, literacy is limited to a few. This means that there are limited opportunities to store and make people aware of social scripts through written documents. **Storage** of social scripts is through **memory.** An **awareness of social scripts** comes though **observing and imitating** the **behavior** of others or being **verbally told** how to act.

In more **modern societies** with higher **literacy rates, written documents** augment observation and oral capacities to communicate social scripts. **Literate societies** also benefit from the much greater capacity a written language provides for storing more intricate social scripts, such as those found in modern corporations. Having the capacity to use communicative strategies found in preliterate societies and the capacity of writing greater benefits the ability of modern societies to store, manage, and communicate social scripts.

NONVERBAL BEHAVIOR

Nonverbal behavior represents a form of communication that includes everything from facial expressions to obscene gestures. **Nonverbal behavior** is often the means by which people are **made aware** of the behavioral preferences of others in social encounters and relationships. A frown can effectively register a behavioral preference. A smile can effectively communicate behavior that is acceptable to someone else in a social situation.

Nonverbal behavior is also a **communication device** that people use to express **their identity** to others. Everything from a tattoo or hairstyle to a piece of jewelry through an eyebrow qualifies. So too does the clothes people wear and how they walk or carry themselves.

IMPRESSION MANAGEMENT

Impression management is a term Goffman (1959) coined to describe **activities designed** to create certain **images** with an **audience.** His emphasis on activities designed to create an impression with others reveals his concern with deliberate efforts by someone to manage how others view him or her. This is difference is from impressions that an audience has of someone that are not managed but simply unfold naturally.

The term **giving off** characterizes performances designed to create a certain impression with an audience. Giving off can be expressed through nonverbal, spoken, or written means. Performances can range from the display of nonchalant indifference by someone walking along a beach to a look of innocence displayed by a child.

People try to **manage** how others view them for a **variety of reasons.** Probably the most obvious is to gain a **favorable impression.** A favorable impression can have two distinct objectives. The **first objective** is to convey an **image** that reflects someone's **ideal self.** The purpose is to manage their impression so that others will provide feedback that affirms that ideal self. The **second objective** is to create the **impression** with an audience that **you are like them** and what they approve of. If successful, this creates a favorable impression that increases the likelihood that they will have a positive attitude toward you.

Whether or not the performance is genuine or fake is not the point. What counts is if the intended image is bought. Even a genuine gesture may not create the impression and/or response by the other person that is desired.

Goffman was mostly interested in managed images designed to gain a favorable impression by others. A different form of impression management occurs when people flaunt their distinctive identity to an audience. Looking Goth is not meant to win approval from those who hate that look. Instead flaunting it is meant to register disapproval from a hostile audience that affirms one's distinctiveness from them.

ROLE DISTANCE AND ROLE EMBRACEMENT

Role distance and **role embracement** are forms of **impression management. Role embracement** refers to efforts by people to **show commitment** to the behavior that they are engaging in before an audience. **Role distance** refers to efforts by people to **express disdain** for a behavior that is witnessed by an audience.

Both **role distance** and **embracement** are **deliberate efforts** to manage impressions. **Expressing disdain** for a **behavior disapproved** of by an audience helps create a favorable impression with them. **Showing commitment** to **behaviors preferred** by others also helps to create a favorable impression.

Self-preferences determine the range of acting someone can engage in when creating an impression of role distance or embracement. If what is required is consistent with someone's self-preferences, there are no obstacles. If, however, what is required involves a deception, then self-preferences can become an obstacle. An example would be when guilt prevents someone from expressing commitment or disdain for a behavior witnessed by an audience.

Audience reactions are shaped by how they **define the situation.** If they think that an **expression of commitment or disdain** is **genuine,** and it is consistent with their behavioral preferences, they are likely to respond favorably. If they think that the performance was faked, they are more likely to respond unfavorably.

INGRATIATION

The term **ingratiation** refers to **an act** that gains a **favorable response** from others. Creating a favorable impression by doing what others like increases the likelihood that others will be disposed to respond favorably. Creating an unfavorable impression by doing something that others dislike increases the likelihood that they will be disposed to respond unfavorably.

Favorable or unfavorable dispositions are not the entire story. Other factors can override a disposition created by an act. For instance, while someone is inclined to react unfavorably, guilt could prevent him or her from doing so. An example would be when a friend is offended but guilt prevents that person from responding negatively. Coercive advantages and deficits can have a similar effect. Someone offended by what a boss does may be disposed to respond unfavorably but concern about consequences may quell that inclination.

TYPES OF INGRATIATION

There are **two types of ingratiation** that are of interest to sociologists. **Genuine ingratiation** occurs whenever **the behavior you personally prefer** receives approval from someone else. Genuine ingratiation is based upon acts that are personally rewarding.

Instrumental ingratiation involves a **behavior** that has been chosen for its **expected outcome.** With **instrumental ingratiation,** you **refrain from your personal preference** and go with what will **benefit you the most.** The expression "kissing up to the boss" is an example of instrumental ingratiation.

COSTS AND INSTRUMENTAL INGRATIATION

Instrumental ingratiation always has at least one cost. It is the cost associated with not being able to do what you prefer. Alternatively, choosing to do what you prefer may bring about the wrath of the other person. That wrath alone may be unpleasant and represent a social cost. Unfavorable reactions may also include the social cost inflicted when others are unwilling to be supportive.

Genuine ingratiation represents a **win/win situation.** What you do is both **self-rewarding** and **socially rewarding** to others because you are complying with their behavioral preferences for you. This is why people prefer situations where social scripts are compatible, because of the potential for people to engage in acts that are self-rewarding while at the same time please others.

CIVIL INATTENTION

If you have ever been on the subway in New York, you have probably encountered what is known as civil inattention. **Civil inattention** occurs when people deliberately refrain from making eye contact or any other contact with someone else. Reading a newspaper or looking down at your feet are familiar methods of civil inattention on the New York subway.

Refraining from making eye contact reduces the likelihood of unwanted confrontations. It is based upon a cultural script that associates making eye contact with an invasion of private space or aggression. The aggressive component is revealed in the dominance game where people try to "stare each other down."

Looking down or away from someone else may have its parallel in the animal kingdom. Averting their eyes is a common behavior among subordinate males in some species. This suggests that civil inattention may be an expression of submissiveness that quells aggressive responses by more dominant males.

Civil inattention involves nonverbal language. But when civil inattention is violated, the result can be an onslaught of verbal or physical assaults. Learning the tactics of civil inattention can save someone a great deal of hassle.

THE LOOKING GLASS SELF

Trying to create a favorable impression with others can be linked to the need of people to have others affirm their ideal self-concept. The concept of the **looking glass self** (Cooley, 1902) offers further insights into this process. Cooley thought the responses of others act like a mirror through which we form our ideal self-concepts.

His basic argument is that **people need approval from others.** That approval is contingent upon becoming like them. Imagining approval by others reinforces the ideal self-concept derived from them through internalization. Disapproval causes a personal sense of mortification. Their disapproval is registered as self-disapproval, which creates a loss of self-esteem.

NEEDING APPROVAL

Cooley provides an interesting insight into one possible dynamic that can help to explain why people come to accept social scripts. He is probably right to suggest that people with a high need for approval are the most likely to form their ideal self-concepts around prevailing social scripts. But not all people form their self-concepts in such a manner. Rebels develop their self-concepts in opposition to prevailing social scripts. For them, disapproval by advocates of those social scripts reinforces their rebellious self-concepts. More will be said about this in the next chapter in the discussion on reference groups.

MANIPULATING OTHERS

Cooley's emphasis on **needing approval** suggests that people are **passive clones** who uncritically devour social scripts. But this neglects the more manipulative side of human nature. Rather than internalizing social scripts, some people use knowledge about such scripts to exploit others.

An example is the unscrupulous home improvement salesman who uses what he knows about the elderly to take advantage of them. Imagining their anger should they become aware of what he has done hardly creates the sense of mortification that Cooley associated with disapproval. For the hustler, taking advantage of people is a source of pride and not guilt or remorse. Legends are created through celebration of such exploits among hustlers and their fans.

CHAPTER 6
SMALL GROUPS

A **small group** is a collection of **at least three people** who engage in a **distinctive set of relationship.** The **nature of interaction** between group members is what makes a small group **distinctive.** Whether or not **cooperation** or **conflict** exists within a group is a fundamental distinction.

Techniques of conflict resolution come into play if conflict exists. If **competition** is the issue, such as when group members are rewarded differently, then agreement on rules and acceptance of outcomes provides a stable format. Agreed upon rules can also provide a stable basis for **compromise.** Should these options not work, then **violence, coercion,** and co-optation may be what causes a group to have distinctive characteristics.

Requiring at least three people distinguishes a **small group** from a **dyad.** This creates the possibility of dynamics that don't occur when a relationship is limited to just two people. An example would be conflict based on the formation of coalitions. A triad is the minimal requirement for a coalition because it requires at least two people who operate against someone else. Coalitions can increase legitimacy or coercive leverage for those who join together. Having at least three people also opens the door for someone in a small group to become a mediator or arbitrator should disputes arise.

Having **three people** as the minimal number in a small group also makes it possible to look at different leadership styles. This is because a **leader** is usually seen as exerting influence on at least several other people. Different **styles of leadership** and the presence of at least two others also makes it possible to talk about other small group dynamics, such as **pluralistic ignorance** and **groupthink.** More coverage of these possibilities occurs later in the discussion.

THE EMPHASIS ON COOPERATION

Much of the **early research** on small groups was **sponsored** by **businesses** and others interested in studying **worker productivity.** The concern with worker productivity prompted many researchers to think about small groups in terms of cooperative relationships. This was in keeping with the idea that a work group should involve cooperative relations where people share resources in pursuit of a production goal.

Later research turned to other possibilities concerning what goes on within a work group and its relationship to the larger organization. This switch in focus raised the possibility of conflict within work groups and/or between official organizational scripts and the demands workers place upon themselves. The discovery of unofficial scripts among workers that creates conflict between them and management prompted studies of techniques for resolving conflict.

The resolution of conflict between labor and management can take on many different forms. Businesses and management often used coercive tactics to get worker compliance. In the past, these coercive tactics ranged from hiring thugs to discourage striking workers to monitoring work sites and threatening to fire uncooperative workers.

Workers can also use coercive tactics to battle for better pay and working conditions. Using strikes to shut down operations became a favorite. Workers also used slowdowns and other strategies to improve their leverage with management. Management often retaliated by hiring scabs to replace striking workers.

The effectiveness of coercive tactics by both labor and management vary considerably. The degree to which either is dependent upon the other is the single more important variable. If replacement workers are easy to find, then management has a coercive advantage. If they are hard to come by, then the advantage often goes to labor because it is hard to run a company without labor.

The coercive power of labor depends upon the costs that they could inflict by withholding their labor. One example involved the teamsters before refrigerated railroad cars were invented. At that time, businesses depended on the horse-drawn wagons driven by teamsters to get their fresh produce to market. The lack of refrigeration gave the teamsters considerable leverage. A surprise strike that left strawberries rotting on hot railroad cars was sufficient to make those businesses listen to their demands.

The history of the labor management relationship is inherently one of conflict because both have opposing goals. Maximizing profit is incompatible with costs incurred by demands for better working conditions and higher wages. Negotiated compromises are more likely when neither has enough leverage to impose their will on the other.

Management efforts to improve worker productivity went from coercive strategies to more subtle ones. The search for more subtle strategies inspired management to turn increasingly to the social sciences for insights. Learning more about group cohesion and leadership types and styles provided a basis for revising strategies for dealing with workers.

The attention here will be on what social scientists have found out about the operation of small groups. Not all of this research concerns worker productivity, though much of it could be related to that topic. The discussion begins with a look at what is meant by group cohesion.

GROUP COHESION

Group cohesion involves the **strength of bonds between members** of a small group. Small groups vary depending upon the amount of cohesion that exists. A **highly cohesive group** is one where all the **members** feel **close and responsible** for each other. A group with little cohesion is one where the bond between members is weak.

Group cohesion results from numerous factors. One is that it can be scripted. An example would be a script that encourages friends in a peer group to feel close and to be responsible for each other.

A script for cohesion may also emerge over time. Before people get to know each other on a job there may be little cohesion between them. Eventually, if they get to know and like each other, an emergent script that reinforces strong bonds between them may emerge.

Sometimes external events increase group cohesion. An example would be when an outside threat increases group cohesion. In many communities, the threat to locate a toxic dump nearby may mobilize people into action. The process of mobilizing carries with it a strengthened bond among neighbors who join together in protest.

The duration of high cohesion in the presence of an outside threat is often relatively short. It lasts as long as the threat exists. After the threat disappears, neighbors may retreat into their own lives. Cohesion is likely to disappear or be severely diminished when this occurs.

Competition between groups can also increase cohesion. A typical example is high school sports rivalries. Schools often schedule pep rallies to boost school spirit before a sporting event. Boosting school spirit is the same as boosting cohesion.

It is easy to see why management was so interested in studying group cohesion. Highly cohesive groups are highly productive. This is because people who feel close and responsible for each other are likely to be cooperative in their endeavors.

An example of manipulating group cohesion for the purpose of improving productivity occurred at one of the huge steel mills outside of Chicago many years ago. Management hired a consultant to improve lagging production at the blast furnaces in the plant. His solution was ingenious. Each day he said nothing but marked a chalk number on the floor in front of each of the blast furnaces. Eventually the workers became curious and asked what he was doing. He explained that he was just marking down the number of tons that each furnace produced the previous day. It was not long before the crews began to engage in some friendly competition. The consultant continued to mark the production of each unit. By creating competition between the crews, the consultant dramatically increased production at the plant.

OFFICIAL WORKPLACE SCRIPTS

Official scripts are **workplace scripts** endorsed by executives. Official workplace scripts result from rational efforts to plan activities. Official workplace scripts are usually written down in more modern societies.

Unofficial scripts are based upon more personal relationships among members of a workplace group. Unofficial scripts are shared informally and are not usually written down. An unofficial workplace script may conflict with the official workplace script endorsed by executives. On other occasions, unofficial workplace scripts reinforce official workplace scripts. An example would be when workers fire themselves up for a project.

A management consultant named **Taylor** created a script that became a popular model for American companies. His script has become known as the **Taylorization** of **work.**

Taylor recommended that **assembly lines** become organized around the **timed repetition of specialized tasks** that are **standardized.** To **standardize** tasks means to have **everyone** do a given task in **exactly the same manner.** There is no allowance for personal variations. The basic strategy has been applied in many industries. An example from the auto industry is sufficient to get the idea. On an auto assembly line, all the workers are assigned repetitive specialized tasks that are done in a standard way. Some workers use a standardized procedure to install windshields, others use a standardized procedure to mount the motor and so forth.

Anyone who has ever worked on an assembly line knows that what Taylor proposed is hardly inspirational. It is flat-out boring and monotonous. Because of this, it is often necessary to have effective ways to monitor and motivate workers to continue with their drudgery. Often the constant monitoring and coercive threats undermine morale even more.

UNOFFICIAL WORKPLACE SCRIPTS

Roethlesberger and Dickson (1939) looked at how **unofficial scripts** among workers can come to influence the efficiency that Taylor attributed to his plan. They found that workers informally discouraged both too much and too little work. Workers classified their more zealous coworkers as **rate-busters.** Those who were lazy and unproductive were labeled **chiselers. Binging,** which involved a punch to the shoulder, was used to discouraged rate-busters and to motivate chiselers.

TASK AND EXPRESSIVE LEADERS

Bales (1951) and his colleagues examined work groups from another point of view. He discovered two different types of leaders that operate within task-oriented groups, such as those found in the workplace. A **task leader** is someone who provides direction and helps the group to remain focused on the task. An **expressive leader** is someone who provides humor and other forms of emotional releases that boost morale among workers.

Both types of leaders make important contribution to worker productivity. A task leader helps the group organize its activities. An expressive leader improves cohesion by elevating morale.

LEADERSHIP STYLES

White and Lippett (1960) offered a different angle on leadership within groups. They identified three different kinds of leaders. **Authoritarian leaders** impose their will upon the group. **Democratic leaders** encourage input from other members of the group in order to arrive at group-based decisions. **Laissez-faire leaders** are friendly but like to keep on the sidelines. Authoritarian leaders are the most active and dominant. Laissez-faire leaders are the least involved and remain largely passive. Democratic leaders are more moderately active in their efforts to reveal and encourage the wisdom of the group.

The implications of these distinctions were not lost on management. **Task leaders** who are **too authoritarian risk alienating workers. Laissez-faire** task leaders might be liked but provide little guidance that is essential to coordinate work activities. Developing **democratic leadership** styles becomes the most popular alternative for task leaders within organization.

DEMOCRATIC LEADERS

The choice of the democratic leadership style was popular in the United States. The idea was that friendly but firm democratic bosses who encourage worker input increase cooperation between labor and management. All of this would increase worker productivity, and therefore company profits.

But this was more of an ideal than a reality. American companies have rarely been run democratically. Those at the top are used to impose their decisions on those below them. Their management philosophy is based upon orders flowing from the top down to subordinates who are expected to comply. It assumes that only they have the wisdom and insight to make decisions.

There are other problems with encouraging democratic leadership in the workplace. One is the potential for workers to take advantage of supervisors who attempt to be friendly and solicit their input. Another is that workers who are used to following directions and being told what to do might become confused should they become involved in making decisions.

MASKING AUTHORITARIAN LEADERSHIP

Americans have had a long history of disdain for authoritarian leaders. The Founding Fathers talked about the necessity to rebel against tyranny. During World War II, our country fought against authoritarian leaders in Germany and Japan. And after that, we waged a cold war against authoritarian rule in communist countries.

All of this history might suggest that Americans despise authoritarian styles of leadership. But this is not exactly correct. Many business and corporate leaders have been known to rule with an iron hand. Some of our presidents have been rather imperial in their style and less than enthusiastic about seeking input from diverse sources in Congress and elsewhere.

Americans in the top positions of leadership in business and government do not always embrace the principle of democratic leadership. Leaders who recognize our aversion to authoritarianism often appreciate that it is wise for them to mask such dispositions or suffer resistance. For them, the task is to mask their authoritarian dispositions by pretending to be democratic leaders.

Pretending to listen gives workers a sense of involvement without disturbing the authoritarian principle that those on the top know best. Having a suggestion box invites the appearance of workplace democracy, even when input is never given serious attention. Encouraging citizens to get out and vote reinforces the image of democratic leadership and majority rule. But it tells us little about the role of authoritarian leaders behind the scenes in Congress and elsewhere who are more inclined to impose their will than to seek compromise.

The strategy of pretending to be democratic is also seen elsewhere. One place is in schools. Many teachers have been taught the difference between authoritarian and democratic teaching styles. Often they are taught that a democratic style is preferable. The problem is that they find it difficult to run a classroom on that basis.

So many learn the tactic of using democratic phrases to lower student resistance to their decisions. It is often much more effective for a teacher to say "class *we* have decided" than it is for a teacher to say "class *I* have decided." This deception probably works better with young children than it does with students in middle school or high school.

WELCOMING AUTHORITARIAN LEADERSHIP

Masking authoritarian styles with a **façade of being democratic** is not always necessary in the United States. Often Americans are quite responsive to and even demand their leaders to be authoritarian. Management books devoted to looking at the wisdom of historical leaders like Attila the Hun reflect this sentiment. The message is that, like Attila the Hun, success in business requires a strong and uncompromising leader.

Events like 9/11 can also create a climate where people seek more authoritarian leaders who are more than willing to use violence rather than negotiations and more democratic resolutions of international disputes. Being quick on the trigger seems more reassuring than relying on a combination of diplomacy and force. More authoritarian rule domestically may also be more acceptable as people are not as resistant to losing guarantees of personal freedom. The easy passage of the Patriot Act after the shock of 9/11 is an example. This legislation vastly increases the powers of the government by reducing personal freedom guarantees.

LEADERSHIP STYLES AND CREDIT

There is another problem with democratic and laissez-faire styles of leadership. It involves the issue of who gets credit for results. A manager who credits workers for results is not likely to get a bonus or promotion. Teachers who allow too much student input run the risk of being defined as weak and ineffective.

Authoritarian leaders are in a much better position to take credit for desirable results. Strong corporate or governmental leaders who claim responsibility for outcomes are more likely to receive more acclaim than those who spread the credit around to others involved in the decision-making process. Some even write books to ensure that people give them proper credit for their alleged accomplishments.

But while authoritarian leaders often relish taking credit for desirable outcomes, they are often quite skilled at denying personal responsibility for bad results. Complaining that too many voices drowned out their wise advice is a clever way to blame democracy for the problems. Another ploy is to complain that life is complex and one cannot always anticipate all of the problems. This complaint is rarely voiced when they take credit for desirable outcomes, which may have had more to do with luck and circumstances than their wisdom.

EFFECTIVENESS

There is no easy answer to the question of leadership styles and their relative effectiveness. An **authoritarian leadership** style favors someone who has **unusual expertise** or is able to **recognize and act on good advice.** One problem is that authoritarian leaders, by their very nature, may not be inclined to seek such advice. Additionally, the personalities of authoritarian leaders often frighten people. This often discourages them from offering fresh advice.

Authoritarian leadership becomes **less effective** when circumstances demand **innovative solutions** that exceed what someone knows or is able to process. Under these circumstances, the **disposition of democratic leaders** to **seek and encourage** advice can produce more effective outcomes. But to be effective, a democratic leader must still be able to judge the relative merits of different viewpoints.

Laissez-faire leaders are the most effective when **surrounded by smart people** who are capable of making good decisions. Too much interference by a leader may cancel the benefits of their expertise. Multiple inputs may also degrade their performance when such inputs come from less-qualified sources.

THE IRON LAW OF OLIGARCHY

Robert Michels (1911) proposed a **perspective on leadership** that differs from the focus on leadership styles. Michels based his theory upon his study of political parties in Italy at about the turn of the last century. The **iron law of oligarchy** states that **overtime leadership** within a political group becomes **concentrated** among a few. These few form an oligarchy that is isolated from other members. An **oligarchy** differs from **authoritarian leadership** in that it involves several people rather than just one people. It differs from democratic leadership because an oligarchy relies on input among a select few, rather than the majority within a group or society.

In a true oligarchy, leadership is shared among the few who are at the top. In reality, oligarchies often form around a strong leader and his advisors. Janis (1971) discusses some of the shortcomings that can arise from such a situation.

GROUPTHINK

Groupthink is the term that Janis (1971) used to describe situations where a strong leader is surrounded by yes men or women. It describes a situation where decision making by a leader goes unchallenged. **Mindguards** are self-appointed protectors of a leader's viewpoints. Mindguards discourage critical thinking by others who surround a strong leader. Nor are they inclined to challenge the leader.

Mindguards are often quite familiar with and close to the strong leader. They know that the best way to ingratiate the boss is to be supportive. Whether or not they truly agree is a separate issue. If they do agree, then **genuine ingratiation** is involved. If they pretend to agree, then their response qualifies as **instrumental ingratiation.** In either instance, the effect is to discourage opposing viewpoints.

The end result is a situation where everyone overtly agrees with what the leader says. The effect is to strengthen the positions of the authoritarian leader. This can be disastrous when the leader is wrong. Many believe this is exactly what went wrong during the war in Vietnam. The problem is that President Johnson surrounded himself with people who told him what he wanted to hear, rather than sound advice.

PLURALISTIC IGNORANCE AND GROUPTHINK

Pluralistic ignorance occurs when people make **erroneous assumptions** concerning the **script preferences** within their **own group.** Pluralistic ignorance occurs when definitions of the situation do not match reality. The general idea is that pluralistic ignorance creates an appearance of consensus when it does not really exist.

Pluralistic ignorance is likely to occur when the viewpoints of a strong leader are protected by mindguards in a group from dissenting viewpoints. This suppression of alternative viewpoints gives the appearance of consensus. Clever leaders exploit pluralistic ignorance by using mindguards to stifle dissent.

INOCULATION THEORY

Groupthink applies to dynamics within a group where mindguards discourage members from questioning the wisdom of a strong leader. **Inoculation theory** shifts the focus to the role of leaders in protecting members from outside influences. McGuire (1961) suggests that rather than totally isolating members from outside views, it might be better to give them a small dose to immunize them.

McGuire based his idea upon the principle of a medical vaccine. In medicine, a vaccine involves giving someone a small dose of a germ, which triggers the immune system's defenses against that particular disease. McGuire wondered if this same principle works with ideas.

McGuire and his colleagues ran a series of experiments to see if this might work. Their basic strategy was to give people a small dose of an alternative viewpoint and then see if it would inoculate them against that idea. Their research suggests that leaders may actually increase resistance to opposing ideas by exposing their members to a small dosage. Of course, it would not be necessary to inoculate members if there is little chance that they will ever encounter alternative scripts.

There is one clarification concerning the comparison between the human immune system and what McGuire proposed. With the human immune system, the vaccination automatically triggers the immune system's defenses. With ideas, giving a small dosage of an opposing viewpoint or script is not enough. It is also necessary to accompany the dose with persuasive arguments against that viewpoint. These critiques are what provide defenses against exposure to an offensive idea.

INOCULATION THEORY AND MORAL ENTREPRENEURS

It is easy to see how inoculation theory can be applied to moral entrepreneurs. Inoculating an audience against an alternative script helps a moral entrepreneur peddle his or her preference. Inoculating an audience against alternative interpretations of events reduces the effectiveness of those explanations.

There are different ways to inoculate, or create resistance, to an opposing script. Characterizing poor Americans as lazy and responsible for their plight has been used to discredit government programs. This argument was evident during the 1990s when critics of government welfare programs insisted that they encourage laziness among the poor. The result was the successful promotion of an alternative script that forced poor Americans off welfare and into jobs. The fact that the majority of poor Americans lived in families where at least one person had a job under the old welfare system went unnoticed.

ANOTHER SOURCE OF GROUP DISTINCTIVENESS

The difference between **primary** and **secondary groups** is another basis upon which groups are distinctive. Cooley (1902) defined a **primary group** as one that is characterized by **intimacy** and **familiarity.** Everyone knows each other and takes each other personally into account.

Identifying a primary group as **three or more people** who are **familiar** with each other and have **personal intimate relationships** is useful. But Cooley **assumed** that **familiarity and intimacy** means **that people like each** other and **feel responsible** for each other. This assumption of **cooperation** and **high cohesion** is a problem because many times familiarity and intimacy can personalize and make conflicts more intense.

For Cooley, the family represents the prime example of a primary group. Cooley must be forgiven for his choice of the family to illustrate what is a primary group. His choice is based upon an idealized image of families. It prevented him from considering the possibility that the family can be stressful and even violent. A family is not likely to function as a cohesive unit under such circumstances.

There is nothing wrong with thinking about primary groups as based upon face-to-face interaction among people who are familiar with each other. Nor is there anything wrong with assuming that familiarity is conducive to expressive relationships based upon taking the entire person into account. The problem is associating familiarity with cooperation and cohesion.

The defining quality of familiarity does not eliminate the possibility of conflict within a primary group. The old saying that "familiarity breeds contempt" captures this possibility. Even friendships among people who regularly get together as a primary group can involve personal conflicts and disputes. The same possibility exists for relationships between parents, children, and siblings within a family.

SECONDARY GROUPS

A **secondary group** is based upon more **impersonal, official,** and **fragmented** exchanges. Secondary groups are more likely to be found in the workplace than on the playground. They also have come to replace primary groups in other realms, such as politics and business. In politics, town hall meetings where everyone can express their opinion have been replaced by sound bits and television commercials. At one time, taking a loan out at the local bank was an exchange between people who grew up together and knew each other's families. Today, transactions at a bank are considerably more impersonal. The ultimate is using an ATM.

Sociologists have documented this general shift in more modern societies from primary to secondary group involvement. Sociologists have documented the extent to which people in a modern society are more likely to feel isolated and alone. Sociologists have also documented the extent to which leisure time activities in modern societies often take place in primary groups that alleviate these feelings. Everything from bowling leagues and hiking clubs to the popularity of group travel tours reflects this dynamic. The search is really about finding more expressive and satisfactory relationships outside the impersonal world of work and urban living.

IN-GROUPS AND OUT-GROUPS

Sumner (1906) defined an **in-group** as the one that you belong to at a given point in time. An in-group is your membership group. An **out-group** refers to outsiders.

Sumner based his concept of ethnocentrism on this distinction. Ethnocentrism occurs when members of a group view themselves as superior to outside groups. Sumner assumed that ethnocentrism is normal among members of a group.

REFERENCE GROUPS

For many years, sociologists went along with Sumner's thinking. It seemed to make sense that members of an in-group would celebrate the superiority of their social scripts. Eventually, sociologists began to realize that this is an oversimplification. It is entirely possible that people may identify with an outside group. Poor immigrants coming to America often identified more with the middle and upper classes than their impoverished neighbors. Seeking upward mobility requires abandoning the assumption that people automatically identify with the group to which they belong at a given point in time.

ANTICIPATORY SOCIALIZATION

Sociologists studying social mobility in the United States found that the concept of ethnocentrism had limited application for their purposes. Social mobility studies focused primarily on the movement of people from a lower to higher social class. This suggests that people may actually identify with the class to which they aspire and not the one that they belong to at the time.

This prompted Merton and Kitt (1950) to argue that the group we identify with may not be our membership group. Merton and Kitt argued that when people identify with an outside group, they often seek to join them. **Anticipatory socialization** describes the process of taking on the characteristics of an outside group in order to gain access and acceptance. Taking on the characteristics of people in an outside group can involve either genuine or instrumental ingratiation.

Identifying with outsiders is not limited to social mobility or anticipatory socialization. A co-opted worker who comes to identify with management is one illustration. To be co-opted does not require workers to engage in anticipatory socialization to join the ranks of management. It may involve nothing more than simply coming to agree with the management point of view.

POSITIVE AND NEGATIVE REFERENCE GROUPS

A **positive reference group** is a group that **someone identifies** with. It may be the group that someone **belongs** to or an **outside** group. If it is an outside group, people may seek to join it.

A **negative reference group** is a group that someone **dislikes** or even **despises.** A negative reference group may be a **group that we belong** to or it may involve an outside group. If it is our membership group, we are likely to try to leave and seek involvement with an outside group that we admire and identity with.

For some, their family is a positive reference group, while for others it represents a negative reference group. The same is true for groups that we presently belong to in the workplace. Examples of out-groups that are negative reference groups can be found among those who despise country western or rock and roll music.

With social mobility, our current membership group or class may be our negative reference group. But care must be exercised when considering this possibility. People can have relatively neutral feelings or even ambivalent feelings about the group that they are about to abandon in their quest for social mobility. Such feelings may not rise to the level of repudiation that is associated with negative reference groups.

SOCIAL SANCTIONS AND REFERENCE GROUPS

Social sanctions are **responses by others** that **increase or decrease** the likelihood that someone will repeat a behavior and/or stay in a relationship. Usually **approval** by others is assumed to be a **reward** that **encourages** behavior and wanting to continue a relationship. Conversely, it is often assumed that **disapproval** by others is a **social cost** that **discourages** a behavior and/or continuing in a relationship.

All of this generally holds true when those responding with approval or disapproval are a positive reference group. Perhaps it is because when people we identify with approve of us, they reinforce our ideal self-concept. Disapproval by people we identify with may cause doubts about our ideal self-concept and a loss of self-esteem.

These self-concept dynamics also help explain why approval by people in a negative reference group **discourages** rather than encourages a behavior. When people we hate approve of what we do, they are essentially telling us that we are like them. Conversely, when people we hate greet us with disapproval, we are sure that our rebellious self-concept remains intact. Thus, disapproval from a negative reference group can operate as a reward in that it encourages us to repeat the behavior that produced it. Whether or not we care to stay in the relationship may be more problematic.

why are they vaguely encouraging conformity

REVERSE PSYCHOLOGY

Experts on raising children remind us of these dynamics when they talk about reverse psychology. **Reverse psychology** requires approving of a behavior that is actually offensive. If children identify with their parents, reverse psychology is not necessary.

Rebellious children thrive on disapproval from parents. Disapproval affirms their need to be different. These children are unresponsive to normal patterns of parental approval and disapproval. What is needed is an alternative strategy. Rather than disapproving, which only encourages the rebellious child, a better strategy is for parents to pretend that they approve of behaviors that they want to discourage.

This is not always easy. Parents may find it extremely difficult to approve of behaviors that they find deplorable, even when they recognize that it is nothing more than a tactic. Approving of what they disapprove of may threaten their own sense of self. Plus they may not want to be on record as approving something that their friends and neighbors frown upon.

PART 3
STUDY GUIDES

CHAPTER 7
ORGANIZATIONS

Organizations

  Large Scale

  Task Groups

Types of Organizations

  Corporations

  Government Agencies

  Schools

  Churches

  Firefighters

  Police

  Unions

Bureaucracy

  Bad Image

Organizations as Task Groups

  Task Specialization

  Command Structure

  Written Memos

  Leadership Styles

Organizations: Then and Now

  Traditional

  Modern

Workplace

    Secondary Relationships

    Primary Relationships

Organizations as Family

Organizations and Personal Expression

Organizations as Hierarchies

    Chain of Command

Flow Charts and Job Descriptions

Top-Down Organizations

Democratic Workplaces

Social Power

    Coercion

        Reactance

    Authority

        Charismatic

            Routinization of Charisma

        Traditional

        Rational-Legal

Organizations

    Ideal-Types

    Iron-Cages

    Question of Efficiency

Obstacles to Efficiency

    Peter Principle

    Parkinson's Law

    Goal-Displacement

Corporate

    Downsizing

    Reorganization

CHAPTER 8
SPHERES OF ACTIVITIES

Sphere of Activity

    Defined

    Script Analysis

Science as a Sphere of Activity

    Sociologists of Science

    Scientific Method

    Empiricism

The Economy

    Technology

    Division of Labor

    Consumption Scripts

Types of Societies

    Foraging

    Hunting and Gathering

    Fishing

    Planting

    Herding

    Agricultural

    Industrial

    Postindustrial

Social Scripts and Technological Innovation

Education

    Storing Knowledge

    Transmitting Knowledge

Religion

The Military

    Military-Industrial Complex

Healthcare Scripts

Who Provides?

Who Receives?

Healthcare in the United States

CHAPTER 9
SOCIETIES

What Is a Society?

Scripts and Societies

Shared Scripts

Disputed Scripts

Determining Consensus/Conflict

Genuine Agreement

The Appearance of Agreement

Ideal Culture

Real Culture

Pluralistic Ignorance

The Conflict Model of Society

Group Dynamics

Civility

Ethnocentrism

Dominant Group

Dominant Ideology

Coercive Advantage

Credibility Advantage

Minority Groups

False Consciousness

Identification with the Aggressor

Conflicted Social Selves

Marginal People

Counter Ideologies

Mainstream Scripts

Subculture

Counterculture

Revolutionaries

Personality Development

Modal Personal

Diversity and Modal Personalities

Social Change

CHAPTER 10
SOCIAL STRUCTURES

Social Structures

The Scope of a Social Structure

The Duration of a Social Structure

Scope and Duration of Social Structures

Structure v. Randomness

Anomie

Players and the Content of Their Relationship

Social Change

Role Theory

Status

Status Occupant

Status Relationship

Social Roles

Role Relationship

Role-Sets

Role Conflict

Cultural Diversity and Role Conflict

The Significance of Role Conflict

Sanction Tests

Script Boundaries and Script Tests

Script Confrontations

Imagining Outcomes and Script Confrontations

Role-Making

    Passive Image of People

    Active Image of People

Personal Expression and Role-Making

Master Status

CHAPTER 7
ORGANIZATIONS

An **organization** is a **large-scale collection** of people with a **script** that allocates and coordinates **diverse skills** in **pursuit of a goal.** An organization is like a task group but with more people and more task specialization. In a small task group, the coordination of activities is mostly handled through oral communication, with little necessity for written memos. Also, the amount of task specialization in a small group is usually limited. Although some task allotment can be based upon different skills, often skills are more interchangeable.

Greater specialization within an organization demands effective means for coordinating activities. A general rule of thumb is that the capacity for written communication, such as memos and e-mail, permit greater specialization within an organization. An organization limited to oral communication is limited in its capacity to coordinate specialized activities. This is why modern organizations are so much more complex than ones found in ancient societies such as the Roman Empire.

TYPES OF ORGANIZATIONS

All organizations are scripted to "organize" the activities of people with different skills in pursuit of a goal(s). Different types of organizations are characterized by their goals. **Corporations** are organizations scripted to provide a product or service to people and make a profit. A **government agency** is an organization, like the State Department or Pentagon, that coordinates activities to provide a government service. **Schools** are educational organizations. **Churches, synagogues,** and **mosques** are religious organizations that convey sacred texts and messages to parishioners.

The **police** and **firefighters** represent still other types of organizations. The scale of these organizations differs depending upon whether or not they are in a small town or major metropolis. **A union is** another type of organization where the hierarchy is defined by the difference between **union officials** and the **rank-and-file** members. There are many also many **service organizations** such as the Red Cross, the United Way, and the Lions Club. Service organizations are sometimes referred to as **voluntary organizations** because much of the membership consists of people who volunteer their time.

BUREAUCRACIES

The word **bureaucracy** is often used as a synonym for **organization.** It is most likely with government organizations. Referring to governmental organizations as bureaucracies is common. It is less likely to be used with corporations, although the expression corporate bureaucracy is sometimes used.

The basic idea of a **bureaucracy** is like a **bureau** (chest of drawers), it is an **organization of units** (departments) arranged from the **top down.** With a government bureaucracy, this top-down arrangement represents a **hierarchy of power,** with administrators at the top giving the orders to subordinates in charge of lower departments.

The term bureaucracy conjures up images of a bungling governmental organization that causes grief for those having to deal with it. Few people seem to rejoice over their experiences with government bureaucracies. People associate bureaucracies with red tape, endless waits, and other frustrating experiences. Who hasn't had a bad experience dealing with governmental agencies such as the IRS or a city official over a traffic ticket?

Government organizations can be frustrating to deal with because, like any other large-scale organization, treatment is impersonal and governed by adherence to scripted rules. This adherence to rules is what standardizes the activities of the many people doing a specialized task. Standardization of specialized tasks is a feature that organizations use in pursuit of their goals. Imagine the chaos if clerks issuing drivers licenses was free to do whatever they choose.

It is the rule based standardized practices employed by organizations that deny personal expression that cause frustrations. Although government organizations are often singled out, dealing with any organization can be frustrating. Banks once had tellers that, some felt, could give them personal attention. Now bank transactions are more likely to be with an ATM or online. Ever try to deal with an automated phone menu?

Frustrations experienced by customers and clients are often mirrored by what is felt by employees of large-scale organizations. Just as relations with customers and clients are rule bound, the tasks of employees can be highly scripted. Employees are told what to do and discouraged from personalizing the job. Moreover, those responsible for bonus and promotion decisions often have never met the personal being evaluated. The same is true for firing decisions.

ORGANIZATIONS AS TASK GROUPS

The major differences between **organizations** and **small task** groups is the amount of **task specialization, reliance on written memos** to coordinate these specialized tasks, and the existence of an **official power hierarchy** or **command structure.** In other regards, what we already have learned applies to the analysis of an organization. One question concerns the compatibility between the official organizational script and unofficial scripts that shape activities among subordinates. If they are compatible, then the organizations is likely to be efficient. Cohesion within the organization is also likely to be high.

If script disparities exist, the question becomes how does this affect operations? Something like joking between workers on an assembly line may be discouraged by management but really improves productivity because it helps them let off steam. On other occasions, scripted activities by subordinates may deliberately or inadvertently disrupt the smooth flow of operations.

Styles of leadership are also important to take into consideration when examining organizations. Is top management authoritarian, democratic, or laissez-faire? Authoritarian leaders are the most likely to encourage groupthink. Groupthink can degrade decision making when tasks involve uncertainties and complexities. Authoritarian leaders can also alienate subordinates who feel that they have no input or control. Alienation reduces cohesion and morale among workers' morale. This, in turn, can reduce productivity. Happy workers are usually more productive.

Democratic leaders can be effective decision makers when matters are more complicated because of their willingness to listen to alternative points of view. Democratic leaders can also improve cohesion and the morale of workers to the extent that workers feel that their concerns are being heard. A potential downside of a democratic leader is that seeking too much advice may cause procrastination or muddled decision making.

Laissez-faire leaders seem like an unlikely fit in organizations because the task of top management officials is to lead. The first question is, why would an organization such as a corporation ever hire a laissez-faire leader? The answer is that normally they would not hire a hands-off leader. Hiring decisions in corporate America favor authoritarian leaders who will either stay the course or turn things around. The term corporate gorilla is used to describe an authoritarian leader who is brought in to change a company.

But being a **corporate gorilla** can have its costs. Sometimes a leader brought in because of his track record as an authoritarian leader has loss his zeal and does little once on the new job. At that point, that person has become a laissez-faire leader. But all is not necessarily lost. When unknown or uncontrollable outside events dictate the fortunes of a corporation, then having a leader who does little to lead may not make any difference. The presence of a mellow leader may also improve morale and productivity, especially if they had been badly damaged by a recent corporate gorilla.

Also remember the difference between a democratic and laissez-faire leader. A democratic leader actively seeks advice. A laissez-faire leader does not. But this may not matter. A hands-off approach to leadership can work when top subordinates are self-motivated and willing to work together.

ORGANIZATIONS: THEN AND NOW

Weber (1922) made a distinction between **traditional** and **modern organizations** that continues to have relevance today. A **traditional organization** is a large-scale operation where **appointment of top official** is based upon **personal relationships,** such as **family** or **friends.** The emphasis on selection from friends and family reflects the tremendous importance of **personal loyalty** in traditional organizations.

Personal loyalty trumps **expertise** in traditional organizations. Caesar would rather have a loyal friend or family member as the head of his armies than someone who might be brighter but could not be trusted. Family connections continue to play a huge role in the selection of rulers and ministers to head important government agencies in underdeveloped or developing nations, such as Saudi Arabia. Government appointments signify how close someone is to the Royal Family. The higher the appointment, the closer the family connection.

Modern organizations use **impersonal written official scripts** to govern their activities. Selection is likely to be based upon standardized criteria meant to establish ability or expertise. Retention or career advancement is also based upon more impersonal standardized criteria. Task requirements are likely to be spelled out in detail and discourage significant personal input.

Weber thought that **traditional organizations** are most likely to be found in **gemeinschaft** societies, where primary relationships prevail. While this may be true, elements of traditional organizations can be found in transitions that take place in more modern societies. Look at what happens to a business that began as a family operation in a city like Chicago. As long as it stays within that family, elements such as family and friendships are often featured. Even if the company becomes larger, its owners may still see it and their employees as a large family. But what happens if the company is bought out or merges with larger company? Often the image of being members of a family who are loyal to each other is replaced by an impersonal organizational plan that treats employees as a number and cost to be reduced. At that juncture, an emergent script containing the impersonal elements of the modern impersonal organization evolves.

PRIMARY RELATIONSHIPS AND THE WORKPLACE

Primary relationships that emphasize **expressive personal relationships** do exist, but to a limited degree in modern organizations. A prime example is affairs between employees on the job. The reason affairs are discouraged is because personal involvement can compromise impersonal requirements necessary for the coordination and completion of tasks.

Sometimes friendships formed on the job extend beyond the workplace. An example is when cops who become friends on the job, live in the same neighborhood, or have family events together. Some can separate their personal and job demands quite easily. Usually bosses are more inclined to switch to an impersonal mode when on the job, while subordinates often try to have personal relationships when it benefits them.

Primary relationships and groups can also come into play with unofficial work group scripts that conflict with official organizational ones. Workers on the job can use primary relationship or group dynamics to pressure compliance. Isolating those reluctant to comply, gossip, and so forth can be powerful devices to encourage compliance with the unofficial behavioral preferences of the group.

PLAYING GAMES

Corporate leaders today often draw upon the **imagery of primary groups** to exploit workers. A common ploy is to define the corporation as a family. This is often meant to create the impression that, like a family, the corporation is someone who thrives on loyalty.

Experiences with a number of American corporations expose how cynical this ploy can be. Enron was particularly adroit at using this family imagery to manipulate employee loyalty. Enron continued with this practice even when the leaders knew that the company was going down the toilet.

Those at the top of Enron who preached the gospel of family and loyalty to employees did so even as they were selling off their stock. Promoting rosy images concerning the future of Enron was meant to discourage employees from selling their shares. Those at the top did this to keep the price of Enron stocks up so that they could profit more as they sold their own stock in the company and prepared to abandon ship.

Trying to conjure up positive images through references to themselves as large families is only one tactic corporations use. Manipulating terminology is also a popular device. Today nobody is ever fired. That sounds too harsh. Instead, employees are downsized.

Another manipulation that corporate executives use is to express heartfelt sympathy for workers who have been downsized. This is often little more than an effort to conceal their callused attitude toward workers. It also has some practical considerations.

Corporations realize that sometimes they may be overzealous in their cuts. Trying to create a positive image of how they feel about their employees can be helpful it they have to rehire some of those that they fired. The same is true if times improve and the company needs to hire more people to keep up with demand. Having a favorable corporate image toward employees can also work with survivors of downsizing who continue to work for the company.

PERSONAL EXPRESSION IN MODERN ORGANIZATIONS

Anyone who has worked at a McDonald's knows the extent to which personal expression is limited. The standardization of tasks can leave little room for personal expression. Management often views personal expression by workers as a threat to the official script that tries to maximize efficiency and productivity.

One exception to limits on personal expression involves top executives. One need only think of famous CEOs like Bill Gates of Microsoft. The company is almost synonymous with him. Of course, as the founder of Microsoft, Gates was well situated to impose his personal preferences on the company.

But distinctive personalities of CEOs are not limited to people who start a company. When companies get into trouble, they often hire strong-willed CEOs who are noted for their unique personalities and skills. You already know these leaders as corporate gorillas.

Some companies also encourage, rather than discourage, personal expression among their employees. This is most likely to occur in companies or departments that supply creative products and services. The emphasis on creativity is the key because creativity and standardization do not go together.

ORGANIZATIONS AS HIERARCHIES

Organizations are faced with the **challenge of coordinating activities** among diverse tasks. The most familiar means for accomplishing this objective is to form a **chain of command** from the top down through the levels of the organization. A chain of command involves different levels of leadership and decision making.

At the top is the person who is in charge of the organization. In corporations, this person is usually referred to as the CEO, which stands for Chief Executive Officer. The job of the CEO is to issue directives that flow down through the various levels of the organization. Just below the CEO are executive vice-presidents who head various departments within the organization, such as those responsible for production and sales.

The same organization structure exists in governmental agencies such as the Department of State or the Justice Department. The only real difference is the terminology that replaces that of designations such as CEO. For instance, the person who heads the Department of State is called the Secretary of State. Deputy Secretaries of State are subordinates to the Secretary of State, and so forth.

The Justice Department is headed by the Attorney General. Within the Justice Department, agencies such as the FBI have their own head who is below the Attorney General in the chain of command. As within any modern organization, the activities of the various units and their heads are formally scripted.

FLOW CHARTS AND JOB DESCRIPTIONS

A **flowchart** presents a picture of the power structure in an organization. A flowchain maps the chain of command with an organization. It delineates those who give and those who take orders at the various levels within the organization.

Job descriptions tell people in an organization what they are supposed to do. In modern organizations, these scripts are usually written down. But even though these job descriptions are typically written down, both oral or written instructions may be used to convey job responsibilities to employees.

Flowcharts and job descriptions are based upon an official organizational script. These accounts formally lay down the organizational plan. An official organizational script can be thought of as an ideal. Whether or not it is matched by how people within an organization actually behave is a separate issue.

TOP-DOWN ORGANIZATIONS

In a **top-down organization** everything from **job descriptions** to **orders** flow from the top executives down through various layers of subordinates. Employees are expected to comply with official rules for completing their tasks. Managers are expected to follow orders from those above them and convey those orders to those below them.

DEMOCRATIC WORKPLACES

Not all organizations are **strictly top-down** in their format. Some **retain the chain of command** aspect but encourage more **democratic decision making.** This involves listening to subordinates rather than only imposing orders on them. The attitude by many corporate executives that they know best discourages more democratic allocations of responsibilities.

Allowing workers to have more to say about how they go about their tasks can be extremely beneficial. They often have imaginative insights that can be drawn upon rather than letting them fume in frustration. Releasing the imaginations of managers to do more than just parrot orders from the top can also be constructive. The same is true of managers who adopt a more democratic style of leadership and reach out to their subordinates for decision input.

ORGANIZATIONS AND SOCIAL POWER

What Max Weber (1922) had to say about social power has had a large impact on how sociologists look at power in society and within organizations. Our present concern is to see how different forms of social power operate within organizations. This requires first looking at how Weber defined social power.

SOCIAL POWER

Social power is the ability to get people to do what you want them to do. **Coercion** is the most obvious form of social power used by executives and managers in an organization. Their coercive leverage is based upon the control over bonus, promotions, and firing decisions. To the extent which people are dependent upon the organization to meet their financial needs is the extent to which the organization can coerce compliance.

The use of coercive power by executives and managers in an organization depends upon knowing what employees are doing. The more an organization relies on coercive control the more it must monitor the activities of its employees. Monitoring ranges from drug tests and cameras to reading employees e-mails or using phone or computer records to count the number of sales calls a day.

Reactance, a term coined by Brehm (1966), helps explain a potential reaction by workers to excessive monitoring and control. **Reactance** is a motivational state characterized by a strong desire to restore freedom when lost or to protect freedom when threatened by loss. The likelihood of reactance is the strongest in societies that emphasize personal freedom. It is less likely in societies that have a cultural emphasis that prioritizes belonging and being supportive of your group. In these societies, people are more conditioned to sacrifice their personal freedom.

To the extent that excessive monitoring and control trigger reactance among workers is the extent to which they can be expected to resist further losses of freedom. By restoring freedom, management decreases the potential for worker slowdowns or other resistances to official organizational decrees. This suggests the one benefit of democratic workplaces is that they reduce the likelihood and severity of reactance becoming an obstacle to productivity.

REWARDS AND PUNISHMENT

Some argue that it is more effective to use rewards than punishment as inducements to comply. Rewarding workers for compliance and doing a good job is seen as better than punishing them by docking their wages. In reality, there is little difference between the two because rewards are withheld in the absence of compliance, which is not that different that docking wages. The only difference is that withholding a reward deprives someone of what they have yet to possess, whereas docking wages would deprive them of what they already are entitled to.

AUTHORITY

Authority exists whenever **subordinates choose to comply** with **orders** issued from someone above them in an organization. The term **volition** is often used to characterize this element of choice. It is what distinguishes authority from coercion.

Authority is considered **legitimate power** because subordinates acknowledge the right of those in power to exercise it and expect compliance. Weber identified three different types of authority. Charismatic authority is based upon personality. With both traditional and rational-legal authority, legitimacy resides with the social position rather than with a specific personality.

CHARISMATIC AUTHORITY

Charismatic authority derives from the **personal magnetism** of a leader within an organization. Because of their personalities, charismatic leaders inspire others to follow them. This is different from coercion because those who comply with a charismatic leader do so voluntarily.

Personal hierarchies of credibility come into play with charismatic leaders. The charismatic leader ranks high in terms of personal credibility. Those who follow have considerably less personal credibility.

Sometimes charisma flows automatically from the personality of a leader. At other times, charisma is more manufactured. **Manufactured charisma** involves efforts to deliberately enhance the credibility of a leader.

MANUFACTURED CHARISMA

Manufactured charisma is a form of **impression management.** It comes in a variety of packages. One version is to announce truthful accounts of spectacular personal accomplishments that the audience may not have known about. The stories that reveal such extraordinary feats can be told by the leader or by admirers.

Another version of manufactured charisma is to lie or stretch the truth about someone's accomplishments. Such deceptions work if people become more enamored with and therefore more willing to follow someone else. The danger of faked accounts is the risk of exposure. Finding out that the war record of a beloved leader was faked can precipitate irreversible anger and rejection. The same is true for a corporate leader who is discredited when false claims about his or her personal history are revealed.

THE ROUTINIZATION OF CHARISMA

Even the most charismatic leaders suffer a similar fate. The basis of their leadership stops with their deaths. But there is a method for preserving their legacy.

Weber used the expression **routinization of charisma** to describe the process by which leadership is passed on from a charismatic leader to subsequent generations. It makes selection of subsequent leaders "routine." An example is when a charismatic leader promotes a script that has his eldest son replacing him at the head of the family business. A charismatic leader who founded a business may plan for this succession long before he or she dies. By naming the company Smith and Son establishes this continuity. A father could also establish this continuity through a will.

Whether or not the son possesses the charismatic personality and abilities of his father is another issue. Blood does not insure that it is so. But that is a separate issue.

Many small businesses in the United States that evolved into complex corporations have relied on family members to supply top leadership positions. The Ford Motor Company is one example. The Upjohn Pharmaceutical Company followed this pattern for several generations until it selected a CEO from outside those with family connections to the original founder.

Creating a script that uses family to routinize charisma is only one option. Another option is for a charismatic leader to designate a successor. It might be a close advisor or someone that the charismatic leader mentored.

TRADITIONAL AUTHORITY

Traditional authority within an organization rests upon a commitment to do things in a customary way. If asked why they comply, subordinates reply because that is just how things have always been done. For tradition to be the basis of an authority structure in an organization, that organization must have had a long enough history to establish what is customary.

A script that routinizes the charisma of a founder of an organization could serve to create a custom concerning who gives and takes orders in an organization. This can occur in political as well as corporate contexts. An example would be if the script for choosing a political leader in a small village favors a family who had a relative that saved the community long ago.

Scripts other than ones based upon a charismatic personality in the past can emerge as a basis for traditional authority. For example, the choice of a political leader may be based upon a competition to see who is the brightest or strongest among candidates for the position. Because scripts involving traditional authority are based upon custom, it is entirely possible that people may no longer remember its origins.

RATIONAL-LEGAL AUTHORITY

Rational-legal authority is based upon deliberate and rational planning that results in a master script. Weber used the idea of rational planning to distinguish it from traditional power where authority unfolds more naturally over time. Writing a modern constitution is what Weber had in mind when he spoke of rational-legal authority.

Our Constitution is a prime example. Our Constitution stipulates the powers of the President, Congress, and the Supreme Court. These stipulations script the authority of people who come to occupy the relevant offices or positions within these branches of government. Notice the conspicuous absence of heredity as a scripted means for accessing positions of authority under rational-legal criteria.

What Weber meant by rational-legal authority also pertains to modern organizations that are formally designed and planned. Formally articulated flowcharts, chains of command, and job descriptions are the norm. So too is the impersonal and fragmented nature of relationships that are dictated by task requirements.

SOCIAL HIERARCHIES OF CREDIBILITY

Both **traditional** and **rational-legal authority structures** intersect with **social** and **expert hierarchies of credibility.** Positions such as CEO, CFO (chief financial officer), President of the United States, Secretary of Defense, and so forth are based upon expertise. Moreover, those occupying these positions of authority usually rank higher in the social hierarchy of credibility with their organizations than subordinates.

This gives them an advantage as moral entrepreneurs both within their organizations and with outside audiences. People are more willing to listen to what they have to say about their own organizational scripts or scripts in other sectors of society. It is this credibility or persuasive advantage combined with being able to gain compliance within their organization by virtue of their position of authority that contributes to their influence.

COERCION AND AUTHORITY

When studying organizations, it is important to distinguish compliance by subordinates based upon authority and compliance based upon coercion. Compliance based upon authority is more stable because subordinates choose to comply. Coercion may be successful, but because people are being forced to comply the potential for reactance is always there.

MODERN ORGANIZATIONS

To the extent that a modern organization is a system of authority it is likely based upon rational-legal authority. Official flowcharts are designed to map the chain of command that scripts whom has power over whom. Job descriptions tell people what is expected of them.

But just because the official organizational script is rationally planned does not guarantee that employees with volition comply with it. Without volitional compliance authority does not exist. Any compliance that does exist is probably due to coercive pressures.

MODERN ORGANIZATIONS AS SECONDARY GROUPS

The **impersonal rules** and **regulations** that govern a modern organization or bureaucracy mean interaction is based upon **secondary relationships.** Another factor contributing to the characteristic of secondary relationships in a modern organization is the recruitment of people on the basis of their expertise rather than personal loyalty. The fragmentation of activities around specialized tasks and discouragement of personal expression are also factors.

THE MODERN ORGANIZATION AS AN "IRON-CAGE"

Weber marveled at the **rational structures** that guide and coordinate activities within a modern organization. But he was alarmed by their **impersonal nature** that he likened to an **iron-cage.** By this he meant that a modern organization represents a cage that excludes personal expression and bonds.

More recent sociologists identify this as a form of alienation, where the personal experiences that occur in primary relationships are largely missing in modern organizations. **Alienation** occurs whenever people are deprived of the satisfaction gained from personal contacts, the opportunity for personal expression, and control over their lives. All of these are compromised by the power structure within modern organizations that operate almost as if members are complete strangers.

THE MODERN BUREAUCRACY AS AN IDEAL-TYPE

When Weber compared traditional to modern organizations, he thought of each as an **ideal-type.** The contrast between modern and traditional organizations is based upon exaggerating their most distinctive features. Weber realized that in reality, organizations only approximate these idealized features.

THE QUESTION OF EFFICIENCY

People often confuse the **impersonal nature** of modern bureaucracies or organizations with the question of **rational efficiency.** Everyone can relate to frustrations people have dealing with bureaucratic rules. A separate issue is that of efficiency.

Ideally, an organizational script provides for the efficient coordination of the diverse activities assigned to its various members. But when considering the question of efficiency, it is important to remember that it represents an ideal-type. The extent of efficiency in organizations can vary tremendously.

Sometimes when we think about the inefficiency in bureaucracies we are tempted to question the extent to which they are essential for modern life. But to understand the necessity of living with organizations in modern society requires only one consideration. The increase in complexity and specialization within task areas makes some form of organizational structure absolutely necessary. Leaving the coordination of complex and specialized tasks to luck or random chance is worse than dealing with the inefficiency that can occur within modern organizations.

PERSONAL DYNAMICS AND MODERN ORGANIZATIONS

Weber meant us to think about the impersonal scripts that govern modern organizations as ideal-types. But thinking about the characteristics that Weber associated with modern organizations is only a beginning. **Personality** is still a factor that affects what transpires within modern organizations.

Personality can **dampen the alienating effect** that impersonal scripts have on employees. The personality of a boss can make the difference between a pleasant workplace and one that is riddled with tension and hostilities. A fair and friendly boss can do much to elevate worker morale.

Questions of personality and how it influences worker morale arise in other contexts as well. **Personal dynamics** often play a role in **evaluations, bonuses,** and **career advancements.** This can raise questions about fairness that undermine worker morale. Playing favorites can also diminish organization efficiency by creating unnecessary tensions in the workplace.

PRIMARY GROUP DYNAMICS

Because modern organizations involve scripts that favor impersonal task-related activities, the role of primary group dynamics can be easily obscured. **Primary group** dynamics occur in settings ranging from conversations around the watercooler to the workplace itself. The study by Roethlesberger and Dickson mentioned in the section on unofficial workplace groups illustrates primary relationships can directly affect workplace activities.

Their study discovered that workers often create production behavioral preferences and sanctions that may differ from what the formal organization script dictates. The unofficial norms of the workers decided what they thought was a proper work pace. Those who worked too fast were labeled rate-busters. Chiselers were those who didn't keep up with the group's production norm. Binging, which was a pop to the shoulder, was used to slow down rate-busters and to increase the output of chiselers.

FACTORS THAT DIMINISH RATIONALITY AND EFFICIENCY

Lawrence Peter advanced a theory concerning modern bureaucracies that became known as the **Peter Principle.** The essence of his idea is that in modern bureaucracies, people are promoted to their level of incompetence. The Peter Principle identifies a process that defies the idea that modern organizations are rational and efficient.

Here is an example of how the Peter Principle works. Promotions are often based upon what someone has accomplished. If that expertise prevails, and not what is required in the position that one is promoted to, then that person may be promoted to their level of incompetence with that organization. For instance, how does an organization select a supervisor from among a group of workers? Being the most productive worker does not necessarily qualify someone as an equally effective supervisor. Different abilities and skills are likely to be involved.

Modern organizations that are truly rational and constantly trying to improve their efficiency are mindful of the Peter Principle. One organization puts its workers through simulations in order to measure their abilities and skills as managers. In one exercise, candidates are assigned different positions on an issue. The one who is the most effective in getting others to agree is seen as having the most managerial potential.

Parkinson's Law looks at another potential area of inefficiency within a modern organization. His law states that work expands to meet available time. This means that a rational organization allocates work hours on the basis of time needed. This eliminates the possibility that people with time on their hands will make work just to fill their extra hours. The problem is that this work generates tasks, memos, and directives that are unnecessary and can lead to a further waste of time.

The danger of what Parkinson discovered is present in many organizations that are top-heavy with administrators. Educational organizations have seen this development in recent years. A general trend has been for a growth in the number of administrators beyond what is necessary. This means that there is an excess number of administrative hours that are available, which is likely to generate unnecessary projects that can sap the energy of others within an institution such as a university. The result is professors spend an increasing amount of their time responding to unnecessary administrative initiatives that distracts from their research and teaching responsibilities.

E-mail provides another example of how the relation between time and work can become distorted. At first it was embraced as a means for improving communication efficiency within organizations. Compared to written mail, e-mail offers the prospect of quick exchanges of messages and memos.

The problem is now people complain about the amount of time that they waste responding to unnecessary office e-mails. It turns out that the ease of e-mail contributes to the mischief administrators with too much time on their hands can make. The expectation of a rapid and timely replay further disrupts the work schedules of those receiving unnecessary messages.

Many corporations who are aware of Parkinson's Law have responded by downsizing and then hiring consultants on a per task basis. The benefit is that it reduces the cost of full-time employment and increases efficiency. Companies also save money by not providing health and other benefits to consultants.

Goal-displacement represents another irrational development that can occur within modern bureaucracies. Goal-displacement occurs when adherence to the rules takes precedent over the organization's goals. With goal displacement, compliance with the rules takes precedent over goal-attainment.

To prevent goal-displacement, those in charge must be mindful of the necessity to periodically review organization scripts. Encouraging employees to provide feedback on which rules work and which do not can be extremely helpful. It also helps them remember that rules are not written in stone.

One problem is that employees often are not interested in trying to change scripts that can improve the link between rules and outcomes. Changing job requirements can be seen as threatening. Having to learn new rules threatens the complacency of workers who are content complying with a familiar script. This is most likely to occur among workers who do not identify with corporate goals and are more interested in just picking up their paycheck.

CORPORATE DOWNSIZING AND REORGANIZATION

In recent years, the terms corporate downsizing and reorganization have become familiar terms to American workers. **Downsizing** is just a fancy word for firing employees. It just sounds less harsh.

Corporate reorganization refers to **changing scripts** that govern activities within a corporation. Corporate downsizing often triggers efforts to reorganize activities because fewer people are left to accomplish the same tasks. Those not fired are called **survivors.** Often survivors feel a combination of elation and guilt over not losing their jobs. Survivors also feel anxiety over their future. This helps motivate them to comply with the new and/or additional tasks asked of them because of corporate reorganization.

Corporate mergers are a common reason for downsizing and reorganizing a corporation. Mergers often eliminate competition by merging two or more companies. But once companies merge, downsizing becomes the means for eliminating job duplication. Reorganization of the merged companies is often necessary to bring the acquired company in line with that of the script of the dominant partner or to create new scripts for the combined entities.

CHAPTER 8
SPHERES OF ACTIVITIES

So far we have seen how social scripts influence everything from solitary acts that are preliminary to interaction with someone else to relationships within dyads, triads, small groups, and large-scale organizations. But sometimes sociologists take on even more ambitious projects and try to examine spheres of activities.

A **sphere of activity** encompasses a **general area of activity** within a society that is bound together by a **common theme.** What has already been said about the analysis of social scripts can be applied to studying spheres of activities. The difference is that a sphere of activity encompasses much more than a single group or organization. It potentially includes all activities within a given sphere.

Some **spheres of activities** of interest to sociologists include religion, education, economics, politics, medicine and healthcare, law, science, police, and military. To become an expert in a given sphere of activity, a sociologist must be familiar with the scripts that govern the activities of people within that sphere. Sociologists often concentrate their research to a particular sphere of activity.

Only a few spheres of activities have been selected for review at this time. Other spheres of activities will be covered more extensively later on. But even then, coverage will not be exhaustive of all possibilities that interest sociologists.

SCIENCE AS A SPHERE OF ACTIVITY

Sociologists of science look at how social scripts shape scientific activities within a society. There are many different script angles that can be investigated, such as how scientific activities are organized or how the results of scientific research are disseminated and used in that society. Attention here will be limited to a single issue. It concerns the distinction between ideal and real scripts.

The behavioral preferences associated with the scientific method in the United States originated in European countries centuries ago. It was at that time that science began to distinguish itself from religion. The key difference was in terms of how religious scholars and early scientists approached the study of nature.

The **Holy Scriptures** dictated how religious scholars affiliated with the Roman Catholic Church went about studying nature. If the Scriptures said that perfection exists in Heaven, these thinkers insisted that is where one would encounter the perfect circle or sphere. This is why Church astronomers were convinced that the moon was a perfect sphere and that planetary orbits form perfect circles. Any observations that contradicted their characterizations were summarily dismissed as unreliable. It was thought that human observation is simply no match for God's infinite wisdom.

105

Early scientists such as Copernicus and Galileo found themselves on a collision course with Church authorities when their theories and observations contradicted religious dogma. Eventually, observations accumulated by astronomers and other scientists began to erode the monopoly in knowledge that Medieval theologians had concerning nature. It was out of these developments that the scientific emphasis on observation emerged.

Empiricism is the term used to describe the method of science that replaces faith with an observation. It suggests that scientists ultimately select and reject ideas about nature on the basis of observable data. Empiricism is the foundation of modern science. This represents one of the most pervasive claims of science.

Many scientists and outsiders believe that this ideal image of science is what prevails in scientific communities. But there is a difference between an ideal and reality. Sociologists who have studied the activities of scientific communities have often found that empiricism is not always strictly adhered to.

Some violations originate in the personalities of scientists who find that their devotion to empiricism diluted by their ambitions. Initial research results are presented not with caution, but with the air of high drama. Nowhere is this more evident than in medical research, where desperate patients and doctors yearn to hear about new cures for diseases like cancer and Alzheimer's disease.

Other violations that collide with the ideals of science reside in the organizational settings in which scientific research takes place. Universities clamor to hire researchers who are able to secure grants because it can greatly enhance their institutional reputation and finances. Selling research proposals to granting agencies may involve more hype than devotion to empiricism.

The fact that researchers have found disparities between ideal and real scripts in science is suggestive of how sociologists can approach the study of any sphere of activity within a society. Virtually any of the distinctions we have made concerning social scripts can also be applied. Issues involving the scope of scripts, how scripts are peddled, and so forth are all relevant.

THE ECONOMY

The **economy** of a society represents a major sphere of activity. The economy of a society is based upon scripts that shape how it goes about producing, distributing, and consuming its goods and services. A key consideration when looking at the economy of a society is its technology.

Technology refers to knowledge and tools people use as means for adapting to their environments. **Tools** allow people to go beyond the limitations of their physical capacities. Tools range from stone axes and gourds used for carrying water to ladders, cars, and computers.

The **division of labor script** determines who does what tasks. Some scripts exclude children from work until they reach a certain age. Others allocate tasks on the basis of gender. Men do different tasks than women. And still other scripts are less discriminatory in how they allocate tasks.

The **consumption script** within a society determines who has access to what goods and services. In some societies, goods and services are shared equally among members of the community. In other societies, those at the top have the greatest access to goods and services, while those at the bottom suffer economic deprivations.

TYPES OF SOCIETIES

Scholars like Lenski and Lenski (1978) classify societies based upon the technology that is featured. The degree of technological sophistication varies from what is found in foraging to industrial societies. More sophisticated technologies generally require a more complicated division of labor scripts. This is because the number and specialization in jobs increases with technological advancements.

The least technologically advanced society is one that forages for subsistence. In foraging societies, people search for food and consume it on the spot. The earliest humans were foragers.

Hunting and gathering societies are more sophisticated. This sophistication is registered in the strategies that are used to kill animals. Sometimes a simple tool like a club is required. On other occasions, the community kills animals by stampeding them over a cliff.

Hunting and gathering societies also learn how to make better use of the animals that they have killed. The capacity to use fire for cooking is one improvement. Knowing how to use animal hides for clothing is another. Knowing that some bones can be used as clubs, while smaller ones can be used as crude needles to sew hides together are other improvements over the technological capacity of a foraging society.

Hunting and gathering societies are also more sophisticated than foraging ones in their ability to identify different edible fruits, nut, and berries. Knowing how to use natural containers to carry fruits, nuts, berries, or water back to the campsite is another advantage over foraging societies. Learning how to weave baskets or make pottery for this purpose represents an even greater technological advancement.

The division of labor script in hunting and gathering societies is based mostly on gender and age criteria. Men hunt if they are old enough. Women and children gather.

Social scripts also come into play elsewhere. Scripts often suggest what activities are the most valued. Often these values are expressed through stories such as those that document the exploits of great hunters. The fact that as gatherers the women and children provide the majority of the nutrition may be rarely celebrated or completely ignored.

Fishing societies, like hunting and gathering societies, are more sophisticated than ones that rely entirely on foraging. Their proximity to fish in streams, lakes, or the ocean is what shapes their technology. The tools used to catch fish range from trying to skewer them with a stick or trapping them in nets.

Planting and **herding** societies are more technologically advanced than hunting and gathering ones. The advantage of a planting society is its ability to find and plant seeds so that food can be grown locally. Being able to harvest food next to where they live is a huge advantage over being nomadic. It takes much more effort to trek about seeking edible fruits, nuts, berries, or plants than growing them in one's backyard.

Herding societies must be knowledgeable about the breeding and raising of stock such as goats, sheep, and cattle. Its main advantage is the fact that it is not necessary to expend time and energy trying to find game. Another advantage is that in a hunting society, the animal must be killed, which means that the community cannot take advantage of other possibilities, such as using its milk or wool.

Agricultural societies represent technological advancements over planting and herding communities. They benefit from knowledge about how to build irrigation systems and plows that dig more deeply. This permits agricultural societies to increase their efficiency within existing areas by providing water and more effectively turning over and replenishing the soil. These improvements in planting technologies also allow them to expand into areas in which planting in the past was difficult if not impossible. Agricultural societies can also benefit from more effective techniques for feeding, raising, and breeding animals.

Industrial societies are based upon machine technology that improves the capacity of people to produce goods. Industrial manufacturing is usually located in and around cities. Cities provide the hubs around which raw materials and finished products are transported. Industrial revolutions witness a migration of labor from rural agricultural settings to cities.

The industrial revolution began in England with the advent of power looms in cities such as Manchester during the 1700s. Power looms greatly enhanced their capacity to produce textiles such as cotton cloth, which had previously been woven by hand. Eventually the industrial revolution spread to other countries, as did the capacity of people to imagine new and inventive ways to improve on the capacity of human labor. The industrial revolution began in the United States after the Civil War and centered on industries such as steel and oil. The steel industry grew with the expansion of railroads and the shift from wooden buildings in cities to ones structured with steel girders. The oil industry grew from providing kerosene for lamps to products needed to lubricate and fuel machines and internal combustion engines.

Postindustrial society, which is characterized by information and computer technologies, is the most recent shift in technology. Some of these jobs pay well. But a major theme has been the shift from good-paying manufacturing jobs to lower-paying ones in the service sector of the economy. This change has also seen advanced industrialized countries shifting their manufacturing sites to underdeveloped and developing countries where labor is cheap.

SOCIAL SCRIPTS AND TECHNOLOGICAL INNOVATION

The discussion on the economic sphere highlighted the relevance of consumption and division of labor scripts. But social scripts can also influence the emergence of technological innovations. Scripts that value tradition are likely to thwart technological innovations because they reinforce continuing to do things as they have been done in the past.

Scripts that value exploration and creativity are more likely to encourage efforts to improve existing technologies. The drive for profits in capitalistic societies can provide this type of incentive. Technological inventions are the means by which capitalists try to stay ahead of the competition.

EDUCATION

Every society must provide a means for preserving and transmitting its knowledge. Much of this knowledge involves technology. But knowledge exists in other areas as well. Some of it involves the basic values and beliefs of a society. Other knowledge involves everything from political scripts to learning about its history.

Educational scripts designate who is responsible for storing and transmitting knowledge. A storyteller in a low-technology society is one example. Another example is when a specialist such as a shaman teaches his son the tricks of the trade. A shaman is someone who acts as the conduit between nature and others in the tribe. A shaman is seen as having the power to cure illness and predict the future.

Until the industrial revolution, technological knowledge was pretty much transmitted by the family through on-the-job training. A notable exception was the development of guilds in more advanced agricultural societies to train neophytes in skills ranging from painting and sculpture to building Cathedrals. In these guilds, neophytes learned from masters of the craft.

These guilds represented an early development toward shifting more and more technological education outside the family. Today, going away to school to learn a trade or prepare for a job is commonplace. Technological advancement has been the primary reason for this shift from the family to schools. Not all of this was deliberately scripted. Sometimes script changes were prompted by events that made it less and less possible for families to prepare their children for jobs.

A classic example is when farms were no longer able to sustain successive generations in a family. This meant that more and more children would have to leave the farm and seek employment in cities. The growth of technologically based schools to train workers in manufacturing and other jobs became essential.

In the area of agriculture, deliberate efforts contributed to the impact events had on farms. During the 1800s, our government recognized the need to establish colleges devoted to agricultural training and research. Land-grant colleges, such as Michigan Agricultural College, cropped up everywhere (now known as Michigan State University).

Other universities, such as the University of Michigan, developed more around professional schools such as law and medicine. Eventually these institutions became more complex in order to accommodate the growth of knowledge. As the American economy shifted from agriculture and manufacturing to its present postindustrial economy, the burdens on educational scripts have increased. Pressure has also increased on parents to find ways to send their kids to college. What was a luxury in the past has become essential for increasing numbers of people today.

Until relatively recently, literacy was never a major concern for most societies. This is because being able to read and write was not a job prerequisite. Generations of workers in the past were able to learn on the job by observing and being told what to do. Now scholars are becoming increasingly alarmed over estimates that as many as 20 percent of Americans are functionally illiterate and whose limited skills prevent them from even filling out a job application form.

RELIGION

One sphere of activity that has been of interest to sociologists from the beginning is that of religion. The primary reason is the history of sociology parallels great transformations that were taking place in Western societies because of the industrial revolution that impacted on religion. Since those early days, a major concern among sociologists has been studying the compatibility of religion and changes brought about by the industrial revolution.

Just a moment ago we looked at the shift in educational scripts that place the primary responsibility for transmitting job-related knowledge on schools. During the early years of these changes, these schools in the United States had a religious affiliation. In fact, among private colleges such as Harvard and Yale, abandoning the requirement of chapel is a fairly recent development.

The creation of public schools, colleges, and universities has been more secular given the Constitutional restrictions involving the separation of church and state. Parents who wanted to retain a religious core for their children's K-12 education opted for private schools where this restriction did not apply. This preference came with a cost because those parents had to pay tuition plus taxes used to finance the public schools.

More recently, moral entrepreneurs for the fusion of religion with education have promoted a number of new scripts. One has been for universities to sponsor charter schools that are taxpayer-funded alternatives to public schools. Some charter schools are versions of private schools in the past that were explicitly religiously based. One difference is that religious beliefs are packaged in more secular vocabulary, such as family values, to circumvent Constitutional issues. A similar strategy has been to promote voucher plans that allow parents to enroll their children in private schools. Often key backers of voucher programs are Catholic and Christian schools that are struggling with funding problems. An infusion of public funds is seen as a solution that also provides more opportunities to proselytize.

Whether or not such scripts are seen as desirable is based upon personal values, beliefs, and norms. So too are other political hot potatoes involving everything from abortion to paying religious organizations with public funds to deliver services to what in the past have been left to the government. All of this reminds us that controversies involving the convergence between religious scripts and those in other spheres, such as education and politics, are likely to be with us in the foreseeable future.

THE MILITARY

Sociologists were first systematically brought in to study the military in the United States during World War II. Much of the focus was influenced by earlier sociological studies of workers. What the military and government wanted was a more systematic understanding of the social dynamics that affect military success.

Sociologists who study the military in the United States examine scripts pertaining to virtually all military matters ranging from the Pentagon and Department of Defense as organizational structures to combat effectiveness. During the Vietnam War, interest in what is known as the **military-industrial complex** was rekindled. The **military-industrial complex** refers to a network of politicians, the military, and those in private industry that manufacture weapons.

The main concern at the time, and even today, is with the conflict of interest between of people in these different segments of society. Senators and Representatives try to get government money to help industries in their districts that produce weapons. Former military procurement officers are hired by these weapons industries to influence legislators and procurement decisions by the military. Prominent military personal, such as astronauts or generals, are also hired by these industries to peddle their influence.

HEALTHCARE

Another major sphere of activity within a society involves healthcare. **Healthcare scripts** designate **who provides** and **who receives healthcare** in a society. The complexity of healthcare scripts varies depending upon the sophistication of medical knowledge. In low-technology societies, a shaman who is believed to have magical powers may be the sole provider of health remedies. As more becomes known about the medicinal value of plants and other substances, the role of healer can change. But the growth of medical knowledge does not necessarily mean the abandonment of spiritual solutions. Even in a modern society such as the United States, the debate over spiritual and medical approaches to healthcare is not fully resolved.

HEALTHCARE IN THE UNITED STATES

The United States is the only advanced industrial nation in the world that bases its medical system on a pay-for-service basis script. Other industrial countries extend health protection to their entire populations. In the United States, healthcare is still rationed on the ability to pay for services.

The only notable exceptions are Medicaid and Medicare. Medicaid provides some help for the poor. Medicare provides assistance for the elderly. Both programs typically pay for less than 50 percent of the healthcare costs of the poor and elderly who are eligible for their benefits. With Medicare, the patient is responsible for paying what is not covered. Medicaid patients are not required to make up the difference, which is one reason why many medical providers in the United States refuse to treat them.

Americans who do have health coverage pay for it either through insurance policies or out-of-the-pocket payments. Some like to herald the fact that tax dollars spent on healthcare in the United States are less than in other industrial countries. Because tax dollars are only spent in the United States on Medicare and Medicaid, compared to other countries where complete coverage in paid through tax revenues, this point is misleading to say the least. The point is that we pay vastly more out-of-the-pocket expenses through insurance premiums and co-payments that are not necessary in these other countries. And, of course, we must also remember that those Americans lucky enough to have insurance through their employer are really paying through foregone wages.

Recent estimates about how many Americans go without health coverage at some time during a given year is about 40 million plus. But even for people with some coverage from Medicaid or Medicare, the risk of financial ruin is one family health crisis away. The sad fact remains that in the United States healthcare remains rationed on the ability to pay.

Americans continue to have the most expensive healthcare system in the world, despite the enormous gaps in coverage. Attempts to bring down the costs through the use of Health Maintenance Organizations (HMOs) had some initial success, but those gains have eroded. Containing costs to keep expenses down remains an issue. Physicians complain when cost containment lowers the fees that they receive for their services. Both physicians and patients complain when cost containment eliminates what they deem to be important services.

It is difficult to know with certainty whether or not the United States will develop new scripts that make the healthcare system more accessible and affordable. Expect healthcare providers and their lobbyists to resist these goals. Expect them to resist any changes that threaten their profits.

CHAPTER 9
SOCIETIES

So far we have looked at social scripts and how they shape social behavior in settings that range from dyads and triads to small groups, organizations, and spheres of activities. Now attention shifts to the study of societies. We begin by looking at what is meant by a society.

WHAT IS A SOCIETY?

A **society** is a **collection of people** who **share a territory** defined by **political boundaries.** People living in the United States represent a society because they all live under the same political system. People living in France represent a society because they all live in an area defined by political boundaries. A community of hunters and gathers that wander about looking for food is a society even though the political boundaries that define them are more fluid.

SCRIPTS AND SOCIETIES

One of the most fundamental questions that sociologists ask when studying a society is the extent to which social scripts are shared or disputed. Script consensus exists if there is an agreed upon social script that is shared by members of a society. If script consensus exists, people in that society share a common culture.

Script disputes among members of a society means that the society is divided and that script conflict exists. If script conflict exists, it is still useful to see if there are areas of script agreement. It is still possible for common cultural themes to be shared by members of a society who have script disputes in other aspects of their lives. In more severely divided societies, there may be little common ground.

DETERMINING SCRIPT CONSENSUS AND CONFLICT

When trying to determine whether or not script consensus or conflict exists within a society it is important to proceed with caution. Observing a high degree of conformity may mean that it is determined by an underlying agreed upon social script. If people within a society have internalized the same set of behavioral preferences and related values and beliefs this would be true.

But a high degree of conformity in a society could be caused by another factor. A dominant group may be able to impose its will on others. When some impose their will on others in a society, at least some conformity is coerced. This would create an appearance of consensus rather than a genuine consensus based upon sharing the same behavioral preferences and related values and beliefs.

Whenever a cultural theme is discovered in a society, the next questions concern its scope. The scope of a social script refers to the number of people in a society who subscribe to its behavioral preferences and related values and beliefs. If script consensus prevails, that number may cover most people in the society. With coercion and the appearance of consensus, the number of people who subscribe to the cultural theme is less, which means that the scope of the script is less.

The existence of deviance within a society suggests that at least some do not subscribe to a given social script. If the amount of deviance is limited to a few individuals, then scripts disputes are between them and the mainstream of the society. As the number of people defying a social script increases it becomes more group based. Group-based deviance creates the opportunity for mobilization and more effective challenges to the mainstream or dominant group that controls society.

IDEAL VERSUS REAL CULTURE

There is a potential difference between the **ideal** and **real** culture of a society that must be taken into consideration when conducting research. What people often report is the celebrated idealized version of their culture. When this reported ideal culture does not match reality, researchers can get an erroneous picture of a society.

For instance, when asked what they value, Americans often cite personal freedom, freedom to say what they want to say, democracy, equality, and so forth. When asked what they loath, Americans often cite dictatorships because oppressive governments suppress the aforementioned values. But care must be taken to separate out how Americans idealize themselves and their actual practices.

Celebrating democracy is not the same as practicing it. Slaves and women were not permitted to vote by the Founding Fathers. Former male slaves were given the vote in 1865, almost a century later, and then Southern states did everything possible to discourage them from exercising this fundamental right in a democracy. Women did not get the vote until 1920, and it took decades more for any of them to be elected to Congress.

During the Cold War and the fight against communism, the United States financed and supported military dictatorships around the globe. Oppression at home by these dictators was rationalized or overlooked because they were seen as good allies in the war against communism. Now that the Cold War has been replaced by the War on Terror, the United States is supporting oppressive dictatorships in the Muslim world while simultaneously declaring that the United States is the global champion of freedom.

Americans who are quick to denounce authoritarian leaders elsewhere may also suffer from a gap between how they idealize themselves and reality. The style of President Bush is that of an authoritarian leader. He proudly declares that it is his way or the highway to countries that he disagrees with or critics within the United States. Using force and coercion to impose his will on others is seen by many as a valuable quality. These same supporters mock those favoring diplomacy as naïve and/or cowards who lack the guts to do what is necessary. The fact of the matter is that diplomacy favors the democratic style of leadership that seeks diverse points of view and compromise.

PLURALISTIC IGNORANCE

Pluralistic ignorance is another potential research obstacle. Pluralistic ignorance occurs when people are afraid to express their true feelings. Rather than risk ridicule or worse, they simply report what they think others favor. This same guarded disposition may encourage them to tell researchers what they think others would tell them or what they think the researcher wants to hear.

THE CONFLICT MODEL OF SOCIETY

The **conflict model of society** directs attention to **studying certain factors** should **script disputes** between **groups** or **segments** of society exist. Disputes or script conflicts between groups or segments within a society is different than disputes over personal script preferences in an encounter or relationship. Although interpersonal disputes may reflect larger disputes in a society, they are resolved between those involved in the encounter or relationship. Disputes between groups or larger segments of a society go beyond interpersonal dynamics to group dynamics.

GROUP DYNAMICS

If script disputes exist between groups or larger segments of society, one of two things can happen. **Civility** occurs when an **attitude of tolerance** and **respect** for differences exists. People cherish their own preferences and traditions but are willing to let others pursue their preferences.

The **concept of civility** is especially relevant to the United States because we are a nation of immigrants. But most new immigrants did not find themselves warmly greeted by those already here. **Discrimination** was a much more common experience. America as the land of opportunity was an ideal, while discrimination the practice.

The alternative to civility is the display of **ethnocentrism** by at least one of the groups or segments involved in a script dispute. Ethnocentrism means that one or more of the groups or segments thinks their behavioral preferences and related values and beliefs are superior. Rather than practicing civility, one or more of the groups or segments tries to impose its social scripts on others in the society. **Civility gives way to proselytizing** as one or more of the groups or segments within the society promotes its agendas.

The fact that the United States represents a **diverse multicultural** society is celebrated by some and condemned by others. **Cultural conservatives** condemn diversity courses on campuses. Courses on African American history, the history of women in the United States, Native American history, or the history of Hispanics are attacked. Cultural conservatives want to turn the clock back to when only white European history was taught.

DOMINANT AND MINORITY GROUPS

The **dominant group** in a society is the **group** that **power** and **credibility** advantages. Because of **power,** the dominant group can **impose its will** on other groups in the society. But control is not based upon coercion alone. A dominant group is also more likely to rank higher in the social hierarchy of credibility. This gives its moral entrepreneurs an advantage over those advocating for other groups in society.

A **dominant group** uses its combination of **coercive power** and **credibility** to protect arrangements in society that it benefits from. Members of the dominant group are also referred to as the **advantaged** or **privileged.** Sometimes they are referred to as the **haves** in a society.

Minorities are **groups** within a society who **suffer deprivations** because of their **relative power** and **credibility deficiencies.** Without sufficient coercive power, they are unable to force the dominant group to treat them more favorably. Without sufficient credibility, they are unable to persuade the dominant group to treat them better. The result is that the social scripts of the dominant group prevail at their expense.

There are other terms used to describe minorities. Sometimes they are referred to as the **disadvantaged** or **underprivileged** in a society. Minorities are also referred to as the **have nots** in a society.

DOMINANT AND MINORITY GROUPS IN THE UNITED STATES

Historically, the **dominant group** in the United States has been **white Anglo-Saxon Protestant men** (WASP). The Founding Fathers, who were white Protestant men whose families migrated from the British Isle, were the impetus for the development of this privileged group. England, Scotland, and Northern Ireland were their countries of origin.

Identifying the dominant group as comprised of WASPs does not mean that everyone with those characteristics was advantaged. Many were not so fortunate and suffered deprivations, although those deprivations were not as severe as those experienced by African slaves and Native Americans. The points to bear in mind when talking about the dominant group are the characteristics of those in charge of a society and not whether or not everyone is so lucky.

Historically, minorities in the United States have included **African Americans, Native Americans, Asian Americans, Hispanics,** and **women.** Catholic Americans, like those who migrated from Ireland during the middle of the 1800s, also can be seen as a minority if for no other reason than only one president in the entire history of the United States was a Catholic. His name was John F. Kennedy. No African American, Native American, Asian American, Hispanic, or woman has served in that office.

The point has already been made that the conflict model of society looks at the power and credibility advantages of the dominant group in a society. Both enhance their control and capacity to sustain arrangements that benefit them at the expense of minorities. Now we will look more closely at the coercive and persuasive advantages of dominant groups.

COERCION

Dictatorships are the prime example of how a dominant group can impose its will through violence. But threats of physical harm, imprisonment, and torture are not the only coercive means that dictators employ. Dictators also control economics circumstances that they can use to their advantage. Providing economic advantages to supporters and denying them to detractors is a form of coercion.

What has been said about dictators applies to dominant groups who can use violence and economic coercion to impose their will on a society. The disdain that Americans often have for the use of violence and economic coercion by dictators can obscure this reality. To the extent that the dominant group in the United States controls politics and the government is the extent to which it has access to violence (or the threat of violence) to impose its scripts on others in society. To the extent that the dominant group controls the economy is the extent to which it can use the economy to impose its control on the rest of society.

DOMINANT IDEOLOGIES AND FALSE CONSCIOUSNESS

A **dominant group** benefits from a **persuasive advantage** over **minorities** because it usually ranks higher in the social hierarchy of credibility. It uses this persuasive advantage that allows it to peddle its dominant ideology. A **dominant ideology** represents the values, beliefs, and behavioral preferences that structure arrangements in society to the advantage of the dominant group.

A **dominant ideology** contains the **behavioral rationalization** that the dominant group uses to justify its advantage. It justifies their advantage and rationalizes the plight of minorities. It abates guilt over its disproportionate wealth, power, prestige, and comfort.

When **moral entrepreneurs** for the **dominant group** are able to get **minorities** to buy into its **dominant ideology,** it creates **false consciousness. False consciousness** exists when minorities internalize values, beliefs, and behavioral preferences and arrangements that serve the dominant group at their expense. False consciousness placates minorities and convinces them that they deserve their plight. False consciousness can be an extremely effective means for social control.

IDENTIFICATION WITH THE AGGRESSOR

Freud argued that when **confronted with an aggressor,** people reduce their sense of threat by coming to identify with the aggressor. The basic idea is that people are less likely to harm us if we are like them. Freud thought that this conversion occurs unconsciously.

This concept has been used to explain why some prisoners in Nazi death camps came to identify with their captors. It has also been used to explain why some people who have been kidnapped, like Patty Hearst, came to identify with their captors. Patty Hearst was the granddaughter of a wealthy American who was kidnapped by a militant group. She was caught on video surveillance tapes appearing to participate in some bank robberies. Questions about whether she chose to be there or was forced to be there are still not completely clear. What is clear is that people who thought that she was there as a result of identifying with her captors because of how they threatened her were more sympathetic than those who thought she chose to be there.

Identification with the aggressor can be extended to talk about identification with those who have power over others in a society. To the extent that discrimination denies people protection and opportunities is the extent to which they might come to identify with those who have power over them. This could explain why some minorities come to identify with the dominant group. Identifying with those in power says that you are like them and deserve to be treated accordingly.

PERFORMANCES

Minorities who come to **identify** with those with **power** over them switch their social selves. A **switch** in **social selves** implies that when this occurs, minorities have come to internalize the values, beliefs, and behavioral preferences of the dominant group. Such a switch means that their performance, designed to win a favorable response by those in power, represents genuine ingratiation.

A different possibility is when minorities become familiar with appearances favored by the dominant group but it does not require a switch in their social selves. Instead minorities fake their presentation of self to win a favorable response by the dominant group. In this situation their performances represent instrumental ingratiation.

CONFLICTED SOCIAL SELVES

Usually it is difficult for minorities to completely abandon their original identity. This means that the potential for a **conflicted social self** always exists for minorities who undergo an identity switch. The magnitude of that conflict depends upon the amount of conscious or unconscious guilt they experience. Some experience little guilt and get on with their lives. Others feel like a traitor to their group of origin.

MARGINAL PEOPLE

A **marginal person** is someone who is **caught between two cultures.** We have already seen that it can apply to recent migrants who are caught between the scripts from their original society and those that confront them when they relocate. But the tensions experienced by marginal people goes beyond those caused by a conflicted social self.

Social rewards and costs can also be involved. Appearances and performances that result in more favorable treatment by members of the dominant group may have a downside with friends and family in someone's group of origin. They may be offended and feel betrayed. The result is that they may impose social costs such as ridicule, scorn, or even outright rejection.

Another problem is that switching appearance to ingratiate members of the dominant group may have some benefits but not what is desired. For instance, minorities may gain access to a dominant group and its activities only to find that they are not completely accepted. The result is that they are marginal in their new setting and marginal among those that they have left.

COUNTER IDEOLOGIES

Counter ideologies are used by **moral entrepreneurs** for **minorities** to improve their situation within a society. Counter ideologies use value and belief appeals to persuade members of the dominant group to stop discriminating and allowing more opportunities for minorities. An example would be when a moral entrepreneur for women argues that it is unfair for men to earn more money than women for the same job.

That appeal is based upon the value of fairness. It is different from an appeal that challenges what members of a dominant group believe is true about minorities. For instance, men may have denied women opportunities in accounting because they believe that they are more able. Showing them data that documents that women are just as good at accounting as men might persuade them to change their mind.

The obstacle faced by minorities is that they are usually lower on the credibility hierarchy than those in the dominant group. They start out at a credibility disadvantage. This is why minorities benefit when someone from the dominant group becomes a moral entrepreneur for their cause.

MAINSTREAM SCRIPTS

A **mainstream script** is an **agreed upon social script** within a society with a **scope** that encompasses **most people.** In this context, mainstream can be thought of as what is normal or typical in a society. Matters become more complicated when trying to define the mainstream in a multicultural society.

The most obvious choice would be to define whatever is associated with the dominant group as mainstream. But what about the lifestyles of the rich and famous? They are certainly associated with the dominant group but hardly what most would define as mainstream. Most people have little chance to emulate the elite in their society.

Another strategy is to define mainstream as what a dominant group endorses. By this definition, all music that is acceptable to the dominant group would be considered mainstream. It could include everything from classical and big band music to jazz.

From a conflict perspective, what is significant is not what the dominant group permits but rather what it finds offensive. It is not necessary for the majority of Americans to agree on one form of music to appreciate what most view as offensive. Heavy metal and rap are often singled out in this manner. Censorship often follows the path of what the dominant group does not like.

The music industry offers yet another way to think about what is meant by mainstream. Mainstream music is what is played on Top 40 radio stations. What is played on alternative radio stations qualifies as music countercultures.

The advantage of thinking about mainstream music is that the music tastes of consumers and not those of the dominant group prevail. What the dominant group prefers or dislikes is less of an issue. Equating mainstream with what is popular can be applied to everything from sports, television programs, and movies to literature.

SUBCULTURES AND COUNTERCULTURES

A **subculture** is usually defined as a group that **differs** from the **mainstream** in a society but is still **compatible** with mainstream values, beliefs, and behavioral preferences. A **counterculture** is usually defined as a group that **opposes mainstream** values, beliefs, and behavioral preferences. The implication is that the mainstream in a society is more tolerant of subcultures than they are of countercultures. The reason is that the mainstream is likely to find countercultures too threatening and disruptive.

In the absence of genuine mainstream views shared by the majority within a society, it is necessary to modify the original conceptions of subcultures and countercultures. The same basic difference is retained with one difference. The dominant group, not the mainstream, becomes the reference point. A subculture is a group within society with differences but it is still sufficiently like the dominant group so as not to offend them. A counterculture is a group that the dominant group views more negatively and is likely to try to control or eradicate.

COUNTERCULTURES AND REVOLUTIONS

All **revolutionary groups** represent **countercultures** because they oppose the **dominant group** and its **ideology.** They seek to transform society and replace the dominant ideology with the behavioral preferences, values, and beliefs contained in their vision of the future. This is just as true of those involved in the American Revolution as it is of Castro's rise to power in Cuba.

Whether or not a revolution is violent or peaceful depends upon the circumstances in a society. In some societies, the only means for bringing about significance change is through the barrel of a gun. In other situations, minorities are able to use persuasion to mobilize people and successfully pull off a nonviolent revolution.

It is crucial to appreciate the defining characteristic of revolutionaries. They want to transform society by changing the prevailing social scripts. Conversion from a capitalist to communist society, or from a communist to capitalist society is an example. Notice that revolutionaries are not content with becoming more acceptable to those in power so that they will be treated better. Their game is not to ingratiate the dominant group but rather to change society.

PERSONALITY DEVELOPMENT

So far we have seen that script consensus or conflict are two possibilities that we may encounter when we study a society. These different possibilities have different implications for the development of personality. If only a single script exists within a society and virtually everyone internalizes it, then all of their social selves will be similar. If that agreed upon social script does not contain contradictory messages, those social selves will not cause problems for them.

If an agreed upon social script contains contradictory messages, then those who internalize it will experience tensions. An example is when a father is expected to be a friend to his son but also is responsible for disciplining him. Having to punish his son for disobeying contradicts being a friend to him. One resolution is to interpret the punishment as coming from love and treating him like a friend.

Multicultural societies create the potential for the development of conflicted social selves. The possibility that a child will be exposed to and internalize elements from diverse and even contradictory role models means that it cannot be assumed that children will be cultural clones of their parents. The fact that the parents may have script disputes between them means that children may internalize elements into their social self that are contradictory.

MODAL PERSONALITY

The assumption that all societies have an agreed upon cultural script helped forge a link between anthropology and psychology many years ago. Freud's argument that the personality of a child is created early by parental responses was the key. The basic idea was that an agreed upon cultural script that shaped how children are raised by their parents in a given society created a typical personality type.

The term **modal personality** describes the **typical personality type** in a society. The basic idea is that agreed upon scripts shape personalities in early childhood. It is then that the internalization of such scripts and child-rearing practices shaped by those scripts create a modal personality in a society. Although the psychologists and anthropologists formalized the idea of a modal personality, the concept is hardly new. Examples of modal personality depictions are everywhere. One example is when someone warns us that the French are extremely rude to outsiders. Another example is when a travel writer tries to describe the typical Spaniard. Sometimes an unconscious bias limits such descriptions to Spanish men. When Spanish women are included, a modal personality approach occurs if the implication is that all Spanish women match the description.

Politicians often use similar characterizations. These characterizations are more commonly known as stereotypes. A modal personality type was implied when President Reagan referred to Russia as the Evil Empire. Other politicians use modal personality types to characterize everyone from the French to people living in the Middle East.

The problem with this approach is that it encourages stereotypes that allow for little variation. The culprit is assuming that there is one agreed upon script that defines all people within a society. The existence of multiple scripts presents different possibilities.

DIVERSITY AND MODAL PERSONALITIES

The assumptions that go into the modal personality profile are severely strained by applications to societies with multiple scripts. Sociologists who are not alert to the possibility of multiple scripts run the risk of creating stereotypical images of people in a society. Trying to develop a modal personality profile of the typical Spaniard when serious differences in regional scripts exist may prove to be futile.

If you check closely, you will find significant cultural and historical differences among Spaniards. Those living in Madrid, the Basque region of the North, Barcelona in the West, and in Southern regions that were conquered by the Moors from North Africa many centuries ago have different cultural traditions. Knowledge about these differences is at least a starting point in breaking stereotypes based upon the assumption of a single agreed upon script.

But to assume that all people living within a given region share an identical script and have the same personalities is foolish. There is a huge difference between realizing that exposure to a given cultural script can influence aspects of behavior and equating everyone's personality with that script. What is often the most memorable about a trip are the unique characters that one encounters along the way.

MODAL PERSONALITIES AND SOCIAL CHANGE

The existence of a modal personality severely limits the possibility of social change within a society. If virtually everyone is shaped by the same script and comes to internalize and use it to rear their children, the only source of change would have to be from the outside. Having a few mavericks that differ would not be enough because their influence would be limited given the overwhelming opinion against them.

This is not to argue that change from the outside is not relevant. History is replete with examples of dominant societies conquering other societies and imposing their will upon them. The problem is that assuming script consensus and uniformity of personality development forfeits the search for more subtle dynamics within a society. To say that the women's movement in the United States was completely imported from elsewhere is misleading at best. Being fooled by the appearance of consensus should not be an option for sociologists. Yet, many sociologists were unaware of how pluralistic ignorance can conceal what people really believe and thought that only a few malcontented women were unhappy. The magnitude of change that has occurred tells us something quite different. There was much more discontent than surface appearances suggested.

PERSONALITY, CONFLICTING SCRIPTS, AND SOCIAL CHANGE

Societies within which conflict over social scripts exists are much more vulnerable to social change than ones in which consensus reigns. If the dominant group effectively utilizes coercion and false consciousness, social change may be unlikely. Sufficient coercion may discourage those who disagree with the prevailing script from expressing their dissent. Sufficient false consciousness may prevent minorities from recognizing their common plight.

Social change is more likely to occur when moral entrepreneurs for minorities are able to mobilize them to challenge the prevailing script. But this requires overcoming false consciousness and convincing minorities that the cost of going along with the status quo is greater than the cost of challenging it. Successful moral entrepreneurs for minorities may create their own message or learn messages from others. Lenin found his voice by reading Marx.

CHAPTER 10
SOCIAL STRUCTURES

Social structures are **patterns** of **interaction** that are repeated over time by people involved in social relationships in a given society. Social scripts determine the players and shape the patterns of interaction. A society where husbands are the breadwinners and wives are stay-at-home moms is an example of a social structure. It is a social structure because how husbands and wives interact is scripted and the pattern is repeated over time.

A different social structure would be one where wives are the breadwinners and husbands stay at home and care for the children. To qualify as a social structure, such a pattern would have to be relatively common and repeated over time. Sometimes a pattern of interaction that is quite rare in a society comes to involve more people who repeat it overtime. It is at that juncture that what began as rare and highly personalized scripted relationship is transformed into a social structure.

Although wives as the breadwinners and husbands functioning as "Mr. Moms" are still relatively rare in the United States, another relatively new pattern (social structure) is not. It is the dual income family. With the dual income family, both mom and dad work. One variation is when mom's income only supplements the earnings of dad. Another variation is when the family relies more on income from mom than dad.

THE SCOPE OF A SOCIAL STRUCTURE

For a pattern of activity to qualify as a social structure, it must be relatively common. Exactly how many must repeat a pattern over time is hard to say. But if enough manifest the pattern over time, it is likely to capture the attention of sociologists.

At that point sociologists are likely to try to determine the scope of the social structure in question. The **scope of a social structure** is the **number people/percentage of people** whose activities follow a certain pattern. Sociologists have a variety of data sources, such as surveys and census reports, that they can use to arrive at a figure.

The difference between the scope of a script and social structure is important to bear in mind. The scope of a social script is the number of people who agree with it. The scope of a social structure is the number/percentage of people that structure their behavior in a certain way. People can agree with a script and not practice it. An example would be a woman who reads *Ms. Magazine* and agrees with the liberated scripts presented there but in her own life functions more like a traditional housewife.

THE DURATION OF A SOCIAL STRUCTURE

For a pattern of activity to qualify as a social structure, it must be repeated over time. The **duration of a social script** is how long it lasts. There is no cut-and-dry rule that states what period of time is required before a pattern of activity that is repeated can be considered a social structure.

If a pattern of activity is repeated enough, it is likely to come to the attention of some sociologists. At that point, research on how long it has been in place will help establish its duration up until then. But the duration of a social structure includes how long it lasts into the future. It is always easier to ascertain duration in the past than to speculate about its future if for no other reason than data on the future is always forthcoming.

Sociologists often speculate on how long an established social structure in a society will last into the future. Sometimes it is a guess, while on other occasions more rigorous analysis of past and current trends is used to make a forecast. Only the future can dictate which speculation is right.

Studies of past and current societies provide insights into some possibilities concerning the duration of social structures. Vocabulary such as rituals, fashions, and fads signify different duration possibilities. A ritual by definition describes a pattern of activity (social structure) that has a long duration. Fads and fashions suggest shorter time frames for structured activities within a society.

THE SCOPE AND DURATION OF A SOCIAL STRUCTURE

When studying structured activities in a society, it is always important to remember the differences between the scope and duration of a social structure. The scope is the number/percentage of people within a group, community, or society who engage in a certain type of patterned activity. The duration of a social structure is how long it lasts.

An example will help illustrate the difference. The popularity of tattooing is something that sociologists might want to study. A beginning point might be to look cross-culturally at the history of tattooing and then establish when it became popular in the United States. Establishing when it became popular creates a time line for mapping its duration. Suppose that that it started in California in fringe groups and then spread to include larger numbers across the country. That information would help establish its scope. Further research might document its scope more exactly.

Even though tattooing has grown in popularity in the United States, it never represented a mass movement. For it to qualify as a mass movement, many more Americans would have had to gotten tattoos. A different comparison point in terms of its scope would be to look at the number/percentage of young people who got tattoos during a given time period.

STRUCTURE VERSUS RANDOMNESS

While the scope and duration of social structures can vary significantly, there is one point that is important. Social structures regardless of their scope or duration have a form that is repeated over time. Randomness would be just the opposite. Random interaction means the absence of any patterning. Random relationships are chaotic and totally unpredictable. The present has no bearing on what happens in subsequent encounters if chance or randomness prevails.

But just as nature abhors a vacuum, so do relationships abhor randomness. Randomness would make it impossible for participants to predict what will transpire in subsequent encounters. Definitions of future situations based upon past experience would be no guide as to what will happen next. This benefits no one. Structure improves the prospect of benefits for at least one of the participants.

This does not mean that the social patterns in a society are structured through eternity. If nothing else, history documents social patterns that can and do change in societies. Breakdowns in established social patterns can create relatively chaotic conditions, such as what occurred during the French Revolution, but over time history documents that new social structures are likely to arise from the ashes of past ones.

ANOMIE

Anomie refers to situations where the behavioral preferences contained in social scripts become weak or diluted (Durkheim, 1897). With anomie, the capacity of social scripts to structure activities is diminished. A state of anomie can be contrasted to situations where social scripts structure relationships.

Some sociologists view anomie as undesirable because they favor continuity and order in relationships. The problem is that these sociologists often fail to ask whom benefits from order and continuity in arrangements within a society. In Medieval Europe, order and continuity perpetuated a feudal system of exploitation. The nobility and clergy prospered at the expense of peasants.

While anomie is seen as undesirable from the perspective of those who benefit from arrangements in a society that are weakened by it, disadvantaged minorities in that society may welcome it as an opportunity for social changes that may improve their situation. Within this context, anomie is not a continuous state of chaos but rather a situation where the weakening of social scripts and the activities that they structure increases the potential for social change. Who welcomes this change is a separate issue.

DESIGNATING PLAYERS AND THE CONTENT OF THEIR RELATIONSHIP

The **social scripts** that structure social relationships have two distinct impacts on activities within a society. The first involves the part scripts have in designating **who are the players.** Scripts that discriminate facilitate access to patterns of activities for some, while denying access to those patterns of activities for others. Scripts also differentiate between players who interact with each other. The difference between a parent and child is a designation that differentiates between two types of players.

Secondly, social scripts determine the **content of relationships** between participants. A script for relationships between parents describes what is considered appropriate behavior for them. The script for relationships between parents and their children describes a different relationship.

SOCIAL CHANGE

Social change occurs whenever there is a **change** in the **players** and/or the **content** of a **relationship.** Social change can involve a few people, as when two friends no longer see each other as such, or a more generalized change in patterns of activities within a society. Affirmative action represents a more generalized change in society that not only changed players, but also changed the content of interaction among those involved in an activity. A change in content would be when men no longer tell sexist jokes while standing around the office watercooler because of the presence of female colleagues.

Whenever sociologists study social structures that exist within a society, the basic logic remains the same. First they identify the players. Then they describe the content of their relationships. Role theory has proven extremely useful in this regard.

ROLE THEORY

Role theory began as an effort by anthropologists to better understand how social scripts come to shape human activities. Their most basic insight is that behavioral preferences don't just float about in a society. Instead, the behavioral preferences contained in social scripts become attached to certain social positions.

Anthropologists discovered that different social positions, such as chief of a tribe, village elder, shaman (religious leader), young man, women, and children, are not viewed the same. Even agreed upon social scripts can assign different behavioral preferences to people depending upon the position they occupied. Behavior that was seen as appropriate for a chief was not seen as appropriate for other men. Behavior that was seen as appropriate for adult males was not seen as appropriate for young males. Behavior that was seen as appropriate for women was seen not seen as appropriate for adult males, and so forth.

The vocabulary of role theory makes it possible to systematically explore this basic insight. Learning this vocabulary and being able to apply it is an essential ingredient in learning how to think like a sociologist. Care must be taken to separate the various dimensions suggested by this vocabulary. These are the most important terms: (1) **status**; (2) **status occupant**; (3) **status relationship**; (4) **role**; (5) **role relationship**; (6) **role-set**; (7) **role conflict**; (8) **role behavior**; and (9) **sanctions.**

STATUS

A **status** refers to a **social position** within a group or society. A **status occupant** is someone who is in a social position at a given point in time. An example of a status is that of a teacher. Someone who is a teacher occupies that position and therefore qualifies as a status occupant.

Before looking at social roles, a word of caution is necessary. There is another usage of the term status that is common in sociology. This usage equates status with social prestige. Someone who is a status seeker is someone who seeks more prestigious positions in society.

Whenever the same term is used in two or more ways, ambiguity results. The problem with ambiguous terms is that one is never sure which meaning to apply. The solution is to establish separate terms for the different meanings.

Therefore, the term **status** will be used exclusively here to refer to a social position within a group or society. From this perspective, to talk about the status of women in American society is to talk about the social positions that they occupy. The term prestige (not status) will be used to describe the amount of social esteem that is given to people in a group or society. Often personal prestige is based upon the occupation one has. An example are studies that show the prestige of United States Supreme Court Justices is much higher than that of average lawyers. In fact, many studies show that among Americans, being a Supreme Count Justice is one of the most prestigious jobs in society. Custodians and manual laborers often rank at the bottom of the American prestige hierarchy.

STATUS RELATIONSHIP

Because the dyad represents the minimal unit of analysis for sociologists, a single status (social position) is not enough. A **status relationship** is a relationship between two and only two social positions and the people who occupy them in a social situation. A status relationships features pairs of social positions. Here are some examples of status relationships: (1) parent-child; (2) coach-athlete; (3) employer-employee; (4) teacher-student; (5) physician-patient; (6) husband-wife; (7) girlfriend-boyfriend; and (8) roommate-roommate.

Status relationships define who the players are by the positions that they occupy. The social scripts (behavioral preferences) the players bring to their social encounters or relationships define what behaviors they feel are appropriate for themselves and the other person, given the positions that they occupy. The social roles (behavioral preferences) people in different social positions (statuses) have for themselves and each other is one of the main research concerns of sociologists.

STATUS OCCUPANTS

Role theory encourages us to look at people in terms of the social positions that they occupy in a social encounter or relationship. A status occupant is someone who happens to be in a specific social position at a given point in time. Looking at two or more people who are interacting with each other as status-occupants reminds us that the behavioral preferences that they bring to those situations are status specific. The same person may have different self-preferences depending upon the position that he or she occupies. The self-preferences of someone in the position of a boyfriend may be different from that same person's self-preference when in the position of husband.

Similarly, when interacting with someone else, the position that person is in can make a big difference. A mother who teaches at a university may relate differently to her children than students. A potential conflict could occur if one of her children takes a class from her. That conflict would occur if her interaction preferences for the child as her child differ from her interaction preferences for that child as a student.

So far, we have talked about how behavioral preferences are status (social position) specific. We turn now to role theory for new vocabulary to describe what we have been calling behavioral preferences until now. The key term is that of a social role.

SOCIAL ROLES

A **social role** refers to the **behavioral preferences** that people involved in social encounters or relationships **attach to a given status.** A role defines what is considered to be acceptable or unacceptable behavior for a status occupant. It establishes what kinds of behaviors participants find enjoyable or dislike.

ROLE RELATIONSHIP

A **role relationship** refers to the behavioral preferences of people engaged in a status relationship. An example would be the role relationship between a husband and a wife. The role relationship consists of their self-preferences as husband and wife and the interaction preferences that they have for each other as a husband or wife.

Compatibility exists if what he thinks is appropriate behavior for him as a husband matches what she thinks is appropriate behavior for him as a husband. Compatibility also exists when what he thinks is appropriate behavior for her as a wife matches her self-preference for herself as a wife. Full role compatibility makes for harmonious relationships.

Role conflict occurs whenever there are disputes concerning what is appropriate behavior for them given their respective social positions. Role conflict creates tensions within relationships. It creates a behavioral dilemma. If what a husband prefers to do conflicts with what his wife thinks is appropriate, he faces such a dilemma. To comply with her preference means he forfeits his self-preference. This amounts to a cost for him. To comply with his self-preference means he offends her, and this invites the potential for a social cost.

ROLE-SETS

A **role-set** refers to the **total set of behavioral preferences** that converge on someone by virtue of the **statuses** (social positions) that the person occupies at the time. A role-set can also be thought of as a series of overlapping status and role relationships. Let me explain.

Let's look at the hypothetical role set for a woman who is divorced with children and returning to college. Immediately, we can infer some of the social positions that form the basis for her role-set. She is a mother (social position), divorced (social position), and a student (social position). But each of these positions does not exist in isolation. The position of mother links to her daughter and son as separate status-relationships. Her position of being divorced links to her ex-husband as a status-relationship. Her position of being a student links separately to each of her professors as status relationships.

All of these overlapping status relationships form a matrix. To fill in the matrix requires looking at all the separate role relationships that she is involved in. Mapping all the role relationships requires looking at all behavioral preferences (roles) that intersect around her and form her role-set. This includes her self-preferences and the interaction preferences of everyone else for her based upon the social position(s) that they and she occupy.

There is a separate role relationship for each status relationship. There is one with her daughter and a separate one with her son. Both role relationships include self-preferences and interaction preferences. To complicate matters more, each of the people that she has a status/role relationship with has their own role-set.

The role-set of her son would be the total set of roles that focus on him by virtue of the positions he occupies. One status/role relationship might be with his father who is her ex-husband. But he may also have multiple status relationships with different friends that add to the mix. The son also has a status/role relationship with his sister (her daughter). If the son is in school, he is involved in many other status/role relationship that function as inputs into his role-set. If he plays little league baseball, more status/role relationships come into play.

Returning to focus on the divorced mother with children who is going back to college helps establish the significance of all this. While her role-set is limited to all the behavioral preferences that impinge upon her dynamics with those other people in her role-set, they are also affected by what is going on in their role-sets. It is easy to see how role conflict can arise within the role-set of someone.

ROLE CONFLICT

Role conflict exists when script disputes exist within a role relationship or the role-set of a specific person. **Personal role conflict** exists when self-preferences conflict. An example is when a mother is motivated to make good grades, but this takes time away from being with her children. The problem is that her self-preferences as a student clash with her self-preferences as a mother.

Interpersonal role conflict occurs when interaction preferences that two or more people have for someone else collide. An example is when your boss wants you to work overtime, but your girlfriend wants you to go to the beach. Being in the positions of employee and boyfriend are the basis for the role conflict. If what your boss prefers and what your girlfriend prefers are compatible, then no role conflict exists.

Combinations of personal and interpersonal role conflict are relatively common. The simplest version is when your self-preference clashes with the interaction preference someone else has for you. More complicate combinations involve multiple self-preferences and interaction preferences.

CULTURAL DIVERSITY AND ROLE CONFLICT

Cultural diversity exists when multiple cultural scripts exist within a society. As a nation of immigrants, the United States offers a rich palette of cultural differences. Exposure to cultural diversity invites the possibility of role conflict beyond what is generated from within a community.

Cultural diversity and role conflict converge under several conditions. The most obvious is when people from different cultural traditions in a society interact. At that point, role conflict occurs when the behavioral preferences of those interacting reflect different cultural traditions.

The other possibility does not require interaction between people from different cultural traditions within a society. All it requires is exposure to the practices in another culture. An example would be when a Caucasian suburban child comes to identify with Native American views on the environment that relish preserving it. If this clashes with the views of her parents, the foundation for role conflict between them exists. It exists because behavioral preferences cover both the actions of others and the attitudes that they express. All it takes is for the child to assert that the attitudes of her parents about the environment are wrong.

THE SIGNIFICANCE OF ROLE CONFLICT

Role conflict creates a behavioral dilemma. To comply in one direction automatically means that you deviate in another direction. The dilemma is trying to decide how to behave when both rewards and costs are likely to follow.

SANCTIONS TESTS

Sanctions are the reactions of self or others to a behavior that increase or decrease the likelihood that it will be repeated. A **sanction test** is an effort to find out what will happen. The test could involve others or self.

Sanction tests provide feedback that informs subsequent definitions of a situation. Experiencing guilt when you did something serves as a **self-sanction test.** An **interaction sanction test** occurs when you get feedback from others involving how they react to certain behaviors. Having people laugh at a joke is feedback that may encourage you to tell it to others.

Sanction tests can be either deliberate or unplanned. An example of a deliberate sanction test is when you inform your parents that you smoked pot, knowing that they disapprove. An example of an unplanned sanction test would be the reaction of your parents if they caught you smoking pot.

SCRIPT BOUNDARIES AND TESTS

Script boundaries refer to the range of behavior that is permitted within a behavioral preference (role) contained in a social script. A **script test** is an effort to test the boundaries of a behavioral preference. A script test differs from a sanction test in that the purpose of a sanction test is to gauge reactions to a behavior. The purpose of a script test is to gauge what you can get away with.

Children often test the boundaries of parental interaction preferences for them. An example would be when a child knows that his/her parents forbid crossing the street alone. Knowing this, some children will try to test the boundaries of that parental decree. Perhaps playing on the grass next to the curb is the first test. Getting no reaction may prompt them to play along the gutter with one foot in it and the other on the grass. Getting no reaction may prompt them to test further by playing a game with friends in the street. You get the picture!

SCRIPT CONFRONTATIONS

Script confrontations represent direct challenges to a behavioral preference contained in a social script of others. These challenges reverberate back to the values and beliefs that sustain that behavioral preference. With script confrontations, the issue is not determining script boundaries but rather an effort to challenge the behavioral preference itself.

The intent of Dr. Martin Luther King Jr. was to confront the Jim Crow laws in the South that legally mandated racial segregation. He was not interested in testing whether or not Caucasians would tolerate serving African Americans at their restaurants under certain restricted circumstances.

The decision by Dr. King to confront racist scripts took sanction possibilities into account. The expectation for severe reactions was understood. But Dr. King's commitment to confronting these behavioral preferences exceeded his anticipations of consequences that included the possibility that he would be assaulted, jailed, or even killed.

IMAGINING OUTCOMES AND SCRIPT CONFRONTATION

Imagining outcomes that could result from a script confrontation is an element in how someone defines a situation. Imagining how others might react is often incorporated into deliberate script confrontations. Protestors challenging racial discrimination in the South often relied upon their predictions that police would respond violently to discredit them. Getting images of police violence on film helped discredit the pattern of racial segregation in the South. In the summer of 2001, some protesters capitalized on this expectation in Genoa, Italy, during a meeting between the heads of the most economically advanced countries in the world. The more militant protestors who threw cobblestones at the police relied on them to respond with physical force. The hope was that film of the police reacting with physical force would serve their protest objectives.

Script confrontations that try to provoke a violent reaction can backfire. Moral entrepreneurs can use the actions used to provoke the violent response to discredit the protestors and justify police reactions. A familiar example is when the police defend their actions by saying it was necessary to protect property and lives. Characterizing protestors as thugs discredits them and diminishes their credibility.

ROLE-MAKING

There are two contrasting views that sociologists have about people and social roles. Some role theorists view people as clones of social scripts. The basic idea is that people come to accept whatever roles are scripted by their society. This is based upon a passive image of people who internalize whatever script is presented to them.

The alternative possibility assigns a more active image to people. It sees people as actively engaged in the process of promoting their behavioral preferences. The discussion on different negotiation tactics people use to press their behavioral preferences reflects this interpretation of people and social roles.

Role-making also features a more active image of people. **Role-making** occurs when people modify, adjust, and create new social scripts. It does not deny the possibility that people will internalize social scripts or elements within social scripts. But it does suggest that people are not necessarily captive of what they may have preferred in the past.

Sometimes role-making by certain people has a dramatic effect. Martin Luther is a prime example. So too is Calvin. Their modifications and adjustments of religious scripts led to the Protestant Reformation.

The extent to which people are passive clones of social scripts or engage in role-making is an empirical question. There is no reason to assume either. But like so many other concepts, learning to think like a sociologists requires taking both into account when examining actual social encounters or relationships.

PERSONAL EXPRESSION AND ROLE-MAKING

Personal expression exists when social scripts permit personalities to be interjected into social exchanges. Some scripts permit considerable latitude for personal expression. Other scripts limit the potential for personal expression.

What is true about personal expression and social scripts can be applied to social roles. The social roles attached to statuses differ according to the extent that they script behavior. Some roles permit a lot of personal expression. Roles defining friendship are an example because the role of a friend invites personal expression. The opportunity for participants to actively engage in creating or making roles increases in situations that allow for personal expression. The more scripted a role, the less the opportunity for role-making. An example is a job where everything is scripted and workers have little or no input.

MASTER STATUS

The fact that someone may occupy more than one social position at a time has been established. A **master status** is a status (social position/category) that becomes central to how people interact with someone else. A master status assigned to someone need not be the preference of that person for it to have significance.

An example is that of an ex-convict. Ex-convict is clearly a social position or category. It qualifies as a master status if it becomes the basis upon which people interact with someone.

Often racial, ethnic, and gender categories function in the same manner. It happens to African Americans to the extent that Caucasians treat their being African American as their master status. It also happens with African American friends and colleagues who define their being African American as the center of their existence. It happens to Arab Americans when others treat their being Arab as their master status. It happens to women to the extent that being a woman is a master status that trumps all other categories that she represents.

Master scripts are labels that restrict how people interact with someone. It is a label that dominates how they define situations involving that person. It can be the source of extreme frustration for the person who is confined to a master script because it limits the extent to which people want to hear anything else about them.

PART 4
STUDY GUIDES

CHAPTER 11
POLITICAL AND ECONOMIC SCRIPTS

Who Benefits?

Political Scripts

The Foundations of Political Power

Types of Political Power

Types of Authority

    Charismatic

    Traditional

    Rational-Legal

Master and Cultural Scripts

Coercive Power and Authority

The American Political System

The Constitution

    Preamble

    Separation of Powers

    Interstate Commerce

    Power of States

The Bill of Rights

Additional Amendments

The Supreme Court

    Original Intent

    Living Document

Economic Scripts

The Political Economy

    Capitalist Political Economies

    Socialist Political Economies

Peddling Political Economy Scripts

CHAPTER 12
AMERICAN CONTRADICTIONS

Values

Value Contradictions

Sacred and Secular

The Individual and the Collectivity

    Individual

    Team

War and Patriotism

    Perception of Threat

    Who Benefits?

Freedom and Equality

The Principle of Hedonism

    Personal

    Collective

        Hedonistic Calculus

Value Clusters

    Capitalist Political Economy

    Socialist Political Economy

Life, Liberty, and the Pursuit of Happiness

Democracy in America

    Ideal Culture

    Real Culture

Work and Play

The Work Ethic and Family Values

Materialism and Self-fulfillment

CHAPTER 13
CONFORMITY AND DEVIANCE

Definitions

    Conformity

    Deviance

Rewards and Costs

    Self

    Social

Dominant, Mainstream, and Minority Groups

Autonomy and Anonymity

Sociological Theories of Deviance

    Is Any Act Inherently Deviant?

    Labeling Theory

        Moral Entrepreneurs

    The Medicalization of Deviance

    Social Organization

        Social Disorganization Theory

    Subcultures and Deviance

        Subculture

        Counter-Culture

        Deviant Subculture

    Differential Association

    Techniques of Neutralization

        Inoculation Theory

    Control Theory

Positive Reference Groups

Negative Reference Groups

Modes of Adaptation

Conformity

Innovation

Rebellion

Retreatism

Ritualism

Opportunity Structures

Conflict Subculture

Criminal Subculture

Retreatist Subculture

Reducing Deviance

Psychological Interpretations

Sociological Interpretations

Deviant Careers

Primary Deviance

Secondary Deviance

Deviant Label

Deviant Identity

The Culture of Poverty

CHAPTER 14
CRIME AND THE CRIMINAL JUSTICE SYSTEM

Laws

Legitimacy

Coercion

The Use of Coercion

What Is a Crime?

    Law

    Deviant

State Endorsed Behavioral Preferences

    Laws

    Executive Orders

    Regulations

    Ordinances

The Issue of Harm

    Laws

    Regulations

Criminal and Civil Law

    Criminal

    Civil

Jurisdiction

    Federal

    State

Crime Data

    Uniform Crime Report (UCR)

    National Crime Victimization Survey (NCVS)

Types of Crimes

    Street

    Organized

    White-Collar

    Blue-Collar

    Corporate

    Patriotic

Victimless

Status

The Enforcement of Laws

Police

Constitutional Restraints

Discretion

Profiling

The Blue Line

Prosecutors

Powerful

Arrest Warrants

Charging

Plea Bargaining

Judges

Warrants

Search

Arrest

Arraignment Hearings

Jury Trials

Sentencing

Mandatory Sentences

Corrections

Jails

Prisons

Punish

Rehabilitate

Recidivism

Cruel and Unusual Punishment

Privatization of Prison Labor

Federal Prison Industries

Jobs

War on Crime

Decriminalization and Deregulation

More Politics

CHAPTER 11
POLITICAL AND ECONOMIC SCRIPTS

At one time, sociologists paid little attention to how scripts shape political or economic arrangements within societies. Some of this neglect was based upon specialization within the social sciences. Specialization granted political science and economics the right to explore such arrangements.

POLITICS

Politics deals with government. Those who control government have an opportunity to translate their script preferences into laws and policies. Those who control government have access to its coercive power to enforce such laws and policies.

This gives them a coercive advantage over others in a society. Controlling what often amounts to a governmental monopoly on coercion means that those who control government can impose the scripts that they prefer on others in a society.

Sometimes those who control government are government officials. An example would be a dictator. On other occasions, government officials may be pawns to powerful families or business interests.

WHO BENEFITS?

Whenever sociologists look at political scripts in a society, they ask one fundamental question. Who benefits from those social scripts? The answers are based upon who has the most access to the government, who influences the most laws and policies of the government, and who is able to use the coercive power of government to their advantage.

Those who benefit the most from political scripts are likely to be within the dominant group in a society. Minorities are those who benefit the least from the political scripts within a society. Changes in who occupies governmental positions, such as through elections within a democratic society such as the United States, can tilt the advantage scale in one direction or another. But often the top echelon in American politics simply circulates to top positions within other sectors of society, such as education, private foundations, or business, when they are out of office. Some who worked on trade agreements while in Washington join the foreign companies that they negotiated with when they find themselves out of office. Then these same people often reappear in government roles in the next election cycle.

Thinking about who benefits from laws and government policies is closely related to economics. Many laws and policies affect the economy of a society. This means that to ask whom benefits from laws and government policies is often closely linked to the economic interests of different groups in a society.

Before examining the intersection between political and economic scripts, it will be useful to look at some of the basics. We begin with some general considerations about political scripts. This discussion will be followed by specifics involving the American political system. Once this has been done, attention will shift to some general considerations about economic scripts and how they can intersect with political scripts.

POLITICAL SCRIPTS

The government of a society is one of the most significant spheres of scripted activities in a society. A government can be thought of as the source of political decisions. Some governments are quite simple. In a foraging or hunting and gathering society, there may be no formal script. Government may represent nothing more than the emergence of a charismatic leader at the time of crisis to help the community adapt. Formal scripting surfaces when a society decides to institutionalize a role such as that of a chief. Other options include the scripting of a council of village elders. More complexity occurs with the advent of royalty and their courts in agricultural societies. And finally, modern constitutional governments represent the highest degree of political scripting because of the extent to which activities are defined.

THE FOUNDATIONS OF POLITICAL POWER

The essence of any government is its capacity to govern. Governing is based upon power. Power is the capacity to get people to do what you want them to do. It is this capacity to compel compliance that enables a government or political system to implement its decisions or mandates. This means that a key consideration when looking at political scripts is the foundations upon which they can compel compliance.

TYPES OF POLITICAL POWER

Max Weber's perspective on social power was discussed in the chapter on organizations. The purpose at that time was to indicate the significance his various types of authority have for studying organizational structures. Now his insights will be applied to the topic of political scripts

Weber began by defining **coercion** as imposing a political script on citizens. In a political system ruled by coercion, people have no choice but to comply. Not to comply carries with it the threat of losing all of one's possessions, imprisonment, torture, and even death. The basis for all of this is the government's virtual monopoly on coercion through its control of the police and military.

Weber contrasted governments based upon coercion with governments that operate as systems of **authority.** A government is a system of authority if adherence to its directives does not involve coercion. The absence of coercion means that a system of authority involves volition. Volition means that people agree to go along with political decisions.

TYPES OF AUTHORITY

Sociologists also talk about political systems of authority as forming the basis for a **legitimate government.** It is **legitimate because people agree** with the script that defines it. This can be contrasted to a government that rules through coercion. Rule through coercion means that the government it not seen as legitimate.

The first type of authority involves **charismatic authority.** The essence of charismatic authority is personality. It is the personality of the charismatic leader that compels others to follow.

With charismatic authority, the political script is subtle and more in the background than it is with traditional and rational-legal forms of authority. This is because the relevance of the script bears only on what personality characteristics people will see as unique and compelling. Weber noted that charisma is often associated with religious beliefs that confirm for someone the quality of possessing "gifts from God."

Weber realized that not all systems of authority are based directly on the characteristics of a charismatic leader. The problem is that a leadership crisis can occur with the death of a charismatic leader. The **routinization of charisma** is a term that Weber used to explain how the qualities of a charismatic leader are preserved.

One solution is to create a script that that passes on his qualities as a leader through inheritance. His eldest son, who presumably inherits his unique qualities, becomes the next in line to succeed the charismatic leader, and so on for generations in the future.

Traditional authority is often based upon the routinization of charisma in the past. Traditional authority is based upon customs. Transforming charismatic authority into traditional authority is found with the royal line of succession. Presumably, credibility for royal lines of succession to the throne is based upon the exceptional accomplishments of someone in the past. The only problem with the script is that there is no guarantee that those in line for succession will possess the qualities of the original charismatic leader. Some turned out to be uninspiring and quite stupid!

Weber reserved the designation of **rational-legal authority** for modern societies that are governed by a constitution. The existence of a constitution that deliberately calculates and plans governmental activities is why Weber called it a rational form of government. The legal component derives from the fact that the behavioral preferences endorsed by a constitutional government are commonly called laws.

All forms of authority are based upon social scripts. The difference between types of authority involves the circumstances that give them credibility. Rational planning is the essence of rational-legal scripts. Custom is the essence of traditional authority. But even charismatic leadership exists within the context of social scripts. Weber said so much when he observed that charisma is often thought of as a gift from God.

MASTER AND CULTURAL SCRIPTS

Rational-legal authority represents a master script that has been deliberately planned and written down. **Traditional authority** is based upon a cultural script that has created a customary way of governing in a society. **Charismatic authority** is rooted in the **values and beliefs** of a society that celebrate certain unusual personality traits.

COERCIVE POWER AND AUTHORITY

What Weber had to say about authority remains useful. But it would be a mistake to assume that a modern political system that is structured by rational-legal scripts is never coercive. The fact that our political system in the United States is based upon rational-legal documents doesn't mean that it functions completely as a system of authority where compliance in volitional. Coercion also applies.

What ultimately distinguishes the government in the United States from other groups and organizations is its virtual monopoly on coercive power. When people treat its decisions and as legitimate, then it functions as a system of authority. But its coercive power is never entirely absent.

Some comply and pay their taxes because they believe that this is a legitimate function of government. But not everyone believes in the Sixteenth Amendment. For them it is the coercive power of the government that compels compliance. Pay your taxes or go to jail.

THE AMERICAN POLITICAL SYSTEM

The American political system formally began with the break from England after the Revolutionary War. **The Declaration of Independence** represents a formal challenge and justification for the war. **The Constitution** and **Bill of Rights** represent a master script or what Weber called a rational-legal foundation for government. The Bill of Rights is the first ten Amendments to the Constitution. Additional Amendments to the Constitution were also the product of rational discourse. Rational discourse is what produced these deliberately conceived written scripts.

Sometimes people confuse the function and significance of these documents. The Declaration of Independence mentions God on several occasions. But the Constitution never mentions God and the First Amendment forbids Congress from making "no law respecting the establishment of religion . . ."

This confusion arose in 2002 when a federal court decided that the pledge of allegiance violates the establishment of religion clause with its phrase "One nation under God." Some claimed that the Declaration of Independence with its references to God justifies the Pledge as amended in 1954. (Before 1954 the aforementioned phrase did not exist.) Others cited the First Amendment as the document of proper reference.

From a Constitutional viewpoint, the Declaration of Independence is irrelevant to the decision. This is because only the Constitution and its Amendments represent the master script that judges can use to decide constitutional matters. Whether or not the Declaration of Independence or popular opinion supports the decision is a separate issue that moral entrepreneurs are free to use.

Only judges, and ultimately the Supreme Court, have the Constitutional authority to decide on such matters. This is why the appointment of judges, especially for the Supreme Court, is so important. These are lifetime appointments. Once appointed, such judges are free to interpret the Constitution as they see fit. What counts is not the Declaration of Independence or popular opinion. What counts is how a judge interprets the Constitution, its Amendments, and earlier decisions.

THE CONSTITUTION

The Preamble to the Constitution states: "We the People of the United States, in Order to form a more perfect Union, establish Justice, insure domestic tranquility, provide for the common defense, promote the general Welfare, and Secure the Blessings of Liberty to ourselves and our Posterity, do ordain and establish this Constitution for the United States of America."

The Preamble reveals some of the most fundamental values and behavioral preferences of the Founding Fathers. It scripts the job of government. The government must provide for defense from outside threats and insure domestic tranquility. The military does the former and the police insure domestic tranquility. Securing personal liberty from government action is not only stated here, but it is further elaborated in the Bill of Rights, which was added some years later to the Constitution.

Most of this is familiar. But there is one part of the Preamble to the Constitution that is often ignored. It is the job of government to provide for the general welfare. This value is most likely to be ignored by conservatives who exclude the poor and less fortunate from the government obligation to provide for the common welfare. Eliminating programs for the poor and less fortune through tax cuts that disproportionately favor the wealthy does not seem to promote the general welfare of society.

Beyond the statement of values and behavioral preferences in the Preamble, the most basic contribution of the Constitution is its plan for separating powers between the Executive, Legislative, and Judicial branches of our government. This formal separation of powers scripted what had evolved over centuries in England involving royalty, Parliament, and a judicial role going back to the Magna Carta.

The Tenth Amendment clarifies and formalizes something that some believed was inherent in the Constitution. It affirms the principle that powers not delegated to the federal government by the Constitution are reserved to the states or the people. The right for states to govern themselves is based upon this amendment. The clause "or the people" can be used to legitimate additional amendments beyond the first ten that are known as the Bill of Rights.

The acknowledged rights of the federal government involve defense, waging war, and regulating interstate commerce. Regulating interstate commerce has been the principle vehicle for justifying the federal war on drugs. But questions concerning federal, state, and local jurisdiction with the war on drugs remain. Disputes of this nature are featured in movies and cop shows when the Feds (FBI/DEA) interfere with local narcotics enforcement teams.

The Constitution and its amendments form the core of the American political script. The Supreme Court is the ultimate interpreter of the script. The justices of the Supreme Court have demonstrated remarkable flexibility when interpreting these documents. This interpretive flexibility is what makes the selection of new justices to the Supreme Court a source of extreme political tension and debates.

The amendments to the Constitution represent some of the most important elements in the American political script. They are the foundation of some of the most intense debates within American society today. Some of the most important ones have been listed for the purpose of reference and class discussion.

Take, for instance, the Second Amendment, which gun proponents insist justifies personal gun ownership. Look carefully at the wording of the amendment. Does it say that you and I as individuals have the right to bear arms? Or does it say that you and I have the right to bear arms for the single purpose of maintaining a militia? If the purpose is to maintain a militia, then this amendment has nothing at all to do with someone's alleged right to possess a gun for personal protection or to protect his family.

The terrorist acts of 9/11 in the United States prompted Constitutional interpretations by Attorney General Ashcroft that are controversial. Some claim that many people are being held in violation of the Fifth Amendment. Notice that it explicitly states that no one should be deprived of life, liberty, or property without due process. To argue that terrorist suspects can be held by the military without due process is seen as constitutionally suspect. To suggest that due process applies only to citizens is equally suspect because the amendment refers to "person" and not citizen.

Another area of controversy includes the Bush Administration's decision to try alleged terrorists in military courts. The Sixth Amendment states that the accused shall enjoy the right to a speedy and public trial by an impartial jury of the state and district wherein the crime shall have been committed. Shifting jurisdiction to military courts is one issue. Another issue is by what stretch of the imagination can the government argue that a panel of military officials represents an impartial jury from the state and district in which the crime is alleged to have occurred. Not providing counsel for the accused, or not telling the lawyer of someone who has been accused where that person is being held, are seen as further Constitutional violations by some observers.

THE BILL OF RIGHTS

The **Bill of Rights** represents the **first ten amendments** to the Constitution. All of these amendments were ratified on December 15, 1791. Since then, more amendments to the Constitution have been passed. What follows are the most familiar, and probably most significant, of these amendments.

I. Congress shall make no law respecting the establishment of religion, or prohibiting the free exercise thereof; or abridging the freedom of speech, or the press; or the right of the people to peacefully assemble, and to petition the Government for a redress of grievances.

II. A well-regulated Militia, being necessary to the security of a free State, the right of the people to keep and bear Arms, shall not be infringed.

IV. The right of the people to be secure in their persons, houses, papers, and effects, against unreasonable searches and seizures, shall not be violated, and no warrant issue, but upon probable cause, supported by Oath or affirmation, and particularly describing the place to be searched, and the persons or things to be seized.

V. . . . nor shall any person be subject for the same offense to be twice put in jeopardy of life or limb; nor shall be compelled in any criminal case to be a witness against himself, nor be deprived of life, liberty, or property without due process of law; nor shall private property be taken for public use, without just compensation.

VI. In all criminal prosecutions, the accused shall enjoy the right to a speedy and public trial, by an impartial jury of the State and district wherein the crime shall have been committed, which district shall have been previously ascertained by law, and to be informed of the nature and cause of the accusation; to be confronted with the witnesses against him; to have compulsory process for obtaining witnesses in his favor, and to have the Assistance of Counsel for his defense.

VII. Excessive bail shall not be required, nor excessive fines imposed, nor cruel and unusual punishments inflicted.

X. Powers not delegated to the United States by the Constitution, nor prohibited by it to the States, are reserved to the States respectively, or to the people.

ADDITIONAL AMENDMENTS

XIII. Neither slavery nor involuntary servitude, except as punishment for crime whereof the party shall have been duly convicted, shall exist within the United States, or any subject to their jurisdiction.

XIV. . . . nor shall any State deprive any person of life, liberty, or property without due process of law . . . nor deny to any person within its jurisdiction the equal protection of the laws.

XV. The right of citizens of the United States to vote shall not be denied or abridged by the United States or any State on account of race, color, or previous condition of servitude.

XVI. The Congress shall have the power to lay and collect taxes on incomes, from whatever source derived . . .

XIX. The right of citizens of the United States to vote shall not be denied or abridged by the United States or any State on the account of sex.

XXIV. The right of citizens of the United States to vote . . . shall not be denied or abridged by the United States or any State by reason of failure to pay poll tax or other tax.

XXVI. The right of citizens of the United States who are eighteen years of age or older, to vote shall not be denied or abridged by the United States or by any State on account of age.

THE SUPREME COURT

The **Supreme Court of the United States** decides on the Constitutionality of laws passed by Congress, the States, or local jurisdictions. The idea that those seated on the Supreme Court are impartial interpreters of the Constitution, the Bill of Rights, and other amendments, represents an ideal not a reality. Down through the years, Supreme Court judges have demonstrated an amazing versatility in their reading and application of these documents.

Original intent is a doctrine some believe should be used by Supreme Court Justices when deciding cases. This viewpoint contends that when questions concerning the interpretation of these documents arise, the only guideline should be what those who wrote the Constitution or various amendments had in mind at that time. Although proponents claim that this rids judgments of personal bias or preference, in reality proponents often use their claims as to what the authors had in mind to advance their own personal agendas.

The fact that these documents themselves may be the product of personal bias and the times is conveniently ignored. Nor do proponents of this approach admit that their own personal bias can crop up through the process of selectively trying to read the minds of those who wrote such documents. And finally, proponents rarely admit that there is probably no such thing as a "literal" interpretation of the words and expression of those authors, since any linguist acknowledges the latitude of meanings that can be read into any word or statement.

Others believe that Supreme Court justices should view the Constitution and its amendments as a **living document** that continues to grow and evolve. The argument is that unless justices move beyond original intent, no progress is possible. The doctrine of original intent would never have allowed former male slaves and women to get the vote because they were excluded by the Founding Fathers from exercising this right.

Proponents of the living document doctrine are the most likely to admit that their judgments involve interpretations of the Constitution and its Amendments. Trying to apply words written centuries ago to contemporary judgments is an interpretive process. Those who favor the original intent doctrine are more likely to deny that their judgments are interpretations.

The **interpretative latitude** inherent in the Constitution and its amendments is why the nomination and confirmation of Supreme Court judges has become such a central concern of political parties and other interest groups in the United States. The stakes are enormous because the Supreme Court can approve or reject virtually any Act of Congress, Executive Order, or regulation. Whatever interpretative bias exists is serious since all justices have a life-time appointment.

ECONOMIC SCRIPTS

Economic scripts were discussed in the chapter that dealt with some spheres of activities that sociologists study. Economic scripts determine how goods and services are produced, distributed, and consumed in a society.

Production scripts deal with the division of labor in a society. Production scripts designate who does what. **Distribution scripts** cover how products and services are made available to customers. **Consumption scripts** involve who has access to the goods and services in a society.

Increasingly, sociologists and other scholars have come to recognize that it is virtually impossible to look at economic scripts in isolation. Production, distribution, and consumption scripts are all tied to political scripts. Scripts that define the role of government in an economy are central.

THE POLITICAL ECONOMY

The term **political economy** refers to the **intersection** between **economic** and **political scripts** in societies. Different societies embrace different scripts involving the relationship between government and the economy. The difference between a capitalist political economic script and a socialist political economic script is the most important one.

Both **capitalist** and **socialist political economic scripts** represent ideal-types. **Ideal-types** exaggerate certain characteristics that may not be fully replicated in actual situations. Ideal-types are helpful when making comparisons.

A **capitalist political economic script** is based upon the contention that **the government that governs the least governs the best**. A **socialist political economic script** is based upon the contention that **the best government is one that provides the greatest good for the greatest numbers**.

Both contentions involve **values.** Freedom and independence from government interference are values that sustain a capitalist political economy model. A commitment to the collectivity over the individual is the value that sustains the socialist political economy model.

There are also **beliefs** or **truth claims** made about these two models. Advocates of the capitalist political economy model claim that the economy works best if left alone. Some proponents of the capitalist political economy model even claim that it is mutually beneficial to all in a society. Critics claim that if left alone, the capitalist political economic model creates a greater disparity between the rich and poor and government intervention is necessary to curb the greed of those at the top. This is why they embraced a socialist political economy model.

Proponents of the capitalist political economic script claim that government intervention threatens economic viability. Both President Reagan and President George W. Bush advocated deregulation on this basis. Both Reagan and Bush extended this argument to include tax reductions for the wealthy (tax deregulation) so that they could create more jobs. Critics counter that deregulation in general, and tax deregulation specificly, benefit those at the top at the expense of those at the bottom. Instead of creating jobs, tax cuts were retained as wealth by those at the top.

Critics of the socialist political economy model often disparage government as inefficient and incompetent when compared to the private sector. This is why they argue for privatizing tasks traditionally done by the government, ranging from garbage collection and schools to private Social Security accounts. These arguments are countered by the claim that efforts to privatize government functions are really an attempt by business to make profits by reducing wages and services.

CULTURAL THEMES

Whether or not a **society favors a capitalist or socialist political economic script** depends upon **cultural themes.** Of particular significance are cultural values. Because of the emphasis on freedom by the Founding Fathers, a capitalist political economic script has an advantage in the United States. European societies are more inclined toward socialist political economic scripts. This is evident in the extent to which government programs provide healthcare and other benefits to their societies.

CAPITALIST POLITICAL ECONOMIES

Adam Smith listed the central feature of a **capitalist political economy** in his book *The Wealth of Nations.* His book was written during the 1700s but still has currency among many political economists today. His basic message was the **less government the better.**

Advocates of this position celebrate market forces. Like Adam Smith, proponents of capitalism believe that the wisdom of market forces are superior to the human capacity to plan. Most argue that if left to the natural interplay of market forces, the economic results will provide the greatest good for the greatest number in a society.

Critics complain that what is missing from this happy scenario is the possibility of a monopoly. These critics argue that the logical goal of capitalism is monopoly and not the competition that Smith and his followers thought drive the economy. Critics envision a future where various segments of the economy will be controlled by a few corporations which, given their leverage, negates competition. Without competition they can determine prices with the result that consumers requiring their services or products will suffer.

The absence of government intervention is the key to understanding the script for a truly capitalistic society. The term **laissez-faire** describes the script for minimal involvement in society by a government. Other features of capitalism are the private ownership of all economic resources and the celebration of the quest for personal profits. Sometimes competition is added to this list, but this is not really something that capitalists welcome. The problem is that genuine competition undermines personal profits.

Monopoly is the true goal of all real capitalists. A monopoly occurs when one company controls an entire market. Today, shared monopolies are more likely than single monopolies. A **shared monopoly** exists when four or fewer companies control more than 50 percent of the market. This is quite common in the United States.

The reason that monopoly is the ultimate goal of capitalism is that it maximizes profits. Monopoly represents the absence of competition, which drives prices and profits down. Shared monopolies are not what ambitious capitalists want. Shared monopolies exist when it is not possible to create a single monopoly.

SOCIALIST POLITICAL ECONOMIES

The basic difference between capitalist and socialist political economies revolves around the role of government. Socialist political economies are based upon the assumption that government must be involved if the goal to deliver the greatest good to the greatest numbers is to be realized. This can be scripted in a number of different ways.

For a **socialist political economic script** to exist, **government** must **regulate production** and/or the **distribution of goods** and **services.** One possibility is that government owns all means of production and controls distribution as well. Another possibility, and one more prevalent in Europe, is for production to remain mostly in private hands, but government programs are used to increase the availability of goods and services to citizens. This places the role on government more on the distribution than production side of the process.

This usually means higher taxes than in a country like the United States, where government programs to help the less fortunate are constantly in jeopardy. Slashing taxes in the United States, a popular refrain of conservatives, is just another way to deny benefits for those who do not have the resources to access them. In European countries, taxes subsidize healthcare for everyone, whereas in the United States, healthcare is rationed on the ability to pay. European governments also spend more on housing, education, retirement programs, and other social programs than we do in the United States.

Moral entrepreneurs for the capitalist political economic model in the United States have successfully linked socialism to discredited Marxist regimes. It has been a successful selling ploy. Conveniently missing from these accounts is the fact that virtually all of the advanced economic countries in the world today do more for their citizens than we do here in the United States.

PEDDLING POLITICAL ECONOMY SCRIPTS

The contrast between capitalist and socialist political economies is striking. It is particularly useful when comparing how different social philosophies inform these options. Quite clearly, the capitalist model favors the individual and personal economic benefits. The socialist model is based more upon the attempt to provide the greatest economic benefits for the greatest numbers.

Many proponents of the capitalist political economy model in the United States claim that the best government is no government. What they really want to promote is limiting government if it encroaches on their profits. These same capitalists are more than willing to accept government intervention when it sustains or improves their profits.

Relying on government to protect or increase profits has been common among capitalists in the United States. Most of our foreign policy since World War I has been a captive to this interest. It is why the government of the United States helped to overthrow the freely elected socialist government in Chile and replace it with a dictatorship. More often than not, claims that our foreign policies are designed to promote freedom are only a ploy to challenge governments that are not friendly to American capitalism.

Advocates of a capitalist political economy that limits government often contradict themselves in areas besides foreign policy. A prime example is when a corporation forces taxpayers to help them fund an operation. This has become a standard operating procedure of American companies who threaten to move to where governments will give them the best package of financial incentives. Those incentives usually involve tax breaks that other taxpayers must cover.

Using taxpayer money to finance the profit of a corporation is not limited to tax breaks. Pharmaceutical companies benefit enormously from taxpayer dollars that fund university drug research around the country. This means that much of the research and development costs are picked up by taxpayers. This amounts to a subsidy that enhances corporate profits through taxpayer contributions.

Extorting money from taxpayers has become a favorite tactic of sport owners who threaten to move unless the local citizens pass bond issues to help finance the building of a new stadium or arena. This tactic helped George W. Bush parley a relatively small investment in the Texas Rangers baseball team into a windfall when it was sold at an enormous profit after he and the other investors forced the community of Arlington to finance a substantial portion of the Ranger's new stadium complex. The good folks of Arlington subsidized the profits gained by Bush and the other investors. Such governmental subsidies clearly contradict the public posture of moral entrepreneurs for capitalist political economies who argue that government must stay out of the business of business.

CHAPTER 12
AMERICAN CONTRADICTIONS

A **coherent agreed upon script** is sustained by **values** and **beliefs** that are **consistent.** A **coherent agreed upon script** provides for stable and predictable interaction. The existence of **value contradictions** creates an underlying instability that makes predicting interaction more difficult.

VALUES

A **value** is a **generalized principle** or **standard of judgment** that influences the behavioral preferences in a social script. Because it is a generalized principle or standard, a value creates an underlying commonality to more specific behavioral preferences. If someone values freedom, then that person will endorse scripts that enhance it and condemn those that deny it.

Compliance with self-preferences that reflect a value is personally rewarding. Compliance creates a self-reward because values represent core elements in someone's ideal self-concept. Behavior that is consistent with those values affirms that ideal self-concept.

Compliance with the interaction preferences of someone else is likely to prompt a social reward. If values are agreed upon and shared by people who interact with each other, self-rewards and social rewards are mutually gratifying. This value consistency is what provides for script coherence across behavioral preferences.

VALUE CONTRADICTIONS

Value contradictions cause complexities that undermine stability in social relationships. Value contradictions appear in two distinct ways. The first involves a conflicted social self. If someone internalizes contradictory values, then a reward/cost dilemma can arise. Compliance with a behavioral preference reflecting one value produces a self-reward, while at the same time creating a self-cost associated with violating a behavioral preference reflecting the contradictory value.

The second involves situations where groups in a society hold contradictory values. These contradictory values are the basis for widespread role conflict. It is widespread compared to specific behavioral preferences. An example from the 1960s can be used to illustrate this point. Hippies generally despised or distrusted all authority. This value manifested itself in more specific behavioral preferences, such as despising or distrusting the authority of parents, the police, and political leaders. This value disposition collided with that the dominant group and many other Americans who admired and celebrated these same authorities.

Meanwhile, for many Americans the value line drawn between the most ardent hippies and supporters of traditional authority was not so clear. Many who leaned toward more conventional behavior toward authorities also had admiration for the free spirit of hippies who defied those conventions. There were also hippies who, while defying societal conventions in both appearance and behavior, had some misgivings.

This mixture of personal and interpersonal dynamics involving value contradictions in a society produces an unstable combination of rewards and costs. This chapter looks at some value contradictions that cause conflict and tension among Americans. The conflict results from conflicting value messages.

SACRED AND SECULAR

Americans have been and remain conflicted over the extent to which society should be governed by religious principles. Those on the **sacred** side think that religion should permeate all aspects of life, including government. Those on the **secular** side think that religion should be confined to the personal lives of people and not be allowed to intrude upon government.

The sacred/secular value dispute becomes most intense when the focus is on government. This is because the First Amendment specifies that Congress shall make no law that restricts the free exercise of religion. However, the same amendment also stipulates that government shall not make any law "respecting the establishment of religion."

The latter is often interpreted as the separation of church and state declaration. In the election where Bush won a second term as President, the sacred and secular value dispute was pronounced. On one extreme were Christian fundamentalists who advocate the infusion of their religious values on government. Bush signaled that he was on their side with coded language that usually avoided direct references to God and the Scriptures by substituting terms like "faith-based initiatives." Bush also signaled his support for more sacred intrusions on government by proposing a Constitutional Amendment against gay marriage. His efforts to reverse the governmental right for women to have an abortion signaled his proreligion values. Since reelection Bush has reinvigorated governmental opposition to stem cell research based on the religious argument that life begins at conception.

On the other extreme there are secular advocates who think that that any reference to God or religion should be strictly forbidden. Any religious reference, such as "In God We Trust," which appears on currency should be eliminated. So too should prayers by public officials or by others on property paid for by taxpayers. People on this side are also the most adamantly against religious displays such as the Ten Commandments in places paid for by taxpayers.

Many Americans feel ambivalence about the sacred/secular value dispute. Many are willing to allow for some religious expression such as "Under God" but feel that denying government funding for stem cell research goes to far. A value contradiction often underscores this ambivalence, such as valuing the potential for saving lives through stem cell research more than concern that destroying a fertilized cell is the equivalent of murder.

Sometimes issues are so subtle that many don't recognize the underlying value contradiction. For instance, the government clearly permits marriage ceremonies based upon religion. To deny this would violate the First Amendment. But this is separate from the legal status of marriage as recognized by the government. Contrary to conventional wisdom, you cannot get married by Elvis in Las Vegas. Elvis can preside over the ceremony but only someone authorized by the government can sign the marriage certificate and make it legal. Because it is unlikely that an ordained minister, priest, or rabbi is likely to be present, that task is performed by a local justice of the peace.

THE INDIVIDUAL AND THE COLLECTIVITY

Another contradiction Americans experience is based on values that celebrate both the **individual** and the **collectivity.** This contradiction is illustrated by the relative amount of emphasis Americans place on **individual** versus **team** accomplishments.

The celebration of the individual can be traced to the Founding Fathers of the United States. The Declaration of Independence talks about the individual right to life, liberty, and the pursuit of happiness. The Bill of Rights gives voice to the importance of the individual through its protections against government.

The fact that the Founding Fathers were overwhelmingly Protestant may also have set the scene for the American fondness for the individual. Max Weber (1904–1905), a German sociologist, outlined the significance of Protestantism in this regard. A fundamental element in the Protestant Reformation is a diminished role for the clergy in the everyday lives of parishioners. Whereas Catholics depend upon the Church to mediate salvation through rituals such as confession, for Protestants the matter of salvation is either predetermined or left to their own acts.

The Protestant fondness for individualism is also compatible with the emphasis on a capitalist political economy that was favored by the Founding Fathers and subsequent generations of successful and influential business elite. The contention that capitalism is the product of individual effort is a familiar claim by moral entrepreneurs. But the American fondness for individualism is registered elsewhere as well. In sports, we are addicted to selecting someone as the Most Valuable Player (MVP) on a team.

Notice that MVPs are normally associated with team sports. This creates a conflict with an emphasis on being a team player. Anyone who has played a team sport recognizes this inherent conflict. Coaches love the cliché that states "There is no I in the word team." Yet these same coaches indulge themselves in the annual ritual of selecting who is the MVP on the team.

As sports in America moved from amateur to paid athletes competing in professional sports, the emphasis on the individual became even more pronounced. To move on to professional sports requires developing impressive individual statistics. Having been on a winning team is less important than amassing personal data that is attractive to scouts and professional franchises.

For the few who graduate to professional team sports, the pressure to amass personal statistics continues. Professional athletes are paid according to data on their individual accomplishments. Status and respect becomes intertwined with how much an athlete is paid. Those raking in unbelievable money often go through the ritual of thanking their coaches and teammates, but most Americans associate esteem with money and not playing a supportive role.

This does not mean that team accomplishments don't matter to sports fans in the United States. The morale of entire cities often rises and falls with the success of its professional sports franchises. The same is true with colleges and universities that often pay their coaches in major sports like football and basketball more than they pay the president of their school.

The dynamic tension between American values that celebrate both the individual and the team are not limited to the world of sports. American corporations are constantly struggling with this duality. Witness the number of corporations that present themselves to their employees as a family. Their point is that family members are loyal. Family members form a team.

Yet these same corporations give bonuses and promotions on the basis of individual accomplishments. This means that to be successful, someone who seeks advancement must be able to impress their bosses with their unique accomplishments. The problem is that crass individualism may be seen as suggesting that someone is not a good team member. So someone with career aspirations must learn how to balance giving credit to the team while siphoning off enough personal credit to get the attention of their bosses.

During 2002, Americans also witnessed greed by corporate officials who lined their own pockets at the expense of their shareholders and employees. Lying about revenues and expenses to inflate stocks to enrich themselves was common. But the outrage many Americans expressed over these excesses of individualism at the expense of collectivities, such as employees, illustrates the shifting dynamic that exists between the American fondness for individualism and loyalty to the team.

WAR AND PATRIOTISM

The value contradiction between the individual and collectivity plays out elsewhere in American society. It is closely related to the relative emphasis on **war** and **patriotism.** It surfaces whenever the United States decides to go to war.

One expectation is that when the **United States is threatened,** its citizens must be prepared to **sacrifice their personal interests** for the **good of society.** The ultimate sacrifice is a willingness to give one's life for the good of the society. A **patriot** is defined as someone who is willing to make this ultimate sacrifice for the "team."

But the Vietnam War and invasion of Iraq suggest less than a comfortable fit between war and patriotism in the United States. A critical factor is the extent to which someone accepts that these wars were/are necessary for the security of the country. An opponent of the Vietnam War may have been so because he or she did not believe that American security was at stake. Moral entrepreneurs for the Vietnam War insisted that the very existence of the American way of life was at stake and that those who opposed the war were unpatriotic. Moral entrepreneurs against the Vietnam War insisted that it was a waste of young American soldiers. Among those who served and died in Vietnam, some did so because they thought it was their patriotic duty, while others were forced by the draft to serve.

Moral entrepreneurs for the invasion of Iraq and the continued presence of American forces there insist that it is the centerpiece in the War on Terror. Those who oppose the invasion of Iraq argue that it wastes valuable resources that could be better used elsewhere to fight terrorist threats to the United States. Those within this camp add that the war in Iraq increases hatred and terrorist recruits. Proponents of the war counter that it is better to kill terrorists in Iraq than at home.

Values come into play when moral entrepreneurs use emotional labels to brand the opposition. Moral entrepreneurs for the war in Iraq question the patriotism of those who oppose it. Moral entrepreneurs against the war smear Bush when they question his real motivation. Was Bush trying to avenge Saddam Hussein's attempt to assassinate his father and other family members? Was Bush trying to promote opportunities for his buddies in the oil industry? Linking alleged motivations to the question of whether or not it is worth the loss of American lives creates the emotional linkage.

There is another issue that shapes value disputes involving patriotism and war that can be best illustrated by the game of chess. The game of chess presents an interesting metaphor for war. The most expendable are the least educated and those of the lowest rank. They are the equivalent of pawns in the game of chess. These are the ones most likely to die in a war effort. Those at higher ranks and skill levels are more protected and therefore less exposed to death.

This hierarchy of risk within the military is one point. The other point is, who benefits the most from the military involvement? Is it the king? In societies without a king, is it the most advantaged within a society?

This issue is the center of a debate within American society. Why is it that the American military has often supported dictators in some countries while not in others? The reality is that we have a long history of supporting dictators that give American companies access to their natural resources, cheap labor, and markets.

More recently, the terrorist attacks of 9/11 have encouraged our government to support dictatorships who express a willingness to support our efforts to eliminate future acts of terrorism against us. Critics complain that this strategy makes the United States look like hypocrites because of our frequently declared policy of encouraging democracies around the world. Giving military aid to dictatorships is hardly the best method for encouraging this objective!

The question of who benefits from American military excursions around the world is becoming more and more relevant. The war on terrorism is a case in point. So far, terrorists have primarily targeted economic symbols such as the World Trade Center, governmental facilities such as the embassies in Africa, and military installations such as the Pentagon. Exactly how much of a threat does this pose for the average American?

To the extent that other potential targets, such as sports arenas, shopping malls, nuclear power plants, water supplies, are seen as credible is the extent to which more Americans will share in a sense of threat. To the extent that the perception of threat is associated with urban areas is the extent to which rural Americans may be more concerned about healthcare than dying from a terrorist attack. To the extent that any or all of these possibilities is perceived as having a negative economic impact on jobs is the extent to which more Americans will support the War on Terrorism.

It is interesting to think about contradictory claims associated with the war on terrorism. Some moral entrepreneurs in the United States view it as a religious crusade against Muslim heretics. Others caution that it is really not a religious crusade against Islam, but rather a war against radicals who fail to understand the Koran. Still others claim that it is really a war over fundamental values such as freedom and democracy. And some wonder why our government is willing to bomb some governments that suppress these values but not others that are equally offensive.

An even more fundamental contradiction for many Americans involves different philosophies for dealing with conflict resolution. Some believe that the only solution is coercion. Proponents of this viewpoint are also likely to believe that spanking children is essential to control them. The coercive alternative to conflict resolution is compatible with the American background script that celebrates violence.

Others in the United States believe that diplomacy is a better way to deal with conflicts. Negotiations and compromise is the preferred strategy. Proponents claim that violence only begets more violence. Moral entrepreneurs for the coercive alternative like to label advocates for negotiation and compromise as wimps.

Whether force or compromise is the most effective depends upon circumstances. Meanwhile, our own personal values and beliefs about the efficacy of either strategy influence the policies that we are willing to support. Only hindsight can tell us what didn't or might have worked in a given situation.

FREEDOM AND EQUALITY

The concepts of **freedom** and **equality** are familiar to anyone who knows much about the Founding Fathers and the history of the United States. These terms are found in documents ranging from the Declaration of Independence to the Constitution and the Bill of Rights. Less appreciated is the fact that these two concepts are not really compatible when one looks at their political implications.

The **Founding Fathers** declared that **liberty** or **freedom** is **natural right** of all people. In reality, the Founding Fathers did not exactly mean what this implies. Certainly, they were not about to extend these rights to slaves. Instead, their principle concern was to use this claim to justify their revolt against the British.

Freedom for the Founding Fathers was more than an abstract principle. For most of the Founding Fathers, there was a more practical issue. Most of the Founding Fathers had grown rich and prosperous during the colonial period. Freedom for them meant the right to preserve their wealth in the face of threats by the British to take it through taxation or other means.

The Constitution and Bill of Rights that became the core of the new American government after the Revolution were designed to protect citizens from tyranny. The Bill of Rights limits the potential for governmental tyranny through provisions that guarantee rights to assemble, due process, and so forth. But these rights did not necessarily protect the disadvantaged, such as slaves or workers, from abuses by the dominant group.

The contention that the best government is one that governs the least served the vested interests of the Founding Fathers as the dominant group at that time. Cries that government is too big and must be limited is a common complaint of moral entrepreneurs for the dominant group today. In the absence of governmental intervention, the powerful and wealthy are free to exercise their advantages at the expense of the less fortunate in society.

Another way to characterize what freedom means to the dominant group is that it helps them preserve and enhance their advantages. This spin on what freedom means collides with the concept of **equality.** To be free is not to be equal. To be born equal is not the same as having equal opportunities.

The call for equality is more likely to come from those who are relatively disadvantaged within a society. Freedom for those who are disadvantaged means little without opportunities. Their call for equality is not necessarily a call to eliminate all disparities within a society. Often it is nothing more than a plea for fairness and an opportunity to improve their situations.

Those who are disadvantaged can appeal to the good will of the dominant group and hope that they will be charitable. But dominant groups are usually reluctant to give up their advantages. The dominant group views calls for equality or more fairness as threats to what they have accumulated. The disadvantaged often rely on the government as a means for improving fairness and equality, which is why the dominant group often promotes a limited role for government. Members of the dominant group often see government as a threat to their advantages.

This is why their moral entrepreneurs constantly complain about taxes. Reducing the tax base is one of their favorite ploys for reducing the potential for government programs that threaten their advantages. These moral entrepreneurs often exploit antigovernment sentiments or the strains that taxes do place on Americans who are struggling with making ends meet.

During the 1980s, the Reagan Administration advanced this agenda with the claim that leaving wealth in the hands of the wealthy would trickle down to the masses through their investments in the economy and job creation. This made tax reductions for the wealthy seem like an act of benevolence. The reality is that this strategy contributed to an unprecedented growth in the gap between the richest and poorest Americans.

More recently, the Bush administration successfully peddled a tax reduction script that disproportionately benefits wealthy Americans. Their justifications for these reductions ranged from dusting off the trickle down theory to claims that it was essential to jump-start a faltering the economy. When these claims seemed to falter, some in the Bush administration resorted to the charge that it was unpatriotic not to support their tax reductions.

Attacks on taxes and big government as threats have been quite effective. Such attacks help distract attention from how corporate and other interests of the dominant group contribute to the plight of many. For instance, rather than blaming bank mergers and decisions for families losing theirs farms, some militant groups in states such as Montana are convinced that the government is to blame. The fact that eviction notices are usually served by government officials such as sheriffs reinforces this perception that helps prevent them from directing their anger toward banks or corporate America.

Issues among Americans concerning freedom and equality intersect with the contradiction that exists between celebrating the individual or collectivity. Cultural scripts that feature the individual play into the hands of moral entrepreneurs who celebrate the virtue of freedom over equality. It helps sell their message that freedom trumps a commitment by Americans to their fellow citizens. It allows them to disguise personal greed as a virtue.

THE PRINCIPLE OF HEDONISM

The principle of hedonism was borrowed from British philosophers such as Jeremy Bentham. The basic idea of **hedonism** is that the pursuit of pleasure should be the measure of all morality. Hedonism comes packaged in two different scripts.

Personal hedonism views hedonism as an individual right. This is what the Declaration of Independence emphasizes when it talks about the right of individuals to pursue happiness. Because of its emphasis on the individual person, hedonism favors capitalist political economy scripts.

Collective hedonism shifts the focus from the individual to the collectivity. It is based upon what Bentham described as the **hedonistic calculus.** The hedonistic calculus is a principle that states that the best society is one that creates the greatest pleasure for the greatest numbers. The concepts of collective hedonism and the hedonistic calculus favor socialist political economy scripts.

VALUE CLUSTERS

A **value cluster** is a set of values held by people. The term was not used at the time, but the distinction between a **capitalist** and a **socialist political economy** model represent value clusters. Now it is possible to elaborate on this distinction.

A **capitalist political economy** model celebrates **freedom,** the **individual,** and **personal hedonism.** This translates into the value cluster that asserts that the individual should be free from government interference and be allowed to maximize his or her personal pleasure. This is basically a win/lose model of society where some are allowed to benefit at the expense of others.

A **socialist political economy** model **celebrates equality,** the **collectivity,** and the **collective hedonism.** This translates into a value cluster that asserts that government must provide equality of opportunities for all of its citizens and provide the greatest good for the greatest numbers by curbing excessive accumulation of wealth and power by some at the expense of others. This is basically a win/win compromise model of society that requires the more advantaged to help those less advantaged.

Although America is often defined as a capitalist political economy, and certainly leans in that direction, Americans are more ambivalent than its most outspoken advocates admit. Many Americans have conflicted social selves that waffle between seeking to maximize personal hedonism for themselves and feeling a certain amount of guilt about it being at the expense of the less fortunate. Sealing themselves off from reminders of those who need help is one method for dealing with this personal dilemma. This is why some are so enthusiastic about eliminating "street people" from their sight lines, out of sight out of mind. Other signs of an underlying tension are behavioral rationalizations such as "I deserve what I got" which implies that those less fortunate deserve their plight.

Another sign of the tension between personal and more altruistic dispositions is a cycle. The 1920s were a period of personal excess in the United States that celebrated the lifestyles of the rich and famous. The Depression of the 1930s encouraged more people to support government programs to help the less fortunate. World War II brought Americans together as a collectivity. Soon after the war, new prosperity saw an increase in personal gains as people became were able to buy cars and houses in the suburbs. The civil rights movement of the late 1960s reminded people that not everyone was prospering. Some were being left behind or left out. Civil rights legislation to correct racial imbalances was soon followed by the War on Poverty. During the 1970s and 1980s there was a return to a personal emphasis. Looking out for number one (oneself) became the operating principle.

LIFE, LIBERTY, AND THE PURSUIT OF HAPPINESS

The Founding Fathers championed the **principle** that people have the **right** to **life, liberty,** and the **pursuit of happiness.** They believed that a tyrannical government is the biggest obstacle to these natural rights. A tyrannical government can jeopardize the realization of these virtues. But just being free from oppression is not enough. People must also have access to the resources that make life, liberty, and the pursuit of happiness a possibility.

Probably the most popular attempt to reconcile the issue of freedom with the opportunity for happiness is contained in stories associated with Horatio Alger. These stories, which were written during the early 1920s, feature poor heroes who pull themselves up by their bootstraps and become rich and successful through honesty and hard work. These stories feature freedom as a necessary condition for the realization of these virtues. For people who are free from tyranny, these virtues are the instruments by which happiness is measured by money and success is acquired.

These stories reinforced the claim that free people can become whatever they want to be. The only obstacle to success, wealth, and happiness is an unwillingness to engage in honest hard work. Missing from this happy scenario is any consideration of how circumstances affect outcomes.

The capacity of the American economy to absorb millions of poor migrants into its industrial growth is such a circumstance. Originally, many of these newcomers to the United States were poorly educated and unable to read or write, but jobs in meat processing plants and other factories absorbed them nonetheless. Whether their relative success was due to this economic circumstance or their devotion to honest labor is debatable.

Yet, a popular theme that continues is one that blames poverty on personal qualities rather than circumstances. Congressional motivation for welfare reform in the 1990s was based primarily on the claim that welfare undermines a commitment to hard work. The fact that the majority of poor Americans were working at the time was largely ignored. The fact that many

Americans who have moved from welfare to the workforce are still poor suggests that more than motivation is required for the good life. Equally important is access to jobs that pay enough to make the pursuit of life, liberty, and happiness a genuine possibility.

But what is the solution as good paying manufacturing jobs give way to service sector jobs that pay less? One solution is to improve education to make the American workforce more attractive to our own and outside companies. But as the demand for a more educated workforce increases, Americans seem immersed in squabbles based upon individual rather than collective calculations. Voucher programs are sold as alternatives to decaying public schools that may help some but are likely to leave large numbers of American youngsters behind.

Cultural scripts associated with values such as individuality, freedom, and personal hedonism make it difficult for Americans to understand issues from a more collective framework. A related problem is that corporate America, with its obsession with quarterly statements, has reinforced a short-term view. Increasing funds to improve decaying educational infrastructures and obsolete programs are greeted with alarm by those who believe that it will increase business costs.

But not providing funding creates some dire long-term possibilities. Population projections suggest that not too long from now the majority of people entering our labor force will be minorities. Does this mean that in the future minorities who already are educationally deprived, as measured by enrollments in colleges and universities, will be even more disadvantaged? If so, what does this mean in terms of the Founding Fathers contention about the right of people to life, liberty, and the pursuit of happiness?

There is also a potential threat for Americans who are relatively well educated. Some of them were unconcerned when lower-skilled American jobs were lost to Third World countries. Now some of them are worried that American companies will import more highly skilled cheap labor from other countries. This has already been going on in high-tech areas, where companies get special permission to import skilled labor from countries such as India. The practice has also displaced many high-tech workers in the United States.

More recently, some companies have started to use skilled labor, such as high-tech engineers in India, through electronic interfaces that allow communication from remote sites with headquarters in the United States. This allows for coordination of efforts without requiring the physical presence of these workers in the United States. The advantages are these companies pay workers in India far less than if than if they were in the United States. This strategy is likely to grow in importance because companies need not worry about immigration issues that might stop the flow of foreign labor.

All of this, coupled with the frenzy among American corporations to downsize (fire) white-collar jobs to cut costs, has created a new realization. Many of those fired are unable to get a job in spite of their desire and motivation to work. Moreover, many highly skilled workers who were downsized but recovered by becoming outside paid consultants are finding their jobs in jeopardy when the economy declines. Companies first cut costs by downsizing. Under worsening economic conditions, cutting consultant costs becomes more of a reality. So much for the Horatio Alger stories.

All of these comments point to a single incompatibility that the Founding Fathers never dealt with concerning the right people have to life, liberty, and the pursuit of happiness. Life, liberty, and happiness require resources. In the absence of opportunities and access to these resources, the contention that people have a right to life, liberty, and the pursuit of happiness becomes an empty cliché.

DEMOCRACY IN AMERICA

One of the **most cherished values** in American history is our commitment to **democratic principles.** When considering this commitment, it is crucial to distinguish between it as a **cultural ideal** and a **reality.** This is the source of it as a fundamental contradiction within our society.

The reality has been that since its inception, those in charge have systematically attempted to exclude many people from the democratic process. This can be seen in terms of the most fundamental element of any democratic system, which is right of all citizens to express their views through the vote. Women did not receive this right until 1920. That was more than a century after the government was formed. And then it barely passed Congress.

The fact that slaves represented as much as 20 percent of the colonial population did not persuade the Founding Fathers to give them the right to vote. That right was not received until after the Civil War with passage of the Fifteenth Amendment to the Constitution. Even with this right, generations of African Americans were denied it through Jim Crow laws in the South.

During the 2000 election campaign for president between Bush and Gore, more problems emerged concerning obstacles to democracy. In states such as Florida and Illinois, outdated machines and voting procedures affected whether or not thousands of votes cast by African Americans and other minorities were counted. Publicity concerning these events cast doubt upon whether or not President Bush was really elected through a democratic process. Some still believe that it was the Supreme Court decision that ended recounts in Florida that elected Bush.

Distortions such as these, and the limited willingness of local and state governments to remedy them, contribute to the contradiction between democracy as an ideal and a reality in American society. The tremendous influx of money into elections is another factor that adds to this distortion. The same is true of the enormous impact well-funded lobbyists and political action committees (PACs) have on the political process.

WORK AND PLAY

Many Americans have difficulty with **play** because it is associated with unproductive self-indulgence. Yet, the principle of hedonism talks about the right to happiness. This suggests that it is okay to be happy, even if happiness is derived from play.

The problem is that many Americans have internalized the **work ethic** to the extent that for them it is the only legitimate source of happiness. Happiness obtained through unproductive and self-indulgent playful activities is seen as wrong. Play is for children, not adults. For these people, play creates guilt rather than pleasure.

For others in American society, play is a more significant source of happiness than their work. The pleasure that they derive from work is virtually nonexistent. This makes leisure time activities their most important source of pleasure.

The contradiction between valuing work and play can lead to an interesting dynamic. Those not entirely comfortable with play as a source of pleasure may find it necessary to convert it into work. An example is someone who gains pleasure from jogging but feels guilty about it being an unproductive activity. One solution is to legitimate their indulgence by entering officially sanctioned races. This allows them to see their everyday jogging rituals as preparation for competitive and therefore productive events.

THE WORK ETHIC AND FAMILY VALUES

Many Americans experience conflict over **values** that celebrate both **work** and **family.** For some, the tensions revolve around a **conflicted social self.** Many who have internalized a strong work ethic find that it conflicts with their family obligations. When the boss demands more hours at work, they feel compelled to comply. To do otherwise would make them feel guilty. But the hours spent on the job are hours that are lost to spending time with their families. This makes them feel guilty. The fact that the number of weekly hours on the job has increased to nearly 50 for male employees and 45 for female employees makes this conflict all the more acute.

Role conflict involving work and family values is not limited to feelings of guilt. Some who prefer to spend time with their family may worry about losing their jobs should they offend their boss. Or someone who prefers work compared to time spent with the family may feel pressures from the kids and spouse.

In the past, the script gave Dad a pass on raising the kids and spending time with the family. His primary obligation was as a breadwinner. This provided men who internalized the role of breadwinner with an excuse for not spending enough time with the family.

Meanwhile, the same script gave the daily burden of raising and dealing with the kids to dear old Mom. This played well with stay-at-home Moms, but caused problems for women who worked outside their homes. For working Moms who internalize their role as homemaker and who also feel a responsibility toward their jobs, the conflict can be extremely stressful.

Some moral entrepreneurs blame this stress on scripts that encourage mothers to seek careers. Women who work are characterized as women who choose a job over their families. But working moms often do not have a choice. For single moms, the only option to work in the past was often some form of welfare. But welfare reform has insisted that to qualify, single moms must spend more time getting trained or working. Married women have also found that work outside the house has become increasingly necessary to help the family make ends meet.

Moral entrepreneurs who insist that the primary role for women is to raise their kids and support their husbands often ignore these circumstances. This simply worsens the guilt many women feel when they are unable to fulfill mother and wife roles that they have internalized. Tensions are only increased when their husbands and children complain about their failures as wives and mothers.

Sometimes the pressure moms experience comes from moral entrepreneurs who represent different positions concerning work and family. But contradiction between demands of work and those of the family don't always involve a collision between different moral entrepreneurs. Sometimes the same moral entrepreneur promotes the contradiction. An example is when a politician preaches the virtue of being a stay-at-home mom but refuses to support legislation requiring employers to pay a living wage for the head of a household, which forces more mothers to work.

A related contradiction arises from quarters that preach family values and who were also the principle backers of welfare reform. This is especially pronounced when family values are associated with a traditional role for women as mothers and wives. One of the consequences of welfare reform has been to take poor moms out of their households by placing them in training programs or the workplace. This means that they have less time to spend with their families. This is hardly the stuff of what family values suggests.

MATERIALISM AND SELF-FULFILLMENT

Materialism is a preoccupation with possessing expensive items such as clothes, cars, and houses. **Self-fulfillment** involves engaging in activities that are intrinsically valuable. Contradictions arise when people value materialism as a symbol of success, but find the effort deprives them of behavior that is more fulfilling.

Conspicuous consumption involves the lavish display of wealth through the possession of valued goods, such as fashionable clothes, large houses, and prestigious cars. Conspicuous consumption for many is the means by which they get affirmation from others by impressing them and getting positive feedback. Advertisers have effectively sold Americans on the virtues of consumption as the measure of self-worth.

But unless someone inherits wealth, conspicuous consumption usually requires accumulating wealth. The cost is the long hours necessary to accumulate that wealth. Those long hours deny the time for other valued activities, such as spending time with children and family. The dilemma revolves around the ego rewards brought about by work and the capacity to conspicuously consume and guilt over unfulfilled opportunities elsewhere.

Some successful people reach this point and decide to quit or cut back on their work schedules. Now rewards from more fulfilling activities are diminished by costs incurred by less ego reinforcement through conspicuous consumption. Although the tension between materialism and other fulfilling activities can be experienced by a person, the contradiction can be expressed through cycles. President Kennedy said, "do not ask what your country can do for you but what you can do for your country." This inspired many to join the Peace Corps as a more fulfilling opportunity than pursuing material goals.

The 1960s were also the time when hippies renounced materialism and sought fulfillment by dropping out of society. This was seen by some as a threat the very existence of our economy. But advertisers are clever and it did not take them long to capitalize by bringing consumerism to alternative pursuits. As work became less fulfilling, many Americans turned to leisure time activities such as jogging. Soon joggers were inundated with products guaranteed to improve their performance and pleasure. Work was necessary not to conspicuously consume, as with lavish homes and lifestyles, but to pay for more fulfilling leisure activities.

CHAPTER 13
CONFORMITY AND DEVIANCE

Conformity occurs whenever someone complies with a behavioral preference contained within a social script. Conformity can be with self-preferences or behavioral preferences of someone else. Conformity with self-preferences yields self-rewards. Conformity with the preferences of someone else yields social rewards from that person.

Deviance occurs whenever someone violates a behavioral preference contained within a social script. Deviance that violates self-preferences yields self-costs, such as guilt or a loss of self-esteem. Deviance that violates the preferences of someone else yields social costs from that person.

DOMINANT GROUPS, THE MAINSTREAM, AND MINORITIES

Both **dominant groups** and the **mainstream** can back their behavioral preferences with power and credibility advantages over minorities. Most sociological theories of deviance that will be covered in this chapter are based upon a concern by dominant and mainstream groups in America to better understand the actions of those who deviate from the behavioral preferences contained in their social scripts.

Through grants and scholarship, sociologists obliged and formulated explanation for social deviance. Dominant and mainstream groups used these explanations to exercise their credibility and power advantages over groups that engaged in behavior that offended them. Juvenile delinquents, especially those in gangs, came under the most scrutiny and efforts by representatives of dominant and mainstream groups, such as the police, to control their behavior.

Quite often, the juveniles who drew the most attention were in poor minority communities. Moral entrepreneurs for dominant and mainstream groups captured the credibility advantage because of their relatively high location in the social hierarchy of credibility. This allowed them to identify juvenile delinquents with minority communities. This deflected attention away from misdeeds committed by children in their own communities and funneled police and other community resources toward the control of minority children.

This is not unlike early research on small groups by sociologists that was funded by business and government interests that wanted to learn more about workers in order to better manipulate them. Business and government agencies represented dominant and mainstream groups at the time. Workers were minorities that suffered a power and credibility disadvantage.

But the fact that control was the objective and minorities the target should not be allowed to distract from the numerous insights sociologists gained concerning human dynamics. Many of the concepts developed within the context of studying deviant groups as defined by dominant and mainstream groups have a more universal application. An effort will be made to expand these insights and apply concepts from sociological theories of deviance to other situations.

AUTONOMY

Autonomy is the capacity to function independently from others. It is the opposite of dependence. **Anonymity** exists when people and their activities are not known to others. Both are relevant to sociological research on deviant groups.

Workers had little autonomy and therefore little anonymity when confronted by management. If management wanted to send in sociologists to study them, there was little that they could do about it. To not cooperate, or at least tolerate the presence of researchers, could have serious repercussions.

Sociological access to street gangs was more complicated. Street gangs, especially violent ones, have a certain degree of autonomy that makes it difficult for outsiders to control them. The violence that provides a measure of autonomy for street gangs can also be used to deny access to outsiders like sociologists. Preventing others from observing them created a certain measure of anonymity for street gangs.

To study street gangs, sociologists had to either gain the trust of the gang leader(s) or have access to an informant that had insider information. Those sociologists who had direct access or access through an informant to a street gang usually published the results of their research in journals or books. Dominant and mainstream groups often drew upon this knowledge to control such street gangs in the future.

Whether by design or unintentional, the knowledge generated by sociological research and theories on street gangs and other "deviant" groups had a common outcome. In the hands of representatives for dominant and mainstream groups, this knowledge reduced the amount of autonomy for such "deviant" groups because it could be used to control them. Insights into their activities also helped the police and other agencies to develop more effective and often subtle ways of gaining information about them.

SOCIOLOGICAL THEORIES OF DEVIANCE

Early sociological theories of deviance took for granted definitions of deviance as provided by dominant and mainstream groups. Most shared the opinion of dominant and mainstream groups that deviance was a threat to society. This meant that behavior that offended dominant and mainstream groups also concerned sociologists studying it.

Only later did sociologists step back and realize definitions of deviance and what constitutes acceptable behavior results from a social process. What makes a behavior deviant is not its character or any specific quality. Rather, it results from a social process whereby those with the most credibility are able to persuade people that a certain behavior is unacceptable.

Our discussion begins with this crucial insight and then proceeds to look at other sociological theories of deviance. To do so disrupts the chronological order in which the theories emerged, but chronology is mainly significant to those who are interested in studying the history of sociological thinking about deviance. To use the insights provided by these theories to advance your ability to think sociologically does not require an elaborate acquaintance with historical questions such as which theorist influenced whom.

IS ANY ACT INHERENTLY DEVIANT?

In a **society** where there is a **single agreed upon script,** members often believe certain behaviors are inherently deviant. Interpretations concerning what constitutes a deviant act are taken for granted. Certain acts, by their very nature, seem offensive and wrong. This attitude is reinforced to the extent that members have limited exposure to social scripts from other communities or societies.

Becker (1963) took issue with the contention that certain acts are **inherently deviant.** By this he meant that there is nothing in the act itself that makes the act unacceptable. **No act is universally condemned.** Acts considered deviant and unacceptable in one society may be seen as acceptable and encouraged in other societies.

You might wonder about this point. Aren't certain acts such as murder universally condemned? Don't all societies have norms against killing?

Suppose that one found out that all societies have some restrictions on murder. Does this mean that murder represents a universal form of deviance? Upon closer inspection, the details from different cultures reveal how misleading this statement would be. The generalization conceals the fact that cultural scripts vary enormously over who can or cannot be murdered. In some societies, the script allows a man to kill his wife if she is unfaithful. Other societies would condemn such an action and declare it to be deviant.

Another example involves the death penalty as a type of murder. Many countries do permit the government to kill citizens who violate certain norms. The United States is the only advanced industrial country that does so. Organizations such as Amnesty International routinely condemn the United States for this practice.

Anthropologists have long argued that the incest taboo is a cultural universal. The incest taboo prohibits sexual relationships between parents and children, siblings, or other designated relatives. Doesn't this cast suspicion on Becker's claim that no act is inherently deviant? The problem is that even anthropologists provide exceptions to this rule, such as royal marriages between siblings. But this is not the only evidence contrary to the claim that incest taboo is a cultural universal. Some data suggests that as many as 20 percent of American women have been sexually assaulted by a member of their family.

LABELING THEORY

Labeling theory begins with the contention that **no act is inherently deviant.** If no act is inherently deviant, it must not be something about the act itself that causes people to condemn it. It must have to do with social dynamics.

Labeling theory focuses on how moral entrepreneurs use their credibility advantages to define certain behaviors as deviant/unacceptable. The label in labeling theory is when moral entrepreneurs successfully "label" certain acts as deviant/unacceptable. This deviant label not only condemns the act, but simultaneously the stigma it attaches to the behavior tarnishes the reputation of anyone who commits it.

Moral entrepreneurs for **dominant** and **mainstream groups** play a key role in the labeling process. Becker's and other labeling theories were concerned about the credibility advantage of these moral entrepreneurs (social hierarchy of credibility). When Becker was criticized for being biased in favor of minorities, he responded by saying if he did advocate for them, it was merely to help balance the playing field. This translates into suggesting that he was using his credibility as a sociologist to give minorities a voice, rather than simply being drowned out by moral entrepreneurs for the advantaged within society.

MORAL ENTREPRENEURS

Originally, sociologists associated **moral entrepreneurs** with **dominant** and **mainstream** groups in society. They placed the focus on moral entrepreneurs who use ideas associated with the dominant ideology in a society to promote and try to favorably interpret results associated with social scripts. Their job was to justify existing arrangements that benefit the dominant group.

But now, sociologists recognize that there are also **moral entrepreneurs** who use counterideologists to discredit existing arrangements in a society that disadvantage minorities. The result is that sociologists look at the interplay between moral entrepreneurs for the dominant/mainstream groups and moral entrepreneurs who promote the interests of minorities.

A vital element is looking to see if moral entrepreneurs for dominant/mainstream groups have a credibility advantage over moral entrepreneurs for minorities. If so, the interest becomes trying to see why? Is it because moral entrepreneurs for the dominant/mainstream groups represent people in society who are more esteemed and are themselves high on the social hierarchy of credibility? Or is it because moral entrepreneurs for dominant/mainstream groups are themselves more highly esteemed and located higher in the social/expertise hierarchy of credibility than moral entrepreneurs for minorities?

A related set of questions can be applied to moral entrepreneurs for minorities. If the credibility deficit is based upon the fact that they are lower in the social/expertise hierarchies of credibility in the society, what can be done? Would having advocates better positioned in society to advocate for them increase the effectiveness of their messages meant to critique existing arrangements that disadvantage the minority in question. Or would it be better to inventory the values and beliefs of those in dominant/mainstream groups and play off them in presentations designed to gain credibility?

Moral entrepreneurs from the ranks of dominant and mainstream groups who promote counter ideologies for minorities are often more successful. But minority moral entrepreneurs such as Dr. Martin Luther King Jr. were able to draw on their reputations as ministers to enhance the credibility of their messages among members of dominant and mainstream groups. This is because ministers are among those who rank relatively high on the social credibility scale in the United States. The charismatic personality of Dr. King also did much to enhance his credibility among both minorities and members of dominant and mainstream groups in America.

The role of charismatic personalities in social movements is important for another reason. Usually the dominant group mobilizes its moral entrepreneurs to stigmatize those who promote a counter ideology. It takes an extraordinary person to reverse these deviant labels. It is what transforms a Joan of Arc from an outcast to a heroine.

THE MEDICALIZATION OF DEVIANCE

The **medicalization of deviance** occurs when moral entrepreneurs attach a medical label to deviant acts. An example would be when moral entrepreneurs label homosexuality as a disease. The point that no act is inherently deviant helps expose the mischief involved when medical concepts are applied to deviant acts.

Medical labels suggesting that a behavior is sick or unhealthy are meant to demean, discredit, and stigmatize a behavior. Medical labels are meant to imply that an offensive behavior is pathological. Pathology is the study of disease in medicine. The implication is that the behavior in question is a like a cancer on society.

A **sociopath** or **psychopath** is someone completely without a conscience. But these terms have often been used more casually to label someone who engages in a behavior that offends a group as sick. The term "psycho" is a variation on this labeling process.

If certain behaviors are defined as pathological, then what constitutes healthy behavior? You guessed it! **Healthy behavior** is behavior that conforms to the script that a moral entrepreneur favors.

A group that can define their behavioral preferences as healthy, while successfully condemning those of others as others as sick, has a credibility advantage. A religious group that can persuade audiences that an act they find offensive is "sinful" enjoys a similar credibility advantage. The only difference is that the former draws on medicine as an authority, while the latter draws on the Scriptures as an authority.

SOCIAL ORGANIZATION

Social organization occurs when a **single agreed upon social script** coordinates the activities of people within a society. It is that agreed upon social script that structures relationships between people. Many early sociologists associated a healthy society with one where there is a high degree of social organization.

Their reasoning was based upon an analogy between the health of an organism and societies. With an organism, life requires that the various parts (organs) work together in harmony. Disease occurs with breakdowns in the parts or the coordination between them.

The basic idea was that for a society to survive, all of its various activities (parts) must be coordinated. The problem with the analogy is that it reinforces the status quo in a society that may be structured by a dominant group that benefits at the expense of minorities. Another problem is that, unlike organisms, societies rarely die. While some societies have become extinct, the more common historical pattern is for social change to take place.

Thinking about the survival of a cultural tradition as the issue is more meaningful than talking about the literal survival of a society. The "death" of Rome was the collapse of the cultural institutions that shaped activities in the Roman Empire. Those who admired these cultural institutions and the grandeur that was once Rome depicted the conquering forces from the north as "barbarians." Western scholars enamored by the glory of Rome called the period after the fall of Rome the "dark ages." The Renaissance in Italy marked a return to the cultural traditions that were once Rome.

Terms like the "dark ages" and the Renaissance demonstrate that historians are not above the use of labels to identify social scripts and their related values and beliefs that they admired or condemn. Bias concerning behavioral preferences, values, and beliefs can creep in, even among scholars trying to be objective. The philosophical period labeled the Enlightenment is a case in point. Enlightenment thinkers believed that "reason" is the path to philosophical, political, and religious enlightenment. Monks and theologians who embraced "faith" as the true path thought enlightenment scholars audacious to think that human reason could ever match the infinite wisdom of God.

SOCIAL DISORGANIZATION THEORY

Social disorganization theory begins with the assumption that social order is good and social disorder is bad. The reasoning was based upon the aforementioned comparison between organisms and societies. A healthy society, just like an organism such as a human being, is one where all the parts work together.

Social disorganization theorists view **deviance** as the basis for **social disorder.** Deviance is unhealthy because it disrupts normal routines in society. An underlying assumption is that these normal routines are essential for survival. These theorists did not consider the possibility that these normal routines benefit the dominant group at the expense of minorities.

Assuming that deviance represents a social problem that must be addressed, these sociologists went about explaining what causes it. Their answer rested upon a comparison between traditional (gemeinschaft) and modern (gesellschaft) societies. Traditional societies were associated with small rural communities, while modern societies were associated with urban life concentrated in cities.

These sociologists argued that **social control in traditional societies** is effective because it is **based upon personal relationships** where everyone knows everyone else. It is these **informal (interpersonal) methods of social control** that the community exerts over those who defy its behavioral preferences that makes it so effective. Anyone who has lived in a small town knows that gossip and the threat of being isolated or "shunned" can be an extremely effective means of social control.

What happens when people **migrate from rural farms and communities** to **cities** is that this **interpersonal control dynamic** loses its effectiveness. City life is more anonymous and impersonal. Social control moves from informal methods of social control to more formal ones. Police replace family and neighbors as the means by which deviance is controlled.

The personal control dynamic is not entirely lost in cities. If the police are from the neighborhood that they patrol, their personal knowledge can be useful. The problem is that the community surrenders its personal methods of social control to the police, who become a substitute control mechanism. This separation is often depicted in crime movies or television shows. Once someone from the neighborhood becomes a cop, that person may be viewed differently by former friends.

There have been efforts more recently to capture some of the personal control dynamics in city neighborhoods. **Community policing** involves providing more personal contact with cops. Bringing cops into schools is one tactic. Another is to create a version of the "beat" cop who walks around the community getting to know families and shopkeepers.

The success of such programs is a topic of debate. One problem is that these cops often are not from neighborhood families. Being friendly is not the same as having personal connections with blood relatives and relatives by marriage. Another problem is that urban neighborhoods are more in flux today. Families come and go. This is a change from migration patterns in the past where people from a certain ethic background, such as Irish or Italian, have several generations living in the same urban neighborhood.

SUBCULTURES AND DEVIANCE

Although criminologists and sociologists often talk about deviant subcultures, the term is really a misnomer. If these were truly subculture theories, then the focus would be on groups that differ yet are still basically compatible with the mainstream in society. A more accurate portrayal of these theories is to see them as counter-cultures.

This is because most of these theories deal with juveniles or other groups that act out scripts that are offensive to a dominant group or the mainstream in a society. A subculture may differ, but it is not offensive to a dominant group or the mainstream in a community or society. The term counter-culture is a more appropriate designation for deviant groups, such as juvenile gangs or drug subcultures.

Even though it is more appropriate to identify these theories with counter-cultures, sometimes it is easier to just call them deviant subcultures. What is important is to remember is that whenever you see terms such as deviant subculture, be sure to remind yourself that this really is a counter-culture. The same holds for any references to subcultures in the discussion.

DIFFERENTIAL ASSOCIATION

Sutherland (1947) employed a **basic socialization model** in his explanation for deviance. Sutherland proposed that deviants are people exposed to two different scripts. The first script is the one that they learn at home. Sutherland associated this script with an agreed upon set of community values.

The second script comes through interaction with members of a deviant subculture. This script represents what we have called a counter-ideology because it embraces values, beliefs, and behaviors that are at odds with the mainstream. Exposure to the deviant script counters the socialization that a deviant received at home and in the community. Someone becomes a deviant when socialization into the deviant script takes precedence over the mainstream script.

Sutherland never really answered two key questions. The first question is where do deviant subcultures come from if deviance requires socialization? Presumably this could not arise out of consensus within a community. But where could one come from if this theory requires the existence of a deviant subculture in the first place? Presumably it would have to be imported from outside the community.

This explanation ignores the possibility that deviance can originate among those who never fully internalize the mainstream script. The self-concepts of such individuals form around opposing what everyone else seems to prefer. This possibility also helps to explain something else.

The second question not answered by Sutherland is, why are some kids attracted to a deviant subculture, while others will have nothing to do with it? Why is a deviant subculture a positive reference group for them, while for other children in the same neighborhood it is a negative reference group that they despise?

What is it that inoculates some children from involvement but not others? Even children from the same family, where parents have tried to inoculate them against recruitment by a gang, can react differently. Whatever the reasons, the point remains that only those with a predisposition toward the script of a deviant subculture will be attracted to it.

It is this predisposition that a deviant subculture can influence. A deviant subculture legitimates what the community condemns. A deviant subculture reinforces a predisposition rather than creating it. Matza and Sykes elaborate on this dynamic.

TECHNIQUES OF NEUTRALIZATION

Matza and Sykes (1961) do not really address the question of why some join a deviant subculture while others refuse. But they do provide an insight into how interaction with members of a deviant subculture can result in buying into their script. The insight involves what they call techniques of neutralization.

Techniques of neutralization are **behavioral rationalizations** that a deviant subculture provides to help its members overcome socialization into mainstream values. These rationalizations are excuses that are used to justify a delinquent act. An example would be justifying violence toward others as self-defense. Another would be to argue that stealing is a payback for what society owes them.

Although the concept was developed in conjunction with studying juvenile gangs, techniques of neutralization are common in more mainstream organizations. The military relies heavily on techniques of neutralization to help reluctant recruits rationalize killing. Many of the behavioral rationalizations are the same as found with violent juvenile gangs. Some familiar ones are defining someone as the enemy, it is a matter of survival where, if you don't kill him he will kill you, or don't let your comrades down.

The military also likes the label "collateral damage" to describe the killing of innocent civilians. It helps soldiers and pilots rationalize their actions. The term also plays well with audiences at home who prefer not to think about the loss of innocent life.

Corporations have their own "techniques of neutralization." Employees are downsized not fired. Downsizing is usually characterized as caused by global forces that corporate officials had no control over. This deflects attention away the possibility that mismanagement is what created the need.

INOCULATION THEORY

Inoculation theory offers an insight into how techniques of neutralization can be countered. If those who embrace a mainstream script give their children some exposure to various techniques of neutralization, it may immunize them against those rationalizations. The danger is that mentioning them may do more to pique their curiosity than it does to immunizing them.

CONTROL THEORY

Hirshi (1969) proposed that people who **identify** with the **scripts, values,** and **beliefs** of **dominant** or **mainstream groups** are more likely to **conform** to their preferences. Another way to state this is to suggest the importance of dominant/mainstream groups to be positive reference groups. As positive reference groups, they are more effective agents of social control.

What interested Hirshi is how can dominant/mainstream groups increase the likelihood that youngsters will identify with them and treat them like a positive reference group? Hirshi noticed that this is most likely to occur with children who have close personal ties to their parents. Those who do not form personal ties are more likely to deviate.

Given this observation, Hirshi makes a simple recommendation. If you want to discourage juvenile delinquency, you must encourage youngsters to immerse themselves in activities that conform with mainstream scripts and get them to build closer ties with their parents. Have them join the boy or girl scouts. Take them on family vacations. Read to them.

But his theory has a serious limitation. It is likely to work best with youngsters who already view their parents as a positive reference group. For them such immersions are likely to strengthen their resolve not to join deviant groups.

Trying to get rebellious kids who view their parents as a negative reference group to change is a more difficult challenge. Without an ideal self-concept based upon parental behavioral preferences, values, and beliefs, it is difficult or impossible to conceive of parental affirmation as creating closer ties with them. Instead, whatever parents disapprove of is likely to be incorporated into the rebellious child's ideal self-concept. This kid is not likely to be a happy camper on a family vacation!

MODES OF ADAPTATION

Merton (1979) begins with the assumption that there is an agreed upon socially shared mainstream script that determines what goals are legitimate in a society. Making money and being successful in America is an example of a shared goal. Merton is not interested in judging that goal.

Merton also assumes that **this mainstream script** dictates **acceptable means** for obtaining these goals. These assumptions prompted Merton to frame his theory around a somewhat unusual definition of conformity. **Conformity** occurs when people use **legitimate means** in pursuit of a **culturally legitimate goal.** An example would be when people in the United States use acceptable means to make money.

Merton proceeds to identify four modes of adaptation. All four represent types of deviance. This first involves innovation.

Innovation occurs when people use **unacceptable means** in pursuit of a culturally acceptable goal, such as monetary success. Stealing is an example of innovation.

Rebellion involves deviants who **reject** a **culturally legitimate goal.** An example would be people who reject the goal of monetary success. Rejection of the goals means that neither conformity nor innovation is an option for them. Political activists who challenged materialism in American society during the 1960s are an example.

Retreatism is the **dropout version** of **rebellion.** It involves people who may initially buy into cultural goals and the means for attaining them but change their mind. A good example is a student who majored in business but decide to forgo all of that and join a hippie commune.

Ritualism is a form of deviance that occurs when people in an organization become obsessed with rules. It approximates what is meant by **goal displacement.** Goal displacement was discussed in the chapter on organizations. An example is when a government bureaucrat becomes obsessed with following the rules and refuses to allow any exceptions.

INTERPRETING MERTON

Merton is often seen as talking about how an individual adapts to societal scripts. This interpretation encourages describing someone as a conformist, innovator, or someone who has retreated from society or engages in ritualistic behavior. But there is a more sociological interpretation.

A more sociological interpretation views his perspective as dealing with social circumstances. Members of the dominant group in American society are much more likely to conform than become innovators. The reason is that members of the dominant group have access to legitimate opportunities to pursue the goal of monetary success. Those confronted with fewer legitimate opportunities for monetary success are more likely candidates for innovation.

Social circumstances may also influence those who decide to retreat from society and pursue alternative lifestyles. Many who became hippies were from middle-class or even upper-class families. Many of them found spiritual experiences and the sense of community found in communes more meaningful than the material comforts that they grew up with.

Social circumstances can also help explain why some people within an organization become ritualistic rulemongers. Being able to force others to comply can be a power trip brought about by reactance. Reactance would occur when people feel confined and need to assert their independence or control.

OPPORTUNITY STRUCTURES

Cloward and Ohlin (1960) look at how **blocked opportunities** relate to different types of deviance. **Blocked opportunities** refer to situations where people are denied access to opportunity structures within a society. Merton's concept of innovation inspired their thinking.

Cloward and Ohlin identify three different types of deviance that result from block opportunities. Their sociological emphasis can be seen in the fact that they attribute blocked opportunities to social scripts that deny some access to the means for improving their lives. A sociological emphasis is also evident because they describe these reactions in terms of activities within a deviant subculture, rather than the response of a single person.

A **conflict subculture** occurs when **violence** results from **blocked opportunities.** The psychological theory that frustration causes violence helps to explain this dynamic. In this theory, frustration refers to goal-blockage. This is synonymous with blocked opportunities.

The **violence** created by blocked opportunities need not be directed at the source of the frustration. Those who feel frustration toward the dominant group that denies them access to opportunity structures may decide to take it out elsewhere. Freud would have labeled this **displacement** because it redirects anger from its original source to others. An example would be when members of a poor community take their anger out on each other.

A **criminal subculture** directly parallels Merton's notion of innovation. It represents a response to blocked opportunities that encourages property crimes such as stealing. With both conflict and criminal subcultures, the magnitude of the activities is seen as directly related to the degree that access to the cultural goal of monetary success is denied.

A **retreatist subculture** parallels what Merton described as retreatism. People in a retreatist subculture resort to substance abuse as a response to denied opportunities. Frustration over denied opportunities causes them to withdraw into a world of drugs.

All **three of these possibilities** can be used to **identify different components** of what is often defined as a drug subculture. **Violence** is most likely to involve drug dealers as they fight for turf and payment from users. Stealing and other **property crimes** are most likely to be committed by drug users to pay for their habit. Those **using drugs** are also the most likely to qualify as being involved in the retreatist aspect of an overall drug subculture.

REDUCING DEVIANCE

The **theory of blocked opportunities** offers a **sociological approach** to reducing violence, property crimes, and substance abuse. Eliminating the contributing factor of block opportunities is the key. Providing education, job training, and access to good jobs would diminish the numbers of people experiencing block opportunities and the consequent violence, property crime, and substance abuse.

A **psychological approach** is quite different. A psychological approach explains violence, property crimes, and substance abuse as a personal deficiency. The remedy is to help individuals overcome their deficiencies and stop those behaviors.

The advantage of the sociological approach is that it is more efficient. Eliminating the root cause would reduce or eliminate the need for individual therapy. The main problem with the sociological approach in the United States is opposition by the dominant group to spending taxpayer dollars to help eliminate opportunity barriers for those left out or behind. A related problem is that improving wages that would improve opportunity structures for workers is a cost that the dominant group opposes.

DEVIANT CAREERS

Lemert (1967) offered a different explanation for deviance. He began by defining **primary deviance** as an initial behavior that violates societal norms. He was not interested in explaining why this might occur.

What interested him more are public reactions to such an act. Lemert proposed attaching a **deviant label** to someone often causes subsequent deviant acts. This is especially likely if a **deviant label** becomes a **master status** for someone. Without society attaching a deviant label to someone, that person may never commit a deviant act again.

Secondary deviance occurs when a deviant label causes someone to engage in future acts of deviance. This can easily happen when someone who has engaged in an act of primary deviance is not given a second chance. An example would be when someone who regrets having committed a crime such as shoplifting can't shake a deviant label. People are unwilling to stop labeling that person as a deviant.

At some point, that person may come to internalize that deviant label. This switch in identify can have dramatic consequences. It is the stuff out of which **deviant careers** are made. A deviant career involves someone who develops a self-identity based upon being labeled deviant by others. Fulfilling that **deviant identity** is what causes a deviant career to unfold.

Breaking the cycle that concerned Lemert requires people to refrain from using an act of primary deviance as a justification for attaching a lifelong label on an offender. Treating an initial act of deviance as a mistake is a beginning. This is especially true with youngsters for whom a deviant label might be just enough to tip the scale toward a lifetime of difficulties.

For those who commit a crime and do the time, a similar response can be extremely critical. If people continue to label them as criminals, that label may be enough to sway ex-convicts that want to go straight into a life of crime. Giving ex-convicts a chance to get jobs can mean much more than just giving them a legitimate path to earning money. It gives them the opportunity to break free from stigmatized labels.

THE CULTURE OF POVERTY

In the United States, people like to base their explanations on characteristics of individuals. This is consistent with the American emphasis on individualism. No where is this more evident than with explanation of poverty.

Poverty is often explained as brought about by personal defects. Saying that people are poor because they are lazy fits into this pattern. It provides a behavioral rationalization to the effect that, who wants to help those who won't help themselves. It blames those who are poor for their plight, rather than their lack of resources and access to opportunity structures.

A variation on this theme is to attach blame to what is known as a **culture of poverty.** The culture of poverty refers to alleged attitudes that are seen as causing people to be poor. The general idea is that the poor are socialized into being poor.

There is a long list of negative attitudes attributed to the poor that are used to buttress this perception. One is that people are poor because their culture encourages them to be lazy. Another is that the culture of poverty teaches people to be pessimistic rather than optimistic. And yet another is the argument that the culture of poverty fails to teach people the importance of deferring immediate gratification so that they can save for the future.

Notice that none of these allegations address the issue concerning resources and access to opportunity structures. That would suggest that the decision by the advantaged not to make opportunities more available is what causes poverty. Blaming the poor as personally or culturally deficient is often used to justify the claim by the advantaged that it would be a waste of time and money to try to help them.

Some of the attitudes that are attributed to the poor are blatantly ridiculous. To say that not deferring gratification is the cause of their plight assumes that they have anything to save for the future. It also suggests that problems with deferring gratification are uniquely a problem with the poor. But what about the massive credit card debts of middle-class families? Isn't this the result of their failure to defer gratification?

Attributing laziness to those on welfare was a principle argument that welfare reform used. The argument was that welfare makes people lazy. The reality was that the majority of people on welfare were from working families. Moreover, the average stay on welfare even before reform was about two years.

Blaming the plight of the poor on their alleged sense of pessimism is fascinating for what it does not reveal. Anyone can appreciate the virtue of optimism, but is optimism about their future realistic for families that are caught in poverty? Psychologists might argue that feelings of pessimism among the poor are realistic given the limits on their resources and opportunities.

What would it take to inspire optimism among the poor? How about increasing access to opportunities? Successful experiences are natural generators of optimism.

Moral entrepreneurs for welfare reform promised that it would accomplish this task. By forcing people off welfare and into jobs, the cycle of pessimism would be broken. The underlying assumption was that having jobs would improve their lives. But preliminary data suggests that the main consequence of welfare reform has been to increase the number of working families that do not earn enough to elevate them out of poverty. In many cases, benefits that poor working families had before welfare reform are no longer available. Is this supposed to make them feel more optimistic?

CHAPTER 14
CRIME AND THE CRIMINAL JUSTICE SYSTEM

The **criminal justice system** is comprised of the **police, prosecutors, judges,** and **corrections officers.** All of their **wages** are paid for by taxpayers. Their **job** is to **enforce laws.**

LAWS

Laws are **behavioral preferences** that have been **officially endorsed** by the **government.** This means that laws are distinct from all other behavioral preferences in society. Groups who get the government to endorse their behavioral preference have distinct advantages.

The **first advantage,** especially in a democracy like the United States, is that behavioral preferences that receive a government stamp of approval can get a boost in legitimacy. This is because legislative actions in a democracy such as ours are based upon the principle of majority rule. Majority rule reflects election results that confer upon elected officials the responsibility to represent the people who elect them.

The **advantage of legitimacy** is more problematic in **dictatorship** where a leader can simply declare his behavioral preferences the **law** of the land. The extent that laws are seen as imposed is the extent to which legitimacy can be problematic. Questions of legitimacy also occur in a democracy if legislative decrees (laws) are seen as reflecting the interests of the few at the expense of the majority within society.

The **second advantage** that accrues to behavioral preferences that have been transformed into laws involves power. Once a behavioral preference has been declared a law, the coercive capacity of government can come into play. Obey the law or else suffer the consequences.

When **legitimacy** is afforded a law, then the coercive capacity of government need not come into play. People will obey because they see the law as legitimate. The **coercive power of the state** is there to "encourage" compliance by those not willing to obey.

The interplay between coercion and legitimacy can be illustrated by looking at traffic laws. States pass speed laws such as 70 mph on limited access highways. If you think that the speed law is reasonable, you see it as legitimate. That legitimacy may be based on your personal opinion, rather than the perception that it represents the majority in your state. If you see it as reasonable or legitimate, you are likely to comply on your own. If you disagree with the law, then it is the coercive power of the state (government) that comes into play. Expression of that coercive power begins with flashing lights and your decision to pull over.

THE USE OF COERCION

Just because the **government** can use **coercion to enforce laws** does not mean that it always does so. A government may have the coercive capacity and laws to back its action to force corporations to stop polluting. But politics may intervene and spare a company from suffering the consequences of remaining out of compliance.

Another important factor is **funding.** Using coercive force requires funding enforcement agencies. Sometimes politicians vote for a law because of political necessity and then reduce or eliminate funding for enforcement. Politicians can also reduce funding for existing laws that they disagree with and thereby diminish the effectiveness of those laws.

Still another factor is the element of **discretion** by enforcement. African American drivers are much more likely to get pulled over for traffic offenses than their Caucasian counterparts. Use of discretion by the police in this manner is often called racial profiling.

Passing laws invites the **potential use of coercive power** by the government. As a sociologist it is **just as important to see what laws do not exist** as it is to look at those that have already received governmental approval. Powerful interest groups for corporations have prevented the passing of legislation that would make it a crime for them to engage in certain activities. If it isn't on the books, then it is not going to be a target of government enforcement.

What is interesting is the extent to which the **movement to get tough on crime** focuses on offenses most likely to be committed by poor Americans. Laws, funding, and enforcement resources are allocated to stop behaviors by the poor that harm others. The problem is that corporations such as the tobacco industry cause more harm but are often given a pass by politicians who control what laws are passed and what resources will be allocated to enforce them. Some 400,000 Americans die each year of tobacco-related disease, but except for use by minors, it is completely legal. Compare this to about 20,000 people who are murdered each year in the most violent times.

WHAT IS A CRIME?

A **crime** is an act that **violates** a **law.** A **criminal** is someone who deviates from the law and is caught and convicted. Words like crime and criminal have enormous significance. These are labels that stigmatize criminal deviance much more than other forms of deviance that just happen not to break any law.

As the heat mounted on President Nixon because of his alleged involvement in the Watergate affair, he publicly declared that he "was not a criminal." Watergate involved a break-in into the Democratic Headquarters by Nixon operatives. The break-in was clearly a criminal act. As the investigation implicated Nixon more, he decided to step down and not risk a conviction.

More recently, a top aid to President Bush provided information to reporters that led to the exposure of someone working for the CIA who had been a deep undercover agent. The allegation is that the top aid leaked the information to discredit a report by her husband that cast doubt on the Bush contention that Saddam Hussein was seeking to get nuclear materials from Africa. Bush initially said that he would fire anyone who leaked the information. When documents surfaced that linked his top aid to the leak, Bush switched and said he would fire anyone who committed a crime. This was more than a change in wording because there is little question about the leak. But legal questions about whether or not the manner by which the information was provided violated the law is a higher bar.

STATE ENDORSED BEHAVIORAL PREFERENCES

Laws are the most obvious and best known form of government endorsed behavioral preferences. Legislative bodies pass laws. Local, state, or federal legislative bodies can pass laws. At the local level, city councils are an example of a legislative body that can issue rules and regulations. At the state level, there are legislative bodies that can pass laws that affect people in that jurisdiction. And, of course, Congress has the power to pass federal legislation.

An **executive order** by the President of the United States is also a behavioral preference endorsed by government. It has the same significance as a law, but is usually not given as much attention nor does it have the same emotional significance. President Ford banned the assassination of foreign leaders through an executive order. More recently President George W. Bush banned foreign aid from going to family planning agencies that even mentioned the word abortion. This executive order represents a governmental act backed by the coercive power of the state. Foreign aid is the coercive lever. Family planning agencies around the world dependent upon American foreign aid risk that aid if they mention the word abortion.

Regulations are another form of government endorsed behavioral preferences that often receive less attention than laws. An example of a regulation is a workplace safety rule. Other governmental regulations are rules that involve everything from automobile and air safety to building codes. Because regulations are not called laws, people often treat them lighter and as less significant. At the local level, regulations are often called **ordinances.** An example would be when a city, because of a water shortage, limits its use on lawns.

Just as with laws, there can be a lot of politics involved in the passing of ordinances and regulations. Zoning disputes in towns, villages, and cities can become extremely tense. A recent decision by the Supreme Court added fuel to the tension. In the past, local governments were allowed to buy private homes if it was for a public purpose, such as building a park, school, or road. The Supreme Court now says that public purpose includes condemning personal homes for a private development project that pays higher taxes. Is more tax revenue a proper interpretation of what constitutes a public good? Critics worry that this interpretation is an open invitation for private parties with influence on local officials to grab private homes for personal profits.

Federal regulatory agencies are there to enforce regulations passed by Congress. The Federal Reserve Board is a well-known federal regulatory agency. It has the power to raise or lower interests rates. Other federal agencies that have regulatory power range from the Federal Communication Commission, the Security and Exchange Commission, and the Federal Energy Commission to the Federal Aviation Commission. Scripts and their behavioral preferences are always involved with how regulatory agencies act upon legislative or presidential orders or when they devise strategies for implementing them.

There is one other point about ordinances, regulations, and laws that warrants attention at this time. Blocking efforts to pass ordinances, regulations, and laws is often a tactic that groups use to protect their own interests. Not having a behavioral preference endorsed by the state permits groups to engage in acts that would otherwise be penalized. Many acts that cause serious financial or physical harm to people by corporations are not crimes because corporations effectively discourage the government from regulating that conduct.

THE ISSUE OF HARM

This chapter is mainly about what people normally associate with criminal acts such as murder, robbery, drug dealing, breaking and entering, and so forth. But before looking at topics related to such acts, it is important to establish that violations of regulations may represent a greater harm to society. A corporate executive who violates a Security and Exchange regulation may only face a fine, but the act may cost people much more than a series of thefts from homes.

During 2002, the American public became inundated with stories about corporate accounting deceptions that cost investors billions of dollars. A fascinating element with all of these stories is whether or not this misconduct violated any state sanctioned behavior preferences. A related issue concerns whether or not violations were of norms sanctioned by a regulatory agency or a legislative body. Pictures of corporate executives being handcuffed meant that they were charged with a crime that violated a federal or state statute passed by a legislative body. Those violating a regulation passed by an agency such as the SEC were more likely to receive a slap on their wrists rather than handcuffs.

SORTING OUT THE DIFFERENCES

There are **two qualities of criminal acts** that, when combined, distinguish them from other forms of government-endorsed behavioral preferences. The first is that **criminal acts violate a legislative script.** Federal crimes violate laws written and approved of by Congress. State crimes violate laws written by the legislative bodies in the various states.

The second condition is that these **legislative acts** carry with them costs that limit the **freedom** of those who violate them. A **criminal act** is one where **conviction** results in the **loss of freedom.** The amount of freedom lost varies from supervision under a probation officer or life in prison to the death penalty.

Costs involving **ordinances and regulations** are different. The loss of freedom is not an issue. What's at stake are **monetary penalties,** that is, fines.

The difference between criminal and civil laws also rests primarily upon the types of penalties that accrue to violations. Loss of freedom versus monetary penalties is the key. Under criminal law, victims are compensated entirely through sentences that deprive the guilty of his or her freedom. Under civil violations, the offended party seeks monetary compensation.

O. J. Simpson illustrates the difference. He was charged and acquitted of murdering his wife and her companion. The families of his wife and her companion then sued him for wrongful death under the civil code. He was found guilty of that civil offense and ordered to pay a large monetary penalty to the families.

CRIMINAL AND CIVIL LAW

The difference between criminal and civil laws can be quite complicated. But there are some features that help to clarify matters. One is the difference in penalties. Another has to do with how these different types of offenses are characterized. All laws, whether civil or criminal, must meet the challenge of constitutionality.

A **civil law** covers an **offense against an individual.** The plaintiff initiates action in a civil litigation through the claim that he or she has suffered an injury or loss due to the behavior of someone else. If successful, the plaintiff will usually seek monetary compensation to remedy that loss or injury.

In cases involving relatively minor infractions, the plaintiff may decide to pursue the matter without representation by a trial lawyer in a small claims court. This is portrayed daily on TV shows such as *Judge Judy*. In other situations, the plaintiff will hire a trial lawyer to pursue the matter in court. In cases involving civil violations, such as breach of contract or in product liability claims, suing for monetary compensation is the most common practice.

Criminal laws cover what are defined as **offenses against society.** A prosecutor initiates action in criminal proceedings. The prosecutor is seen as representing society. With criminal violations, the remedy is punishment. Punishment always involves restrictions on the freedom of anyone convicted of committing a crime.

The difference between criminal and civil laws is scripted. Lawyers learn about these scripts when they attend law school. Often, lawyers learn more about how the system actually works on the job once they are out of law school. That is when they encounter informal scripts that may have not been covered in law school.

FEDERAL AND STATE JURISDICTION

The **Constitution** gives **states** broad powers to determine what **constitutes criminal activities.** Most crimes, along with their prosecution and punishment, involve state statutes that have been found to be constitutional. But there are some areas where the federal government has shared or exclusive responsibility.

Federal jurisdiction comes into play with Congressional acts covering everything from sedition, espionage, kidnapping, and gun registration to clean air, civil rights, organized crime, price fixing, tax evasion, and labor management violations. The difference between sedition and espionage is the former refers to advocating the violent overthrow of the government, while the latter involves selling national military or defense secrets to a foreign government. What is covered by the other terms is self-explanatory.

CRIME DATA

In the United States crime data is primarily gathered through two different vehicles. The **Uniform Crime Reports** (UCR) tabulate data submitted by local and state law enforcement agencies on a monthly and yearly basis. **The National Crime Victimization Survey** (NCVS) is conducted twice a year and asks a large random sample of people to report on whether or not they have been victims of certain crimes.

The **NCVS** includes **crimes** that have **not been reported** to the police. The **UCR** relies exclusively on crimes that have come to the attention of the criminal justice system. Experts generally agree that the omission of unreported crimes in the UCR seriously underreports the actual amount of crime.

Crimes included on the UCRs are called **index crimes.** Index crimes are broken down into two categories. One includes **violent crimes** such as murder, rape, robbery, and aggravated assault. The other list includes **property crimes,** such as burglary, larceny, auto theft, and arson.

Conspicuously absent from these inventories are corporate crimes such as price-fixing and high-status crimes such as insider trading. This can easily distort the issue of what acts cause harm to society. For instance, the number of people killed on the job or through job related diseases is anywhere from three to five times higher than the number of people who are murdered each year. Similarly, the number of people who die from the use of tobacco products, which is legal for anyone over 18, ranges from 10 to 20 times the number of people who are murdered each year.

TYPES OF CRIMES

A **criminal act** is a behavior that violates a behavioral preference that has been endorsed by the state. There are numerous types of criminal acts. Most deal with acts that we normally think about when we think about crime.

STREET CRIMES

Street crimes represent offenses that directly threaten people or property. These are crimes associated with what is reported on the UCR. They are also crimes that are more likely to be prosecuted when committed by poor as opposed to wealthy Americans. Street crimes are the basis for reports that document increases or decreases in crime.

ORGANIZED CRIME

Organized crime conjures up images of the Godfather and the Mafia. The idea of organized crime can be contrasted to an act committed by an individual or individuals on their own. Organized crime requires the coordination of criminal activities that provide illegal goods and services to customers. The goods and services range from selling illegal drugs and gambling to prostitution and loan sharking.

The term organized crime is relatively new. It covers activities previously associated with Irish and German gangs during the late-nineteenth century and Jewish gangs until the emergence of Italian families during the 1920s. More current manifestations can be found in African American, Jamaican, Latino, Asian American, and motorcycle gangs.

WHITE- AND BLUE-COLLAR CRIMES

Sutherland (1940) defined **white-collar crimes** as **illegal activities** of people in **white-collar** or **high-prestige jobs** for **personal gain.** A key element is his emphasis on personal gain. Examples include employee theft of company property, embezzlement of funds, and insider trading.

Although criminologists have generally ignored **blue-collar crime,** it is more significant than previously believed. A blue-collar crime involves illegal activities of workers conducted on the job for personal gain. An example would be when a worker steals materials from a job site for personal use or sale.

CORPORATE CRIME

Corporate crimes represent **criminal acts** that members of a corporation commit to **benefit the corporation.** What distinguishes corporate from white-collar crime is the matter of corporate rather than personal gains. Examples range from violating workplace safety regulations to price-fixing or concealing damaging data about products or services.

Issues concerning prosecution and punishment of corporate crimes are often unique. One simply cannot put a corporation into prison. Trying to prosecute specific members can also be uniquely difficult because of what is known as diffusion of responsibility.

Diffusion of responsibility refers to the spread of responsibility. It occurs when corporate officials say that they weren't responsible for what occurred. It must have been others. Trying to gain sufficient evidence that demonstrates both responsibility and criminal intent is often difficult when dealing with corporations.

Adding to this mix of unique circumstances associated with corporate crimes is the reluctance of many Americans to imprison people in high-prestige occupations, such as the CEOs of corporations. Even if corporate officers cannot duck responsibility through claims involving diffusion of responsibility, they are much more likely to be fined than jailed. In one case, the corporate officer responsible for the plan where GM, Firestone, and Standard Oil conspired to buy up public transportation and then dump it so that they could sell busses, tires, and gas was fined only a few dollars.

PATRIOTIC CRIMES

Thanks to the Reagan administration and its involvement in the Iran Contra scandal, a new crime has been added. **Patriotic crimes** are **crimes** committed by **government officials** in pursuit of what they define as **national interests.** In this case, officials tied to the Reagan administration were accused of violating an act of Congress that prohibited selling products to one country in order to raise money to finance weapons for American allies fighting in Central America.

Although attention given to the Iran Contra scandal gave rise to the notion of patriotic crimes, such crimes are hardly novel in the history of the United States. Lying by government officials in the name of national security has probably been the most frequent offense. An example is when government officials steadfastly denied any involvement in the overthrow of the Allende government in Chile. Another were the lies of military officials designed to conceal from the American public and Congress atrocities committed by our troops during the Vietnam War.

When governmental officials lie to the public, no crime has been committed. But if they lie under oath at a Congressional Hearing, they can be charged with perjury. Perjury is a crime. But trying to get evidence against someone in an agency such as the CIA can be extremely difficult. The CIA reserves the right to censor material that it publicly releases by claiming that it would jeopardize national security.

VICTIMLESS CRIME

In most crimes against people or their property, it is assumed that the victims were not willing partners in the act. This is one basis for describing what constitutes a victimless crime. A **victimless crime** is one where involvement is by choice.

Examples range from illegal **gambling** to frequenting **prostitutes.** Prostitution is illegal everywhere in the United States except in some counties in Nevada where prostitution is legal. Moral outrage against gambling limited legal gambling to Nevada until fairly recently. Now virtually every state has legalized some form of gambling.

Moral outrage is what often condemned victimless crimes such as gambling and prostitution to back alleys. Usually religious groups have been the most indignant about these so-called victimless crimes. This is why victimless crimes are often defined as **moral offenses.** This is because religious groups often oppose offenses such as gambling and prostitution.

Whether or not prostitution and gambling represent victimless crimes depends upon one's perspective. With prostitution, a case can be made that clients are not victims because they choose to participate. Whether prostitutes are victims is an entirely different story. Pimps may use drugs and violence to control their prostitutes.

Gambling offers a different angle. It would be a stretch to argue that the corporations that run casinos in Las Vegas are victims. A better case could be made that compulsive gamblers are victims. But of the total gambling population, compulsive gamblers are a small minority. Is this sufficient to make it illegal and deny gambling as a source of entertainment for the majority?

Gambling also illustrates the fickle relationship between morality and what governments restrict. At one time, moral entrepreneurs who condemned gambling were extremely successful in having their norms endorsed by state governments. Except in Nevada, gambling was illegal across the country. Then, state governments discovered that lotteries were a wonderful source of revenue. Until that time, betting on numbers was associated with what was known as the numbers racket. Now state governments have made their own numbers game legal!

STATUS CRIMES

Status crimes are activities that are illegal only for minors. The term **juvenile crime** means the same thing. Examples range from underage drinking or smoking to truancy.

THE ENFORCEMENT OF LAWS

The **criminal justice system enforces behavioral preferences that have been endorsed by the state.** More specifically, the criminal justice system enforces laws that represent offenses against society. The **criminal justice system** is **separate** from the **civil system.** The civil system is designed to resolve personal disputes. It is also **separate** from **agencies** responsible for **enforcing ordinances** and **regulations.**

The **police, prosecutors,** (district attorneys), **judges,** and **corrections officers** are the main players in the criminal justice system. All of these players in the criminal justice system **work for the government.** All are paid by their respective governmental units to enforce laws.

Only the police, prosecutors, judges, and correctional officers are members of the criminal justice system. This is because they are **full-time employees** of the government. **Juries** are not official members because their involvement is short-lived and they do not make a living from their activity. The **accused** and those convicted of a crime are not considered to be members of the criminal justice system. None of them are paid to enforce the laws. The same holds for **defense lawyers.** The job of defense lawyers is to protect the rights of their clients. They are not paid to prosecute laws.

THE POLICE

The official script for the **police** places them at the frontline of the criminal justice system. Their job responsibilities include obtaining evidence and detaining those suspected of having committed a crime or in the process of committing a crime. The Constitution and its Amendments script places restrains on how the police can discharge their duties.

CONSTITUTIONAL RESTRAINTS ON THE POLICE

Here are some examples of **constitutional restraints.** The Bill of Rights is the primary source of constitutional restraints of the police. An example is the Fourth Amendment that states the police cannot invade the privacy of citizens without probable cause.

This allows **police surveillance** in public areas where there is not a reasonable expectation of privacy. If police want to get surveillance evidence in situations where there is a reasonable expectation of privacy, they must apply for and get a search warrant from a judge based upon their claim that there is probable cause that justifies such an intrusion. Getting a judge to authorize a wiretap of someone's phone line is one example.

The Fourth Amendment also states that a **search warrant** must contain a description of the property to be searched and the persons or things to be seized. The **plain view doctrine** offers an exception to the provisions of a search warrant. It allows the police to seize incriminating evidence not stipulated in a search warrant if it is in plain view of officers conducting an authorized search. The police often take advantage of this exception by getting a search warrant with the unexpressed intent to find additional evidence.

An example would be a situation where the police obtain a search warrant based upon a "reliable" informant who alleges there is a crime being committed in a home. Even though the warrant limits what items can be searched for, once inside officers may use the plain view doctrine to find other incriminating evidence. It may even be about a crime that they had no suspicion about. This tactic amounts to an informal script shared by police.

The **Miranda Rule** is another restraint on police activities. It states that if a suspect has been taken into custody he or she must be advised of their constitutional rights. These rights include the right to remain silent, the right to an attorney (even if he/she can't afford one), and the warning that anything that he or she says can and will be used against them.

If these conditions have not been made clear to someone who is in custody, then evidence against them obtained through questioning by officers can be disqualified. There are a variety of scripts that the police use to skirt the Miranda Rule. One involves what is meant by **custody.** Custody means that someone has no choice but to go with the police. The police might ask a suspect to come downtown to help them clear up some questions that they have. The Miranda Rule does not come into play if someone agrees to go with them because custody means that they had no choice but to comply.

Entrapment represents another restraint on the police. Entrapment occurs when officers induce someone into an illegal act that they otherwise would not have committed for the purpose of initiating prosecution against that person. An example would be when an officer of the Department of Natural Resources (DNR) meets a hunter at a bar and induces the hunter, who would otherwise not poach, into shooting deer under illegal conditions.

There are also restrictions on the use of **excessive force** by the police, but defining what constitutes excessive force can be hard. The problem is that the police are given the right to use necessary force when making an arrest. Exactly what is necessary to get a suspect into custody can spur debates as it did in the *Rodney King* case where police were videotaped beating and kicking him beyond what many observers thought was necessary to get him into custody.

A related issue is that of **deadly force.** The police are armed and can use deadly force under certain circumstances. These circumstances include the threat of deadly violence toward themselves or others. Tensions in communities are often aroused when an officer shoots and kills an unarmed suspect. Some police officers carry a second gun to plant on a suspect should that person turn out not to be armed.

POLICE DISCRETION

Police discretion involves the latitude officers have in applying the law. Time and limited resources make the exercise of discretion a common occurrence among cops. An example is the fact that a traffic cop cannot stop everyone who breaks the speed limit.

Police discretion means selective enforcement of laws. Selective enforcement means that some offenders will not be detained or arrested. Those offenders are essentially above the law.

Controversies involving police discretion arise when discrimination occurs. Discrimination occurs when police discretion favors some, while targeting others. A familiar example is when cops are more likely to stop a car for a traffic violation if the driver is African American.

Sometimes a pattern of discrimination results from a deliberate policy. An example is when the police target the users of crack cocaine rather than those who snort the same drug. Many critics complain that this is not an even-handed way to fight the war on drugs because those targeted are usually poor, while those who have the more expensive habit of using cocaine are usually wealthy.

PROFILING

Profiling is an area that can create constitutional difficulties. A legitimate use of profiling is when the FBI use profilers to come up with possibilities that might be useful for the police. An example might be the profile of a likely domestic terrorist. Because of Timothy McVeigh, one profile singles out a loner who has had military experience and is an outspoken critic of the government.

While such a profile might be useful in directing police attention to certain suspects, a profile is not probable cause. The police would probably run into constitutional issues if they tried to arrest all people who meet the profile of a potential domestic terrorist. If police legally gain additional evidence that justifies an arrest of someone meeting the profile, such as the purchase of materials to make a bomb, then the principle of probable cause might very well justify an arrest.

The issue of **racial profiling** raises some additional issues. One involves police discretion. The question is, do the police violate the equal protection guarantee of the Fourteenth Amendment if they selectively apply laws on the basis of race? This issue applies to situations where officers disproportionately stop African American compared to Caucasian speeders.

Matters become even more interesting when racial profiling involves more than police discretion. The police may stop African American speeders because of a profile that suggests African Americans are more likely to possess illegal drugs than their Caucasian counterparts. But does a profile constitute probable cause? Many legal scholars believe that it does not. They argue that what is necessary for probable cause is more specific evidence that a crime has been or is being committed.

The unstated reason for racial profiling is often a pretense to stop and detain someone with the hope of finding evidence through the **plain view doctrine.** This practice is a ploy cops can use to circumvent the Bill of Rights protection against unreasonable searches. It distorts the original intent for creating the plain view doctrine that allows officers to seize evidence that they just happen to come across without first having to get a warrant.

The events of 9/11 have increased concerns about the abuses that can result from profiling. The primary concern is that Arab Americans will be treated as suspects by law enforcement agencies even if there is no evidence to support the contention. Many worry that the government, in its zeal to protect Americans from terrorists, may do so by violating the civil liberties of those who just happen to be from Middle Eastern countries.

THE BLUE LINE

The **blue line** illustrates an unofficial police script. It is based upon a value and script that enforce loyalty to fellow officers over outsiders. An example is when a police officer knows that another cop is taking illegal payoffs but refuses to disclose this information to the proper authorities. The choice may be based upon an acceptance of the loyalty norm or fear of repercussions from other cops.

PROSECUTORS

Prosecutors are **lawyers** who have been **hired by the government** to represent society in criminal proceedings. Television shows such as *Cops* create the impression that the police are the most powerful entities in the criminal justice system. In reality, the most powerful entity is the prosecutor.

The **power of a prosecutor** is based upon his or her **discretion.** It is the **prosecutor** who decides whether or not to get a judge to authorize an **arrest warrant** and bring a suspect to court. The role of the police is limited to providing evidence to the prosecutor, who then decides whether or not it is worthwhile to proceed and try the case.

The **prosecutor** also decides on what **charges** are appropriate given the evidence supplied by the police. This decision is based upon his or her confidence that a jury will convict based upon the evidence. Deciding how to charge someone accused of the unlawful killing of someone else is a case in point. In most states, first-degree murder requires demonstrating willful and premeditated intent. Second-degree murder is seen as a lesser offense because it does not require all the elements contained in statutes that define first-degree murder. Manslaughter also involves taking someone's life, but is even a lower offense because it does not involve deliberation, malice, and premeditation.

Plea-bargaining further augments the power of prosecutors. Plea-bargaining occurs when a prosecutor agrees to dismiss or reduce charges against a suspect in return for evidence. Some believe that plea-bargaining is a violation of the Constitutional guarantee of equal protection because it gives some special treatment that is denied to others.

There are **many reasons why a prosecutor** may decide to **plea bargain.** One is that the prosecutor is unsure that he or she has enough evidence to convict the suspect on an original charge. When this occurs the prosecutor may ask if the accused will confess to a lower charge and avoid the risk of a more severe sentence.

This works best when the accused has an inexperienced or inept defense attorney. More experienced defense attorneys take such offers as an acknowledgement that the prosecutor is worried about getting a conviction on the original charge. If they see it as a weakness, they may advise their clients to take their chances in court on that charge.

Plea bargains are also used to gain evidence from a suspect that is otherwise not forthcoming. Sometimes this happens when two or more people are suspected of engaging in a crime. The prosecutor offers the best deal to the first one willing to provide testimony or other evidence against the others. One problem with this use of plea-bargaining is that it often relies on the testimony of a suspect that neither the police nor the prosecutor trust. Using people known to lie as witnesses is a dubious practice.

JUDGES

Judges are involved in the **criminal justice system** in a number of different capacities. One involvement is signing **search** or **arrest** warrants. Signing an arrest warrant compels the police to bring a suspect to court.

A judge also presides over the **arraignment hearing,** where the accused registers a response to the charge against him or her. Pleading guilty or not guilty are the two most frequent responses. A judge also decides if the accused will be held without bail or the conditions of his or her **pretrial release.** A pretrial release often involves a monetary guarantee. Sometimes the accused is released on his or her **personal recognizance** without a monetary guarantee.

The Sixth Amendment to Constitution guarantees the right to a trial by an impartial jury. Judges preside over **jury trials.** The main job of the judge in a jury trial is to make sure that what transpires meets constitutional criteria. If the accused waives the right to a jury trial, then the judge is given the right to decide on that person's guilt or innocence.

Trial judges are usually given the responsibility for deciding on the sentence for someone convicted of a given offense. **Mandatory sentences** take away the amount of discretion that a judge may exercise when deciding upon a sentence. Legislative bodies set mandatory sentences. An example is the California three-strike rule that mandates a life sentence for anyone convicted of three or more felonies. An exception to the rule that judges do the sentencing is when the jury is given this responsibility such as in cases when the death penalty applies.

CORRECTIONS

Corrections cover all aspects of **incarceration** and **punishment.** Whether or not it lives up to its name is debatable. Some view punishment is justified even if it has no corrective value. Others view punishment as a deterrent. And still others believe that more education and job training while incarcerated is necessary to increase the likelihood that people will correct their ways when released.

Jails are local facilities that incarcerate suspects for between 24–72 hours, those accused of a crime who have been denied or cannot meet bail conditions, and those convicted of crimes that carry sentences of less that one year. **Prisons** incarcerate people for longer periods of time. **State prisons** hold those convicted of state offenses. **Federal prisons** hold those convicted of violating federal laws.

Recidivism refers to repeat offenders. Questions about reducing recidivism rates are intertwined with philosophies that we have already discussed. Some argue that the purpose of putting someone in prison is solely to **punish** them for an offense. Others add that more than punishment should be involved. They believe that literacy, education, and job-training programs should be used to **rehabilitate** prisoners and reduce the recidivism rate. To rehabilitate someone is to have them lead productive and crime-free lives once they leave prison.

Constitutional issues involving corrections involve a variety of concerns. Perhaps the best known involves protections against **cruel and unusual punishment.** Overcrowding is one factor that has been interpreted as violating this protection. In jurisdictions where this occurs, officials are compelled to release a sufficient number of prisoners to remedy the situation.

More recently, the controversial issue involving the use of prison labor has arisen because the government has endorsed the practice of letting private companies use prisoners as a source of cheap labor. This practice is often called the **privatization of prison labor.**

There is a federal program that gives contracts to private companies to use prison labor. **Federal Prison Industries** produce everything from office furniture and military clothing to working on phone banks. Businesses who use prison labor stress its **rehabilitative benefits** through the learning of job skills. Regardless of this claim, there is no doubt that prison labor provides a cheap alternative to outside labor. One reason is that taxpayers are paying for basic needs such as food, clothing, and shelter.

Businesses that must compete with cheap prison labor complain that it amounts to unfair competition. Businesses that must compete with companies that use cheap prison labor complain about another element in the script. The government often requires that its agencies buy from prison industries. This means that normally private companies are denied the opportunity to even bid for government contracts involving the purchase of items like office furniture and military uniforms.

Allowing American companies to use prison labor has put our government in an awkward position. How can we complain about the Chinese, who use prison labor, when we approved of the practice here in the United States? It makes us look hypocritical.

JOBS AND THE CRIMINAL JUSTICE SYSTEM

Something that is overlooked is the fact that those who make a living in the criminal justice system have a vested interest in crime! **Without crime** people in the **criminal justice system** would **lose their jobs.** This explains why the organization representing correction officers in California was one of the key lobby groups supporting the three-strike rule. The three-strike rule states that anyone one convicted of three or more felonies automatically receives a life imprisonment. What could be better for guaranteeing corrections jobs!

Recognizing that those in the criminal justice system have a vested interest in crime does not mean that they are in favor of crime. What it does mean is that their jobs depend upon keeping public support for enforcement efforts. If the public loses interest in a certain type of crime, it is in the vested interest of those within the criminal justice system to have their moral entrepreneurs drum up concern over another offense.

Scholars familiar with this dynamic involving the criminal justice system in the United States look to see what happens when crime is down. A predictable response is for the criminal justice system to look for new threats. If there is a reduction in coke or crack use, why not switch the focus to ecstasy?

Whether or not ecstasy is really more dangerous to users or others than booze is not the issue. The use of ecstasy is illegal. The use of booze is not.

By targeting ecstasy as a threat to Americans, the criminal justice system helps to sustain public support. The pattern of discovering a new threat is not new. The criminal justice system prospered much earlier when LSD was deemed a threat to American youth. This threat was reinforced by ads that compared the brains of users to that of a frying egg. A similar ad campaign was mounted in regards to the ecstasy threat in the United States.

Another example of how the criminal justice system can benefit from public alarm involves **crack babies.** Not that many years ago, alarm about crack babies was used to sell the war on crack users. The fact that drinking during pregnancies creates as much or a greater risk to babies because of **fetal alcohol syndrome** was silently ignored. Targeting crack mothers gave the criminal justice system an illegal activity to pursue.

All of the fuss about crack cocaine had its results in other ways. Crack cocaine users, who are usually poor, were disproportionately targeted over powder cocaine users who are more affluent. But this selective enforcement went ever further. Sentences for crack offenses were as much as four times higher than for those convicted of peddling or snorting powder cocaine.

In 2000, California passed a regulation that requires placing many of those convicted of a drug offense into a rehabilitation program. This should cause concern to those who have jobs in the correctional system. But those who provide the required rehabilitative services have reason to be optimistic.

THE WAR ON CRIME

Waging war on crime has become a popular political stance in the United States. Politicians who exploit this theme are often less than honest about other dangers to Americans. Those who want to beef up the criminal justice system to get tough on street criminals play on American's fears concerning crimes such as murder, rape, robbery, and so forth. Some of these fears are justified, but what is not mentioned is that many more people in the United States die each year from workplace diseases or accidents than are murdered.

Many **politicians** who play the **war on crime card** simultaneously vote to get **rid** of **workplace safety rules** that protect workers. Often these same politicians vote to get rid of environmental pollution regulations or diminish their effectiveness by reducing or eliminating funds for enforcement. While virtually no taxpayer expense is too high to fight the war on crime, virtually no cost to the profits of businesses that might protect workers and the community is seen as justified.

DECRIMINALIZATION AND DEREGULATION

Decriminalization refers to the process of removing laws from the books or severely reducing the penalties for them. The term has been used extensively in regards to the use of drugs such as marijuana. Proponents of legalizing pot are essentially asking for the government to decriminalize it. Politicians who promote the war on crime vigorously oppose such measures.

Deregulation is the equivalent of decriminalization. Both involve eliminating state endorsement for certain norms or severely limiting penalties. Often politicians who oppose decriminalization of acts, such as smoking marijuana, support deregulation of acts that threaten workers.

Those who advocate deregulation often rant about the importance of getting government off our backs. What they really mean is getting government off the backs of businesses because governmental regulations are seen as a cost that undermines profits. These same politicians have no qualms about getting the government on the backs of others in society, such as those who prefer marijuana to booze. Some don't even have any reservations about endorsing the death penalty even when significant numbers of inmates have been released from death row because of new DNA evidence.

MORE POLITICS AND THE CRIMINAL JUSTICE SYSTEM

Those who advocate **getting tough on crime** often trivialize the constitutional protections afforded all citizens. A common complaint is that only too often someone gets off on a technical point. These are not merely technical points. These technical points cover our **constitutional rights.** What is remarkable are conservatives who in one speech wrap themselves in the Constitution and Bill of Rights and in the next one trash protections spelled out in documents such as the Fourth and Fifth Amendments.

Politicians also exploit another concept. It involves the contention **that no one is above the law.** Conservatives who wanted to impeach President Clinton repeatedly used this refrain to justify their actions. Clinton had, after all, lied under oath about an affair. Lying under oath is a criminal offense. Therefore, the enormous expenditure of funds to impeach Clinton was justified because no one is above the law.

The phrase that no one is above the law was effective but concealed more than it revealed in this case. Police discretion essentially places some above the law by giving them a pass. Discretion exercised by prosecutors and judges places some above the law by giving them a pass or lighter treatment.

The blatant politics of claims that Clinton should be impeached because no one is above the law concealed another reality. Prosecutors often threaten to charge people with perjury but seldom actually go forth with a charge and trial. The reason that prosecutors rarely charge someone with perjury is because perjury is extremely hard to prove.

There is no question that Clinton's sexual behavior offended many people in the United States. There is also no question that many of them believed that he deserved to be punished for violating their sense of morality. The problem for them was the fact that Monica Lewinsky was a consenting adult. This made it a legal act. Moreover, charging him with sexual harassment was not seen as a viable because there was no evidence of quid pro quo or his creating a hostile work environment for her.

Some worry that what happened to President Clinton set a frightening precedent that will encourage opposition groups to attack subsequent presidents on technical legalities. Taking a president to court over matters that the criminal justice system normally spends little time prosecuting can be an effective tactic. One consequence is that it can tarnish a president's reputation. Another consequence is that it makes a president spend time fighting legal battles rather than promoting policies. And finally, the expense of fighting legal battles can drain both personal and party funds.

PART 5
STUDY GUIDES

CHAPTER 15
SOCIAL STRATIFICATION

Stratification Defined

Vocabulary of Stratification

Social Class

Upper Class

Old Money/Upper Crust

New Rich

Middle Class

Upper

Lower

Working Class

Poor

Working

Nonworking

Underclass/Super-poor

Dominant and Minority Groups

Advantaged/privileged/haves

Disadvantaged/underprivileged/have-nots

Magnitude of Stratification

Capitalist Political Economies

Socialist Political Economies

Stratification Variables

Wealth

Power

Prestige

Social Mobility

Intergenerational

Career

Caste and Class Systems

Justifying Systems of Stratification

Divine Right of Kings

Social Darwinism

Distributive Justice

The Protestant Work Ethic

Conspicuous Consumption

Counter-Ideologies

Minorities

Think Tanks

Heritage Foundation

American Enterprise Institute

Backlash

Role of Think Tanks

Political Correctness

Comfort Zones

White Men as Victims

Political Incorrectness

The Independence Card

Scapegoating

Social Class Card

Care-Based Appeals

Care-Based Ads

Minority Options for Improving Mobility

Violence

Civil Disobedience

Persuasion

Social Mobility

Discrimination

Family Resources

CHAPTER 16
AMERICAN MINORITIES

American Minority Groups

Minorities as Trophies

Role Models

Minorities Realities

Disadvantaged

Political Power

Less Household Assets

Lower Life Expectancies

Higher Rates of Poverty

High Infant Mortality

Less Access to Education

Less Social Prestige

Identifying Minorities

Race

Ethnicity

Religion

Gender

Labels

African American

Native Americans

Mexican Americans

Asian Americans

Choosing Labels

Dominant Group

Self-Labels

Dominant Group

Gatekeepers

Discrimination

Self-Fulfilling Prophesies

Affirmative Action

Assimilation Model

Segregation

De Jure

De Facto

Accommodation

Acculturation

Assimilation

Amalgamation

Alternative to Assimilation

Civility

Melting Pot

Factual Material

Native Americans

African Americans

Hispanic Americans

Asian Americans

Recent Trends

Religious Minorities

Women

Minority

Religious Scripts

Gender Stratification

Gender Roles

Feminization of Jobs

Critical Mass

Comparable Pay

Glass Ceiling

Mentors

Gender Segregation

CHAPTER 17
SEX SCRIPTS

Sex Scripts and Biology

Freud

Sexual Prohibitions

Beyond Freud

Script Disputes

Role Conflict

Interpersonal

Personal

Searching for Alternative Scripts

Mainstream Versus Personal Preferences

Suppression

Repression

Sexual Inclinations and Moral Entrepreneurs

Studying Societies

    Questions

        Agreed Upon Sexual Script?

        Differences?

            Dominant Group

            Mainstream Groups

            Minorities

Types of Sexual Scripts

    Societies

        Abstinent

        Permissive

        Ambivalent

Hypocrisy

    Personal Mismatch

Ideal and Real Sexual Scripts

    Research Obstacle

    Social Mismatch

        Abstinent Societies

        Permissive Societies

        Ambivalent Societies

Factual Material

    Cross-Culture Research

    American Sex Scripts

    Abstinence and Contraception

Sexual Orientations

    Heterosexual

Homosexual

Bisexuality

Rape

Sexual Harassment

Pedophilia

Pornography

CHAPTER 18
COURTSHIP, MARRIAGE, AND THE FAMILY

Rituals

Courtship

Mate Selection

Marriage Ceremonies

Arranged Marriages

Romantic Love

Place of Residence

Marriage Partners

Homogamy

Heterogamy

Extended Families

Prepared to Stay

Patriarchy

Sexism

Nuclear Families

Getting Rid of the Kids

Separation Anxiety

Fear of Coping

Midlife

Empty Nest Syndrome

Male Midlife Crisis

Professional Woman Life Crisis

Boomerang Kids

Latchkey Kids

Divorce Facts

Single Parents

Absent Fathers

Role Model

Income

Mothers as Role Models

Wife as Senior Partner

Commuter Marriages

Blended Families

Marriage/Remarriage

Domestic Partners

Sandwich Generation

Dependent Kids

Dependent Parents

Family Poverty Facts

Family Violence

Domestic Violence

Child

Spouse

Elderly

Facts

CHAPTER 15
SOCIAL STRATIFICATION

Social stratification is the **unequal distribution** of **power, wealth** and **prestige** in a society. Stratification creates **layers of difference** between those who benefit the most and the least from the scripts that sustain them. All societies have some degree of stratification because not everyone possesses the same amount of power, wealth, and prestige.

THE VOCABULARY OF STRATIFICATION

Social class is the term most often used to identify the strata or layers that form a **social stratification** system. The **upper class** represents those who have the most power, wealth, and prestige in a society. The **upper crust** consists of "old money" people who primarily inherit their wealth. Social registry networks revolve around these families who, in addition to their wealth, have extraordinary prestige. That prestige is often based upon lineage that traces their family roots to prominent figures. The "**new rich**" may match or exceed the upper crust in wealth but never in prestige. Bill Gates, arguably the wealthiest man in the United States, is too much of a newcomer to gain access to the world of the upper crust.

The **middle class,** just like the upper class, has its divisions. The **upper-middle class** is comprised mostly of professions such as lawyers and physicians along with accountants and business executives. The **lower-middle class** earns less and has less prestigious jobs than those above them. Included are lower-rung managers, small shopkeepers, and skilled contractors in areas such as plumbing, carpentry, and electrical work. Many have high school diplomas and those with college degrees usually receive them from less prestigious public universities.

The **working class** in the past was comprised mostly of blue-collar workers in manufacturing jobs. Job security is a major issue as many of these relatively good paying manufacturing jobs are being replaced by cheap labor in poorer countries around the world. Service and retail jobs are rapidly replacing manufacturing jobs. One consequence is lower pay, fewer benefits, and concern about job security brought about by mergers and consolidations in fields such as banking and retail. Usually, jobs are the first casualties of such mergers and consolidations due to eliminating duplication and cost cutting. Working-class families are less able to finance a college education for their children than more prosperous ones. This greatly dims their future outlook.

The **working poor** are families where at least one member is employed but are not able to earn enough to move out of poverty. The problem is low wages and not a willingness to work. At a minimum wage of $5.15 an hour, a family has to live on less than $11,000 per year not including sales and other taxes. That is about $200 per week or about $800 per month. Housing alone gobbles up a significant portion, to say nothing about owning and maintaining a car for work.

The **nonworking poor** include people who are unable to find work, the elderly who are often living off of social security, the disabled, and minor children living in homes with unemployed adults. The **underclass,** that is sometimes called the **super-poor,** have earnings less than half the official governmental poverty line.

THE DOMINANT GROUP AND MINORITIES

The **upper class** within a **society** is the **dominant group.** But the **real elite** is the wealthiest, most prestigious, and most powerful in the upper class. It is the upper class and the elite within it that constitutes the **advantaged** within a society.

Minorities are those **less advantaged** in a society. Their numbers are small in the upper class and upper-middle class. Their numbers are the highest in the ranks of the working poor, the nonworking poor, and the underclass.

Terms such as **advantaged, privileged,** and **haves** loosely refer to the **dominant group** within a society. Terms such as **disadvantaged, underprivileged,** and **have-nots** refer to **minorities** living in the lowest strata of society. Minorities include groups such as African Americans, Native Americans, Hispanic Americans, women, and so forth.

THE MAGNITUDE OF STRATIFICATION

The **magnitude of stratification** refers to the **gap** between the **top** and **bottom** in a system of social stratification. It can be thought of as the gap between the dominant group and minorities living in poverty. A comparison between the wealth, power, and prestige of the top ten percent and the bottom ten percent would be one way to measure the magnitude of stratification in a society. Knowing whether or not the gap is increasing or decreasing in a society tells us something about trends involving the magnitude of stratification in a society.

Capitalist political economies maximize the magnitude of stratification within a society. The main reason is the limits such a society places upon government intervening to help foster the greatest good for the greatest numbers. Within capitalist political economies, differences in the gap between the top and bottom can vary. The gap between the top and bottom in the United States in recent years exceeds that of all other economically advanced countries including Great Britain, Scandinavian nations, and those such as France, German, and Italy. In fact, in the past few decades, the gap between the top and bottom strata in American society has grown to the point that it is now the greatest since records have been kept.

Socialist political economies rely upon government programs to moderate the magnitude of stratification within a society. The extent to which a country regulates access to wealth and resources, such as education, is the extent to which it can moderate its magnitude of stratification. Disparities between the top and bottom still exist, but the magnitude of those disparities is less than it is in capitalist political economies.

STRATIFICATION VARIABLES

There are **three basic stratification variables** that sociologist study. These variables are often referred to as **social resources.** Stratification exists to the extent that access to these resources is problematic for some segments of society. The variables or resources are **power, wealth,** and **prestige.**

Power is the ability to get others to comply with a script or a set of preferences. It can be based upon **coercion, authority,** or **persuasion.** Those who occupy social positions with the most coercive leverage, authority, or credibility enjoy a power advantage in any social encounter.

Often, power advantages are expressed through access to the political system in a society. Those who shape and influence political decisions are the most likely to get their scripts endorsed by the state. Those who get the government to support their scripts can use its coercive power as an ally.

Wealth refers to the possession of money, property, and other valued objects in a society. It is more than just wages and income. Wealth includes other assets, such as stocks, bonds, and home ownership.

Wealth is the primary means by which people are able to gratify their needs in a capitalist political economy. Socialist political economy scripts are more likely to have basic needs met through government programs. Wealth can also be a means by which people exercise their influence on the political system.

Prestige is the amount of social respect that an individual or group receives in a society. Sociologists are mainly interested in the amount of prestige people receive based upon their jobs or occupations. Physicians, for instance, have considerably more prestige in the United States than teachers, custodians, and blue-collar workers.

Prestige is an important source of **self-esteem** in any society. People in positions with a high degree of social prestige are likely to have high self-esteem. People who occupy positions with low prestige are more likely to suffer from low self-esteem.

Prestige can also enhance the **credibility** of people. The prestige of physicians often makes their opinions about topics outside their area of expertise more credible than when custodians express their views on the same topics. In a society where more prestige is given to husbands as the breadwinners than wives as homemakers, husbands are likely to have a credibility advantage. A persuasive advantage based upon prestige can easily be translated into a power advantage.

Sociologists measure prestige by asking people in a society to rank different jobs and occupations. What is highly valued in one society may be less valued in another. The amount of prestige afforded jobs and occupations can also fluctuate in the same society. An example is when Americans learned that many top executives lied about their corporate revenues and assets in order to enrich themselves. For many, this tarnished the prestige of people in those positions.

SOCIAL MOBILITY

Social mobility refers to **movement** between **social classes** or layers of stratification within a society. **Career mobility** refers to the increases or losses in power, wealth, or status during someone's lifetime. The former is associated with **upward career mobility.** The latter is associated with **downward career mobility.**

Intergenerational mobility involves the extent to which **successive generations** experience upward or downward mobility. This can apply to families or generations defined as a birth cohort. If your parents live better than their parents, then they have intergenerational upward mobility. If baby boomers, those born between 1945 and the early sixties, live better than previous generations of Americans, they can be seen as upwardly mobile.

CASTE AND CLASS SYSTEMS

The distinction between **caste** and **class systems** has been used to characterize different **potentials** for social mobility. In a **traditional caste system,** such as that which exists in India, social mobility is limited. People cannot escape the caste into which they were born. A **class system,** by way of contrast, was used to indicate the **possibility** of **upward mobility** in a society such as the United States.

While the comparison has validity, it obscures as much as it illuminates. Upward mobility in a class system such as ours is much more limited than once recognized. This is partly because many generations of early Americans did experience either career or intergenerational upward mobility. What was missing from the picture is the extent to which these possibilities depend upon economic circumstances. Humble beginnings and ample job opportunities for unskilled and semiskilled labor fueled much early mobility.

Today, the opportunities for upward mobility among poorly educated Americans is severely limited. The demand for more education and skills traps the less fortunate to an extent that previously did not exist. Corporate downsizing and outsourcing jobs to Third World countries has further reduced mobility opportunities for both blue- and white-collar workers in America. The draw of cheap labor is not limited to unskilled jobs. Today, corporations are increasingly outsourcing engineering, financial, and other highly skilled jobs to workers in countries such as India.

Changing economic realities may cause the present generation of Americans to become downwardly mobile. We can already see this in terms of career mobility when successful middle-aged or older executives are downsized to make room for younger and cheaper labor. Not being able to sustain a lifestyle is the hallmark of downward mobility, regardless of whether or not someone is a blue- or white-collar worker.

The prospect of downward mobility for the current generation of students and young workers also exists. The difference is that this involves intergenerational rather than career mobility. Tough job markets and the prospect of limited opportunities in the future will make it difficult for many college students today to match the lifestyles of their parents.

JUSTIFYING SYSTEMS OF STRATIFICATION

Dominant groups who **benefit from arrangements** within a society have a vested interest in perpetuating their advantages. Using their credibility advantage, the dominant group tries to accomplish this by peddling ideas that serve their interests. King James I of England did this when he claimed that Kings are God's lieutenants on earth. Kings have a divine right to rule.

These **ideas** can also be thought of as **techniques of neutralization** that members of the dominant group use to rationalize their advantages. Feeling guilt about having so much while others go hungry? No problem! Just dust off some old arguments to justify your advantage. Getting the less fortunate to buy into the arguments creates **false consciousness** among them. It is false consciousness because internalizing justifications of the dominant group for inequities placates minorities and makes them accept their plight.

Now it is time to look at some illustrations of ideas that the dominant group in the United States has used and still uses to justify and sustain its advantages. These ideas range from **Social Darwinism** and **distributive justice** to the **Protestant work ethic** and **conspicuous consumption.**

SOCIAL DARWINISM

Charles Darwin published *The Origins of the Species* in 1859. In this famous book, Darwin argued that **species** evolve from simple to complex organisms through the mechanism of natural selection. **Natural selection** is the process by which the environment sorts out which species will survive and perpetuate. Species with characteristics that do not match the survival requirements in a given environment become extinct.

Social Darwinism represents a dominant ideology that **justifies human conquest** and **domination** through a misreading of what Darwin meant by natural selection. For Darwin, natural selection involves the survival or extinction of an entire species and not what happens within a species such as humans. The problem with Social Darwinism is that it focuses entirely on "survival" among individuals or certain groups within the human species.

During the nineteenth century, this erroneous application of Darwinism to human events become immensely popular as a justification for European colonialism. The colonial rule of Great Britain over less-developed countries was explained as a manifestation of Darwin's natural selection. The strong survive, while the weak are vanquished.

Adding to the distortion of Darwin has been an attempt to justify patterns of human conquest and domination with an analogy based upon predator/prey relations in nature. The argument is that war and human conquest is just as natural as a lion killing a zebra. The seductive appeal of this contention wears off once one realizes that lions and zebras are two different species. It has nothing at all to do with lions killing lions or zebras killing zebras! Trying to justify what goes on between members of the same species, such as humans, with an analogy based upon what goes on between different species is absurd.

Yet, the popularity of Social Darwinism continues today. Not only is it used to rationalize the role of the United States as a dominant world power, it is also used to justify inequities among Americans in terms of power, wealth, and prestige. The script insists that social inequities are simply a manifestation of the struggle for survival. The rich and the powerful deserve their advantages, while the poor deserve their plight because of their deficiencies.

DISTRIBUTIVE JUSTICE

During the Great Depression, the son of a prominent and wealthy family became alarmed over attacks from voices representing the downtrodden that raised questions about the virtues of families such as his own. The possibility that wealthy families such as his own might be predators troubled him greatly. Later on George Homans would become a social psychologist at Harvard where he developed a theory to alleviate his concerns.

Homans (1961) argued that gaps between the wealthy and poor in a society are really **fair** and **just.** According to Homans, the reason is that those at the top have more to offer. His contention is quite attractive to many Americans. It certainly gives greed a different interpretation.

The bottom line for Homans is that people get what they deserve. This is what Homans meant by **distributive justice.** His basic argument is that an unequal distribution of rewards is just in a society or workplace because of differences in contributions made by those at the top and those at the bottom.

What Homans proposed justifies any gap between the top and bottom in terms of who gets what. If the magnitude of stratification is enormous, all that it takes is for the advantaged to inflate their value. How else could one explain the growing gap between CEOs and workers in the United States? A few decades ago, CEOs earned about 30 times the wages of workers. By 2000, that advantage was more than 300 times the wages of workers. Saying that CEOs had become ten times more valuable in that time span requires an agile imagination.

This does not mean that such claims will fall on deaf ears. The wealthy in the United States have an enormous credibility advantage over those who might argue that such a claim is nonsense. But even if workers don't accept the contention that this is just, it may not matter. Corporate America has the coercive leverage to depress worker wages with threats to move elsewhere.

THE PROTESTANT WORK ETHIC

We have already discussed how the German sociologist Max Weber linked Protestant ideas with the growth of capitalism. What Weber proposed has relevance for scripts that justify inequities in the United States. Reviewing his basic argument is essential for understanding this relevance.

His book focused primarily on **Protestant denominations** that embrace the doctrine of predestination. This doctrine states that God has already chosen those who will enjoy everlasting life. Weber went on to suggest that Protestants understandably experience considerable salvation anxiety. The result is an effort to determine who manifests "signs of grace." All this can also apply to Protestants who do not believe in predestination but for whom eternal life must be earned.

Weber proposed that Protestants look to their own list of virtues for the answer. This list includes virtues such as hard work, thrift, and so forth. Those best manifesting these virtues are the mostly likely to be among God's chosen. Talk about prestige!

This interpretation suggests that working hard is a sign of being among God's chosen. If this is true, then slaves must be among the most likely to have been chosen for salvation. Just mentioning slaves suggests that what Weber had in mind did not include the most exploited at the lowest rungs in society.

Justifying social inequities with religion and the work ethic is just as suspicious as using Social Darwinism or distributive justice to justify them. Perhaps the most convenient distortion is that those at the bottom are lazy and therefore the least likely to be among the chosen. This justifies treating them like expendables.

But the fact that such claims are dubious is not the real point. What counts is who believes them. Believing such claims can unite a dominant group. A dominant group that feels a sense of moral justification is likely to feel comfortable imposing its will on those who it defines as unacceptable.

CONSPICUOUS CONSUMPTION

Conspicuous consumption involves the **lavish display of wealth** through the purchase of expensive items such as cars and homes. The chapter on American contradictions discussed it compared to the quest for self-fulfillment. Now its relevance to scripts that justify inequities within a society can be established.

In a materialistic society such as the United States, conspicuous consumption is elevated to a symbol of accomplishment. The higher the value of what is consumed, the higher one's **prestige.** Prestige afforded by others then becomes the basis for self-esteem. The more people applaud, the better one feels about oneself.

Conspicuous consumption rivals the work ethic as a justification for inequities in the United States. The consumption ethic equates the value of people with their capacity to consume. Because the wealthy set the standards of lavish consumption, they are rated the highest on this basis. Everyone else falls somewhere below them on the prestige scale.

Even though both the work and consumption ethic can be used to justify a system of inequities within a society, there is one fundamental difference. The people Weber talked about would never indulge in the lavish display of their wealth if for no other reason than the Protestant virtue of thrift. This stands in stark contrast to the generation of early industrialists in the United States who thrived on conspicuous consumption. An example is all the mansions that wealthy Americans built to rival European castles.

COUNTER-IDEOLOGIES

Minorities rely upon **counter-ideologies** to challenge the advantages of the dominant group in a society. A socialist political economic script constitutes a counter ideology in a society where a capitalist political economic script prevails. A capitalist political economic script represents a counter-ideology in a society where a socialist political economic script prevails.

Mannheim (1936) identified counter-ideologies that call for massive change in society utopias. A **utopian ideology** is a script that calls for such changes. Utopian ideologists range from Karl Marx to Islamic fundamentalists who want to drastically alter societies around the world.

A counter-ideology embraced by a minority does not necessarily represent an extensive assault on existing social, economic, or political arrangements. Many counter-ideologies in American society involve lifestyles or tastes advanced through the existing political structures. The gay rights movement in the United States is one example.

Many other disputes in the United States involve different tastes, in everything from music to literature. Within this context, those who embrace whatever is popular at a given point in time represent the dominant group. If Top 40 music is primarily available in a given market, then it represents the preferences of the dominant group. The dominant group includes people such as advertisers, station managers, and audiences. Those favoring alternative music that gets little play would represent a minority group.

THINK TANKS

Moral entrepreneurs increasingly rely on think tanks for their arguments. A **think tank** is an **organization** devoted to research and writing to develop positions on certain topics. The most important political think tanks in the United States can be roughly classified as conservative or liberal. Think tanks feed moral entrepreneurs with ammunition that can be used to sell social, political, and economic scripts that they favor.

Conservative think tanks such as the **Heritage Foundation** and the **American Enterprise Institute** have gotten the edge in recent years. Both are extremely well funded and effective in presenting conservative scripts. Their activities include funding scholars to write papers and books that advance conservative points of view. They also provide conservative candidates, talk show hosts, and other supportive moral entrepreneurs with "talking points" to advance agendas that serve the dominant group.

BACKLASH

Historically White Anglo-Saxon Protestant men (WASPS) were the dominant group in American society. The term **backlash** refers to attempts by this group and its allies to reclaim ground lost to minorities. Targets of the backlash movement include racial, ethnic, and religious groups that are seen as causing these losses. Women who challenge male patriarchy are also included as targets.

CONSERVATIVE THINK TANKS AND BACKLASH

Both the Heritage Foundation and the American Enterprise Institute are among the most prominent players. Both fund scholars to develop research and "talking points" that promote conservative agendas. Conservative moral entrepreneurs on talk radio and television use such talking points to fuel their backlash movement.

During the Clinton administration, many conservatives who were displaced in Washington D.C. landed endowed positions at these think tanks. When Bush was elected, many of these "scholars" found jobs in the White House, government, or as advisors. Their ideas, and those developed by others in these think tanks, have shaped and reinforced both domestic and foreign policy directions taken by the Bush administration.

Attacks on affirmative action are just one example. Cries of reverse discrimination are common as an ideological justification for eradicating programs designed to help those who are disadvantaged. The claim that affirmative action is unfair because it favors minorities was loudly proclaimed. A more subtle message has been that minorities are generally less qualified than their white male counterparts. A similar message has been directed at women. That message is that women are less capable of leading companies or governments than their white male counterparts.

Using minority moral entrepreneurs to express these viewpoints has been a clever ploy. Successful African Americans such as Supreme Court Justice Clarence Thomas, who benefited from an affirmative action program at the Yale Law school, rail against affirmative action. Meanwhile, minorities who still suffer from discrimination shudder about their futures and the futures of their children.

The claim that affirmative action represents a form of reverse discrimination often is combined with the notion that minorities are unqualified. The idea that affirmative action and reverse discrimination denies more qualified people admission to universities is a popular refrain. In the *University of Michigan* case, conservative critics of affirmative action used this and the image of racial minorities to attack it.

This case began when a Caucasian male and female student complained that affirmative action cost them admission to the University of Michigan. Opponents of affirmative action rallied to their support. Certainly an injustice was committed. Their high school grades and admission scores were cited to justify their point. But it turned out that minorities with lower grades or admission scores represented only about one-third of all those who were admitted with lower credentials.

Who were the other two-thirds? Many were legacies of parents who had graduated from that university. Others were athletes. Some were preferred because they filled other slots, such as in the marching band. Why weren't these situations targeted? One could argue that these less-qualified students were twice as likely to be the cause of the two applicants' problems as academic minorities who benefited from affirmative action.

One of the most troubling issues involving affirmative action is the focus on admission or job qualifications. Affirmative action was intended to help those who are disadvantaged, which disproportionately involves minorities. Minorities are less likely to get quality education, which means that they are the most likely to be excluded based upon racially neutral criteria. Even with affirmative action, the numbers of African American and Hispanic students in colleges or universities still fall far below their numbers in society. The picture is even worse when looking at graduate programs and professional schools in areas such as law and medicine.

What is interesting about the backlash is that it is not limited to admission or job qualification debates. At one time, varsity sports in high schools and colleges were the domain of men. This privilege began to be eroded with passage of Title IX legislation in 1972. This legislation prohibits discrimination in funding against women athletes in schools that receive any federal aid. The legislation has greatly improved opportunities for women in sports, even though parity with funding for male sports still does not exist.

From the beginning, moral entrepreneurs favoring male athletes have ranted and raved about Title IX. The decibels really increase whenever a male sport is placed in jeopardy by funding for a female one. What causes the anger is the underlying assumption that only men deserve athletic opportunities.

Much is also made of the fact that sports, such as football and men's basketball, are major revenue generators. By a curious twist of logic, this is used to justify the viewpoint that any excess revenues generated by these sports should be given to nonrevenue men's sports. Linking who generates funds with who should get funds is an interesting sleight of hand.

Also missing from such arguments is the point that, while these sports do generate the most revenue, they are also the most expensive to maintain. Head coaches routinely make much more money than the president of their university. Apparently running an athletic program is more important than running the university.

There is strong evidence that Title IX still has a ways to go. Data suggests that between 1972 when the act was enacted and 1997, for every *new* dollar spent on women, two dollars were spent on male sports. Contributing to this disparity is the fact that between 1992 and 1997, new spending on male sports increased $3 for every $1 spent on women. The majority of athletic scholarships, about 59 percent, still go to men. Budgets in athletic departments also favor men three to one over women. The disparity in money spent on recruiting favors male athletes by more than three to one. And a 1997 NCAA study found that about half of Division 1-A and 1-AA college football programs don't cover their own expenses, let alone subsidize other programs.

POLITICAL CORRECTNESS

One of the most effective ploys for discrediting counter-ideologies in the United States has been the concept of **political correctness.** The idea was created by conservative think tanks and first used publicly by President George H. W. Bush. Since then, political correctness has been used extensively to discredit liberals or anyone with the audacity to challenge the dominant ideology.

Political correctness is meant to trivialize serious challenges to the status quo by minorities who have been disadvantaged by the system. Complaints by minorities about demeaning comments or behaviors are dismissed as politically correct. The key charge is that liberals have made Americans hypersensitive to labels.

Here is how conservative moral entrepreneurs use the concept of political correctness to disparage opposing viewpoints. According to them, no one complained about men making sexually offensive remarks around women before crazed liberals imposed their politically correct viewpoints on everyone. Now men have to restrain themselves and not tell jokes that disparage women in their presence. What's wrong? Have women lost their sense of humor?

The political correctness movement wraps itself in attacks on free speech. What it is really about is discrediting a counter-ideology that exposes how such remarks and attitudes contribute to oppression and discrimination against women and other minorities. It is really all about the freedom to let the dominant group regain its lost ground.

COMFORT ZONES

A familiar complaint among white men is that the presence of minorities disturbs their **comfort zone.** Much of this discomfort is caused by disruptions in their **taken-for-granted worlds.** An example is when men complain that the presence of women in the workplace makes them feel uncomfortable. Apparently, the presence of women takes the fun out of telling sexist jokes.

Elsewhere men complain about having to refrain from belching, scratching, and swearing when around women in the workplace. Many dream of the good old days when they were free to be men. These perceived restraints on their freedoms are one reason why they are angry toward minorities. Protecting their comfort zone can easily take precedence over any appreciation about what these jobs mean to minorities who have been excluded for so long.

Notice that disturbing the comfort zone of men in the workplace or elsewhere is the main concern. At golf clubs, men were able to protect their comfort zones from their wives by excluding them. A variation was to have "ladies day," which the guys avoided like the plague. Today many private golf clubs either refuse or erect barriers designed to keep women and other minorities out. This is particularly significant when playing golf with prominent people is an important element in building a successful career.

These examples involving comfort zones illustrate the extent to which white men will go to preserve their advantages. The degree to which political correctness is used by the right to advance its scripts can be measured by the number of times it appears in the titles of articles or books. Its inclusion is a signal that the article or book will be an assault on a counter-ideology or proponents of challenges to scripts that advance conservative agendas.

WHITE MEN AS VICTIMS

The number of commentaries, articles, and books on **white men** as **victims** is staggering. All of them whine about how white men are losing out to minorities. The underlying assumption is that all of this is tragic because white men are really more qualified than minorities.

Whether or not the impression, that minorities are not as qualified, is expressed or remains a subtext, varies. It is left unstated when moral entrepreneurs worry that it might be too offensive. On other occasions, it is given explicit voice. An example is when moral entrepreneurs claim that women are genetically unsuited for leadership. The less than subtle implication is that a woman is born to follow.

Genetics arguments underscore other explanations designed to prevent women access to certain areas. Moral entrepreneurs for a military comprised solely of men often argue that women are genetically not suited for warfare. The claim is that women are genetically programmed to nurture.

Whether or not such arguments are believed is a separate issue. The notion that women are naturally nurturing is arguable. Children are just as likely to be physically abused or killed by their mothers as by their fathers. Does this mean that the military should view women as an untapped killing force?

To the extent that men believe that women are nurturing is the extent to which they will see themselves as victims if they lose military jobs to them. The same pertains to other qualifications, such as the ability to lead or fly a high performance aircraft. The extent to which women are given opportunities to prove themselves is the extent to which women have a chance to alter genetic stereotypes.

The underlying assumption of superior qualifications is what sustains credibility for the claim that white men are victims whenever minorities get the jobs previously reserved for them. Notice how this assumption can lead to different reactions when someone loses a job. Suppose a school district must fire one employee to meet its budget. Also suppose that in this hypothetical situation, one teacher is a white male and the other is a minority.

Try to visualize the different reactions of moral entrepreneurs. Moral entrepreneurs for white men are likely to view the matter as an injustice or tragedy if the white male teacher is fired. These same moral entrepreneurs are likely to shrug their shoulders if the minority teacher is fired.

Moral entrepreneurs for minorities may view the firing of the minority teacher as a travesty. But while their contention might resonate among many minorities, it is likely to be greeted with suspicion or even contempt by those who believe minorities are less qualified. The latter reaction can even occur among minorities who have bought into the notion of white male superiority.

THE NEW POLITICAL INCORRECTNESS

The concept of **political correctness** has revitalized the use of politically insensitive terms and expressions. Notice that the emphasis is on the revitalized use of politically insensitive comments. It is meant to distinguish the new **political incorrectness** from insensitive or offensive talk in the past.

What distinguishes the new political incorrectness is the degree to which it celebrates offensive talk. The **new political incorrectness** is heralded as a fresh alternative to the distortions and constraints imposed by political correctness. When a talk show host characterizes those who advocate improving conditions for women as "Femi-Nazis," his obviously insensitive characterization is celebrated by his audience as a demonstration of his independent thought. He is no captive of politically correct speech.

Being politically incorrect has become a badge of honor among those who view themselves as independent thinkers. The fact that many just parrot what they have heard on the radio doesn't phase them. Nor does the fact that the radio talk show host just mentioned calls his audience "ditto heads" seem to matter. Some even join the host and call themselves "ditto heads," yet still cherish a self-image of being independent thinkers.

Many who practice political incorrectness see themselves as more than independent thinkers. They like to characterize themselves as people who "tell it like it is." The implication is that they cut through political correctness and tell the truth. To say that this characterization is self-serving is a gross understatement.

PLAYING THE INDEPENDENCE CARD

Talk show hosts are not the first to manipulate an audience by playing the independence card. The **independence card** appeals to people who think of themselves as an **independent thinker.** It is the style of **maverick moral entrepreneurs.** It is particularly effective in the United States, where being contrary is celebrated as distinguishing one from the unwashed herd.

A classic example from the world of advertising illustrates how the independence card can be used to manipulate people. Advertisers often use it to sell products. Phillip Morris used this theme to sell cigarettes. Or more accurately, Phillip Morris played the independence card to sell a brand of cigarettes developed for women. The problem was most women smokers at that time were not about to give up their unfiltered brands for a "wimp" cigarette.

What resulted was a successful campaign to market the new filtered cigarette to men through ads featuring the Marlboro Man. The Marlboro Man is the embodiment of independence and machismo. His best friend is his horse. This ad campaign was designed to give men permission to smoke what amounted to a "girly" cigarette by wrapping the product in the image of independence and manliness.

Not too many years later, the same company developed a light beer to compete with the sale of white wine to women. Once again their market forecasts were disappointing. Women did not flock to their new product. So what to do? Why not give men permission to drink what is essentially a "girly" beer? This was accomplished by a series of Miller Lite commercials that featured independent macho men swilling diluted beer with their buddies.

SCAPEGOATING

Scapegoating represents another means by which moral entrepreneurs can discredit a counter-ideology. To **scapegoat** someone is to blame them for problems that they did not create. Sociologists are particularly interested in seeing how blaming minorities is used to help the advantaged within a society.

Blaming minorities is a favorite ploy of some conservative talk show hosts. An example is when women are blamed for the angst working-class white men feel due to the loss of jobs. Clever talk show hosts know how to direct that anger toward feminists rather than those at the top who are responsible for those job dislocations and losses.

Freud's concept of **displacement** helps explain how this works. **Displacement** occurs when people shift their anger from a threatening source to a less threatening alternative. An example would be when someone goes home and kicks the dog rather than release that anger toward a boss. "Don't take your frustrations out on me" expresses the same point.

Ventilating anger toward minorities is safer than directing it toward corporate executives who make the decisions that affect the loss of jobs. Someone who has been laid off risks more if he tells off his boss than if he ventilates against minorities. To ventilate against a boss is practically a guarantee against a positive letter of recommendation that may be needed to secure a new job.

Identification with the aggressor can also come into play. Those who lose their jobs because of decisions by the advantaged may unconsciously realize that their hopes for the future rest with them. Identifying with scripts associated with the advantaged may relieve anxieties about the future. This is not likely to come from identifying with the disadvantaged.

Directing anger toward people who have little or nothing to do with problems people experience protects the powerful from criticism. How people with virtually no power can cause so many problems is rarely addressed. An example is undocumented workers. The reason that the United States has a problem with undocumented workers is because there are employers who want to hire them. In fact, many employers prefer non-English speaking illegal immigrants to legal residents. The reason is that it is easier to exploit non-English speaking illegal immigrants.

This suggests that undocumented workers are not taking jobs from other Americans. Instead it suggests that employers prefer giving jobs to them. But where is the anger toward those employers? It is the job of their moral entrepreneurs to direct that anger elsewhere.

THE SOCIAL CLASS CARD

Minorities by definition are those who are **relatively disadvantaged** in a society. For moral entrepreneurs who represent minorities to play the social class card is to be expected. The **social class card** involves pointing out **gaps between minorities** and those **who benefit the most** from arrangements in a society.

Moral entrepreneurs for the advantaged complain that playing the social class card is wrong. Many would have us believe that social classes don't make a difference in the United States. If this doesn't work, they often resort to highly charged labels, such as calling those who describe such disparities as Marxists. What really concerns them is the little dirty secret about American society. It is the fact that the top 10 percent control more than 60 percent of the total wealth!

CARE-BASED APPEALS

Care-based appeals present everything from politicians, governments, and corporations as concerned about the less fortunate in societies. President Reagan's "trickle down" economic theory is one example. He argued that the best way to help the poor is to give the rich more money through tax-saving programs. The basic idea was that the rich would then invest their additional wealth in the creation of good-paying jobs, and in the process the benefits would trickle down to those at the bottom of society.

Critics charged that this was all a deception and the only ones who would really benefit are those at the top. Data suggests that the critics were right. Under this plan, the gap between the wealthy and the poor increased substantially.

Another example of a political care-based appeal occurred at the annual meeting of the seven richest nations in the world in Genoa, Italy that took place during the summer of 2001. The first official act of the leaders was to donate one billion dollars to fight AIDS. Their purpose was to soften criticism that they are insensitive to the plight of the downtrodden in Third World countries. That one billion dollars seems like a generous offer but in reality it represents less than one-tenth of one percent of the combined national budgets of these wealthy nations.

CORPORATE CARE-BASED ADVERTISEMENTS

Corporations often use care-based appeals to soften negative attitudes about them. **Care-based advertisements** present a corporation as caring about the less fortunate. This ploy has become almost a stock-in-trade for tobacco companies.

One cigarette company featured its donations to help fund a home for wayward teens. Another ad reenacts the distribution of food given to people in Bosnia from one of the company's other divisions. And yet another tobacco company ad features its funding for breast cancer research.

All of these ads are meant to soften images associated with disease and death caused by the use of tobacco. The audacity of ads featuring funds for breast cancer is remarkable, given the lengths to which tobacco companies have gone to market their products to women. What's next? How long before tobacco companies feature donations for research on prostate cancer?

The relevance of care-based ads for social stratification should be obvious. Care-based ads are meant to sustain or improve profits, often at the expense of others in society. With tobacco companies, it involves more than just hooking a new generation on their products. By softening their image, such ads are also meant to diminish the prospect that states and others will sue them in the future.

MINORITY OPTIONS FOR IMPROVING MOBILITY

Minorities are confronted with a number of different options concerning the advancement of their interests. Because of power differentials that favor the dominant group, coercive power has limited potential in the United States today. Minorities who try and confront them are at a coercive disadvantage.

Challenging existing scripts through **civil disobedience** has been a more successful tactic. Civil disobedience is the deliberate violation of a law. The purpose is to bring attention to the law. When Dr. Martin Luther King Jr. and his colleagues sat in at segregated lunch counters in the South, they were engaging in civil disobedience. Civil means refraining from the use violence. Instead it was the police and the Klan that used violence against the demonstrators.

The use of coercion is a limited option simply because those who control government have a virtual monopoly on it. The risks associated with violent challenges are illustrated by what happened to the Black Panthers. During the 1960s, the Black Panthers expressed a philosophy based upon their right to protect themselves from white violence by arming themselves. This was soon interpreted by the white power structure as more than just a defensive posture. It was seen as a call for armed insurrection. The result was a violent campaign by the police against the Black Panthers.

What the Black Panthers may not have realized is that by arming themselves even for self-defense, they made themselves more vulnerable to police violence. The police could always justify the excessive use of violent force by claiming that the Panthers were armed. The result was that many Black Panthers died and most of the others were imprisoned.

What happened to the Black Panthers has happened to others who defiantly arm themselves for what they claim is self-defense. At both Waco and Ruby Ridge, the police killed people who announced that they were armed for the purpose of self-defense. The only difference is that they were whites who were perceived by the dominant group as an armed threat.

Whether or not the intent of all these groups was entirely self-defense is not the real issue. A more relevant point is that the government has a monopoly on coercive power. What happened to the Black Panthers who were killed by the police or those who lost their lives at Waco hardly taps into what this means. Consider what the government could do to a compound of defiant advocates of a counter-ideology. Imagine how long those hardy souls could last against a cruise missile.

The direct action alternative to armed resistance is best captured by the strategy of Martin Luther King Jr. Dr. King advocated **civil disobedience.** Civil disobedience is a method based upon peacefully disobeying laws that are seen as unjust. For Dr. King and others it meant **script challenges** through acts such as sitting in on segregated lunch counters in the South.

Some confuse civil disobedience as a nonviolent strategy for challenging dominant ideologies with violent reactions by those in the dominant group. Dr. King and his followers frequently faced violence by both white citizens and the police. Many still underestimate the courage its takes to engage in peaceful acts of civil disobedience under such conditions.

Armed resistance and civil disobedience are direct challenges to a dominant group. Alternative strategies use **persuasion.** But moral entrepreneurs for minorities often encounter obstacles when trying to use persuasion to advance their agendas. **False consciousness** among minorities can create resistance to messages designed to mobilize them.

Trying to sell a counter-ideology to a dominant group can represent a formidable challenge. Resistance to scripts that might undermine their advantages is to be expected. But without support from at least some within the dominant group, it may be difficult to bring about change with persuasion alone.

SOCIAL MOBILITY

Social mobility has already been discussed. Now the attention will shift from types of mobility to circumstances that influence it. Both **discrimination** and **family resources** are significant factors.

DISCRIMINATION

Americans often **confuse** the significance of **prejudice** and **discrimination. Prejudice** involves a **negative attitude** that some hold about others. Members of both dominant and minorities groups can be prejudiced.

Discrimination is a different because it involves more than just prejudice or bad attitudes. **Discrimination** involves **power.** It occurs whenever a **dominant group** operates as a **gatekeeper** and treats those like it favorably, while denying minorities access to opportunities and valued resources.

There are two sides to discrimination. One side involves **denying minorities** access to opportunities and valued resources. The other side involves **gatekeepers favoring members of the dominant group** when it comes to providing access to opportunities and valued resources.

Both forms of discrimination affect social mobility. Favorable treatment improves the chances people will have to advancing. Unfavorable treatment decreases the chance that people will be able to improve their social class situation.

In the United States, discrimination is based upon factors such as race, ethnicity, religion, and gender. The dominant group has characteristics that benefit them in a system of stratification. Historically, being a white Protestant Anglo-Saxon male (WASP) has been a considerable advantage. Minorities have characteristics that the dominant group uses to deny them access to opportunity structures, which is why they are located

FAMILY RESOURCES AND SOCIAL MOBILITY

Family of origin is often equated with our **birth** family. This is too restrictive because it excludes someone who is **adopted.** Nor does it include **blended families.** A blended family is one based upon divorce and remarriage.

Family resources are one of the keys to understanding social mobility. Family resources include everything from **education, wealth, power, attitudes,** and **networks** or the lack of them. Children raised in families with limited resources are limited in their opportunities for upward mobility.

Before looking more carefully at how family resources can influence both intergenerational and career mobility, a qualification factor must be mentioned. The significance of family resources depends upon economic conditions. A contracting economy reduces the potential for upward social mobility for everyone, but still those with the most family resources are better able to survive or improve their situation.

The significance of family resources is demonstrated by the fact that most of the men who became successful in business during the period from 1776 to 1920 were the sons of ministers. As sons of ministers, they had several advantages. The first is that they were likely to be literate like their fathers. Being able to read and write was definitely a bonus during that period in American history. The second advantage was that their fathers were among the most prominent members of their communities. This meant that their fathers were well connected.

Today, disparities in family wealth affect whether or not qualified students can attend college. Home ownership has become an increasingly significant variable as the cost of higher education has gone up. Families who own their homes can use their equity to secure loans to help pay for college. Families too poor to qualify for mortgages and who pay rent do not have access to this resource.

What many don't appreciate is that people who pay rent are disadvantaged in another regard. People who have a mortgage can deduct the interest on it and their residential taxes on their federal income tax. This means that the real cost to someone with a mortgage of $900 a month may be about the same as the cost to someone who rents for $600 a month. Not only does the homeowner have a nicer place in which to raise a family, but the homeowner also creates equity that can be used for everything from financing the education of their children to funding their own retirement.

Notice that the entire cycle of homeowner or renting can be vicious. Parents who have equity in their homes can draw upon it to help their children meet the down payment requirements for a mortgage. Parents who rent are much less likely to have enough money to help their children in the same way. This is because the vast majority of people who rent have little or no equity to borrow against.

Discrimination by lenders adds more to the woes of minorities in the United States. African American couples with the same financial qualifications are twice as likely to be turned down for mortgages as Caucasians. In fact some studies use Caucasian and African American couples to test local lending practices where the African American couple is given a profile that makes them more qualified than their white counterpart. Guess who is the most likely to get the loan? Once again Caucasian couples are at least twice as likely to get the loan.

Patterns of discrimination such as these also help to explain why in 2002, over 74 percent of Caucasian families owned their homes, while the figure for African Americans was only 48 percent. This means that nearly three-quarters of Caucasian families were able to use home ownership to accumulate wealth. Less than half of African Americans were able to use home ownership as a means for accumulating wealth during that same period of time. This advantage for Caucasian families can be used as a resource to help their children in hard times, as well as improving their prospects of upward mobility generally.

CHAPTER 16
AMERICAN MINORITIES

The general discussion on social stratification provides the background for looking at specific minorities in American society. These minorities are identified on the basis of race, ethnicity, religion, or gender. But before looking more carefully at what these designations mean, it will be helpful to make some more general points.

AMERICAN MINORITY GROUPS

American minorities groups are people in the United States who are **disadvantaged** in terms of **power, wealth,** and **social respect or prestige.** Minorities have the least access to power, have difficulty finding good paying jobs, and the jobs that they do have tend to be ones with low prestige.

The designation minority refers to the circumstances of a group. The fact that some within a racial, ethnic, religious, or gender-based group may be more fortunate is not the point. It is the circumstance of the entire group that counts.

MINORITIES AS TROPHIES

Minorities often become **trophies** or **prizes** that political parties enthusiastically display. It is a form of **impression management. White male politicians** can use an endorsement from a prominent minority leader to create the impression that the politician supports others in that minority community and they support him.

A **related ploy** used by **white male politicians** is to sprinkle **anonymous minority faces** as background images in political photo opts. The intended impression is the same. The speaker supports them and they support the speaker.

At one time, Democrats had a lock on minority endorsements because they were seen as the party that cared for them. But after decades of **affirmative action,** more **minorities** have gained access to success and privilege. That **success** and **identification** with the **dominant group** has prompted many of them to embrace more conservative views once associated almost exclusively with white males of the dominant group in American society. Thus, more minority voices are available to endorse Republican candidates and issues.

Exactly what political party is the party for minorities is not the issue. Images are what count with voters. Republican strategists must proceed with caution because while minority images benefit them with some groups, the same images may not play so well with other supporters. Democratic strategists must also proceed with caution because it is often difficult or impossible to win elections without support from white voters. There is also the problem for both parties that too much support for one minority group may alienate other minority groups.

ROLE MODELS

High-profile minorities, regardless of their political or social views, serve as **successful role models** for others in their minority communities. Affirmative action has played a key role in breaking down discrimination barriers that in the past denied talented minorities from moving up in society. Creating positive role models for minority communities was the prime objective of affirmative action.

Backlash moral entrepreneurs who favor returning to the past when gatekeepers from the dominant group discriminated against minorities have their own spin on affirmative action. To hear them talk you would think that affirmative action programs discriminate against white males. The reality is quite different. Women still represent the numerical majority in the United States, but after the retirement of Sandra Day O'Connor, only one of nine justices on the Supreme Court are women. The number of women heading the top 500 corporations in the United States fluctuates between a few to none. And of course, even Catholics who represent about 25 percent of Americans have had one of their own elected to President of the United States. Women and other minorities such as African Americans and Hispanic Americans are still waiting their turn.

Although **high-profile minorities** are **positive role models** for minority communities, political divisions can taint them. Many African Americans felt a closer affinity with Thurgood Marshall as an African American on the Supreme Court than they do with the much more politically conservative Clarence Thomas. African Americans with more conservative values and beliefs find Clarence Thomas more to their liking.

For practically the entire history of network news programs on television, minorities have been conspicuously absent. Among the national programs, only CBS briefly used Connie Chung as an anchor. ABC, CBS, and NBC all reverted to past practices and in 2005 only white men anchored their evening news slots. Meanwhile the folks at Fox grasped the significance of having female anchors. Market shares for Fox and others that have begun to use more female anchors have improved.

MINORITY REALITIES

Minorities are people **who as a group** are **disadvantaged.** Looking at minority participation in politics is one measure. One minority reality is that minorities are underrepresented in politics. Another minority reality is that they are even more underrepresented at the top levels of American corporations.

Another **reality for minorities** is a **disproportionately small share of wealth.** Wealth is based upon a variety of factors. **Income** is the amount of money paid for work. Whether or not fringe benefits, such as healthcare and retirement programs, are available is a related variable. Fringe benefits paid for by the employer are considered as income.

Household assets are different from income. Household assets refer to everything that a family owns. The single most important form of household assets is the amount of equity that a family has in their home. Home equity is the difference between what is still owed on a home and its market value. Home equity is not available to renters.

Other household assets include everything from furniture, appliances, and TVs to stocks and bonds. Household assets are significant in two regards. The first is that the average value of all household assets is a good indicator of how well different groups are doing. The second is that household assets represent a legacy that children can inherit in the future. The children of minorities suffer substantially in this regard, which contributes to intergenerational cycles of disadvantage.

Minority realities include **lower life expectancies** among **men** and **higher rates of poverty** and **infant mortality.** There is one exception to life expectancy. Although women are disadvantaged on all other wealth, power, and prestige scales, women outlive males in all categories. But for men, the life expectancy differences are startling. For a Caucasian male child born in 2001 the life expectancy 75. The life expectancy of an African American male is 68.6 years (Macionis, 2006: 399). The life expectancy for African American women is about 8 years less than it is for Caucasian women.

Minority realities include **higher poverty rates.** The **rate of poverty** reflects the percentage of people within a racial or ethnic category who are poor. Statistics from 2002 show that about 9 percent of Caucasians lived in poverty, 21 percent of African Americans lived in poverty, and 22 percent of Hispanics lived in poverty (Henslin, 2006: 212).

Minority realities include **higher infant mortality** rates. **Infant mortality** refers to the number of children that do not survive the first year. Access to healthcare during pregnancy and afterward is probably the single most significant factor affecting infant mortality rates. The death rate among disadvantaged infants in the United States who are minorities is twice as high as it is for advantaged children (Macionis, 2006: 398).

Minority realities include less access to **educational opportunities.** As college and university education becomes increasingly important, access to it becomes a critical issue for minorities. A significant problem for minorities is that they are disproportionately from poor communities, where access to quality educational resources from K–12 is more difficult than it is in more prosperous communities. This places them at a disadvantage when seeking admission to colleges and universities. Another problem is the high cost of higher education. Minority families have less income and are less likely than whites to own their homes that can be used as collateral for loans to help pay the bills.

The amount of education for parents is also significant because it can affect aspirations for their children. Parents who are better educated are more likely to encourage reading books, newspapers, and magazines. Parents that are well educated are more likely to give their children access to computer skills that are increasingly essential for school and the workplace.

Minority realities include **lower social prestige** because the jobs that they have are less prestigious. The amount of prestige given to various jobs and occupations often affects **self-esteem.** Members of a dominant group who have more prestigious jobs or occupations are more likely to feel good about themselves than people who work in lowly jobs that are scorned by society. Having high self-esteem is more important than most people realize.

Recent events have conveyed the importance of self-esteem and jobs. Many successful white men who lost their jobs due to corporate downsizing and restructuring found out that they lost more than their wages. Not having their jobs deprived them of their self-esteem. Working at McDonalds is a demeaning alternative to the prestige they experienced as corporate managers.

Minorities, on average, hold jobs that are judged demeaning by others. Their jobs deprive them of the self-esteem many other Americans take for granted. What has happened to some, because of corporate downsizing and restructuring, is a depressing reality for American minorities.

IDENTIFYING MINORITIES

Race, ethnicity, religion, and **gender** are the most common factors that are used to distinguish the dominant group from minorities. Care must be taken not to confuse these criteria. Confusion over the difference between race and ethnicity is one of the most frequent. Some other confusion will also be pointed out.

RACE

Racial differences are based upon **genetic factors** that create different **physical features.** Identifying differences based upon physical features such as skin color seems simple enough until one explores the matter a little more deeply. The problem is that there are few genetically pure races anymore. The genetic pools upon which racial differences are based have become diluted down through the centuries.

This does not mean that racial differences have completely disappeared. What it does mean is that categorizing people on the basis of race has become more a social process than a simple identification. An example is skin color. Lightness of skin color varies significantly among those categorized by the dominant group in the United States as African American.

Lightness of skin color may also affect how the dominant group treats those classified as African American. Does it discriminate on this basis? Are some in the African American community more disadvantaged on this basis?

Geneticists suggest that only about 1 or 2 percent of someone's entire genetic pool affects that person's racial appearance. This means that the genetic pools of groups in the United States are 98 percent or more comparable. This genetic fact suggests that **variations within groups** are likely to be as great as **variations between groups.** It does not mean that everyone is the same. But it does mean is that members of the dominant group and minorities are much more similar than some moral entrepreneurs would lead us to believe.

Take, for instance, intelligence. Caucasian moral entrepreneurs have written extensively on the subject. The essence of their argument is that Caucasians are intellectually superior to minorities such as African Americans.

Usually differences in success are taken as the basis for such contentions. The absence of African Americans in academe, corporate America, and politics is seen as conclusive evidence for the intellectual superiority of Caucasians. Notably absent from these appraisals are the historical effects of discrimination. In fact, denying minorities opportunities based upon the assumption of inferiority is a favorite ploy of dominant groups. The practice guarantees the creation of circumstances that are used to sustain the stereotype.

Moral entrepreneurs for the dominant group resort to a number of different ploys when confronted with minorities who counter this stereotype. One has been to argue that African Americans who have gained access to corporate American or politics are often light skinned. Rather than acknowledging that Caucasian gatekeepers might treat them more favorably, these moral entrepreneurs attribute their success to having the precious Caucasian seed.

Another ploy is to treat success as exceptions. Yes, some minorities are smart, but this is an exception. Caucasians are smarter on average than African Americans. Caucasian males have used also this same argument in regards to successful women.

The most familiar racial categories used in the United States are Caucasian, African American, Native American, and Asian American. Sometimes the terms Hispanic or Latino are used as a racial category, but this is inaccurate. The category Hispanic or Latino is an ethnic designation. Hispanic or Latinos differ amongst themselves in terms of racial differences. Some are distinguished on the basis of a genetic pool favoring European or Caucasian appearance. Others have appearances that are based upon genetic influences from Africa. And still others have racial appearances that reflect the genetics pools of Native populations.

ETHNICITY

Ethnicity is based upon **national** or **cultural origins.** Someone's ethnicity is determined by where his or her family is from. Ethnicity can be used to distinguish people who are classified together on the basis of race. It is what distinguishes Caucasian Americans whose relatives migrated from England, Ireland, Germany, or Italy. It is what distinguishes Asian Americans whose relatives came from China, Japan, South Korea, or India. It is what distinguishes Native Americans in different tribes. It is also what would have distinguished African Americans taken from different communities had slavery not disturbed these linkages.

Ethnic purity as a basis for classifying people has probably always been less than definitive. Centuries of war and conquest around the world have created fluid boundaries that often diluted ethnicity. Marriages between couples with different ethnicity elsewhere and here in the United States have diluted matters even more.

People still define themselves in ethnic terms. Often this requires a degree of selectivity. Choosing between ethnic possibilities is a common practice. Under patriarchy, the ethnic roots of a husband prevails over that of his wife. An example would be a family that defines itself as Italian when the father is Italian and the mother is German.

Contributing to this selectivity is the practice of having a married woman take the family name of her husband. This helps to establish his family's ethnicity as preferred. But patriarchy is not the only factor that affects ethnic identities among Americans. Some Americans who have multiple ethnic lines pick and choose. This is more likely to occur with latter generations rather than with those who first come here.

But even people who have absolutely no ethnic links may become enamored with a culture and define themselves accordingly. It becomes a positive reference group for them. An example would be when someone from a different ethnic background becomes an **Anglophile.** An Anglophile is someone who loves anything that is English.

Questions about **ethnic identities** are different from how **members of a dominant group define people.** What counts is how they define someone. Asian Americans often identify with their ethnic roots, such as being from China, Japan, or India. But the dominant group may throw them all together as Asian Americans. When a dominant group does this, it prioritizes race over ethnicity.

Earlier the point was made that the categories Hispanic and Latino are based upon ethnicity rather than race. As a generic ethnic designation, these terms refer to people who migrated to the United States from areas of this hemisphere that was under Spanish rule in the past. But a careful ethnic application requires more. It requires looking at whether someone is from Mexico, Puerto Rico, Cuba, Honduras, Panama, Columbia, and so forth.

RELIGION

Religion refers to **sacred ideas** that are **believed** or **thought to be true** by those who embrace them. **Religious differences** are often used to distinguish Americans. The vast majority of Americans are Protestants. Catholics are the next largest religious category. Other groups, such as Jews and Muslims, represent relatively small percentages.

Confusion over **religion** and **ethnicity** is common. It occurs when someone from Ireland is automatically thought to be Catholic. The reality is that the first Irish who came to the United States were from Protestant areas in the north. The migration of Catholic Irish came much later.

A similar mistake is often made concerning German Americans. Because of Luther, many automatically assume that Germans Americans are Protestants. Many Germans who migrated to the United States are Protestants. But those migrating from the Bavarian region of Germany are more likely to be Catholic. That area is approximately 80 percent Catholic.

GENDER

Gender involves the biological **difference** of whether or not someone is a **male** or **female.** Males are the dominant group in the United States because of their relative advantages to women. Among men, Caucasian males are the most advantaged. African American men compared to Caucasian males are disadvantaged, although they are somewhat higher in income than African American women. Caucasian women are disadvantaged compared to Caucasian males but relatively better off because of marriage and more job mobility than other minority men and women.

Gender is like race in that genetics and biological characteristics are involved. What interests sociologists about gender scripts are not obvious differences, such as men are not able to get pregnant and nurse infants. More interesting to sociologists is how other alleged physical, emotional, and intellectual differences are used to justify certain scripts.

An example is the issue of upper body strength. Men seem to have a clear advantage in this regard. But as technology advances, the significance of upper body strength diminishes. Using brute strength becomes associated with low-prestige jobs involving manual labor.

But old scripts do not die easily. The military still uses exhaustive physical challenges for its recruits. Men often cite difficulty that women recruits have meeting these challenges as a justification for excluding them from the military. But in a high-technology military, physical strength and endurance is more important for low-prestige activities than it is for driving a modern tank or flying high-performance aircraft.

Another slant on the military relates to the persistence of old concepts involving physical prowess. The days when the best warrior was the leader are long gone. If physical stature were the criterion, Napoleon would never have had a chance. Napoleon was extremely short.

But for the sake of argument, assume that aggressiveness is an essential quality for people in the military. Does this mean that genetics is decisive? Or is there something that can be done to elevate the aggressiveness of both men and women? Why not use steroids and testosterone patches to elevate levels of aggression among men and women who are below the norm?

There is also the issue of violence. Male moral entrepreneurs often characterize women as nurturing. Women are genetically disposed to nurture, not kill. Killing is the stuff of which men are genetically disposed. Missing in this appraisal is the reality that mothers are just as likely to kill their infants and children as fathers.

COMBINING ATTRIBUTES

When looking at **dominant** and **minority groups,** it is often necessary to look at certain **combinations** of **race, ethnicity, religion,** and **gender.** It is Caucasian men who enjoy the most advantage in the United States. But Caucasian men with high prestige religious backgrounds, such as Episcopalian or Presbyterian, are more likely to be among the advantaged than those from lower prestige religious backgrounds. Hispanic men who have Caucasian features have an advantage over those with darker complexions. And finally, although women do constitute a minority group in the United States, Caucasian women have fared much better than their Native American, African American, and Hispanic counterparts.

LABELS

Members of a minority group may describe themselves as **African American, Native American, Mexican American,** or **Asian American.** Some wonder about minorities using these labels to describe themselves. Aren't we all Americans?

The practice of using such labels is hardly new. At one time, self-labels such as Italian American, Polish American, and Irish American were evident. The reason that members of these groups used these labels is because the dominant group often treated them like outsiders. The self-label Italian American was an effort to lay claim to being an American while retaining one's ethnic identity.

Over the years as the situation normalized for many of these minorities, these self-labels began to disappear. It was no longer necessary to claim a rightful place at the American table. Whether or not the same thing will happen to African Americans and other current minorities remains to be seen.

It should also be mentioned that labels such as Native Americans are not always preferred as self-labels. Many prefer the label Indian, even though for some it still smacks of the European invasion centuries ago when Columbus was searching for a route to India. Others prefer their own ethnic identity as a member of a particular tribe.

Questions concerning self-labels are relevant to other minorities as well. Many who are officially classified as Hispanic prefer the label Latino. Others prefer labels that are more specific to their countries of origins. Labels such as Chicano (Mexican American), Cuban American, or Puerto Rican are examples.

CHOOSING LABELS

The **dominant group** can play a significant role in **defining minorities.** The categories on census forms force many minorities to make a choice. People who define themselves as Chinese may have no other option than to mark Asian American. Someone who is both African American and Irish may be forced to mark on the basis of race rather than ethnicity.

One of the most prominent opponents of affirmative action is someone who hates government labels. He is often forced to define himself as African American when he has indicated that if he were to make a choice it would be Irish American. He blames the government and affirmative action programs for emphasizing race at the expense of other labels. This wealthy "minority" has bankrolled efforts to eliminate affirmative action programs around the country.

One can easily appreciate his frustration in dealing with imposed labels by the government, media, or anyone else. What may bother him just as much is another label that moral entrepreneurs who are against affirmative action have peddled. Some equate affirmative action with unqualified. What may bother him is that this taints the accomplishments of all African Americans, including himself, who are exceptionally successful.

He believes that eliminating affirmative action would diminish this stigma. What he may underestimate is the capability of some to stigmatize minorities as unqualified in the absence of affirmative action programs. Ironically, he sees himself as an ally with moral entrepreneurs on the right who criticize affirmative action, but fails to see that these moral entrepreneurs are responsible for defining minorities as unqualified.

His concern with how successful minorities are often defined by the dominant group is totally legitimate. Dominant groups in most societies see themselves as superior to minorities. Ethnocentrism by dominant groups toward minorities is nothing new. But eliminating programs designed to help those minorities is a huge price to pay. The dominant group may continue to define him as a minority while using him to promote their efforts to restore white privilege.

THE DOMINANT GROUP AS GATEKEEPERS

A **gatekeeper** is someone who **controls access** to **opportunities.** Members of the **dominant group** are the **most important gatekeepers** because they control access to the opportunity structures that facilitate upward mobility. In this capacity, they are in a prime position to use race, ethnicity, religion, and gender to their advantage.

Racism and **sexism** involve more than just negative attitudes. Racism and sexism occur when members of a dominant group use their negative attitudes about minorities to deny them access to opportunity structures. **Power** and **credibility** give members of the dominant group the opportunity to act on negative attitudes. This is distinct from minorities who may hold negative attitudes about the dominant group but are not gatekeepers.

Power and credibility make all the difference in terms of opportunities and social mobility. Moral entrepreneurs for the dominant group conveniently ignore this point when they cite negative attitudes minorities have toward the dominant group. Is that just as racist or sexist as when the dominant group disparages minorities? Saying that negative attitudes by anyone toward anyone else are equally distasteful or offensive is not the same as acknowledging how power and control count in terms of opportunities and social mobility.

SELF-FULFILLING PROPHESIES

A **self-fulfilling prophesy** occurs whenever members of the **dominant group** control events to sustain their bias and stereotypes about minorities. One of the favorite tricks of the dominant group in this regard is to deny minorities access to opportunities that would challenge such images. By denying access, the dominant group can claim that the absence of minorities is proof of their inherent deficiencies.

An example is auto racing. Men have created barriers that make it extremely difficult for women to access this world. Only a few have made it to high performance drag, oval, or circuit racing. Many men view this as proof that women don't have what it takes.

For women who crack this barrier, men have a backup strategy. If a woman finishes in the middle of the pack it is seen as proof that women cannot compete at the top level. What is telling about this ploy is the silence over all the men who joined her and finished in the middle of the pack.

Nor are men who despise the intrusion of women into the sacred realm of auto racing willing to admit another reality. Given the thousands of young men in the feeder pool of talent, the odds are severely against any women to reach the top. If the numbers in the feeder pool become comparable, then it would be possible over time to make a more objective judgment about the relative potential for men and women as racers. But there is no reason to assume that these numbers are likely to change in the foreseeable future.

Many men also delight when a woman racer doesn't finish or crashes. This is seen as proof positive that women should never be allowed to race. They endanger the lives of all men.

Notice the difference in interpretation when men crash. They are often celebrated as daring and aggressive competitors. Rarely is much said about how they endanger their fellow racers. When it is mentioned, the comment is often made that racing is a dangerous profession and men are willing to assume the risks. Apparently there is a difference about the gender of those who create the risks.

AFFIRMATIVE ACTION AND SELF-FULFILLING PROPHESIES

One reason for **affirmative action programs** is to give **minorities** a chance to overcome obstacles created by generations of discrimination. Affirmative action is designed to give minorities a chance to disprove negative stereotypes. From this perspective, affirmative action is meant to discredit self-fulfilling stereotypes sustained by denying minorities access to opportunities.

This helps explain one of the dynamics behind the **backlash** against affirmative action. If the script promoted by critics of affirmation action prevails, the effect will be to reestablish barriers that help to sustain stereotypes concerning the limitations of minorities. To regain ground, the dominant group must diminish opportunities that discredit their contention that only they are qualified. The effectiveness of assaults on affirmative action is increased if moral entrepreneurs for the dominant group are able to enlist a minority group member as a spokesperson.

THE ASSIMILATION MODEL

The **assimilation model** for societies requires that **minorities adopt** the values, beliefs, behavioral preferences, and identity of the **dominant group** as a condition for **acceptance** into society. It requires them to abandon their cultural scripts and identities. This is different from a **melting pot model** of society where **group differences** contribute to an **emergent script.** With assimilation, the only script in town that counts is that of the dominant group.

Sociologists reinforced the assimilation model for American society with a theory that described the process. It is based upon the fact that the dominant group has power and control to accept or reject minorities. Their perspective on assimilation clarifies stages involved in the process.

The **first stage** is when the minority group is **physically separated** from the dominant group. Before the advent of television, this isolation reduced opportunities for a minority group to know much abut the dominant group. The term **segregation** refers to such a state.

Separation between minority and dominant groups when mandated by law is called **de jure** segregation. The Jim Crow laws in the South after the Civil War are an example of de jure segregation. **De facto** segregation is based upon more informal and nonlegal scripts for enforcing segregation between minorities and the dominant group.

The **next stage** occurs when **minorities** become **aware** of the scripts and related values and beliefs favored by the dominant group. At that time, members of a minority group become aware of differences between themselves and those in the dominant group, but still retain their own identity. The term **accommodation** refers to this stage.

Acculturation occurs when members of a minority group abandon their own values and identity and take on that of the dominant group. At this juncture, members of a minority group undergo a transformation that is registered in everything from changes in their speech and language to clothing and mannerisms. The dominant group becomes their **positive reference group. False consciousness** is another term that could be used to describe acculturation.

Assimilation refers to the point at which members of the dominant group allow some minorities to participate in their patterns of activities. The condition for this is that minority group members take on the values and identity of the dominant group. But switching reference groups is no guarantee of acceptance. The dominant group can still be selective in deciding on who to admit into their ranks.

The **amount of assimilation** is a key question. **Tokenism** refers to allowing only a few minorities in. Tokenism means that assimilation is only a gesture to relieve pressure and complaints, rather than a genuine commitment to assimilation.

Amalgamation occurs when the dominant group allows **intermarriage** with members from a minority group. Sociologists often see resistance by members of the dominant group to assimilation as being the greatest in areas of intimacy, such as dating and marriage. This is why some sociologists view amalgamation as the final step in the assimilation process.

Until a Supreme Court decision in the 1960s, interracial marriages were illegal in the United States. But even today, dynamics associated with interracial marriages are fascinating to observe. Why is it that there is more acceptance for a Caucasian man who marries an Asian American women than there is when an Asian American man marries a Caucasian woman?

ALTERNATIVES TO THE ASSIMILATION MODEL

The **alternative** to the **assimilation model** is one where **civility** replaces **ethnocentrism. Civility,** in the **minimal sense,** means that the **dominant group** does not **require minorities to identify with them** as a condition for access to jobs and opportunities in society. Minorities are free to remain themselves.

If taken one step further, civility is more than just tolerance of differences. It is an **open mindedness** that invites embracing minority scripts and related values and beliefs in the construction of **emergent scripts.** These emergent scripts are more than just changing past practices of discrimination against minorities and allowing them access to jobs and opportunities. These emergent scripts resemble the melting pot fusion of differences into new script possibilities.

THE MYTH OF THE MELTING POT

The idea of a society as a **melting pot** carries with it the image of diverse cultures blending together into new scripts. This idea of a multicultural society as a melting pot has been attractive to many minorities.

The appeal for many minorities is that they would be able to have access to opportunities without having to abandon their own cultural traditions and identities. The possibility that others might respect their ideas and values and even incorporate some of them into their lives can be appealing. Ultimately, the appeal of the melting pot concept for minorities is that it stands in stark contrast to what the assimilation model demands.

The concept of the United States as a vast melting pot has had appeal for some within the dominant group. Some were worried that differences would tear the society apart as it had done in Europe during World War II. For many of these members of the dominant class, the melting pot image was a form of wishful thinking.

The myth of the United States as a melting pot continues among many Caucasians today. A survey taken during the summer of 2001 by the Gallup poll found a stark contrast in attitudes concerning racism. The vast majority of Caucasians reported that race is not an issue. The majority of African American respondents felt that racism remains a significant problem.

Some moral entrepreneurs for the dominant group in the United States take a more cynical approach to the question of whether or not the United States is a melting pot. They are fully aware that the most significant scripts are those of the dominant group and not some magical mix from our diverse backgrounds. But they calculate that to sell these scripts, it is best to promote the image that they have emerged through the process of a melting pot.

The comments to this juncture have been meant to conceptualize relations between minorities and the dominant group in the United States. Now it is time to take a glance at specific minority groups. What has been selected is meant to create only a thumbnail sketch. There is no real substitute for more extensive reading and exposure to more detailed accounts of these minorities.

NATIVE AMERICANS

Thousands of years before the ancient Egyptians, Greeks, or Romans, the first Americans began to migrate to what is now North, Central, and South America. The migration began during an Ice Age when huge glaciers drained enough water from the Bering Straits to create a land corridor between Asia and what is now Alaska. This means that the first Americans were here centuries before Europeans from England, France, and Spain began to explore this hemisphere beginning in 1492.

When European explorers began to arrive, the number of Native Americans estimated to be living in this hemisphere was in the millions. But numbers alone are not sufficient to describe what greeted Europeans explorers. The number of different tribes and languages among these Native Americans was in the hundreds.

During the colonial period that followed early exploration, Europeans came and settled in large numbers. About 80 percent of the settlers during the colonial period were from England, Scotland, and Ireland. Those from Ireland were predominately if not exclusively Protestant. The arrival of these settlers began the process of driving Native Americans off of their land and onto reservations.

During the colonial period, displacing Native Americans from their land was accompanied by another practice. Both the British and the French enlisted Native Americans as allies. The result was the French-Indian War that lasted seven years until 1763 when the British and their allies prevailed and drove the French from what would become the United States.

After the Revolutionary War, European Americans kept moving Native Americans further west with the promise that they would be safe there from intrusions by Caucasians. But as the demand for more land by Caucasians increased, these Indian Territories were pushed further westward. And in the process, Native Americans were forcefully displaced from their lands. On one of these forced evictions, nearly one-fourth of a tribe forced to move from Georgia to Oklahoma died along the way. This event is known as the Trail of Tears.

Forced marches and murderous attacks by the military were commonplace during the westward expansion in the 1800s. Caucasian historians often use heroic labels such as the Battle of such-and-such to describe military brutality. The Battle of Sand Creek in Colorado was hardly heroic. Soldiers waited until the warriors had left to enter the village and slaughter children, women, and the elderly. Native American groups describe the event as a massacre.

Up until about 1850, the Bureau of Indian Affairs (BIA) was lodged in the Department of War. This was logical because until then, the main objective was to defeat Native Americans and take their land. By then most of the conquest had been accomplished and the military was engaged primarily in mopping up exercises to control Native Americans who left their reservations. This is when the Bureau of Indian Affairs was transferred to the Department of Interior where it remains today.

The Department of the Interior is responsible for managing our natural resources. This meant that the government viewed its policy toward Native Americans as the equivalent to managing natural resources, such as wildlife and forests lands. What a quaint idea!

With this move the government officially made Native Americans wards of the state. The not so subtle implication was that Native Americans are childlike and incapable of managing their own affairs. This was an astonishing stance given that Native Americans had lived and thrived in North America thousands of years before the Europeans first arrived. Essentially all decisions affecting their lives were taken over by the government and the Bureau of Indian Affairs.

This final tragedy for Native Americans occurred in the 1890s at a place called Wounded Knee. By that time, the Native American population had been reduced to about 250,000. Given the estimated millions of Native Americans who lived here before the arrival of the Europeans, many believe that what happened to them qualifies as genocide. Genocide refers to the mass murder of minorities. Another often cited instance of genocide is the mass murder of Jews during World War II by the Germans.

Attempts to assimilate Native Americans into the dominant culture have been only moderately successful. Schools were created for this purpose and a popular practice was for Caucasians living in the East to send their discarded hats and garments to reservations so that Native Americans would have the chance to become more civilized. But many Native Americans resisted the call to abandon their traditions in favor of those of the dominant white culture.

It was not until 1924 that Native Americans were officially given the right to vote. Today, casinos on some Native American lands have help improved the economic situation for those tribes. But even then, costs incurred by having Las Vegas companies run their casinos and other expenses such as tax agreements with state and local governments cut into their profits. The situation for most Native Americans living on other reservations is one of extreme poverty. Those who go to cities to find work often do so to escape the poverty of reservation life. Many of them join the ranks of other Americans who do not earn enough to rise out of poverty.

AFRICAN AMERICANS

The ancestors of African Americans first came as slaves to colonial America in 1609. African slaves were used as a source of forced labor in colonial America. It was during the colonial period that the slave population increased to about 20 percent of the total colonial population. In some areas in the South that proportion was much greater.

The size of the slave population and some slave rebellions contributed to the fear of slave uprisings during the colonial period. This prompted the Founding Fathers to eliminate slave trafficking in the early 1800s. This was not a statement about the immorality of slavery as an institution, even though some states had adopted that position. Instead, it was a practical decision designed to manage the size of the slave population.

It is interesting to speculate what might have happened during the civil rights movement in the United States a century and a half later if this decision had not been made. If the percentage of African Americans had remained at what it was during the colonial period it would have been about 20 percent of the population. This is significantly higher than the figure of about 12 percent at that time. With added numbers would African Americans have had more clout?

Slavery continued to be legal in both the North and the South. The only real difference was that slaves in the North worked mostly as domestics in households, while the majority of slaves in the South were used as field hands. The large agricultural demand for slaves as field workers in the South is why such a high concentration of slaves lived there.

Slavery legally ended in about 1865 with the victory of the North over the South. The Thirteenth Amendment officially ended the practice. The Fifteenth Amendment gave former male slaves and their male descendants the right to vote. That right was crushed in the South by state laws that made it difficult if not impossible for African Americans to exercise their constitutional right to vote.

Southern states passed Jim Crow laws to sustain separation between Caucasians and African Americans. Jim Crow laws mandated separation in everything from restaurants, hotels, drinking fountains, and education to where people could ride on a bus. These states insisted that these practices abided by the Fourteenth Amendment requirement that people must be treated equal. The concept of separate but equal lasted until 1954, when the Supreme Court decided that for African Americans, separate was hardly equal.

Just because the Supreme Court officially ruled against the Jim Crow laws did not mean an end to racism. Supreme Court decisions affect **de jure** segregation. This limited legal discrimination but did not address more subtle **de facto** segregation. De facto segregation occurs in practices but is not officially legal.

In many cities **de facto segregation** is a way of life. Eitzen (1997) reports that 86 percent of Caucasians living in suburbs live in communities with less than 1 percent African Americans. Census data from 1990 provides a flip side to the picture. In Detroit, 61 percent of African Americans lived in communities that are at least 90 percent African Americans. In Chicago, the figure is 71 percent. Moreover, some cities, such as Detroit and Philadelphia, experienced an increase in residential segregation between 1980 and 1990.

The point has already been made that discrimination against African Americans persists in lending practices. Some studies show that African American applicants for mortgages are turned down twice as often as their Caucasian counterparts who have the same economic profile. The same pattern has been found when Caucasian and African American couples were given the same profile and told to test their luck with different banks and other lending institutions.

Another pattern of discrimination has been found among postal workers. African American workers are twice as likely to be fired as their Caucasian counterparts. This pattern exists even when controlling for the amount of education and job reviews.

Data from *USA Today* (1/12/04: 2a) presents a discouraging picture concerning African American political involvement. As of 2002, only one African American had been elected governor of a state. Four Hispanics and Asian/Native Hawaiians have been elected governor. Only two African Americans have been elected to the Senate compared to five Asian/Native Hawaiians, three Native Americans, and three Hispanics.

HISPANIC AMERICANS

To understand the history of Hispanic Americans requires first looking back at the influence of Spain in this hemisphere. Its influence was expressed the most in the Caribbean, the Gulf of Mexico, and in Central and South America. Mexico officially gained its independence from Spain in 1821. At that time, its territory included states such as Texas, New Mexico, Arizona, and California.

At first, Mexico was reasonably open to migration by Caucasian Americans. That attitude changed when Caucasians took over the Mexican province of Texas and declared independence. American historians and movies have cast the Alamo as a noble stand by American folk heroes against the armies of Santa Anna. The truth of the matter is that Santa Anna was attempting to take back the territory that was rightfully Mexico's.

The Mexican-American War fought between 1846–1848 ended with the United States invading Mexico City. The Treaty of Guadalupe Hidalgo (1848) gave control of the Southwest and California to the United States. Provisions of the treaty allowed Mexicans living in the area the right to citizenship and the right to vote. These official rights were countered by de facto efforts by the government and others to undermine them. Still, it is noteworthy that the ancestors of current Mexican Americans were given the vote almost 20 years before African Americans, about 70 years before women, and about 75 years before Native Americans.

Many Mexican Americans who are treated like illegal newcomers to the United States today have a history of legal involvement that goes back more than 150 years. Many more have legally immigrated since then. During this century, the demand for cheap labor from Mexico has been high. Sometimes governmental programs have officially opened the borders for this purpose. One of the biggest programs of this nature occurred between the end of World War II and the early 1960s when large numbers of Mexicans were brought in to work primarily in agriculture.

Mexican Americans are used to cycles of backlash. One example occurred during the Depression when even legal migrants from Mexico were threatened with deportation should they apply for governmental benefits that were available to others. During the 1990s, political attacks from the right on Mexican Americans resurfaced. The newly elected President Bush surprised many conservatives in the summer of 2001 when he floated the possibility of giving amnesty to the more than three million undocumented workers from Mexico who live in the United States.

Conservatives are divided on the issue of migration from Mexico. Some take the stance that immigration threatens the United States. Many from the business community who hire undocumented workers favor increased migration because it provides them with a cheap source of labor.

Today, migrants from Mexico are most likely to work in cities and not agriculture. The men often work as laborers or in light industries. The women are most often employed as domestics or service workers in hotels and hospitals. Many employers actually prefer non-English speaking illegal immigrants because they are easier to exploit. Complaints about excessively low wages or horrible working conditions can always be discouraged by the threat of deportation. The meat packing industry relies heavily on this source of cheap labor.

Although about two-thirds of all Hispanic Americans are of Mexican ethnicity, Cubans who represent only about 5 percent of all Hispanics are the most powerful group. These Cubans arrived in Florida after Castro took over Cuba in 1959. They have prospered and become a formidable political force in Florida and Washington, D.C. About 13 percent of Hispanic Americans are from Central and South America. The presence of Puerto Rican Americans, which represent about 10 percent of all Hispanic Americans, is unique because Puerto Rico is actually a possession of the United States. Their largest wave of migration occurred after World War II when they settled in areas such as New York City.

ASIAN AMERICANS

Relatives of Asian Americans first began to arrive in the United States just after the Mexican-American War. The first were Chinese peasants who were brought over as cheap labor to work in western mines and on the railroad. By about the 1870s, anti-Chinese sentiment ended this practice and Japanese peasants became the source of cheap labor in the west.

During World War II, the government seized the property and imprisoned Americans of Japanese descent. Some of this was a reaction to Pearl Harbor, but that is not enough to explain the different treatment of Japanese and German Americans. It must be remembered that German U-boats were operating not far off the coast of America and inflicting many casualties.

A more complete explanation as to why German Americans were not also locked up requires looking elsewhere. By the time of World War II, Americans of German descent represented a sizeable number. They were also Caucasian.

After the Vietnam War ended, people from Vietnam, Laos, and Cambodia migrated to the United States. More recent trends have seen more migration of high-tech workers from countries such as India. High-tech companies such as Microsoft rely heavily on workers from such countries. This helps explain one of the most striking differences between Asian American migration in the past and today. Today, newcomers from Asia are much more likely to be highly skilled and from middle-class backgrounds.

The actual ethnic breakdown of Asian Americans is interesting. About 23 percent are from China (either the mainland or Taiwan). About 19 percent are from the Philippines. This may surprise those who might think that Japanese Americans are the second largest group of Asian Americans. The reason for so many people immigrating from the Philippines goes back to the Spanish-American War during the 1890s when the United States came to impose its influence on the Philippines. Since then, the United States has had a significant role in politics there, including the support of some dictators who favored our vested interest in Asia. The American military presence in the Philippines has been huge. Until recently decommissioned, our airforce and navy bases in the Philippines were among the largest in the world.

Data on other Asian Americans indicates that those from Japan, Korea, and India are each about 11 percent of the total number of Asian Americans. The percentage from Vietnam is only slightly lower at about 8 percent.

RECENT TRENDS

Results from the year 2000 census reveal some dramatic shifts among minorities within the United States. From 1990 to 2000, the Hispanic population increased by 58 percent! The percentage increase for Asian Americans was only slightly less at about 52 percent. Most of this increase was due to migration. Meanwhile, the African American population has remained relatively static at about 12 percent of the total population. How the politics of these changes will play out in the future remains to be seen.

The rate of poverty among African and Hispanic Americans remains high. It is about three times higher than it is for Caucasian Americans. The situation for educated Asian immigrants who command good paying jobs is much more favorable. Opportunities for poorly educated Asian immigrants brought over to work in garment district sweatshops are not so favorable.

Life expectancy disparities between the dominant group and minorities have already been discussed. But one figure stands out. Today, primarily because of exposure to toxic substances, the life expectancy of a migrant worker is about 49 years. This is about the same as the life expectancy of a Caucasian male in 1900!

RELIGIOUS MINORITIES

The colonial population was predominately Protestant. This religious advantage continued through the American Revolution with the Founding Fathers. But not all Protestants have enjoyed the same advantages.

There is a social class hierarchy among Protestants. Episcopalians and Presbyterians are at the top. Methodists and Lutherans are in the middle. Southern Baptists are often ranked at the bottom.

The social class bias in religion was registered with the election of Southern Baptists such as Carter and Clinton. Some in Washington, D.C. worried about the government being taken over by commoners. There are some in Washington, D.C. and New England who, as Republicans, supported George W. Bush, but worry about his switch to Southern Baptist from his father's Episcopalian roots.

Today, the vast majority of Americans remain Protestant. About 25 percent of the population is Catholic. The fact that we have had only one Catholic president in the history of the United States tells us something about religious minorities. About 3 percent of Americans are Jewish and about 2 percent are Muslim.

WOMEN AS A MINORITY

Religious and other cultural scripts advantage men around the world. Some of this has already been covered in comments about the disadvantages women experience in the United States. But globally, ideological impact of these scripts is even more astonishing. Eitzen (1997) notes that globally, women do about 60 percent of the work but only receive 10 percent of the income and only own 10 percent of the land. A similar bias is registered in hunting and gathering societies where women and children as gatherers provide up to 80 percent of the nutritional value of food but are rarely celebrated in stories and myths. Instead, the stories and legends are devoted to the exploits of men as hunters.

WOMEN AND RELIGIOUS SCRIPTS

Most **religious scripts** emerged in **patriarchal** societies. A patriarchal society is one where men represent the dominant group. Therefore, it is not surprising that these scripts favor men.

Bem and Bem (1980) provide excerpts from religious sources that reflect this bias. Here are some examples from the Bible:

> In the beginning God created the heavens and the earth . . . And God said, Let us make man in our image . . . And the rib, which the Lord God had taken from man made he a woman . . . And the Lord God said unto the woman, What is this that thou has done? And the woman said, The serpent beguiled me . . . Unto the woman God said, I will greatly multiply your sorrow and thy conception; in sorrow thou shalt bring forth children; and thy desire shall be to thy husband and he shall rule over thee.

(Gen. 1, 2, 3.)

> Let the woman learn in silence and with all subjection. But I suffer not a woman to teach, nor to usurp authority over the man, but to be in silence.

(1, Tim. 2)

Bem and Bem also use a prayer of Orthodox Jews to establish the theme of patriarchy in that religion:

> Blessed art Thou, oh Lord our God, King of the Universe, that I was not born a gentile. Blessed art Thou, oh Lord our God, King of the Universe, that I was not born a slave. Blessed are Thou, oh Lord our God, King of the Universe, that I was not born a woman.

A passage from the Koran, the Holy Book of Islam, establishes that religion's view of men and women:

> Men are superior to women on account of the qualities in which God has given them pre-eminence.

Some might argue that these passages are excessively selective. Many religions have passages that encourage men to respect and even celebrate women. But this does not address the basic question concerning minorities. Who has the power, wealth, and real prestige in a society?

The disparities between men and women based upon religious scripts are likely to be the strongest among the most orthodox believers. An example occurred in Afghanistan where, until recently when overthrown by American forces, Taliban leaders imposed an extremely orthodox interpretation of the Koran. Another recent example is when the conservative Southern Baptists adopted a resolution at their recent annual convention that insists wives must accept the authority of their husbands over them.

GENDER STRATIFICATION

Gender stratification refers to the unequal distribution of power, wealth, and prestige among men and women in a society. The amount of gender stratification as measured by the gap between men and women varies from society to society. But the size of the disparity is not what establishes women as a minority in any society. Any disparity is sufficient to classify women as a minority.

PATRIARCHY AND MATRIARCHY

We have already seen that a **patriarchal society** is one where men benefit from the existing arrangements more than women do. Historically, patriarchal societies have been the rule. More recent changes in some societies, such as the United States, involve reducing the advantage gap and not transforming it into a matriarchy.

A **matriarchal society** is one that is run by women and benefits them disproportionately over men. For a matriarchy to exist, women must control the wealth and have the most power and prestige. Because the term matriarchy refers to what goes on in the larger society, it does not pertain to situations where women have control over raising the children or writing checks from their husband's account to pay bills.

Some are tempted to call a single-parent family headed by women a matriarchy. By definition, this is a mistake if for no other reason than she does not have a spouse over which to exercise power. A more accurate characterization is to identify such a family structure as matrifocal. **Matrifocal** means that family life centers on the woman as the head of the household.

SCRIPTS AND GENDER

Sociologists readily acknowledge that there are biological differences between men and women that may explain some scripts that evolved from the past. Differences in physical strength may explain the role of men as hunters and women as gathers. But this physical difference does not explain why male activities are valued more than those of women in that type of society.

Physiological differences also help to explain why traditional scripts give women more involvement with infants who are nursing. But this physiological explanation for different gender roles does not explain why men do not have a more active involvement when an infant is on for-mula and does not require breast milk. Nor does it explain why a father today feels that it is the responsibility of his wife to give a crying infant a bottle in the middle of the night.

Gender role limitations for women in the past and even today do not always rest upon physiological attributes. Patriarchal scripts also celebrate the mental and emotional superiority of men to women. A related attribution insists that women are innately nurturing. This charac-terization suggests that their roles should be limited to nurturing others, such as their children and husbands.

The point was made earlier that some insist that women should never be allowed in combat because they may have to kill someone. The suggestion is that they are incapable of such an act or will not be able to deal with such and event because killing runs against their natural instincts. Whether or not women in combat react much differently than men remains to be seen. The reality is that many men never fully recover emotionally from their experiences in war.

GENDER ROLES

Gender scripts define **gender roles.** Gender roles assign different expectations to people depending on whether or not they are male or female. The learning of gender social scripts involves two facets. The first is when a child **becomes aware** of what is expected of him or her. The second occurs if a **child internalizes** such scripts.

Gender socialization can begin even before a child is born. Gender socialization involves peddling gender scripts and roles. Parents expecting a little girl or boy may have plans for them long before that child arrives. These plans often begin with decisions on how to decorate the baby's room. Pink for girls, blue for boys, and so forth.

Once on the scene, little boys and girls are often confronted with quite different expecta-tions. Little girls are encouraged be quiet, passive, and submissive. Little boys are expected to by noisy, active, and assertive.

A study of award-winning children's books covering the period from 1967–1971 found some interesting disparities. The ratio of male to female pictures favored men 11 to 1. The ratio of male animal characters to female ones was 95 to 1. Guess who this disparity favors in terms of importance?

Other studies of children's literature have found similar disparities. One study found that not one female character had a role outside the home. Although some of these images are changing, there still remains a disparity in terms of what children's books project concerning the potential roles and opportunities for boys and girls.

Disparities concerning future possibilities perhaps could account for an alarming finding from one study. Throughout childhood, there are few differences between boys and girls con-cerning self-assurance and confidence. By high school the self-assurance and confidence of girls begins to decline relative to that of boys. Moreover, some studies also show that by high school, young women have more self-hatred than do boys.

In the past, restrictions on what women could do placed extraordinary pressure on them to get a man. This meant that a failed romance in high school was more than just that. To fail in romance was to fail in your future if you were a young woman. This reliance on men is likely to diminish as women have more opportunities for sports, other activities in high school, and careers. Many men find this loss of control extremely disturbing. Some men even think about themselves as victims.

Data on career potentials is improving. Compared to 1960, only 5.5 percent of graduates from medical school were women. The figure in 1993 was 36 percent. An even more dramatic change has occurred in law. In 1960, only 2.5 percent of graduates from law schools were women. By 1993, that figure had risen to 43 percent. And in fields such as veterinary medicine and pharmacy, the majority of graduates are women.

THE FEMINIZATION OF JOBS

Many of the new opportunities for women today are in prestigious professions such as medi-cine. Sociologists have observed that the prestige of an occupation or profession can fall when minorities are admitted in sufficient numbers. It occurs when the number of newcomers reaches a certain **critical mass.** There are some indications that this is happening in areas of medicine.

Another example is that of public relations. In the past, it was a field dominated by men. Today, the public relations voices of top politicians and corporations are often those of women. There are some indications that this has made the field of public relations less attractive to men.

The term **feminization of jobs** refers to situations where the prestige of a job falls because more women are employed in it. Sometimes it only takes the involvement of a few women for this to occur. On other occasions it takes a much larger critical mass, such as when the majority in a field previously dominated by men are women. Men often flock to new professions or occupations when the involvement of women comes to stigmatize a job. An example has been the almost exclusive involvement of men in the growth of computer software and other high-tech businesses.

Science and engineering fields remain male-dominated worlds. This bias is reinforced and perpetuated by high school scripts that discourage young women from taking advanced placement courses in math and related scientific fields. Scripts that favor involvement by young men in science clubs and related activities also contribute to the bias in these fields.

COMPARABLE PAY

In the United States, the earnings of women are still less than 80 cents for every dollar that is earned by men. Some of this disparity exists because of past discrimination that prevented women from entering and advancing in many careers. This preference for men means that even today, after some changes have been made, more men still have better paying jobs and are in senior positions that pay the most money in corporations.

Even when women have gained access to certain jobs and professions, they often are paid less than men who are in the same positions and at the same level of seniority. Problems get even worse when one looks at how opportunity differences steer men and women into different jobs. Some academic disciplines, such as engineering, medicine, and science, are top-heavy with men. Others such as English give greater access to women. Guess which faculty gets paid the most?

Some universities have come to recognize these disparities. Some are trying to bring the salaries of women professors up to that of men at the same rank and in the same fields. Others have sought to find more women candidates for spots in disciplines that have traditionally been saturated with men.

Comparable pay is a concept that says men and women should be paid based upon their relative worth. The simplest application is when men and women hold the same job with the same amount of seniority. But discriminatory practices often make this a more difficult task in other situations.

While few would complain about disparities in earnings among physicians and nurses, given their disparity in **educational requirements** and **responsibilities,** other comparisons are more problematic. What if college-educated executive secretaries in a university who are responsible for helping a dean or a president run an office are paid less than high school educated truck drivers on campus? What if registered nurses are paid less than men who mow the lawn at a state hospital? Both of these situations have been documented by research.

These comparisons raise serious questions about comparable pay. Shouldn't employees be paid on the basis of their education, skills, and responsibilities? Although some states have attempted to address this issue and create formulas that include these and other factors, it is difficult to know what will happen in the future.

That will be in the hands of politicians and the heads of corporations. Presently, there is more hope at the state level, where more women hold elected offices than in Congress. But any state legislation must also meet constitutional opinions rendered by the Supreme Court, where some judges with lifetime appointments are hostile toward women's issues. What will occur in corporate American is anyone's guess. The paucity of women in top executive decision-making positions does not bode well for comparable pay programs. Yet, corporate executives who realize the importance of recruiting and retaining valuable women employees might feel compelled to take such action.

THE GLASS CEILING

Scripts concerning the involvement of women in corporate America have been changing. Today, about 44 percent of all management positions are held by women. However, barriers remain with the top management positions. In one study fewer that .5 percent of the 4,000 highest paid corporate officials and directors were women.

The **glass ceiling** is a term applied to the process by which women and other minorities are able to rise only so far in a corporation. It refers to the barrier that keeps minorities from breaking through to top positions. This is a metaphor describing the process whereby women watch as men advance into these positions.

There are a variety of reasons that the glass ceiling exists in corporate America and other organizations. One is based upon scripts that describe men as leaders and women as followers. Another is the script that questions whether or not women can emotionally and intellectually handle responsibilities at the top.

A different explanation concerns scripts for mentors in corporate advancement. A **mentor** is someone with experience and knowledge about how to deal with corporate politics. Having a mentor is an obvious advantage. Having a mentor on a promotion committee is even more desirable.

Some corporations recognize that the glass ceiling is preventing them from tapping into the entire talent pool of candidates. One strategy to overcome this barrier has been to encourage more men to mentor promising female employees. This strategy has met with only limited success. One reason is that many corporate executives find mentoring women and other minorities uncomfortable. With women, some male mentors have difficulty separating their profession and personal lives. For many, it is easier to go back and mentor men.

Another factor that affects the glass ceiling involves **gender segregation.** Gender segregation occurs whenever men or women are disproportionately concentrated in certain jobs. The problem is that women are often concentrated in certain corporate "people oriented" areas such as human resources. This disadvantages them compared to men who are concentrated in areas such as engineering and finance, which are much more popular tracks to the top.

Because the numbers of women who have benefited from affirmative action programs greatly exceeds that of other minorities, the glass ceiling phenomena has often been associated with them. But the glass ceiling applies to all minorities when their chances to move on to the highest positions in a corporation are blocked. The same pertains to the issue of job segregation. Sociologists are interested in seeing the extent to which other minorities besides women are concentrated in certain jobs.

CHAPTER 17
SEX SCRIPTS

Some argue that **human sexual behavior** is **instinctive.** The viewpoint that human sexuality is instinctive is sustained by comparisons with other species, where sexual responses seem to be genetically programmed. But if **human sexual behavior** is based upon instinct, then its **expressions** should be similar across **different cultures.**

SEX SCRIPTS AND BIOLOGY

Cultural variability refers to **different ways** people **behave** around the world. **Cultural scripts** are what cause this **variability.** It is reflected in activities ranging from sex to what foods are eaten, how they are prepared, and when they are eaten. Just as some societies prohibit the eating of a food such as pork or have specially prepared food for celebrations, so too do societies vary in terms of what sexual behavior is encouraged or prohibited.

FREUD

Freud was fascinated with how cultural scripts shape human sexual activities. In Freud's theory the **Id** represents the **biological sex drive.** Freud felt that the sex drive is what permits the human species to reproduce. The **Superego** represents **cultural scripts** that have been **internalized.** Freud proposed that tensions arise when the human sex drive becomes repressed due to the internalization of cultural scripts that prohibit its expression.

The relationship between cultural scripts and the human sex drive is more varied than what Freud proposed. Freud focused more on the general category of a repressive script than trying to cross-culturally describe the sexual preferences of people in different societies. Anthropologists are the ones who have documented this sexual variability.

SEXUAL PROHIBITIONS

Kinsey (1948) recognized **variability** in **human sexuality** across **cultures** and **societies.** But he also pointed out another feature of cultural scripts dealing with sexuality within a society. This feature helps inform those doing cross-cultural sex research.

Kinsey claimed that **all cultural scripts** contain certain **sexual prohibitions.** This means that researchers must look for more than just what is sexually permitted or encouraged when they study a group or society. Looking to see what sexual behavior is prohibited is equally important when trying to describe the scripted sexual activities of a group or society.

BEYOND FREUD

Freud utilized a **consensus model** of society that assumes that a single sexual script exists within a given society. While it is always possible that script consensus within a society can exist, those who research sexual behavior have found that sexual preferences (and scripts that support them) can vary widely within the same society. To the extent that these differences are group based is the extent to which group differences in sexual preferences exist within a society.

Researchers have found that sexual preferences and what is sexually arousing result from a complex mix of biology and personal experiences. Often those personal experiences are based upon cultural scripts. But both biological inputs and/or more unique personal experiences can combine to produce atypical sexual preferences.

SCRIPT DISPUTES

The possibility that people may be exposed to different sexual scripts raises the possibility of role conflict. Interpersonal sexual role conflict exists for someone who is confronted by other people who embrace different sexual scripts. Role conflict means that pleasing one means offending the other. This creates a behavioral dilemma based on social reward/cost possibilities.

Personal sexual role conflict occurs whenever someone internalizes incompatible sexual preferences from others. This creates a behavioral dilemma based upon a divided social self. This creates a self-reward/cost dynamic where engaging in a sexual act produces the possibility of both pride and guilt.

The combination of role conflict between sexual self-preferences and those of others is also a distinct possibility. The simplest equation is one where what you prefer is opposed by the other person. Doing what pleases you results in costs incurred by the other person. Yet, pleasing that other person by conforming to his or her sexual preferences has the self-cost of denying yourself the chance to do what you prefer.

SEARCHING FOR ALTERNATIVE SCRIPTS

The **behavioral preferences** contained in **personal social scripts** do not always match those of dominant/mainstream sexual scripts in a society. This creates the possibility that someone may have to suppress those preferences or risk adverse responses to those with more mainstream sexual preferences. With suppression, the person is aware of his or her own sexual predilections but chooses not to express them.

When the **sexual behavioral preferences** of someone are different from those around him or her, another possibility exists. **Internalization** of dominant/mainstream group sexual prohibitions may cause people to repress their real sexual preferences. **Repression,** unlike suppression, is unconscious. It is the unconscious denial of a disposition(s) brought about by an ideal self-concept attained through socialization (internalization) that conflicts with the actual self-concept.

Sometimes the difference between repression and suppression of sexual preferences is difficult to discern. Take, for instance, someone who is gay. If the internalization of prohibitions against same-sex partners is powerful enough, some people may never recognize that they are gay. Others may have clearly understood but refrain from expressing their preference for fear of how others might respond, along with elements of guilt produced through internalization. All of these dynamics may occur over a protracted period until the time that someone "comes out" and declares a gay preference.

These dynamics are not unusual among men and women who have been married but later realize that they prefer same-sex partners. This is different from men and women who marry but suspected or knew about this preference before. Some may even live dual lives within a marriage.

Searching for alternative sexual scripts is nothing more than trying to find groups or communities that legitimate sexual preferences that have been previously repressed or suppressed. An awareness and/or involvement in such communities can do much to relieve guilt and other burdens brought about by internalizing sexual preferences that do not match those contained in someone's personal social script. This is not the same as searching for different sexual partners for the purpose of repeating personal sexual preferences.

SEXUAL INCLINATIONS AND MORAL ENTREPRENEURS

Moral entrepreneurs peddle sexual scripts that influence what is internalized and how people will respond to certain sexual inclinations. Moral entrepreneurs in the United States disagree over what constitutes acceptable sexual behavior. The same act is often condoned and condemned by different moral entrepreneurs.

Moral entrepreneurs often use explanations to legitimate or condemn certain sexual inclinations and behaviors. Biblical references are a popular source of explanations for moral entrepreneurs in the United States. Giving God's stamp of approval or condemnation to certain sexual inclinations or behaviors can be extremely persuasive with some audiences. Those trying to legitimize a behavior condemned on religious grounds may use research data to fortify their claims.

Citing biblical or other references to either normalize or stigmatize certain sexual inclinations is common. It is a method for justifying beliefs that sustains or condemns a sexual script through truth claims. Whether or not such claims are true is not the point. What counts is whether or not people believe them and whether or not interpersonal sexual role conflict results.

STUDYING SOCIETIES

Thinking like a sociologist requires you to ask several questions when researching sexual scripts in a society. The first question is whether or not a **single agreed upon socially shared sexual script** exists. If so, then most are likely to conform, and the potential for sexual deviance is low.

If **diversity** in **sexual scripts** is discovered, then there are a series of other questions to ask. The first is, what groups embrace what sexual scripts? A second is, do they qualify as dominant, mainstream, or minority groups? A third question is, do their advocates have the power to impose their scripts on the opposition? A fourth question is, whether or not advocates are credible? And finally, how do personal or social hierarchies of credibility play out in efforts to persuade?

How conflict is resolved between those holding different sexual scripts in a society depends upon answers to these questions. But thinking like a sociologist also means proceeding carefully when conducting research. Always remember that what people tell you may not necessarily be what they personally think.

Pluralistic ignorance reminds us that what people say can be influenced by perceptions of what others prefer. Those others include members of their group as well as the interviewer. The self-concepts of people may also create distortions, such as when what they say is based upon the need to maintain an ideal self-concept.

Mapping the **sexual behavior** of those being studied alleviates some of these research problems. But it is not always easy to legally gain the access necessary to observe them. If research is publicly funded, another problem arises. Courts on many occasions have reasserted the right to privacy. Research funded by the government must be careful not to violate this right. Getting permission to observe or film from those involved has its own problems. Are those willing to be observed or filmed representative of everyone in a group or society? If not, then research distortions can arise.

TYPES OF SEX SCRIPTS

Cross-cultural research reveals an **amazing diversity** of sexual scripts. What is approved of in one society is often reviled in another. The following **classification system** that identifies **different types of societies** in terms of general sexual themes helps make sense out of this enormous diversity. The typology is an elaboration on a scheme used by Robertson (1981: 208–209).

There are **three basic sex scripts** that distinguish how societies deal with sexuality. These differences involve **basic themes** and not specific sexual acts. These general differences serve as a point of departure for consideration of more specific sexual practices.

ABSTINENT SCRIPTS

The **first type of society** employs an **abstinent sexual script.** A sexually abstinent society is what Freud would call a sexually repressed society. Sex in these societies is limited to the function of reproduction.

The **most severe** abstinent sexual scripts limit authorized sexual behavior to procreation. In extreme cases like the Shakers, all sexual behavior is prohibited. Without recruitment from elsewhere, such societies are bound for extinction.

The **restraints on sexual activities** in abstinent societies are extensive. Scripts severely limit contact between members of the opposite sex from childhood through adulthood. The extensive use of chaperons to monitor interaction between youngsters is common. These practices continue into courtship with scripts that require the presence of an adult whenever a couple is together. Even contact between adult men and women who are not married is normally prohibited.

Adults in an abstinent society **conspire** to **keep children ignorant** about sex. This conspiracy of silence continues into adolescence. The result is couples who are sexually naïve.

These restrictive sexual scripts are normally written into laws in abstinent societies with formal governments. Elevating social norms to laws is indicative of the seriousness with which they are taken. But formalizing these sexual scripts is not always necessary in societies with powerful mechanisms of informal control. Gossip and shunning are often more than sufficient to enforce the rules. Gossip is the less dramatic form of isolation from the group upon which one depends. Shunning is a more official method of making someone an outcast within the group.

Among **Native American** communities the **Arapaho** illustrate what is meant by an abstinent society. Male and female children are kept separate and the adults constantly monitor and chaperon their activities. Because of the efforts to conceal sexuality from the children, youngsters in this society are sexually naïve. Similar patterns have been discovered in rural Ireland where the Catholic Church remains influential.

SEXUALLY PERMISSIVE SCRIPTS

The **second type** is a society with **sexually permissive scripts.** A **sexually permissive script** is open and places few restrictions on sexual activities. In these societies, the parents take a much more active role in making their children aware of sex. Unlike abstinent societies, parents in a sexually permissive society do not attempt to conceal their own sexual behavior from youngsters. The open and tolerant attitude toward sex means permissive societies rarely construct legal barriers in an effort to control sexual activities.

Examples of **sexually permissive societies** range from the Pacific Islands to Europe and elsewhere. The **Netherlands** (Holland) and **Scandinavian countries,** such as **Denmark** and **Sweden,** are modern examples of sexually permissive societies. All of these societies provide an abundance of sexual information to their youngsters. Except for acts of sexual violence, these societies are generally silent in terms of legal restrictions on the sexual activities of consenting partners.

SEXUALLY AMBIVALENT SCRIPTS

The **third type** of society is one with **sexually ambivalent scripts.** This is a society where both **permissive** and **abstinent** themes collide. It is a society with **mixed sexual messages.**

Both **role models** and **moral entrepreneurs** convey these differences. One side declares that sex should be limited to marriage and procreation. The other side views sex more recreationally. It contends that any sexual activity between consenting partners is acceptable. The element of consent implies a prohibition against rape.

Exposure and awareness of these contradictory scripts often creates personal ambivalence. **Personal ambivalence** occurs when someone is undecided or has mixed feelings about something. Personal ambivalence concerning sexual scripts results from internalizing elements from contradictory scripts in society. Personal ambivalence suggests a **conflicted social self.**

The **United States** is a prime example of a **sexually ambivalent society.** Historically, many of the Europeans who settled in the United States held abstinent views. Sex was for procreation. And even in that context, images from the Garden of Eden often equated sexual behavior with sin. This is captured with the religious saying that "In Adam's Fall We Sinned All."

Later, migrants brought with them a variety of sexual scripts. Some of them leaned toward the repressive themes of the Puritans. Others were more permissive.

The times were also changing. The 1960s ushered in an explosive growth in sexual expression. The hippies and free love came to symbolize a much more permissive sexual script.

These different sexual scripts explain tensions and collisions over everything from censorship to sex education in the United States. Some voices express concern that exposing youngsters to sexual material is detrimental. These voices of abstinence cry out against sex education and insist on censoring access to sexually explicit materials. Other voices insist that in an open society such as ours, it is virtually impossible to isolate youngsters from sexually explicit materials. These more permissive voices recommend sex education more on the scale found in European societies, where youngsters are more knowledgeable and make more informed choices.

Perhaps nowhere is personal ambivalence more evident than with young musicians who are sexually explicit in their performances but publicly announce their intent to save themselves for marriage. Such performers are often criticized from both abstinent and permissive moral entrepreneurs. Moral entrepreneurs from the abstinent side deplore their overt sexuality. Moral entrepreneurs from the permissive side deplore their hypocrisy.

The issue of premarital sex contains other contradictions. Premarital sex for young men is to be expected with the understanding that it is best to have it with bad girls. This is exactly how generations of young men in the military have been introduced to sex. This is why prostitution flourishes around American military bases everywhere. Young men who reveal no sexual interest are often seen as the ones to really worry about.

The less-than-subtle message is that sex is really not acceptable with respectable women. Imagine the conflicted social selves of young men who must reconcile their association of sex with whores and sluts and the expectation that a healthy sex life is valuable in marriage. Some make the transition, but many are still trapped in abstinent scripts that associate sexual pleasure with sin.

The United States remains hypocritical on the matter of premarital sexual exploration when it comes to women. Sexually active young women are often labeled "sluts." This label stands in stark contrast to sexually active men who are often praised with terms such as "stud."

More will be said about American sexual scripts in a moment. But first it will be useful to review the difference between ideal and real cultural scripts. This will be followed by some cross-cultural data on sexual scripts. Looking at cross-cultural data will provide some revealing insights into sexual scripts. These observations will help shed some light on sexual scripts in the United States.

HYPOCRISY

Hypocrisy exists when a **person** does not **practice** what he/she **preaches.** It is a personal matter. An example would be parents who forbid their children to have premarital sex, when in fact the parents had premarital sex.

If a sufficient number of people in a group, community, or society do not practice what they preach, then personal matters become a social issue. The issue of personal hypocrisy becomes an issue involving a disparity between ideal and real cultures. Often research on disparities between real and ideal sexual scripts begins by interviewing some people and only becomes relevant at the group, community, or societal level when the numbers engaging in hypocrisy become significant.

IDEAL AND REAL CULTURAL SCRIPTS

Ideal culture refers to the official script that exists in a society. **Real culture** refers to actual behavior. Hypocrisy occurs when there is a disparity between ideal and real culture. When trying to explore human sexuality, it is always important to remember the difference between ideal and real culture.

The difference can pose a problem for researchers. When Kinsey first started to survey Americans about their sexual preferences and behavior, he became suspicious that people were not being forthcoming in their responses. But he found that in personal interviews with nonjudgmental interviewers, people were often more than willing to disclose an amazing diversity of sexual preferences and behaviors.

This is why Kinsey resorted to using time-consuming interviews to compile his data. Apparently, ideal culture was the basis for reporting on surveys. What is left unanswered is why people were so willing to reveal their actual self during personal interviews. Perhaps the supportive, nonjudgmental atmosphere helped release them from preferences associated with the ideal culture and/or their ideal social selves.

A related problem concerns when societies are most likely to have a discrepancy between ideal and real cultures. An abstinent society that is truly abstinent is likely to practice what it preaches. If this occurs, there is no disparity between ideal and real sexual scripts.

But sometimes an abstinent sexual script as the official ideal public image does not match what people do. There is some evidence that the Puritans were not as abstinent as their public image would suggest. Puritans in America had a relatively high rate of births to unmarried women. The fact that these pregnancies were often with future husbands does not diminish the fact that the behavior represents premarital sex that was officially denounced in sermons and other public statements.

Sexually permissive societies that have few sexual restrictions in their ideal cultural image have no problems when behavior matches that script. But like all societies, even sexually permissive ones have some prohibitions. Sexual violence and sex with young children might be examples. To the extent that actual practices stray from the ideal sexual script is the extent to which a mismatch exists.

Sexually ambivalent societies contained multiple and often contradictory sexual scripts. Therefore, they are difficult to research in terms of ideal and real culture because there is no consensus on what constitutes an ideal sexual script. Breaking such societies down into groups based upon sexual script differences makes it possible to pursue the question. Rather than applying it to the entire society, the researcher would be trying to determine the extent to which disparities between ideal images and realities exist. For instance, the ideal culture of hippies was free and open love and sexuality, but the reality was that in some groups the script favored men. It liberated and legitimated men to have free and open sex, but the role of women was more restricted. An example would be where initiating sexual encounters favored men over women.

CROSS-CULTURAL RESEARCH ON HUMAN SEXUALITY

Robertson (1981: 208–211) provides a wealth of cross-cultural information on different sexual scripts. He draws much of the data from a comprehensive comparison completed by Ford and Beach that involved about 190 different societies. Here is a sample of those findings:

> Of all of the societies studied, only about 5 percent had strong scripts both against premarital and extramarital sex.

> More than one-third of the societies scripted various forms of adultery.

> The script for the Siriono in Bolivia states that a man can have sex with the sisters of his wife and with his brother's wives and their sisters.

> There are no restrictions on adultery among the Toda in India. Married men and women are free to have sex with others outside of marriage. The Toda have no term for adultery.

In the Trobriand Islands, the script encourages children to begin having sexual intercourse at about 6–8 for girls and 10–12 for boys.

In his study Kinsey found that 70 percent of American couples had never tried any position other than face to face with the male on top. Kluckholn found in his study of Native Americans that about 87 percent were more imaginative.

Marquesian men who live in the Pacific can perform sexually for hours. Kinsey found that most American men reach a climax within two minutes.

Sex scripts influence how often people have sex. Among the Keraki of New Guinea it is about once a week. Americans average two or three times a week. The Aranda of Australia about three to five times a day. The Chagga of eastern Africa have sex up to ten times per night.

About two of every three societies have scripts on homosexuality that range from tolerating to requiring it. Male homosexuality is scripted much more than female homosexual practices. For purposes of procreation, societies that endorse male homosexuality require some heterosexual activity on their part.

AMERICAN SEX SCRIPTS

As a sexually ambivalent society, the United States has both abstinent and permissive themes. Some of these themes have already been mentioned. The inclination of some parents to conceal sexual information from their children is consistent with an abstinent viewpoint. Advocates of early sex education represent a more permissive theme.

Like many abstinent societies, the United States has also tried at various times to place legal restrictions on sexual behavior. Robertson (1981: 213–214) reviews some of these laws:

About 50 percent of states have laws that make adultery a crime.

Prostitution is officially prohibited everywhere except in certain counties in Nevada.

Until the 1960s, it was a crime to engage in a homosexual act in all states. Even today, sodomy laws that provide strong penalties for oral and/or anal sex remain on the books in many states.

Oral and/or anal sex is a crime in more than thirty states, even when between husbands and wives. Penalties range up to twenty years in prison.

At one time, it was a crime in Indiana for someone to encourage anyone under 21 to masturbate.

At one time, it was a crime to give unmarried couples information on birth control.

In 1976, the Supreme Court established the right for states to restrict sexual behavior, even among consenting adults.

The original Kinsey study of American men (1948) and women (1953) asked people about their sexual activities. Many people who believed sex should remain private were shocked by his research. Others were shocked by what he found out. Here is a sample taken from a discussion by Roberston (1981: 215):

Almost 70 percent of men reported having had sex with a prostitute.

About 85 percent of men reported having had premarital sex. Almost 50 percent of the women reported having had premarital sex. With the women, premarital sex was most likely to be with their future husbands.

Fifty percent of married men and 25 percent of married women reported having had extramarital sex.

More than 90 percent of men reported that they had masturbated. About 60 percent of women reported that they had masturbated.

About 60 percent of men and women had experienced heterosexual oral sex.

About 16 percent of men reported having had as much homosexual as heterosexual experiences. Twenty-eight percent of women reported having had or desired homosexual experiences.

About 37 percent of men had experienced a homosexual act to the point of orgasm.

About 8 percent of men were exclusively homosexual for at least three years prior to responding.

Research like that conducted by Kinsey has not been warmly greeted by those favoring an abstinent sexual script for Americans. Many object to researchers prying into the private sex lives of citizens, even if respondents agree to participate. What may concern these critics more is the possibility that such research will reveal sexual diversity that is at odds with the sexual image of America, that as moral entrepreneurs, they prefer and promote.

ABSTINENCE AND CONTRACEPTION

Recent data on how abstinence and the use of contraceptives by American teens is interesting (*USA Today*, 1/12/04). Government data suggests that nearly half of all teens have sexual intercourse by age 18. The general pattern is that teens are more likely to use contraceptives the longer that they wait. Only 58 percent use contraception if sex occurs within the first month. After four months, the percentages increases to 71 percent. One-night stands were associated with the lowest rates of contraception use.

Teens who take abstinent pledges are most likely to delay sex. But when they do become sexually active, they are 57 percent less likely to always us contraception than teens that have not taken the pledge. Explanations for why teens that tumble from the sexual abstinence wagon are less likely to use contraception were not provided.

SEXUAL ORIENTATIONS

Sexual orientation refers to someone's choice of sexual partners. **Heterosexual behavior** occurs when sex is between males and females. **Homosexual behavior** occurs when sex is between members of the same sex.

Some **terminology** involving **homosexuality** can be confusing. Sometimes the term **gay** is used generically in reference to both male and female homosexuals. Others prefer limiting the term gay to male homosexuals and **lesbian** to indicate female homosexuals.

Homophobia refers to a fear of homosexuals. Negative attitudes about homosexuals are rooted in religion and other scripts. But the fear itself is often based upon unresolved sexual conflicts within the person who is homophobic. Straight males who are secure in their heterosexuality are less likely to be homophobic than a man with unresolved sexual issues.

Gay bashing, which involves beating and even killing gays, is one consequence of homophobia. By bashing gays, a sexually conflicted male accomplishes two objectives. The first is that his gay bashing affirms to himself and all of his friends that that he is totally straight. The second objective is to eliminate the presence of gays who might be an unconscious temptation.

Unresolved homosexual tendencies can have a different manifestation. One possibility is that a man who publicly announces his heterosexual conquests might do so to conceal his own unresolved homosexual conflicts. This helps to explain why some men are obsessed with keeping count of their conquests so that they can brag to their friends.

The expression **"coming out"** refers to a situation where someone publicly acknowledges that he or she is a homosexual. **"Outing"** is a process where others disclose that someone is a homosexual. Outing is a controversial tactic used by more militant gays and lesbians who believe that exposing prominent people who are homosexual will be helpful to their cause.

The issue of **promiscuity** is often raised in discussions on homosexuality. Promiscuity refers to frequent and indiscriminate sex with multiple partners. Some data suggests that gay men are more promiscuous than lesbians. Yet many male homosexuals have relationships that are as stable as their heterosexual counterparts. One must remember that many male heterosexuals are extremely promiscuous and that more than 50 percent of marriages end in divorce.

The concept of **domestic partners** takes the general issue of homosexuality and applies it to the workplace. The term refers to homosexuals who have relationships that mirror what occurs in stable marriages. The question is should **spousal benefits,** such as medical insurance, be extended to the partner of a homosexual employee? The problem is that spousal benefits have traditionally been based upon marriage. But homosexual marriages are not legal in almost all states. Many employers who recognize the value of skilled workers who just happen to be homosexual have changed their scripts and are now providing spousal benefits. This has become a trend among large American corporations such as Disney.

Bisexuality refers to someone who has had both same sex and opposite sex lovers. Some bisexuals continue the pattern throughout their lives. Many others are homosexuals who have had unsatisfactory and limited sex with someone of the opposite sex. An example would be a woman who, after marriage and having children, comes to realize and prefer lesbian encounters. Interestingly enough, children who have been raised in lesbian households seem to be just as well adjusted as those raised in more traditional heterosexual households.

The term **Berdaches** refers to Native Americans men who possess both male and female traits. The Berdaches are androgynous. **Androgyny** refers to anyone who possesses both male and female characteristics in appearance or behavior.

The Berdaches may also have a same sex lover. What is interesting about them is that they are more than just tolerated. Often they are greatly respected and seen as having unique spiritual qualities.

RAPE

Rape involves forced sex. This seems simple enough until one examines sexual scripts. A common sexual script is that in the absence of evidence to the contrary sex is always consensual. This **doctrine of implied consent** creates a burden on women to prove that a sexual encounter was not consensual. Matters would be dramatically reversed if the script demanded that a man prove that a woman he had sex with consented. In the absence of such proof, it would constitute rape.

The issue of consent is central to debates concerning **marital rape.** Men often view marriage vows as implying eternal consent by their wives to any of their sexual desires or advances. This creates the ludicrous conclusion that a married man can never force himself on his wife. It may also mean that a man who is separated from his wife but officially not divorced can never be accused of raping her.

SEXUAL HARASSMENT

Sexual harassment is a special case of unwanted sexual conduct. Sexual harassment requires a number of circumstances. The first is that sexual harassment involves unwanted sexual comments or advances in the workplace. The second is that it must come from someone who is in a position of power. And third, sexual harassment is usually seen as requiring more than one encounter.

There are several distinct types of sexual harassment. **Quid pro quo** involves a situation where someone in power offers job protection or advancement in return for sexual favors by a subordinate. Creating a **hostile environment** involves a situation where sexually inappropriate comments or actions make it difficult or impossible for a subordinate to carry out his or her responsibilities.

PEDOPHILIA

A **pedophile** is an adult who is sexually aroused by children. Adults who act on this disposition can be charged with crimes in jurisdictions that prohibit sexual relations with children. Some pedophiles are heterosexual and others are homosexual in terms of what arouses them.

Revelations involving sexual scandals involving priests and children have become quite frequent. The fact that the children are usually boys has prompted some to declare that this is primarily a homosexual act. Others claim that priests are often sexually naïve and that the celibacy requirement creates frustrations that they act out with boys. But different explanations do not alter the fact that in most jurisdictions, their behavior represents a criminal act.

In some jurisdictions, these acts are criminal beyond the fact that they involve young children. Some states still have legislation that makes anything defined as a homosexual behavior a criminal act. This means that in some jurisdictions, a priest could be charged with both offenses.

Pedophiles who commit heterosexual acts with children can also be prosecuted but often it is under different criminal statutes. Often the behavior comes under a statutory rape law that prohibits sex with a girl who is not old enough. If the statute stipulates 13 years of age, then a pedophile could be charged with statutory rape for having sex with anyone younger than that.

PORNOGRAPHY

Pornography refers to sexually explicit materials that are deemed offensive. It is usually a concern to those who represent the more abstinent or repressive inclinations in the United States. Those with more permissive attitudes about sex and eroticism are less likely to become concerned. A notable exception is when feminists complain about sexual images that depersonalize women and encourage men to view them as nothing more than sexual objects.

The Internet has created some challenging obstacles for those who want to censor what they believe is obscene material. While communities and states can try to censor sexually explicit material, the Internet makes it virtually impossible to prosecute offenders in remote jurisdictions. If a state has passed laws against certain kinds of sexually explicit materials it can prosecute offenders in that state. But exactly how would a prosecutor in the United States go about charging and bringing to trial offenders who live in Scandinavia, Europe, or Asia?

CHAPTER 18
COURTSHIP, MARRIAGE, AND THE FAMILY

Courtship practices, marriage rituals, and **family structures** are often **taken for granted.** People usually take their own practices for granted unless they are exposed to alternatives. A Protestant attending a Catholic wedding ceremony for the first time is an example. Exposure to different customs and practices makes taking one's own customs and practices for granted more difficult.

Mate selection customs are similar. People take their mate selection rituals for granted. Many young people in the United States associate mate selection with dating, falling in love, and deciding to get married. But in some countries young people have nothing to do with the selection process. In those societies parents choose who their children will marry.

Growing up in a community where all families are structured the same way is also similar. Getting used to a pattern, such as a working father and stay-at-home mom with dependent children, can easily make one take that pattern for granted. But data on the United States suggests that such a family structure is not even typical (Lindsey and Beach, 2000: 378). In 1990, only 26 percent of American families met that profile and by 1997 the percentage had dropped to 25 percent. In fact, the number of single-parent families in 1990 was slightly higher at 28 percent and in 1997 at 32 percent.

COURTSHIP RITUALS

Courtship rituals involve **scripted activities** that bring couples together as a **prelude for marriage.** Courtship scripts determine how mates are selected in different societies. One of the most fundamental differences in courtship scripts involves who chooses the marriage partners.

ARRANGED MARRIAGES

Arranged marriages are most likely to be scripted in more traditional societies. An **arranged marriage** is one where the parents decide who their children will marry. With arranged marriages, the interests of the parents and their families takes precedence over the interests of their children.

The practice of arranged marriage has been extensive in India. Henslin (1999: 439) observes that even today about 95 percent of marriages there are arranged. But even there, some changes in the traditional script have occurred. Today, couples have more to say about the union than in the past. More couples are also likely to meet and talk to each other before the marriage ceremony. This was strictly forbidden in the past.

Scripts governing arranged marriages between royalty demonstrate the significance of family interests. European history is full of royal marriages arranged for social, political, and/or economic reasons. Even when the prospective mates have some input into the selection process, there often are scripted limitations. Perhaps the most frequent restriction among royalty is the prohibition against marrying a commoner.

ROMANTIC LOVE

Mate selection through **romantic love** has become the norm in most **modern societies. Romantic love,** as the concept implies, involves mate selection based upon people falling in love. Giddens and Duneier (2000: 2) contend that the romantic love syndrome first occurred among royalty in Europe, where falling in love was captured in sexual fantasies and extramarital affairs. It is the stuff about which romantic poets wrote. This account views romantic love as an outgrowth of arranged and loveless marriages among the aristocracy.

Even though mate selection in modern societies is most likely to involve some form of romantic love, courtship rituals associated with it can vary significantly. Some romantic love scripts require extensive premarital monitoring and chaperoning by parents and adults. Heavy-duty chaperoning structures everything from where young people can meet to the conditions under which it is permissible for them to be together before they get married. The image of church socials and grandma watching the young couple from behind a curtain on the porch captures what chaperoning entails.

Today, dating rituals are less likely to involve parental or community monitoring and chaperoning. Some involves youngsters who have romances but still live at home. Having more working single parents and dual-income families greatly reduces the potential for monitoring them at home. A related factor is that neighbors who in the past could be counted on to monitor are increasingly likely to be disconnected strangers with little interest in keeping an eye on their neighbor's children.

But not all the reduction in monitoring and chaperoning is due to changes of this nature. Another huge factor is the number of young people who are going away from home to attend colleges and universities. This dramatically reduces the ability of parents to monitor their romantic encounters.

Data on the age of first marriages in the United States is also revealing. Hess, Markson, and Stein (1996: 283) report that in the 1950s, the average age for a woman was 20 and 22 for a man. By 1993 that figure had changed to 24.5 for women and 26.5 for men. Contributing to this shift has been the amount of time it takes to finish college and to sort out job prospects.

Youngsters today leave home not only for college but also for their jobs. This further diminishes the potential for courtship monitoring by their parents. It also increases the likelihood that children will marry someone their parents know nothing about.

Both the demand for college and jobs in other communities contribute to the fact that parents are often likely to meet their child's future spouse on only a few occasions before the wedding. Sometimes parents never meet their future son-in-law or daughter-in-law until preparations for the wedding are under way. The same holds true for meeting the in-laws. This stands in stark contrast to the days when youngsters married someone from families in their own communities that knew each other.

All of this is not entirely unique to modern times. A common pattern in the past was for young men who migrated to the United States to postpone marriage until they settled in. This often meant late marriages. Sometimes the woman was from the old country or a community in the United States where she and her family were known to the groom and his family. On other occasions, the bride and her family were virtual strangers. Many times the man was much older than his bride.

These marriages were not usually scripted, like arranged marriages in countries such as India. But more often than not, these were marriages of convenience rather than romantic love. Romantic love was much more likely to be found as a basis of mate selection in subsequent generations.

PLACE OF RESIDENCE

Patrilocal means that the couple will live with his parents. **Matrilocal** means that the couple will reside with her parents. **Neolocal** means that they will establish their own separate household.

Patrilocal and **matrilocal scripts** are usually found in more **traditional societies** where marriages are the most likely to be arranged. Patrilocal and matrilocal scripts are also associated with extended families. **Neolocal scripts** are found in more **modern societies** where romantic love and the nuclear family are more typical.

MARRIAGE PARTNERS

Whether arranged or the product of romantic love, sociologists make a distinction concerning the backgrounds of married couples. **Homogamy** refers to a situation where their racial, ethnic, religious, and social class backgrounds are the same. **Heterogamy** involves a situation where the bride and groom come from different family backgrounds.

Homogamy is found in more **traditional societies.** India is known for the degree to which caste determines mate selection and marriage. In major cities, caste requirements are made explicit in ads seeking mates.

In the **United States, race** remains an obstacle to heterogamy. Religion and ethnicity have become less serious barriers. But just a few generations ago, religion and ethnicity were still powerful factors. Pressures to marry someone from the same ethnic and religious background were powerful. Couples who broke with this script risked being denounced, ostracized, and even disowned by their families.

EXTENDED FAMILIES

An **extended family** is one where **three or more generations** work and live together as a family unit. The emphasis on three generations means that this type of family unit includes children, parents, and grandparents. Extended families are the most likely to occur in preindustrial societies, where members are expected to spend their entire lives living and working together.

Scripts for **extended families** prepare **youngsters** to stay. These scripts prepare them to stay within the family structure throughout their lifecycle. They are taught that **loyalty** and **commitment to the family** is first and foremost. This is necessary because of the extent to which family members depend on each other. Adults in their prime working years provide for the dependent young and the elderly in their families.

As grandparents retreat from their daily work activities, they become available for tasks such as helping take care of the kids. This pattern of interdependence between family members explains why there are no retirement homes for the elderly in these societies. There is also less childcare issues for parents than we find in modern societies.

An extended family is likely to be both a **producing** and **consuming unit.** This means that they are likely to produce what they consume. This is the most likely to occur in low-technology societies where the family unit is the basis for self-sufficiency. As societies become more job specialized, families may have to trade what they have to offer for other goods and services. An example would be when a farm family pays for the services of the village blacksmith with a freshly killed chicken.

POWER AND EXTENDED FAMILIES

Scripts for **extended families** dictate **power structures.** The term **patriarchy** describes one such possibility. While a patriarchal script denies wives power in their marital relation with their husbands, it also means that the father has the ultimate power and authority over his sons and daughters. The main difference is that eventually his sons will enjoy the benefits of the same script, while the future of his daughters as wives and mothers is more limited.

A **patriarchal script** does not mean that differences in power among women do not exist. An example of this difference comes from traditional China, where the mother-in-law is given power over her daughter-in-law. Since the married couple typically lived with the husband's parents, this meant that daughters-in-law were likely to encounter this disparity in power on a daily basis. The good news is that today's daughter-in-law will become tomorrow's mother-in-law to her son's wife.

The power that a mother-in-law has over her daughter-in-law does not qualify as a matriarchy. In a **matriarchy,** women have power over men. This was not scripted for wives in traditional Chinese society. Power with households and society was scripted for men.

SEXISM

The actual amount of sexism in societies with extended family scripts varies considerably. It still is relatively low in societies where men and women share in the productive activities. This creates an interdependence that does not exist when the man alone is the breadwinner. This is why sexism is probably the highest in agricultural societies with a landed aristocracy rich enough to remove their wives and daughters from production. This makes women totally dependent upon their fathers and husbands.

The shift toward less sexism and more equality in contemporary marriage follows a similar pattern. This is why moral entrepreneurs who favor patriarchy deplore women working and having better career opportunities. The less a woman's economic dependence, the less a man can control her through coercion.

One reason that moral entrepreneurs who value patriarchy in the United States attack feminists is because they worry about losing more than economic control. They worry about losing control over the minds of women created by false consciousness. If false consciousness exists, men can still control their wives, even if their wives earn more than they do.

Wives who are better educated and have better job opportunities are less dependent upon their husbands and have more options outside of marriage should it fail. In the past, wives became increasingly trapped in a marriage as their years of economic viability diminished. This economic trap increased the capacity of their husbands to impose their will on them.

THE NUCLEAR FAMILY

A **nuclear family** involves just **mom, dad,** and **the kids.** This means that it is based upon only **two generations** that live and function together. This makes the nuclear family smaller than an extended family, where three or more generations live and work together.

Sociologists believe that the nuclear family is a product of changes in society that demanded the family to be more mobile. This mobility involves two different considerations. The first is mom, dad, and the kids need to be able to pick up and move if a job change is necessary. The second is that the children must be prepared to leave home to pursue their own job opportunities.

The issue of family mobility seems simple enough. It is hard to move an entire extended family to the city when it can no longer sustain itself on the land. But it is not always easy to move the extended families in a tribe searching for buffalo either. The big difference is that a nomadic tribe continues to live and function together as it moves on to search for game. Eventually, the economic forces that exert themselves on extended families will cause them to fragment.

This begins when one or more members of an extended family leave and migrate to cities or other countries in search of work. An example would be when some members of families living in rural Poland at the turn of the twentieth century left in search of opportunities in American cities such as Chicago. If successful, these migrants might send for others to join them, but this usually did not involve the entire extended family. Some stayed back.

Those who migrated to the United States may have taken with them scripts from the old country. But more and more, the families that they started in the United States became transformed into nuclear families. Even when grandparents did live in the home, things were already changing. The traditional work of the family, which might have been farming in rural Poland, no longer was the source of income. Living in the city changed all of that.

Even when the children of those who first migrated inherited a family business, the pattern of them all living together for the rest of their lives often changed. It changed when those children who inherited the business left to set up their own separate households. Further changes occurred when their children left the business and went on to live and find jobs outside the neighborhood.

GETTING RID OF THE KIDS

The number one job of the nuclear family is to prepare the kids to leave. The task of **getting rid of the kids** is just one way to express this reality. The modern world makes it increasingly difficult for the kids to stay.

This is not to say that the task is easy. In fact, it has probably become more difficult today than in the past. In the past, everyone involved in nuclear families generally realized that the kids would eventually leave to set up their own households. But in the past this often meant they would move across the street and still remain nearby. Today, considerably larger distances are involved when they leave for college or jobs and set up households that may be hundreds if not thousands of miles away.

SEPARATION ANXIETY

This may cause a form of **separation anxiety. Separation anxiety** refers to the anxiety children and/or parents feel when the prospect of living apart arises. The concept applies to societies with nuclear families. Separation anxiety is rare in societies with extended family structures.

FEAR OF COPING

Pressures for children in nuclear families to leave the nest raises fears about their ability to cope on their own. Both parents and children can experience this fear. For parents, it may mean a reluctance to let them go. For children, it may surface as resistance to leaving home or the community.

The fear of coping is considerably less for children who have developed good skills for coping on their own. Children with domineering parents suffer in this regard because they have been given few opportunities to develop these skills. Parents who are domineering are also likely to worry about the judgment of their children. Sometimes this is with good reason, because they haven't let their children develop coping skills.

Worry about the coping skills of their children can begin early for some parents. For them, every stage of development is measured against the likelihood that their child will be able to cope and succeed in life. When a child first walks or talks, it used to be little more than a bragging right. Now for some parents, events like these become evidence of whether or not their child will be able to cope on his or her own 18 years later.

This neurotic obsession among some parents with preparing the child extends beyond infancy. Getting the kids involved in sports in the past was often an extension of a parent's ego or unfulfilled dreams. Today, huge numbers of parents believe that it is essential to teach them coping skills for the future. The amount of parental anxiety over grades and college application tests has skyrocketed in recent years. This anxiety has spread to children who increasingly worry about their grades and performances on standardized tests.

Whether or not coping anxiety is healthy for children is controversial. Less controversial is the reality that survival in the future will place more burdens on people than it did in the past, when good-paying blue- and white-collar jobs were relatively easy to access. This may mean that goofing off in high school or college has more long-term costs today than it did in the past.

THE EMPTY NEST SYNDROME

Many mothers dread the day when their children will leave home. Sociologists officially acknowledged this for mothers with the concept of the empty nest. The **empty nest syndrome** refers to feelings of loss and desperation that mother's experience when their kids grow up and leave home.

The empty nest syndrome is most likely to occur with women who are homemakers and view the children leaving as reducing their sense of value. Without daily involvement with the children, their sense of personal significance erodes. But not all women who are homemakers experience the empty nest syndrome. For some, having the children leave is seen as an opportunity to rekindle the romance in their marriages that had been put on hold when the kids were home.

Other women pursue postponed jobs and careers once the children leave. For many of them, their jobs and career aspirations were suspended once the children arrived. Getting a job or pursuing a career offers them opportunities for fulfillment and self-esteem that were deferred for the gratification associated with raising the children.

Although the empty nest syndrome is usually associated with mothers, it can also happen to men. This is often found among fathers who enjoy sports and being involved in a son's development as an athlete. That involvement is changed or even terminated when the son moves on to compete at the college or professional level. The result may be similar to what mothers experience with the empty nest syndrome.

With Title IX and more young women becoming involved in athletics, fathers may experience the same with them. Did Richard Williams, the father who taught and trained both Venus and Serena Williams, experience this when his daughters became professional successes in tennis? While it is hard to generalize, the fact remains that fathers who become involved in their daughters' sports careers are vulnerable to the empty nest syndrome.

Scripts in the past, or even today, that provide fathers with a pass on becoming involved in raising their children make them less prone to the empty nest syndrome. To the extent that fathers do not internalize child-rearing responsibilities or obtain joy from being with their children is the extent to which they are less likely to miss the kids. The more fathers obtain satisfaction and self-esteem from their jobs also affects how much they will miss having the kids around.

The empty nest syndrome is most likely to occur among women in modern societies, where enjoyment derived from raising the children is countered by pressures in the nuclear families to prepare the children to leave home. Traditional societies with extended family structure scripts mean that abrupt departures by the children are extremely unlikely. The fact that generations live and work together insulates mothers from the sense of loss that the empty nest syndrome can cause in modern societies.

THE MALE MIDLIFE CRISIS

The empty nest syndrome is often seen as the female counterpart to the **male midlife crisis.** The reason is that both occur in midlife. But different cultural scripts come into play.

For mothers, it is the background script that assigns value on nurturing. Once the kids are gone, what is there left to nurture? For men, the background script involves the value assigned to becoming successful.

The **male midlife crisis** is associated with guys who become obsessed with being youthful. Fast cars and young women become the quest. The fear of aging seems overwhelming.

Exactly why some men undergo this transformation from respectable, middle-class citizens to riding Harley Davidson motorcycles is an interesting question. One answer is that this is most likely to occur among men who no longer see their career aspirations as likely. Until middle age, one can always say that there is still time to succeed. By adopting youthful profiles, these men are unconsciously turning back the clock to give them more time.

Other men may have simply become bored with their routines. For them, taking on a youthful profile reminds them of the days when being wild and crazy was fun. Others who never were wild and crazy may now have the means to try new challenges such as sky diving or motorcycling.

The fact that many men who experience a midlife crisis get divorced and marry younger women rests on two considerations. The first is that some men associate their failures with their wives. Getting divorced is seen as giving them another chance to realize their career ambitions. The second is when the prevailing script allows men to marry women who are considerably younger than they are. This means that the pool of possible new marriage partners for middle-aged men is considerably larger than it is for middle-aged women.

PROFESSIONAL WOMAN LIFE CRISIS

For many professional career women, the midlife crisis that they face is different from both the empty nest syndrome and what middle-aged men experience. Among those most successful, midlife can trigger a crisis. Women with children who have been successful often regret the lost time spent with them because of work. Many decide to cut back on work so that they can spend more time with their kids if they still are at home. One option is to get involved in a company flextime plan and work out of the home. Another is to become a consultant and work out of the home. Both options often entail less money but are considered worthwhile. If the children have already left home for work or college, these reduced hours give professional women more time to talk with them on the phone and visit. It also gives them more time to spend with their husbands.

Aside from family consideration, there is another component of the midlife crisis for professional women. Many who have become successful experience a desire to fulfill aspects of their personality that devotion to the job denied. One possibility is to do things to develop themselves more fully, such as reading and volunteering time to groups within the community. This desire for self-advancement or fulfillment parallels the male midlife crisis in some regards, but is often less selfish in its manifestations.

BOOMERANG KIDS

The term **boomerang kid** refers to a child who leaves home but then returns. An example would be when a son returns from college to live with mom and dad until he can find a job. Another example is when a daughter gets divorced and returns to live with mom and dad because she can't afford to have a separate household.

LATCHKEY KIDS

Latchkey kids are children who come home after school, but there is no parent or other adult there to supervise them. Instead, the children are given a key to let themselves in when they come home. The work schedules of parents is the main cause of this phenomenon.

The increased economic necessity for dual incomes has increased the potential for latchkey kids. Sometimes a couple can arrange to work on different shifts so that one of them can be available after school. Many times, however, their work schedule will require them to be on the job at that time. For single working moms, the absence of a spouse increases the chances that their kids with be unsupervised at home after school.

One of the great political ironies involves moral entrepreneurs who advocate that mothers return from the job place to the home to take care of the kids. One reason for their concern is unsupervised latchkey kids. Yet, these same moral entrepreneurs strongly endorsed welfare reform that forced poor, single moms to leave their homes to receive job training and to take on full-time jobs. Apparently, the script involving the significance of mothers staying at home was not meant for poor mothers.

DIVORCE AMERICAN STYLE

Currently, in the United States about 50 percent of all marriages ends in divorce. The majority of divorces occur within the first seven years of marriage. Couples who marry young and those who are poor are more at risk for divorce. Women with little education and those with advanced degrees are the most likely to divorce. For men, the pattern is the more the education the less the likelihood of a divorce (Eitzen and Zinn, 1997: 376).

Statistics reveal that about 60 percent of divorces involve children. The rate is higher for African American children than Caucasians. By age 16, 33 percent of Caucasian children and 66 percent of African American children will be confronted by a divorce. By ten years after a divorce, about 66 percent of the children who are involved will have lost contact with their father (Eitzen and Zinn, 1997: 379).

ALTERNATIVE FAMILY STRUCTURES

The contrast between extended and nuclear families is the one that sociologists in the past emphasized. An increase in **childless couples, unmarried mothers,** and **divorced mothers** has generated more interest in alternatives to the extended and nuclear family structures. These alternative possibilities have been around for some time. The difference is that the growth in how many families do not match with the alleged norm of the nuclear family has made it harder to ignore them.

SINGLE-PARENT FAMILIES

Considerable publicity exists about the increase in the number of **single-parent families** in the United States that has occurred in recent years. Most of this has involved single-parent mothers. Two factors have contributed to this growth. One is the number of unmarried women who give birth. Henslin (1999: 447) indicates that about 33 percent of all births during the 1990s were to unmarried women. A sizable portion of these involved teenage pregnancies. The second is the high rate of divorce, which means that even if a woman remarries, she and her children are likely to spend time as a single-parent family.

Some view the problem of teenage pregnancy as involving fathers who refuse to marry and take care of their responsibilities. This is true to a certain extent, but it underestimates the depth of the problem. Even if the father marries, problems remain. If a teenage father works to help the family, he is also likely to fall behind in his education. This can severely diminish his future earning power, given the increased importance of education in the job market. Without education, any job that he can get as a teenager is likely to be a dead-end job with little future. Adding to all of these difficulties is the fact that the earlier people marry, the more likely they will divorce. This means that the married teenage mother is more likely than others to become a single-parent mother in the future.

Single-parent families created through divorce have their own unique problems. Studies show that the income of the mother and her children plummets relative to the income of her ex-spouse. This is partly due to guidelines for child support that result in ex-husbands disproportionately retaining income. Matters worsen because many men pay nothing or are in arrears on their child support payments. Studies show that about 50 percent of divorced fathers are in arrears and of those about half pay nothing.

ABSENT FATHERS

A current debate involves the significance of an absent father. One argument is that this deprives the children of a **role model.** But this significance is often more narrow than what is admitted. Those who advocate this viewpoint usually mean the absence of a male role model for their sons.

One problem with this argument is the underlying assumption that all fathers represent good role models. But what if the father does not represent a good role model for his son? Would the inclusion of such a person within the family structure really improve matters?

A religious organization called the Promise Keepers has sought to encourage fathers to become involved in their families as positive role models. They are particularly encouraged to strengthen bonds with their sons through participation at rallies. All of this may be positive for sons, but what about daughters who are excluded from these events? Moreover, responsible involvement with their families comes with a price tag. Biblical references are used to dictate that his wife recognizes his authority over her.

Questions about the significance of a present father as a role model represent one side of the debate. The other side argues that the real significance of a present father is income. In the **absence of income,** a poor family remains poor. Adding a poor father to the situation only depletes limited family resources.

Combinations of these factors are varied. Having a father present as a good role model and supportive figure for his wife and daughters is obviously a plus. It is even better when he makes a significant income contribution that can help pay for everything from food, shelter, and heathcare to a quality education.

MOTHERS AS ROLE MODELS

In the United States, there are two contradictory scripts involving **mothers as role models.** One script insists the proper role model for mothers is that of a **homemaker.** A mother who fulfills this role model encourages her daughters to do the same. This script also encourages sons to expect this of their wives.

The alternative script emphasizes the importance of mothers as **career role models** with good paying jobs. This script does not necessarily require women to completely forfeit their role as mothers or wives. But for a wife and mother to be successful in the world of work does require some major adjustments in traditional scripts that cast them exclusively as homemakers.

Those who promote scripts that encourage women to have successful careers see it as benefiting both their sons and daughters. For their daughters, it encourages them to become successful. Since success is so much a theme in American society, this encourages them to access what has been restricted to men. Success is also seen as providing economic independence, which affects how power will be distributed in their relations with men as husbands and in the larger society. As role models for their sons, successful mothers shape different expectations that they might have for their future wives.

Moral entrepreneurs disagree about mothers as role models. Those favoring patriarchy support scripts for mothers as homemakers. Those favoring greater independence and opportunities for women outside the home peddle the career script.

Both male and female moral entrepreneurs can peddle either script, depending upon their preferences. Women favoring the stay-at-home role model are likely to question those who pursue jobs and careers. Women favoring the career role model often charge stay-at-home moms with false consciousness. Businessmen who in their personal lives prefer that their wives stay at home send mixed messages when they hire women. And so it goes.

WIFE AS SENIOR PARTNER

Wife as senior partner (WASP) is a play on the more familiar association of WASP with white Anglo-Saxon Protestant men. Wife as senior partner refers to a situation where her job is primary and that of her husband is secondary. This phenomena is a product of changing economic times where in some cases, opportunities for women are better than they are for men.

A corollary of this possibility is the concept of **Mr. Mom.** Because of economic circumstances and choices, some married couples have chosen to reverse roles. This can occur in a number of different ways. One is for her to be the single breadwinner and his role is basically that of a stay-at-home dad. A variation is when his job allows him to take over the primary responsibility for cooking and taking care of the kids and the house.

COMMUTER MARRIAGES

Economic circumstances have changed the profile of the American family. Today, the vast majority of wives work. While wives and mothers have worked in the past, one difference is the increased likelihood that they will not work in the same community. This raises the prospect of both of them commuting.

Commuter marriages come in a number of different packages. One is a variation on the past model of the husband having to travel some distance to work. This possibility simply adds his wife to the equation. Both may have to commute some distance to work. This can create many time struggles for couples, especially if they have children. In large cities, the commute for each of them can easily be an hour or more each way to work.

Another version of the commuter marriage involves couples who live in different communities. In this situation, it is necessary for them to establish separate living quarters in different towns or cities. The separation for some professions is coast to coast. In other instances, the distance between their jobs is too great for them to share a common home location, but may be close enough so that they can meet on a regular basis. An example would be if you worked in Detroit and your spouse worked in Chicago. The greater the distance between them, the more likely they will have to fly when they want to get together. When flying is the option, expenses become an issue that can affect how often a couple will be able to be together.

BLENDED FAMILIES

Because of the high divorce rate and subsequent remarriages, blended families have become common in the United States. A **blended family** includes both natural and stepparents and siblings. Although blended families are not entirely new, the shear number of them today has amplified some of the difficulties associated with them.

The principle difficulty confronting those living in a blended family is the absence of a coherent script. How should the husband and wife relate to their ex-spouses who are often the biological parent of one or more of the children living with them? How should the children relate to an absent biological parent? How should they relate to a stepparent? How should a parent relate to his or her stepchildren that are living with them? Should they treat them differently than their own biological children that are living within the same household?

DOMESTIC PARTNERS

Domestic partners have already been discussed elsewhere. But since domestic couples represent a type of family structure, mention of them here is appropriate. Domestic partners are same sex couples who live together and form a family unity, but because of state laws are prohibited from marrying. Because spousal benefits for employees are often restricted to those who are married and their children, domestic partners are discriminated against in the workplace. The discrimination is based upon legal restrictions that prevent them from marrying and thereby qualifying a spouse for inclusion in benefits such as healthcare.

The fact that many domestic partners have stable and long-term relationships means that they parallel those who can legally marry and qualify for spousal benefits, expect for de facto discrimination against then as same-sex couples. Many companies are beginning to change their policies to include spousal benefits for domestic partners because these companies realize the importance of competing for and retaining valued employees. Some more conservative religious moral entrepreneurs have opposed these changes in policies and have threatened to boycott corporations such as Disney who have adopted this change.

THE SANDWICH GENERATION

The **sandwich generation** is caught with both dependent children and parents at the same time. This is not entirely new since the possibility exists even in societies with relatively low technology. This point was made with the extended family, where adults in their working years are responsible for both their children and elderly parents.

The enormous economic pressures that confront contemporary sandwich generations are unprecedented. Middle-aged couples face rapidly escalating costs for higher education. But trying to save for their children's college education is not their only concern. These same couples are faced with the potential of having to economically help their parents who are living longer than ever. This becomes a worry because living longer increases the risk that a single illness could throw their parents into financial chaos.

FAMILY POVERTY

Because of its reliance on a capitalist political economy script, the United States does not compare well to other economically advanced countries in terms of what it does to help poor families. Giddens and Deneier (2000: 166) cite statistics that sustain this point. In the United States, government programs lift only about 19 percent of poor families up to half of the median income. In Canada, government programs lift about 40 percent of poor families to half the median income. In the United Kingdom, the figure is 63 percent and in Sweden it is 76 percent!

Welfare reform during the 1990s was supposed to lift people out of poverty by forcing them off welfare rolls and into jobs. So far, the results have been less than promising. The truth of the matter is that while the welfare rolls have shrunk, the number of working families earning less than the poverty line has increased dramatically. The reason is poor-paying jobs. Rollbacks in government programs have worsened the situation for many of these working poor, to say nothing of those who cannot find jobs.

Race and ethnicity affect family poverty. The overall rate of poverty for Caucasian families in the United States is about 10 percent. The rate of poverty for African and Hispanic Americans is about three times more. And the rate of poverty for single-parent families headed by a woman is as much as six times higher than it is for the average Caucasian couple.

Discussions on family poverty often conveniently ignore what happens to children. Many moral entrepreneurs prefer to focus on alleged characteristics of poor parents than what happens to kids who by chance were born into a poor family. Eitzen and Zinn (1997) report that almost 25 percent of all children in the United States live in homes below the poverty line.

This is almost twice as high as the poverty rate for the elderly. At one time, the poverty rate for both children and the elderly was high. What changed is the elderly have become a powerful political force. No politician wants to offend them. This is why candidates spend so much time talking about Medicare, Social Security, and other issues that affect the elderly. These candidates know that letting programs such as Medicaid (healthcare for the poor) erode is less likely to cause them problems because the poor are less politically powerful.

FAMILY VIOLENCE

One **image** of the **American family** is that it offers a **safe haven** in a dangerous world. This romantic image is countered by the amount of family violence that occurs in the United States each year. This violence is often called **domestic violence.** Domestic violence occurs between members of a family. **Spousal abuse** involves husbands and wives. **Child abuse** involves parents and their children.

Recently, there has been a chilling addition to this list. It involves **elderly abuse.** Abuse toward the elderly by family members or those entrusted with their care is more prevalent than previously thought. Trying to take care of a spouse with a disease such as Alzheimer's can be exceptionally frustrating, especially for those who are not properly prepared. That anger can result in elderly abuse. Scandals about the abuse of elderly patients in nursing homes have rocked the nation.

Eitzen and Zinn (1997: 382) present some sobering data on domestic violence. A husband or lover beats his wife or girlfriend every 15 seconds. Thirty percent involve severe beatings. Many of the beatings occur when a woman is pregnant. In a given year, anywhere from 25–45 percent of all homicides in the United States result from domestic violence. And about 66 percent of parents use some type of physical violence on their children. The younger the child, the more likely he or she is going to get hit or spanked. The rate of severe violence by parents toward their children was about one in ten homes.

Patterns of family violence are scripted. Some involve official scripts that give men permission to inflict physical punishment on their wives and kids. Abusive men often learn these scripts by watching their own fathers.

What many fail to realize is that mothers are as likely to beat their children as fathers. Some of them learned this script from their mothers who abused them. Mothers who have internalized the script that defines them as nurturing are the most likely to experience guilt. Those who view themselves as disciplinarians like their husbands are less likely to experience guilt.

REFERENCES

Bales, R., and F. Stodtbeck.

    1951. "Phases in Group Problem-Solving: Journal of Abnormal and Social Psychology." 46: 485–495.

Becker, Howard.

    1963. *The Outsiders: Studies in the Sociology of Deviance.* New York: The Free Press.

    1967. "Whose Side Are We On?" *Social Problems.* 14: 239–247.

Bem, Sandra, and Daryl Bem.

    1980. "Homogenizing the American Woman." In W. Clay Hamner (ed.) *Organizational Shock.* New York: John Wiley and Sons, pp. 212–226.

Brehm, Jack.

    1966. *A Theory of Psychological Reactance.* New York: Academic Press.

Cloward, Richard, and Lloyd Ohlin.

    1960. *Delinquency and Opportunity.* New York: The Free Press

Cooley, C. H.

    1902. *Human Nature and the Social Order.* New York: Scribner.

Durkheim, Emile.

    1964. *Suicide.* New York: The Free Press. Originally published in 1897.

Eitzen, Stanley, and Maxine Baca Zinn.

    1997. *Social Problems.* Boston: Allyn and Bacon.

Festinger, Leon.

    1957. *A Theory of Cognitive Dissonance.* New York: Harper and Row

Giddens, Anthony, and Mitchell Duneier.

    2000. *Introduction to Sociology.* New York: Norton.

Goffman, Erving.

    1959. *Presentation of Self in Everyday Life.* Garden City, NJ: Anchor

    1963. *Behavior in Public Places: Notes on the Social Organization of Gatherings.* Glencoe, IL: Free Press.

Hall, Calvin.

    1954. *A Primer of Freudian Psychology.* New York: Free Press

Heider, F.

    1958. *The Psychology of Interpersonal Relations.* New York: Wiley

Henslin, James.

    1999. *Sociology: A Down to Earth Approach.* Boston: Allyn and Bacon.

Hess, Beth, Elizabeth Markson, and Peter Stein.

    1996. *Sociology.* Boston: Allyn and Bacon.

Hirshi, Travis.

    1969. *Causes of Delinquency.* Berkeley: University of California Press.

Homans, George.

    1961. *Social Behavior: Its Elementary Forms.* New York: Harcourt, Brace and World.

Janis, I.

    1971. "Groupthink." *Psychology Today.* Nov. pp. 43–46.

Katz, E.

 1957. "The Two Step Flow of Communication: An Up-Date Report on an Hypothesis." *Public Opinion Quarterly*, 21, 61–78.

Kesey, Ken.

 1996. *One Flew Over the Cuckoo's Nest*. New York: Penguin

Kinsey, Alfred C., et al.

 1948. *Sexual Behavior in the Human Male*. Philadelphia: Saunders.

 1953. *Sexual Behavior in the Human Female*. Philadelphia: Saunders.

Lemert, Edwin.

 1967. *Human Deviance: Social Problems and Social Control*. Englewood Cliffs, NJ: Prentice Hall.

Lenski, Gerhard, and Jean Lenski.

 1978. *Human Societies*. 3rd Ed. New York: McGraw-Hill.

Lindsey, L., and S. Beach.

 2000. *Sociology: Social Life and Social Issues*. Upper Saddle River, NJ: Prentice-Hall.

Mannheim, Karl.

 1936. *Ideology and Utopia*. New York: Harcourt.

Marcionis, J.

 2006. *Society: The Basics*. Upper Saddle River, NJ: Pearson Prentice-Hall.

Marx. Karl

 1967. *Capital: A Critique of Political Economy*. Vol. I. International Publishers. Originally published in 1867.

 1970. *A Contribution to the Critique of Political Economy*. New York: International Publishers. Originally published in 1859.

Matza, David, and Gresham Sykes.

 1961. "Juvenile Delinquency and Subterranean Values." *American Sociological Review*. 26 (5): 712–719.

McGuire, W., and D. Papageorgis.

 1961. "The Relative Efficacy of Various Types of Prior Belief-Defense in Producing Immunity to Persuasion." *J. Abnormal and Social Psychology*. (62) pp. 327–337.

Merton, Robert.

 1979. *Social Theory and Social Structure*. New York: The Free Press. Originally published in 1949.

Merton, Robert, and Alice Kitt.

 1950. In Robert Merton and Paul Lazarsfeld (eds.), *Continuities in Social Research: Studies and the Scope of Method of The American Soldier*, pp. 86–95.

Michels, Robert.

 1962. *Political Parties*. Trans. by Edan and Ceder Paul. New York: Collier. Originally published in 1911.

Ogburn, W. F.

 1957. "Cultural lag as a Theory." *Sociology and Social Research*, 41: 167–174.

Packard, Vance.

 1957. *The Hidden Persuaders*. New York: D. MacKay.

Parkinson, Northcote.

 1980. *Parkinson's Law*. Boston: Houghton-Mifflin. Originally published in 1957.

Peter, Lawrence, and R. Hull.

 1969. *The Peter Principle*. New York: Marrow

Robertson, Ian.

 1981. *Sociology*. 2nd Ed. New York: Worth Publishers.

Roethlesberger, F. and W. Dickson.

 1939. *Management and the Worker*. Cambridge: Harvard University Press.

Rogers, Carl.

 1959. *Client-Centered Therapy*. Boston: Houghton-Mifflin.

Rolling Stone Magazine.

    2002. *"Getting Inside."* July 25: pp. 41–44

Spector, Malcolm, and John Kitsuse.

    1997. *Constructing Social Problems.* Menlo Park, CA: Cummings.

Sumner, William Graham.

    1940. *Folkways.* Boston: Ginn. Originally published in 1906.

Sutherland, Edwin.

    1940. "White Collar Criminality." *American Sociological Review.* 5: 1–12.

    1947. *Criminology.* Philadelphia: J. B. Lippincott.

Thomas, W. I.

    1937. *The Unadjusted Girl.* Boston: Little, Brown.

Thompson, Hunter.

    1967. *The Hell's Angels: A Strange and Terrible Saga.* New York: Random House.

Tonnies, Ferdinand.

    1957. *Community and Society.* East Lansing, MI: Michigan State University Press. Originally published in 1887.

USA Today.

    2004. January 12: D5.

Veblen, Thorstein.

    1979. *The Theory of the Leisure Class.* New York: Penguin. Originally published in 1899.

Weber, Max.

    1958. *Economy and Society.* Ed. and trans. by Hans Gerth and C. Wright Mills. New York: Oxford University Press. Originally published in 1922.

    1959. *The Protestant Ethic and the Spirit of Capitalism.* New York: Scribner's. Originally published in 1904–05.

Webster's College Dictionary.

    1991. Random House.

White, R., and R. Lippett.

    1960. *Autocracy and Democracy: An Experimental Inquiry.* New York: Harper and Row.

GLOSSARY

Above the Law: Term referring to the contention that no one is above the law. In reality, selectivity based upon police, prosecutorial, and judicial discretion places some people above the law on a daily basis.

Absent Fathers: Fathers who are absent from the family and their children's lives.

Abstinent Society: A society where its' scripts limit sex to procreation.

Accommodation: When members of a minority group become aware of what a dominant group values.

Acculturation: When members of a minority group abandon their own values in favor of those expressed by a dominant group.

Acquaintance Moral Entrepreneur: An agent of socialization that we know who uses persuasion to get us to internalize a social script.

Acquaintance Role Model: An agent of socialization that someone knows who gets them to internalize a social script by being a positive role model.

Active Image of People: Image of people that gives them the capacity to modify and alter social scripts.

Actual-Self: A term Rogers used to describe who we actually are.

Ad Hominem Spin: A challenge to a social script based upon discrediting those who support it rather than challenging its content.

Advantaged: Those who benefit the most from arrangements in a society. Also referred to as the dominant group, privileged, and haves.

Affirmative Action: Attempt to give minorities opportunities that have been denied them because of discrimination.

Agent of Socialization: Anyone who shapes the social selves of others by getting them to internalize a social script and/or its related values and beliefs. See initial and sustaining agents of socialization.

Agricultural Society: A farming society that uses technological advances like irrigation systems and plows to more efficiently use its resources.

Alienation: A situation where people become separate from each other, lose control over their activities, and have little emotional involvement in what they produce.

Amalgamation: Intermarriage between minorities and members of a dominant group.

Ambivalent Society: A society with sex scripts that are a cross between abstinent and permissive societies.

Androgynous: Someone with both male and female characteristics.

Anglophile: Someone who loves anything English.

Anomie: Weak or diluted behavioral preferences (scripts).

Anonymity: Not being known to others.

Anticipatory Socialization: A process whereby someone becomes like members of an outside positive reference group in order to gain access and acceptance.

Arbitration: A situation where a third person is given the power to resolve a dispute between other parties.

Arranged Marriage: A situation where parents or other adults decide who will marry whom.

Assimilation: A form of conflict resolution where a dominant group requires minorities to give up their own identities and take on its identity as a precondition for access and acceptance. Also refers to when minorities are actually allowed into dominant group networks.

Attributing Scripts to Others: Process involving the scripts someone beliefs that other people bring to a social encounter. See definition of the situation.

Authoritarian Leaders: Leaders who impose their scripts on followers.

Authority: A form of legitimate power. Involves a degree of volition on the part of those who comply.

Autonomy: Ability to operate independent from others.

Background Scripts: Scripts containing general cultural values, ideas, or beliefs that provide the context in which more specific scripts unfold and are enacted.

Backlash: Attempts to set back minority progress.

Backlash moral entrepreneur: A moral entrepreneur who tries to discredit minorities and their achievements in an effort to restore privilege to white Protestant Anglo-Saxon men.

Backstage: Theatrical terms to describe behavior that is not observed by an audience. It is synonymous with private behavior.

Behavioral Dilemma: A situation where role conflict assures that the choice of behavior will have negative sanctions.

Behavioral Preference: A behavior someone thinks is acceptable or unacceptable or a behavior that someone enjoys or hates.

Behavioral Rationalization: Excuses people use to justify their behavior to themselves and others.

Behind-the-Scenes Guru: Someone largely out of sight who scripts messages for a public moral entrepreneur.

Belief: A truth claim about reality.

Belief Conviction: The extent to which a claim about reality is thought to be true.

Berdaches: Native American men who have both male and female characteristics.

Binging: Technique by members of a work group to slow down rate-busters and increase the work of chiselers by punching them in the shoulder.

Bipolar: Personality characterized by dramatic mood swings between manic and depression.

Bisexual: Someone who has had both same- and opposite-sex lovers.

Blended Families: Includes step-parents and siblings.

Blue-Collar Crime: Illegal acts committed on the job by people in the working class for personal gain.

Blue Line: Code of silence among police officers.

Boomerang Kids: Kids from nuclear families that return after having left.

Bootstrapper: Spontaneous moral entrepreneur.

Capitalist Political Economy Script: Embraces the laissez-faire principle that the best government is one that governs the least. In reality, it is a formula that maximizes the gap between the rich and poor in a society.

Care-Based Advertisements: Ads featuring care giving by a corporation. Designed to reverse a negative image.

Care-Based Appeals: Attempts by moral entrepreneurs to sell a script by characterizing those who endorse it as caring souls.

Career Mobility: The movement upward or downward in a system of stratification during one's lifetime.

Caste System: A system of social stratification with no opportunity for social mobility during one's lifetime.

Chain of Command: Hierarchy of power or authority within an organization that exists to provide direction and coordination of activities.

Character Assassination: Using ad hominem characterizations to destroy someone's reputation.

Charismatic Authority: When governmental compliance is based upon the personality of a leader.

Charismatic Leader: When the personality of someone is the basis for compliance.

Child Abuse: Violence by parents or other adults in a household against a child.

Chiselers: Those in a work group who do not hold their own. See Freerider.

Civil Disobedience: The peaceful breaking of laws to protest them.

Civil Inattention: Diverting eye contact.

Civil Law: Laws covering offenses against the individual for which monetary compensation can be sought.

Civility: An attitude of respect for people who are different.

Claims-Making Spin: Effort by moral entrepreneurs to employ alleged facts about the consequences of social scripts to peddle or challenge them.

Coalition: When two or more people or parties join resources against others.

Coded Message: A disguised message displaying support for a group but not so obvious as to turn off other audiences.

Coercion: A form of conflict resolution where one party is able to impose or force its script on others against their preferences.

Collective Hedonism: Principle that the best society is one where the greatest good is created for the greatest number of people.

Comfort Zone: Term often associated with white men who complain that the presence of women and other minorities makes them feel uncomfortable.

Coming Out: When people publicly announce their homosexuality.

Commuter Marriage: When a couple must live separately because of job demands. Also refers to couples where one or both live together but their commutes to work diminish the amount of time they have together.

Comparable Pay: Paying men and women according to the amount of education, skill, and responsibility required rather than what biased gender scripts allow.

Compatible Interpersonal Scripts: A situation where the behavioral preferences two or more people have for someone else are consistent.

Compatible Personal Social Scripts: When personal preferences people bring to a social encounter or relationship match.

Compatible Self-Scripts: A situation where the preferences someone has for himself or herself are consistent.

Competition: A form of conflict resolution governed by agreed upon rules where participants agree to accept whoever wins. Competition is win/lose situation.

Compromise: A form of conflict resolution where those involved give up something in order to arrive at an agreement. Compromise is a diluted win/win situation because all parties to an agreement benefit less than if they were able to impose their will on the others.

Conflict: A clash over outcomes in a relationship, group, or society.

Conflict Model of Society: Applies to societies where there are multiple cultural scripts that favor some at the expense of others.

Conflict Subculture: Term used to describe people who become violent when confronted with blocked opportunities.

Conflicted Social Self: Results from internalizing incompatible components from multiple scripts.

Conformity: Behavior that complies with a social script. Merton's definition is unusual in that it defines conformity as using legitimate means to attain a cultural goal, such as material success.

Consensus Model of Society: Applies to a society where there is a single agreed upon script.

Conspicuous Consumption: The lavish display of wealth.

Consumption Ethic: A script that embraces consumption and judges people according to the value of what they consume.

Consumption Script: Determines who has access to what goods and services.

Control Theory: Theory that suggests close ties with parents and involvement with groups that reinforce mainstream values decreases deviance.

Conversation Filler: Something to talk about that fills a conversational void.

Cooperation: When members of a group voluntarily share their resources to work toward a common goal.

Co-optation: Form of conflict resolution where an individual/group gets an outsider who originally disagrees with them to come over to their side.

Corporate Crime: Illegal acts committed by officials that are intended to benefit the corporation.

Corporate Gorillas: Corporate executives (CEOs) brought in from outside the company and given broad powers to improve its bottom line.

Corrections: Component of the criminal justice system that oversees the punishment set by sentences.

Cost: The actual or anticipated reaction of self or others to a behavior that discourages the likelihood that someone will repeat the behavior that produced the reaction and/or continue in the relationship.

Counter-Culture: A group within a larger society that is distinct and incompatible with it. May or may not seek to challenge the script of the larger society.

Counter-Ideology: A set of ideas that oppose existing scripts and arrangements in a society. See Utopian Ideology.

Courtship Ritual: Scripted activities that bring couples together for marriage.

Credibility Advantage: Extent to which what someone says is believed more than others. See personal, expertise, and social hierarchies of credibility.

Credibility Deficit: Extent to which what someone says is less likely to be believed than what others offer.

Credibility Factor: The extent to which someone is believed.

Crime: A behavior that violates a law.

Criminal Justice System: Governmental agencies responsible for enforcing laws.

Criminal Law: An offense against society for which loss of freedom is the most frequent punishment.

Criminal Subculture: Term that is used to describe people who steal when confronted with blocked opportunities.

Critical Mass: Point as which the number of women in a job or profession results in diminished prestige. See feminization of jobs.

Culture: A social script or blueprint that structures generalized customs, rituals, and other activities in a society.

Culture of Poverty: Attitudes attributed to poor people that can be used to blame them for their plight.

Cultural Clone: An agent of socialization who parrots cultural scripts in a society.

Cultural Diversity: When different cultural scripts exist within a society. See cultural pluralism and multiculturalism.

Cultural Innovator: An agent of socialization that modifies or alters a cultural script.

Cultural Lag: Time it takes for societies to adopt their social scripts to technological innovations.

Cultural Pluralism: Same as cultural diversity or multiculturalism.

Cultural Relativism: A situation when members of a group or society respect the scripts of others. It is the opposite of ethnocentrism.

DEA: Acronym for Drug Enforcement Administration.

Decriminalization: Eliminating existing laws or dramatically reducing penalties associated with them. See deregulation.

De Facto Segregation: Segregation based upon customs rather than laws.

Definition of the Situation: Process involving how people interpret or size up a situation. Perceptions people have of themselves and others involving behavioral preferences and likely consequences for compliance or deviance.

Degree of Personal Expression: The extent to which a social script allows or encourages people to express themselves.

De Jure Segregation: Segregation based upon laws.

Democratic Leaders: Leaders who encourage inputs and collective decision making.

Demographics: Data on the distribution of people with certain characteristics in a given geographical area.

Dependence: A situation where someone must rely on others for gratification.

Deregulation: Eliminating a government regulation or diluting it by reducing penalties.

Deregulation: Form of decriminalization that focuses on regulations that are intended to protect people from harm in the workplace and elsewhere.

Desegregation: Eliminating restrictions on where minorities live, work, and play. See assimilation.

Deviance: Behavior that violates a social script.

Deviant Label: A label used by moral entrepreneurs to stigmatize a behavior and people who engage in it.

Deviant Subculture: A term that criminologists and some sociologists use to describe a group that violates the scripts of either the dominant group or mainstream. Synonymous with the term counter-culture.

Differential Association: Theory that deviance is learned by hanging out with deviants.

Diffusion of Responsibility: Spreading the blame.

Diffusion of a Social Script: The spread of a script from one group, community, or society to another.

Disadvantaged: Those who benefit the least from arrangements in a society. Also referred to as minorities, underprivileged, and have-nots.

Discretion: Refers to the amount of latitude or judgment that members of the criminal justice system can exercise.

Discrimination: Practices by the dominant group that deny minorities opportunities.

Displacement: Psychological mechanism that directs anger and frustration toward less threatening people than those who cause it in the first place.

Dissonance: A state of discord between what someone believes and what someone does.

Dissonance Reduction: Effort to relieve tensions brought about by discord between what someone believes and what someone does. One method is to change the behavior to bring it into accord with the belief. Another is to change the belief to bring it into accord with the behavior. Perceiving the behavior as not volitional and forced is also a way to rationalize it and reduce dissonance with a belief.

Distributive Justice: An attempt to justify gaps between the rich and poor by exaggerating how much the rich contribute to society.

Division of Labor: The way a society allocates work activities.

Doctrine of Implied Consent: Assumption that unless a woman can prove otherwise, all sex is consensual. Places the burden of proof on the woman rather than having the man prove that she consented.

Domestic Partners: Couples of the same sex who live together.

Domestic Partner Benefits: When benefits, such as healthcare, are extended to the same-sex spouse of an employee.

Domestic Violence: Violence within the family. Includes child and spousal abuse.

Dominant Group: People who benefit the most from arrangements in a society. Also called the advantaged, haves, and privileged.

Dominant Ideology: Ideas that serve the vested interests of the dominant group in a society.

Duration of a Social Script: How long a script has been in place.

Duration of a Social Structure: How long a patterned way of interacting lasts.

Dyad: A relationship between two and only two people. It is the minimal unit of analysis for sociologists.

Economic Scripts: Scripts that determine how goods and services are produced, distributed, and consumed.

Educational Script: Determine who is responsible for storing and transmitting knowledge in a society. Educational scripts also affect who receives this knowledge.

Elderly Abuse: Abuse of elderly by members of their family or other caretakers.

Emergent Social Script: The script that unfolds overtime and structures the relationship between two or more people.

Emotional Challenge: Using emotional appeals to discredit a social script.

Emotional Contagion: The spread of emotional arousal in a group or crowd.

Emotional Spins: Efforts by moral entrepreneurs to peddle or challenge a social script by playing off the emotions of an audience.

Empirical Question: A question that is answered by data and not speculation.

Empiricism: Scientific doctrine that observable data is the ultimate basis for judging knowledge claims.

Empty Nest Syndrome: Occurs when a mother experiences a loss and sense of purpose when the children leave.

Entrapment: When police officers induce someone to engage in a crime that they otherwise would not commit.

Ethnicity: Cultural differences between people based upon scripts acquired in the communities or countries that they come from.

Ethnocentrism: Refers to a situation where members of a group or society believe that their scripts are superior to those of others.

Everyday Life: Activities that occur in our daily lives.

Expertise Hierarchy of Credibility: Credibility based upon the amount of respect people have for the knowledge of someone.

Expressive Relationship: A relationship that encourages the expression of personal feelings and opinions. A relationship where participants are aware of each other's personal feelings and opinions. See primary relationship.

Extended Family: Three or more generations that live and work together as a family unit.

External Costs: Negative reactions by others to someone's behavioral choice.

External Mechanisms of Control: The real or imagined reactions that increase or decrease the likelihood that a behavior will occur or be repeated. External sanctions mean the same thing.

Factual Challenge: Using data to discredit a social script. See claims-making spin.

Fads: A relatively short-lived but intense pop culture activity. Fads can be a private source of gratification, such as collecting popular action figures, whereas fashions are always public expressions.

False Consciousness: When members of a minority group buy into a dominant ideology.

Family Violence: Violence between spouses and/or children in a family.

Fashions: Fashions, like fads, are pop culture phenomena that tend to have a relatively short shelf life. But unlike fads, fashion statements are always a public expression of someone's personal identity

FBI: Acronym for the Federal Bureau of Investigation.

Federal Regulatory Agencies: Federal government agencies who are supposed to make sure that people and companies are complying with regulations.

Feminization of Jobs: When a job loses its prestige because too many women have it.

Fishing Society: A society that subsists on fish.

Flowchart: An organizational map or diagram that shows who has power over whom and the location of staff positions.

Folkways: Low-octane behavioral preferences. Less intense behavioral preferences.

Food Scripts: Designate when and what to eat and what is appetizing.

Foraging Society: One where people search for and consume food as they come across it.

Formal Mechanisms of Social Control: Sustaining conformity through impersonal agencies, such as the police.

Formal Script: A script that has been deliberately planned, designed, and written down. Formal scripts shape interaction among people engaged in secondary relationships. A corporate flowchart is a prime example.

Freerider: Someone who enjoys the benefits of belonging to a group but makes few or no contributions.

Frontstage: Theatrical term describing behavior that is seen by an audience. It is synonymous with public behavior.

Functionalists: Sociologists attracted to comparison between organisms and societies.

Gatekeeper: Someone who controls access to valued resources.

Gay: Male homosexuals. Sometimes used as generic term for male and female homosexuals.

Gay Bashing: Violent attacks on gays.

Gemeinschaft Society: A predominately rural society scripted more in terms of primary than secondary relationships.

Gender: Differences between people as determined by scripts assigned to them on the basis of their biological sex.

Gender Roles: Scripted expectations for males and females in a society.

Gender Script: Scripts assigned to people on the basis of their biological sex.

Gender Segregation: Disproportional concentration of men and women in certain jobs and professions.

Gender Socialization: Teaching gender roles. See internalization.

Gender Stratification: Unequal distribution of power, wealth, and prestige based upon gender scripts.

Genocide: Mass murder of minorities.

Genuine Ingratiation: Occurs when a performance that ingratiates others is honest and self-gratifying.

Gesellschaft Society: An urban society scripted more in terms of secondary than primary relationships.

Gestures of Disapproval: Reactions by participants in an encounter or relationship that establish behavioral boundaries and attempt to discourage interpersonal deviance.

Getting Tough on Crime: Based upon philosophy of locking up criminals and throwing away the key. Its focus on street crimes deflects political attention away from illegal acts that can be more harmful to society.

Giving-Off: Form of impression management where people try to impress others. See Conspicuous Consumption.

Glass Ceiling: Point at which advancement within an organization or corporation stops for minorities. They have advanced far enough to see the top but can't break through to those top positions.

Goal-Displacement: When adherence to organizational rules takes precedence over focusing on the organization's goals.

Gossip: Idle chatter about someone else. See malicious gossip.

Group Cohesion: The strength of bonds among members of a group.

Group Recruitment: Involves efforts by a group to attract new members by advertising its social scripts and the activities that the scripts shape.

Groupthink: A situation where a strong leader and mind-guards discourage critical inputs.

Halo: Ad hominem characterizations that portray usually a public figure as pure.

Healthcare Script: Determines who provides and receives healthcare in a society.

Healthy Behavior: Behavior that is approved of by a social script.

Hedonism: Principle that people should seek to maximize pleasure.

Hedonistic Calculus: Principle that the best society is one that maximizes pleasure and minimizes pain for its members.

Herding Society: A society that knows how to breed and raise animals for subsistence.

Heterogamy: Marrying someone from a different background.

Heterosexual: Prefer sex with partners of the opposite sex.

Hierarchy of Credibility: Refers to difference concerning who is most likely to be believed in a group, community, or society. See personal and social hierarchy of credibility.

Highly Scripted: When the amount of behavior controlled by a social script is extensive. See scope of a social script.

History: Using written documents to study the past.

Homemaker: A stay at home Mom. More recently includes Mr. Moms.

Homogamy: Marrying someone with the same background.

Homophobia: Fear of homosexuals.

Homosexual: Prefer sex with partners of the same sex.

Hostile Environment: When sexual harassment creates an atmosphere that makes it difficult for a subordinate to work.

Household Assets: Everything a family owns, such as a house, cars, and furniture.

Hunting and Gathering Society: A society that subsists on game, vegetables, and fruit that is brought back to the village for consumption.

Hypocrisy: When what someone says does not match what someone does.

Id: Freud's term for biological drives associated with sex and aggression.

Ideal-Culture: Scripts that celebrate certain values and images that members have of themselves and their society.

Ideal-Self: A term that Rogers used to characterize who we think we ought to be. See social self.

Ideal-type: Exaggerating features in a concept.

Identification with the Aggressor: When fear of others compels someone to become like them in order to psychologically relieve the threat of harm.

Identification with Outsiders: When a member of a group identifies with people not in that group.

Imposing Scripts on Others: Refers to a situation where someone, a group, or society forces others to comply with a script. Involves the use of coercive power.

Impression Management: Efforts to manipulate how people view us.

Incest Taboo: Script that prohibits sex between parents and their children, siblings, and other designated relatives.

Incoherent Script: A script that contains value, belief, or normative that lack a logical and meaningful connection. A social script that contains internal contradictions lacks coherence.

Incompatible Interaction Preferences: When two or more people have conflicting behavioral preferences for someone else.

Incompatible Personal Social Scripts: When personal preferences people bring to a social encounter or relationship conflict.

Incompatible Self-Preferences: When the self-preferences of an individual conflict with each other.

Independence Card: Selling a script or product by appealing to an audience's sense of independence.

Index Crimes: Crimes featured in the Uniform Crime Reports.

Industrial Society: A society where most of its work activities are in manufacturing.

Informal Mechanisms of Social Control: Sustaining conformity through intimate and personal relationships.

Informal Script: A script that shapes behavior among people engaged in primary relationships but is not formally planned or written down.

Ingratiation: When a behavior provokes a favorable disposition or response by someone else.

In-group: The group one belongs to at a point in time.

Initial Agent of Socialization: The first person who gets someone to internalize a social script and/or its related values and beliefs.

Innovation: Merton's terms for a situation where someone uses unacceptable means to reach a cultural goal such as material success.

Inoculation Theory: Idea that if you give people a small dose of an offensive viewpoint, it will inoculate them against that viewpoint.

Instrumental Ingratiation: When the only reason for engaging in an act is to gain a favorable response from someone else.

Instrumental Relationship: A relationship that is task-oriented. See secondary relationship.

Interaction Compliance: When people do what others prefer.

Interaction Preference: Component of a personal social script that someone applies to other people. Includes what behaviors someone feels are appropriate by others and/or the behaviors of others that someone enjoys or despises.

Interaction Script Test: Behavior that elicits a response by others that provides feedback about their interaction behavioral preferences.

Intergenerational Mobility: Amount of social mobility between family or age cohort generations.

Internal Costs: Negative feelings of guilt or low self-esteem that someone experiences because of a behavioral choice that person made.

Internal Mechanisms of Control: Control of behavior through personal feelings, such as pride, guilt, and self-esteem. Based upon internalization.

Internalization: When someone comes to personally accept a social script that was originally held by others.

Interpersonal Role Conflict: Role conflict based upon what other people believe is appropriate behavior for someone in a given status. The conflict may involve what the person in that position prefers and what someone else believes is appropriate behavior. It may also involve incompatible roles multiple others hold for someone in a given status.

Interpersonal Sexual Role Conflict: A clash between someone's own sexual inclinations and what others feel is appropriate.

Interpretive Latitude: The extent to which a script and its content are open to interpretation.

Iron Cage: Term describing the impersonal nature of modern organizations.

Iron-Law of Oligarchy: Tendency of leaders within an organization to become isolated from the rank and file. See Groupthink.

Jails: Locally holds suspects awaiting trial and those with sentences of less than one year.

Job Descriptions: Script that tells people the tasks they are assigned within an organization.

Kinship Network: An extensive set of relationships in a traditional society based upon blood and marriage. Although less elaborate kinship networks in modern societies may involve adoption, blended families, domestic partners, and so forth.

Labeling Theory: Theory that states no behavior is inherently deviant. It is moral entrepreneurs who label certain acts as deviant.

Laissez-faire Leader: A hands-off leader who gives minimal inputs.

Laissez-faire Political Philosophy: Belief that the government that governs the least governs the best.

Latchkey Kids: Kids who are given a key to let themselves in after school.

Law: State sanctioned behavioral preference. Behavioral preferences that have a governmental stamp of approval.

Legitimacy: A script is legitimate whenever people approved of it.

Legitimate Government: A government is legitimate to the extent that people approve of its basic structure.

Literate Society: A society that has a written language.

Living Document: Principle that applications of the Constitution and its Amendments by the Supreme Court should be allowed to evolve and not be limited to allegations concerning the original intent of the Founding Fathers.

Looking Glass Self: Process of judging ourselves through real or imagined approval or disapproval by others.

Magnitude of Conflict: Varies depending upon the intensity with which conflicting behavioral preferences are held.

Magnitude of Sanctions: Extent to which a behavior is rewarded or inflicts costs.

Magnitude of Stratification: The gap between the top and bottom in a system of stratification.

Mainstream Script: A script that the majority of people in a community or society agree with.

Mainstream Values: Agreed upon values that sustain a mainstream script in a community or society.

Malicious Gossip: Idle chatter meant to disparage the character of someone else.

Mandatory Sentences: Sentences mandated by legislatures that take discretion away from judges.

Manufactured Charisma: When images designed to improve the charisma of a leader are deliberately manipulated rather than letting charisma unfold naturally.

Marginal Person: Someone caught between two groups or cultures.

Marital Rape: When a husband forces his wife to have sex.

Mass Culture: Popular culture driven by mass media such as radio, television, music, videos, and so forth.

Master Script: A deliberately constructed script that governs diverse activities among a large number of people. A master script is like a master plan.

Materialism: A preoccupation with owning expensive items, such as clothing, cars, and houses.

Mate Selection: Means by which marriage partners are selected in a society.

Matriarchy: A situation where women control valued resources and have power over men.

Matrifocal: Applies to a single-parent home headed by a woman.

Matrilocal: When a married couple lives with her parents.

Maverick Moral Entrepreneur: A public moral entrepreneur who characterizes himself or herself as an independent thinker.

Media Bias: Occurs when the mass media favors certain social scripts and their related values and beliefs over others.

Mediation: A situation where one person is given the responsibility of trying to help others reach a compromise.

Medicalization of Deviance: Stigmatizing a behavior that is seen as unacceptable by labeling it as sick.

Medical Labels: Labeling acts as healthy or pathological (diseased).

Melting Pot: When diverse scripts merge together to form a new combination.

Mental Rehearsal: Preparing for a social encounter by imagining it.

Midlife Crisis: Occurs when men who no longer believe in their career dreams regress to youthful behavior.

Military-Industrial Complex: Network or relationships between politicians, the military, and industry that has a vested interest in securing funding for military weapons and supplies.

Mindguards: Those who reinforce the position of a strong leader by stifling criticism.

Minority Group: People who received fewer benefits within a society. Also called the disadvantaged, underprivileged, and have-nots.

Miranda Rule: Requires police to make suspects aware of their Constitutional rights.

Mixed Audience: An audience that holds differing behavioral preferences, values, and beliefs.

Modal Personality: Typical person in a society. Only applies to societies where a single agreed upon script creates the basis for a common personality type.

Modes of Adaptation: Different choices people make concerning the pursuit of a cultural goal, such as material success.

Moral Deficit: When audiences view the value behind a behavioral preference as deficient.

Moral Entrepreneur: An agent of socialization who uses persuasion to get people to accept the behavioral preferences in a script along with its related values and beliefs.

Moral High Ground: Selling a social script and its related values and beliefs by appealing to its moral superiority.

Moral Offense: Term often used to describe victimless crimes.

Mores: High-octane behavioral preferences. Behavioral preferences that are seen as very important by people.

Mr. Mom: Term used to describe a stay-at-home Dad.

Multiculturalism: A term that describes a society where more than one cultural script exists.

Mutually Beneficial: Refers to a relationship where everyone benefits from the behaviors of each other. See unilateral benefits for the opposite.

National Crime Victimization Survey (NCVS): A survey conducted twice a year by the Justice Department that asks respondents if they have been a crime victim.

Need For Approval: Assumption that people are driven by the need to get approval from others in order to maintain a positive self-concept.

Negative Reference Group: A group that you disdain.

Negative Role Model: A person that someone else thinks is an example of a bad role model that should be scorned.

Negotiating Social Scripts: Tactics people employ to encourage compliance with their interpersonal behavioral preferences.

Neolocal: When a married couple live independently from their parents.

Net Balance of Rewards and Costs: The proportion of rewards and costs from an encounter or relationship compared to imagined returns from alternative encounters or relationships. A net balance favoring rewards encourages continued participation, while a net balance where costs exceed rewards discourages further participation.

New Rich: People who have recently become wealthy and do not have famous American ancestors.

Nonverbal Behavior: The language of gestures. Communication between people based upon observation rather than speech or written language.

Norm: A behavioral preference that is shared by members in a group or society.

Novel Behavior: Behavior that is unusual. Contrasted to familiar, predictable, and repetitious acts.

Nuclear Family: Family unit based upon parents and their children.

Official Script: The script that a group, community, organization, or society presents as describing how things are done.

Old Money: Wealth associated with families that go back generations.

Organizational Hierarchy: Script describing who has power in an organization, beginning with those at the top.

Organized Crime: The mob.

Original Intent: Principle that Supreme Court decisions should be based entirely upon allegations concerning what the Founding Fathers meant.

Out-group: A group that one does not belong to at a given point in time.

Outing: When someone without permission publicly announces that someone else is homosexual.

Parkinson's Law: Work increases to meet the amount of time that is available.

Participant Observation: Research based upon living with and observing the behavior of people.

Passive Image of People: An image of people that sees them as submissive clones of social scripts.

Patriarchy: A situation where men control valued resources and have power over women.

Patrilocal: When a married couple live with his parents.

Patriotic Crimes: Illegal acts committed by governmental officials in the name of national security.

Patriotism: Willingness to sacrifice self for the collectivity.

Peddling Social Scripts: Process involving attempts to sell a script. See moral entrepreneurs.

Pedophile: An adult who is sexually aroused by children.

Permissive Society: A society with open and tolerant attitudes about sex.

Personal Ambivalence: When someone is undecided or has mixed emotions about certain behaviors. See conflicted social self.

Personal Expression: Acts or performances based upon someone's personality rather than a social script.

Personal Hedonism: Hedonism or the pursuit of pleasure seen as an individual right.

Personal Hierarchy of Credibility: Persuasive difference among people in a group or society based upon their personalities.

Personality: The total set of beliefs, emotions, and behavioral disposition of a person.

Personal Rationalization: Excuse someone uses to abate personal guilt.

Personal Role Conflict: Conflict resulting from a conflict self.

Personal Sexual Role Conflict: Occurs whenever people feel guilty or wrong about their own sexual feelings and inclinations.

Personal Social Script: The behavioral preferences of a specific person. Contains both interaction preferences and self-preferences.

Peter Principle: Notion that within organizations, people get promoted to their level of incompetence.

Plain View Doctrine: Allows police to seize evidence that is in plain view without a warrant.

Planting Society: A society that subsists on food that it plants, cultivates, and harvests.

Plausible Deniability: When leaders purposively distance themselves from the actions of subordinates that they inspired.

Plea Bargain: Agreement by prosecutor to reduce or eliminate charges against one suspect if that person provides testimony or other evidence against other suspects.

Pluralistic Ignorance: Refers to a situation where participants make erroneous assumptions about what scripts they prefer.

Political Correctness: Product of conservative think tanks that identifies attempts to show respect toward minorities as mindless censorship. A favorite line is to suggest that next we will have to use the label vertically challenged to describe people who are short.

Political Economy Scripts: Scripts that shape the relationship between economic and political institutions.

Political Incorrectness: Flip side of political correctness with the emphasis on having the freedom to use whatever labels we want when describing people we don't like. Labeling all feminists dykes is a favorite among conservative moral entrepreneurs. Appeals to people who view themselves as independent thinkers.

Political Scripts: Government scripts.

Pop Culture: Themes and activities that ordinary people find appealing and incorporate into their lifestyles.

Pornography: Sexually explicit material that is seen as offensive.

Positive Reference Group: A group that you see as similar to you and with which you have a positive identity.

Positive Role Model: Someone that someone else identifies with.

Postindustrial Society: A society where work activities are centered around computer and information technologies.

Preaching to the Choir: Peddling a social script to people who already accept it.

Primary Deviance: An initial deviant act.

Primary Group: Three or more people who are familiar with each other and engage in intimate face-to-face encounters.

Primary Relationship: An intimate and personal relationship where people are expected to take each other into account as specific personalities.

Principles of Social Exchange: Different ways that interaction can be structured.

Prison Industries: Practice of letting private companies use prisoners as a source of cheap labor.

Prisons: State and federal institutions that incarcerate inmates for more than a year.

Private Behavior: Behavior that occurs behind closed doors and is not monitored by outside members of the group, community, or society.

Private Script: A script that shapes social behavior that is out of sight from audiences.

Privatization of Prison Labor: Giving contracts to private companies that allow them to use prison labor at extremely low wages.

Professional Woman Crisis: When professional women come to question their career priority and begin to think about more meaningful pursuits.

Profiling: Involves police stopping and detaining people based upon characteristics that are not direct evidence of a criminal violation. Violates probable cause rules.

Promiscuity: Frequent and indiscriminate sex with multiple partners.

Prosecutors: Lawyers who work for the government and represent the people in criminal proceedings.

Proselytizing: An extreme form of ethnocentrism where members of a group try to persuade others to abandon their ways and join them.

Protestant Ethic: Set of virtues such as thrift and hard work that are often associated with Protestantism.

Public Moral Entrepreneurs: An agent of socialization who gets people to internalize a social script through persuasion.

Public Role Model: An agent of socialization who is a public figure that gets people to internalized a social script by an example of a positive role model.

Public Scripts: Social scripts that shape interaction that takes place in front of an audience.

Putting People on Notice: Letting people know the consequences for interpersonal deviance.

Quid Pro Quo: Promising something in return for an act.

Race: Differences between people based upon a physical characteristic such as skin color.

Racial Profiling: It occurs when police stop and detain people solely or disproportionately on the basis of their race.

Racism: When members of the dominant group use negative attitudes toward minorities to deny them opportunities.

Rate-Buster: Someone in a work-group that is an overachiever.

Rational legal Authority: A system of authority based upon a script that is deliberately calculated, planned, and written down.

Real Culture: Refers to the scripts that shape actual behavior. Compare to the ideal culture.

Rebellion: Term Merton uses to describe people who reject a cultural goal, such as material success. This rejection makes the choice of means moot. Rebels are more likely than retreatists to challenge existing scripts.

Recidivist: Someone who returns to prison. Also known as a repeat offender.

Reference Group: A group that you identify with at a given point in time.

Regulations: Government scripts that prohibit certain behavior.

Regulatory Agencies: Local, state, or federal agencies who are supposed to enforce government regulations.

Rehearsal: Preparation for interaction with others. Includes both mental and actual behavioral practice.

Religion: Set of sacred beliefs.

Resocialization: A change in behavioral preferences brought about by a change in situations.

Retreatism: Term Merton uses to describe people who drop out of society.

Retreatist Subculture: Term used to describe people who withdraw from society when confronted with blocked opportunities.

Reverse Outcomes: When the outcomes of planned activities are the opposite from what was intended.

Reverse Psychology: When members of a negative reference group pretend to approve of a behavior they find offensive in order to discourage it from being repeated.

Revolutionaries: People who want to overturn a prevailing script in a society and replace it with their own.

Reward: A response by self or others that increases the likelihood a behavior will be repeated and/or that one will continue with the encounter or relationship.

Rites of Passage: Rituals associated with lifecycle events.

Ritualism: Term Merton uses to describe people who are obsessed with following rules. See goal-displacement.

Rituals: Ceremonies and other activities that express significant values or events.

Role: The behavioral preferences attached to a status.

Role Conflict: Incompatible behavioral preferences for status-occupants.

Role Distance: Showing disdain for a performance.

Role Embracement: Showing a commitment to a performance.

Role-making: Modifying or changing social scripts.

Role Model: An agent of socialization who gets people to internalize behavioral preferences and related values and beliefs by example. Types of role models include public, vicarious, and acquaintance.

Role Relationship: A scripted relationship between two status-occupants.

Role-Set: A series of two or more interconnected role relationships.

Romantic Love: Mate selection based upon falling in love.

Routine Social Behaviors: Familiar behaviors.

Routinization of Charisma: Creating a script for those who succeed as charismatic leader.

Sacred: Attitude that religion should permeate all aspects of life, including government.

Sanctions: The real or imagined reactions of self or others that affects the likelihood that a behavior will occur or be repeated. See rewards and costs.

Sanction Test: An effort to measure the magnitude of rewards and/or costs associated with compliance or deviance from a behavioral preference contained in a social script.

Sandwich Generation: Generation caught between supporting dependent children and parents at the same time.

Scapegoat: Blaming minorities for problems that they have no control over. Shifts attention from decisions made by rich and powerful people.

Scope of a Social Script: The number of people who share or agree with the behavioral preferences in a social script.

Scope of a Social Structure: The number of people who engage in a pattern of activities.

Script Analysis: The process of looking at how social scripts shape social behavior.

Script Boundaries: The range of behavior that is permitted within the behavioral preferences (role) contained in a social script.

Script Coherence: The degree to which elements in a social script are compatible.

Script Compatibility: The degree to which scripts are in agreement.

Script Confrontation: A direct challenge to a behavioral preference (role) contained in a social script of others.

Script Test: An effort to determine the boundaries of a behavioral preference (role) contained in a social script. Can involve either self-preferences or the behavioral preferences of others.

Script Typologies: Contrasting social scripts between or within groups, communities, or societies.

Secondary Deviance: Deviance caused by labeling someone a deviant. See self-fulfilling prophesy.

Secondary Group: When three or more people engage in relatively fragmented and impersonal relationships with each other.

Secondary Relationship: An impersonal relationship where people are expected to limit their involvement to formally scripted behaviors.

Secular: Attitude that religion should be absent from official public activities and policies.

Segregation: Physical separation of people based on characteristics such as race, ethnicity, religion, and gender.

Self-awareness: Knowledge or beliefs someone has about himself or herself.

Self-compliance: When what someone does conforms to his or her self-preference. Creates a self-reward.

Self-Cost: A response by someone to his or her own behavior that decreases the likelihood that the behavior will be repeated and/or that the person will remain in the encounter or relationship.

Self-Disclosure: The extent to which people are willing to reveal their personal behavioral preferences, values, and beliefs to others.

Self-Esteem: Feeling good about oneself. See self-worth.

Self-Fulfilling Prophesy: When a dominant group manipulates circumstances to sustain negative attitudes about minorities. Also applies to minorities who buy into these negative images for the same reason. The notions of secondary deviance and deviant careers are based upon this concept.

Self-Labels: How minorities define themselves.

Self-Preference: Component of a personal social script that contains the behavioral preferences someone has for himself or herself and/or what someone enjoys or despises doing.

Self-Reward: A response by someone to his or her own behavior that increases the likelihood that it will be repeated and/or that person will continue in the encounter or relationships that produced it.

Self-Sanction Test: Behavior by someone that informs him or her about the self-rewards and/or costs.

Self-Worth: The degree to which people value themselves. It is the degree to which someone feels worthwhile. Self-worth and self-esteem are the same.

Separation Anxiety: Anxiety parents and children in a nuclear family may feel over the eventual departure of the children. See empty nest syndrome.

Sexism: When members of a dominant group use negative images toward women to deny them opportunities.

Sex Scripts: Social scripts that shape sexual behavior.

Sexual Harassment: Unwanted sexual comments or advances by someone with power over a subordinate.

Sexually Ambivalent Scripts: Sex scripts that convey mixed messages.

Sexual Orientation: Preference for same or opposite sex partners.

Sexual Prohibitions: Behaviors that are condemned in a sexual script.

Sexual Role Conflict: Incompatible sexual scripts. Can be personal, interpersonal, or a combination of both.

Shared Social Script: A situation where members of a group, organization, community, or society have the same behavioral preferences and/or enjoy or despise the same behaviors.

Shunning: Practice of isolating members who offend a group.

Sick Behavior: A label attached to a behavior that is disapproved of by a social script.

Silent Majority: Ploy used by President Nixon to suggest that the majority of Americans who don't express their opinions agree with him rather than protesters.

Single-Parent Families: A family with one parent.

Small Group: A collection of at least three people who engage in a distinct set of relationships.

Smears: Using ad hominem attacks to discredit, defame, or vilify someone, usually a public figure.

Social Awareness: Knowledge or beliefs someone has about other people.

Social Behavior: Behavior based upon the actual or imagined presence of someone else.

Social Change: A change in participants and/or a change in social scripts and activities.

Social Classes: Divisions within a system of social stratification based on the unequal distribution of power, wealth, and prestige, such as upper crust, new rich, upper middle, lower middle, working, working poor, poor, and super-poor.

Social Class Card: When moral entrepreneurs for the disadvantaged point out disparities in power, wealth, and prestige.

Social Cost: Actual or anticipated response by others that decreases the likelihood that someone will repeat a behavior and/or continue in the encounter or relationship.

Social Darwinism: Attempt to justify inequities within and between societies by distorting what the famous biologist Charles Darwin said.

Social Disorganization: Increased deviance due to less effective informal mechanisms of social control.

Social Encounter: Interaction between two or more people on a given occasion.

Social Hierarchy of Credibility: Differences in credibility based on the social position or location of people in a group or society.

Social Mobility: Movement up or down by people within in a social class structure.

Social Movement: Deliberate attempt to challenge and alter existing scripts and arrangements within a society.

Social Organization: Occurs when a single agreed upon script effectively coordinates all activities in a society.

Social Power: The ability to get others to comply with your wishes, even if it is against what they want.

Social Prestige: The amount of respect people have for someone.

Social Rationalization: Excuses shared and offered by members of a group to justify their behavior.

Social Relationship: A series of social encounters between two or more people that take place over time.

Social Reward: The anticipated or actual response by others that increases the likelihood that someone will repeat a behavior and/or continue in the encounter or relationship.

Social Sanction Test: Behavior by someone that is designed to gauge how others will react to compliance or deviance from behavioral preferences contained in their personal scripts.

Social Script: A single or set of behavioral preferences.

Social Script as an External Constraint: When a social script is imposed on someone else, it operates as an external constraint. See coercion.

Social Script as an Internal Constraint: When a social script becomes internalized and a personal constraint on behavior.

Social Self: The component of personality that results from internalization.

Social Stratification: Unequal distribution of power, wealth, and prestige in a society.

Social Structure: A pattern of interaction that persists over time.

Socialist Political Economy Script: Script that encourages government to create policies that insure the greatest pleasure for the largest number of people in society.

Socialization: Process by which someone first becomes aware of scripts and then internalizes them.

Society: People who live together within the same political jurisdiction.

Sociology of Emotions: An area of study in sociology that looks at how social scripts shape emotional experiences and expressions.

Sphere of Activity: A general area of activity within a society that is bound together by a common theme, such as religion or education.

Spinning a Message: Interpretations of social scripts by moral entrepreneurs that are manipulated to influence audiences.

Spousal Abuse: Violence by one spouse against the other.

State Sanctioned Behavioral Preference: A behavioral preference that has received a government stamp of approval. See law.

Status: A social category or position.

Status Crimes: Acts that are illegal only for juveniles.

Status-Occupant: Someone who is seen as being in a given social category or position at some point in time.

Stereotypes: Stubborn generalizations about people in another category or group that resist information to the contrary.

Street Crimes: Direct threats to people or their property. Crimes normally associated with those reported on the Uniform Crime Reports, such as murder and robbery.

Subculture: A group within a society that is distinct from yet compatible with it.

Superego: Freud's term for the social self.

Superficial Relationships: A relatively shallow relationship that persists over time but where self-disclosure is low.

Sustaining Agent of Socialization: Someone who reinforces what was originally internalized from someone else.

Switching Identities: Ingratiating gatekeepers by switching either deliberately or through identification with the aggressor's public identity.

Taken-for-Granted Scripts: Scripts that become so familiar that people never question them.

Talking Points: Points that moral entrepreneurs use to peddle their scripts. Often provided by think tanks.

Taste Cultures: Everyday consumption preferences.

Taylorization of Work: Work activities scripted around repetitive, standardized, specialized tasks.

Techniques of Conflict Resolution: Different ways that script disputes can be resolved.

Techniques of Neutralization: Rationalizations or justifications for deviant acts.

Think Tanks: Organizations devoted to researching and promoting special interest topics.

Tokenism: When the dominant group only allows a few minorities to assimilate. The purpose is to give the appearance of change.

Traditional Authority: A system of authority scripted by customs.

Triad: A relationship between three people.

Two Step Process: Process by which the ideas of a public moral entrepreneur are conveyed to audiences through acquaintance moral entrepreneurs.

Uneven Playing Field: When the rules governing a competition favor some participants over others.

Uniform Crime Reports (UCRs): Crime data tabulated by the FBI that is submitted by local and state enforcement agencies.

Unilateral Benefits: When benefits or rewards in a social relationship flow in one direction.

Unofficial Script: Informal script that is not officially endorsed by leaders in a group, organization, community, or society.

Unofficial Workplace Scripts: Worker scripts that are not known and/or officially recognized by corporate officials.

Utopian Ideology: A counter-ideology script that seeks large-scale changes in society.

Value Cluster: Set of values held by people.

Value Intensity: The severity with which emotional sentiments are held.

Values: Emotional sentiments expressed as generalized likes or dislikes that reflect what people admire, celebrate, feel is important, or what they hate or despise.

Vicarious Role Model: A character portrayed in a play, movies, or on TV that serves as a role model for someone.

Victimless Crimes: Illegal acts such as gambling where the "victim" chooses to participate.

Violence: Inflicting physical bodily harm on someone.

Volition: Voluntary.

War on Crime Card: Whenever politicians use get-tough-on-crime postures to ingratiate voters.

WASP: Term originally applied to white Anglo-Saxon Protestants. More recent usage refers to Wife As Senior Partner.

White Collar Crime: Illegal acts committed by people in relatively high-prestige jobs for personal gain.